GETTING STARTED IN
POWERBOATING

THIRD EDITION

Bob Armstrong

International Marine / McGraw-Hill

Camden, Maine ▪ New York ▪ Chicago ▪ San Francisco
Lisbon ▪ London ▪ Madrid ▪ Mexico City ▪ Milan
New Delhi ▪ San Juan ▪ Seoul ▪ Singapore ▪ Sydney ▪ Toronto

The **McGraw·Hill** Companies

10 9 8 7 6 5 4 3 2 DOC DOC 9 8 7 6

© 1990, 1995, 2005 by International Marine

Library of Congress Cataloging-in-Publication Data
Armstrong, Bob, 1937–
 Getting started in powerboating. / Bob Armstrong.—3rd ed.
   p.   cm.
 Includes index.
 ISBN 0-07-144899-3 (pbk.)
 1. Motorboats. 2. Boats and boating. I. Title.
 GV835.A76 2006
 797.1′25—dc22   2004027626

Questions regarding the content of this book should be addressed to
International Marine
P.O. Box 220
Camden, ME 04843
www.internationalmarine.com

Questions regarding the ordering of this book should be addressed to
The McGraw-Hill Companies
Customer Service Department
P.O. Box 547
Blacklick, OH 43004
Retail Customers: 1-800-262-4729
Bookstores: 1-800-722-4726

Illustrations by Joe Comeau unless otherwise noted. Illustrations on pages 20, 22 (top),
84, 85 (top), 89, 125, 139 (top), 153, 154, 231, 235, 236, 237, 241, 242, 243, 244 courtesy
the author. Photos courtesy the author unless otherwise noted. Photos on pages 90, 91,
95, 111, 117, 119, 121, 126, 134, 135, 138, 139, 152 by Ed McDonald.

Dedication

This book is dedicated to the memory of
Joseph A. Savino, September 20, 1920–April 28, 1989.
And to his widow, Betty J. (Biddle) Savino.

For more than a dozen years I lived aboard, operated, and cared for their boats. Had they not been willing to let their captain be a writer as well, this book—and countless magazine articles—could never have been written. Had they not also given me the freedom to run other boats when the opportunities presented themselves, I would not have had the experience on which to base much of my writing. For these considerations, I thank them.

More important, through all those years they were true friends who treated me like family. For that, and many other reasons, I miss Joe very much. Still.

But Joe Savino's death did not end my association with the family. I continued to operate and care for their trawler yacht until Betty sold it in 1991. At that time, it would have been so easy for her to dismiss me as merely a "former employee." But that never happened. She has remained a friend—the kind of steadfast friend who knows when I could use a pat on the back and when I'd be better off with a kick in the backside. I can never thank her enough for the moral support, encouragement, and counsel she's given me over the years since her husband's death.

One of my few regrets in life is that I never publicly expressed my gratitude and appreciation to Joe Savino while he was still living. I hope, by now including her in this dedication, I've avoided making the same mistake with Betty.

Contents

PART THREE: The Hows of Powerboat Handling

PART FOUR: Enjoying Your Boat

Preface

So you've been thinking about taking up the sport of powerboating? That's understandable. It looks like so much fun! But how do you start? If you're like many people new to boating, your first step is to visit a nearby dealer or go to a boat show or two. Then suddenly you feel overwhelmed. What appeared to be so simple soon seems surprisingly complex. You quickly discover there are more kinds of powerboats than you'd ever imagined. You look around and realize you just don't know where to begin.

Well, powerboating is always fun, and you'd probably have a pretty good time with any boat. But it's much *more* fun when you have the right boat and are comfortable handling it in just about any circumstance. That's why I've written this book. I'm in no better position to tell you exactly which boat is "right" for you than I am to choose the person you should marry, but I *can* offer practical suggestions for finding the boat of your dreams. Those suggestions are set forth in Part One.

Parts Two, Three, and Four are designed to help you get off on the right foot when you begin to operate your new pride and joy. There's no substitute for experience, of course, and the more time you spend at the wheel, the easier it all becomes. But by taking advantage of someone else's experience, you can get off to a much happier start and make the learning process all the more pleasant. The boat-handling and other operating tips I offer can help you to avoid many of the mistakes beginners usually make—mistakes that often spoil the great fun you can have on the water.

You may wonder why I've written a third edition. Well, it's simple. Times change. Things happen. And eventually, what was once right on target no longer hits the mark. This is true in many fields. In the world of pleasure boats, outboard motors are a prime example. When I wrote the first edition, four-stroke outboards were just coming on the scene. By the second edition, there were more of them around, and it looked like they might catch on, but two-strokes were still dominant and four-strokes were available only in limited sizes and models; the largest was a mere 90 horsepower, still small by the day's standards.

Now four-stroke outboards predominate. Indeed, some companies now make nothing but. Just a few two-strokes remain, and even they have changed and evolved. So what I wrote previously is, in the case of outboards, simply out of date. And this is only one example of change, albeit a dramatic one. There are many others, and not just in propulsion. This new edition reflects such changes.

And then there's experience. Since I wrote the first edition, I've had 15 additional years of experience as a captain, instructor, and boating writer. Although none of that experience would lead me to recant anything I originally wrote about boat-handling and boat sense, what I've learned on the water has given me the opportunity to refine and improve some operational techniques. Despite 40 years of experience all told, I'm still constantly learning, and to me, that's part of the fun of powerboating. It never gets to the point of "been there, done that."

Recently I helped develop and field-test an intensive, two-day, hands-on certification course for new boaters, which once again got me thinking about how to explain things in the most effective way possible. If you really want to get to know a subject, try teaching it; you won't believe how much you'll learn from your students!

Finally, all the "Why didn't you mention (insert your topic of choice)?" questions I've received from readers over the years have prompted me to add new material I didn't cover thoroughly (or in some cases at all) in the earlier editions. As a result, this third edition contains more of what you need to know to get started in powerboating than either of the previous two, and that includes references to some valuable websites that didn't even exist when the earlier editions were published.

Any one of these factors might have been, by itself, enough to prompt the creation of a revised edition. Taken together, they left me no choice. So here it is: the third edition of *Getting Started in Powerboating*. Dig in, read on, and get out on the water and enjoy!

PART ONE

Choosing the Right Boat

1

No Boat Is Right for Everyone

To many people, the ideal powerboat would have a top speed somewhere approaching Mach 1 (or at least feel that way), have the living space of a penthouse condo, be as impressive as the Taj Mahal, operate on the budget of an economy car, and never need maintenance. Of course, it should also be comfortable at slow speeds for those times you're not in a hurry and should be small enough to make it easy to find room in the most crowded marina or anchorage.

But it should be big enough to allow you to bring along all your friends (when you have a boat, you have a lot of friends) yet not so big that you can't handle it yourself. It should also be large enough to make those open ocean passages you dream about (to faraway places with strange-sounding names or just to the town on the other side of the bay) with fuel capacity to match. But then it shouldn't be so huge that you can't get close to shore when you reach your destination.

I think you get the picture: it would be nice to have a boat with all the features you could ever possibly want. Nice, but not possible. *Every boat is a compromise of sorts.* The laws of physics, hydrodynamics, aesthetics, economics, and other practical considerations force you to give up one thing to gain something else—in nearly every aspect of every situation. You simply cannot put 10 pounds of coffee in a 5-pound bag. So you have to decide what you want most in a boat and be willing to give up what you want least in order to have it.

If it's any consolation, this is the number-one rule of boat buying, and it applies to everyone.

Even the ultrarich buyer of a custom-built mega-yacht has to live with trade-offs. That's right—even when its price is in the millions, no boat, no matter how large or luxurious, can have everything or be everything the owner might wish for. So I repeat boat-buying rule number one: Every boat is a compromise. Remember this, and you'll save yourself a lot of grief as you make choices to get the boat that's right for you.

We'll look more closely at the details of the choices as we go along. But for now, let's get our feet wet by exploring some generalities.

Size

We often tend to think that bigger is better. But when it comes to boats, it ain't necessarily so. Sure, bigger boats offer more amenities, the ability to carry more people, and greater fuel capacity (which usually, though not always, equates with greater range), and they're often more comfortable than smaller boats when the going gets rough. But size should be a lesser consideration than many others. Because a basic truth of powerboating is that although you can have more *kinds* of fun in a larger boat, you can't have any *more* fun in a megayacht than you can in an outboard-powered dinghy. And sometimes you can only have less.

I say that with full acknowledgment that "How big is it?" will be one of the first questions people ask when they find out you have a boat. I also recognize that despite the many greater pleasures of owning a boat, being a "yachtsman" is often perceived as a status symbol. And the bigger the boat, the greater the perceived status. But being one who enjoys boating for boating's sake, I firmly believe our goal should not be to have as much boat as we can afford, but rather to have only as much boat as we can really use.

Putting economic aspects aside (OK, no one buys a boat to save money, but we've come a long way from "If you have to ask how much it costs, you can't afford it," and you must face the truth that bigger boats not only cost more to buy, they cost more to maintain, operate, berth, insure, etc.—so the economics are important), there's another downside to bigger boats. They need more water! Not only in area—operating room, so to speak—but usually in depth as well. That means there are many places you can go in a small boat that are inaccessible to larger craft and places that give the operator of a small boat a wide margin of error while requiring a much greater degree of care and precision from the skipper of a large boat. So *where* you plan to go boating should have a strong influence on your decision as to how big a boat you need. (Where you go boating affects other decisions also. We'll get to them all in good time.)

Many years ago, I had a neighbor who learned the "size versus use" lesson the hard way. He had wanted a boat for years, and when he came into a moderate inheritance he finally could afford one, so he got it—a 26-foot inboard cabin cruiser with a flying bridge. It was a nice boat. Very nice. But not for him. You see, he wanted to use his boat not only on the ocean at our hometown's doorstep but also on a nearby lake. So he kept his boat on a trailer for flexibility. But given the 11-foot tidal range in our native state of Maine, he couldn't launch or haul a boat this size at his convenience. To use the ramp on the estuary from which we gained access to the ocean, he had to wait for the right stage of tide—half flood or higher. So quite often the boat was stuck on land when he wanted it in the ocean, or in the estuary when he wanted to take it to the lake. Yes, his cruiser could sit on a trailer, but it wasn't really a trailerable boat. No wonder he traded it the following year for a 19-foot outboard runabout. The 19-footer was truly trailerable and suited his

needs perfectly. And though I've suggested that larger boats can be more comfortable in heavy seas, I have to emphasize that this isn't always true either. I feel much more secure taking rough stuff in a 25-foot center-console fishing boat designed to go to sea than I do in a 60-footer that was designed to be a dockside "cocktail barge." So let's save the size question for later, when you have a better idea of all your needs.

Accommodations

"How many does it sleep?" will probably be the second most often asked question you get from acquaintances. And it can be an important consideration. But not yet. While it's true that today's family cruisers in the 26- to 30-foot range offer more amenities and comfort than most boats in the 36- to 40-foot range did 25 years ago, it's too soon to surmise that you need a cabin at all, much less a certain number of berths. Don't get me wrong; you may well end up with a family cruiser. Ever since the Electric Boat Company took yachting out of the exclusive grasp of the very rich and made boating a practical recreational outlet for nearly everyone with the introduction of the ELCO Cruisette in 1915, the family cruiser has been the mainstay of popular boating. And I would have to agree with the consensus that there's probably no better all-around practical choice. But if accommodations—that is, places to sleep, a galley to cook in, a dedicated area for dining (even if it also converts to a sleeping area), and a head with a full shower—don't really figure in your boating plans, you don't need a cruiser. If your activities are by day only, perhaps a boat with a larger open cockpit would be more suitable. Remember, a cabin takes up space. The more amenities you want, the more space it takes. If those amenities are important, fine. But if they aren't, why pay for them and lose other features you might want more? Features such as a working cockpit for fishing, or room to stow scuba gear, or better access to the water for swimming, or more room simply to soak up the sun? Ultimately, how you plan to use your boat should dictate what it is. And that brings us to . . .

Activities

Although it's true that you can fish from any boat, swim or dive from any boat, or take any boat cruising, not every boat allows you to conduct these activities with equal ease and comfort. So consider the number-two rule of boat buying: Your boat should make your favorite on-the-water activity easy. Of course, your boat will quite likely be a family boat, and the wishes of other family members should have influence also (which takes us back to rule one, compromise), so a pure fishing, or diving, or any other type of truly dedicated craft may be too highly specialized for all your needs. On the other hand, once you get to the 25-foot range, most boats offer a degree of convenient multiple use, even if they can't be all things to all people. What you have to decide is which uses count most for you and your family.

You probably know the needs of your favorite on-the-water activity better than I do. But in the excitement of looking at new boats, you might forget. So let me run over a few of the most popular activities with a nod toward the boat features you'll need to enjoy them.

Fishing

A stable platform tops the list of fishboat features. All boats roll in a trough, but good fishing boats have an easy roll that doesn't go far enough or happen quickly enough to throw you off balance. When you check out a possible choice, be sure your sea trial includes seeing how the boat behaves at trolling speeds and sitting still in a seaway. If it isn't comfortable, keep looking.

Room for anglers to move around as they fight their catch would probably be the second biggest need. This means plenty of cockpit space, open deck, or both. If a boat has a "fighting chair," the cockpit must be large enough that there's still ample space around it. "Clean" space is important, too. That is, deck hardware—cleats, chocks, etc.—should be hidden or recessed so that anglers can't snag lines (or shins) while fighting their catch. And the cockpit sole shouldn't be too far off the water.

You should also have rod holders, rod and tackle stowage, a bait prep center, perhaps outriggers for trolling, and an aerated well for holding live bait. The list of features should also include places to stow your catch and easy means of getting the catch aboard (which means a transom door in larger craft). Since fishing can be both wet and messy, the cockpit should be self-bailing and contain facilities (pump, hose, etc.) for easy and frequent washdown; a fishing cockpit is not a place for the delicate or fancy—in either facilities or participants (Figures 1-1A and 1-1B).

Low-speed maneuverability is also important unless you plan to fish "dead boat," which is impractical for trophy-sized catches. That generally means you'll want twin-screw power whether it's needed for any other reason or not. Often it will be needed simply to provide more total horsepower, because it's a given that the best fishing areas are not always close to the best living areas. Hence, many anglers want a boat that will get to the fish and back in a hurry. This usually means plenty of horsepower. Visibility from the helm is also critical. On larger boats the console is often elevated with a flying bridge to provide a higher vantage point for better all-around visibility. In many regions (south Florida, for one) a tower is added to raise the observation point even higher. In large boats the main station may be so far from the action that a separate console is needed in the cockpit.

Of course, many of these features are options you can add to any boat anytime. But you should consider them from the start, because it may be too difficult (or expensive) to include them later.

Swimming and Diving

If all you wear is a bathing suit (or less), all you really need for this activity is a boarding ladder—an easy way to get back aboard from the water. But if you add flippers, mask and snorkel, air tank and regulator, buoyancy compensator, weights, wet suit, and other scuba paraphernalia, ease of getting into the water becomes as important as ease of getting out.

Room to move around near the boarding area is important, too, so cockpit space can be as valuable for swim/dive boats as it is for fishing boats. The only difference is that the cockpit sole can be higher off the water as long as the ladder is ad-

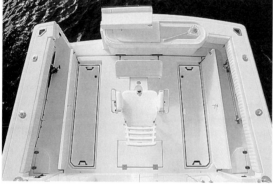

FIGURES 1-1A AND 1-1B. *This Rampage 38 is a fine example of a well-rigged sportfisherman. The efficient cockpit includes a tackle center with large stowage drawers and a molded fiberglass sink with removable cutting board (top). It also features two large fish boxes (with macerators) under the sole, a custom 55-gallon live-bait well in the transom, a swing-out transom door, and ample room for a fighting chair (bottom) with working space around it. (Courtesy Rampage Sport Fishing Yachts)*

equate. This is especially true if the boat has a transom platform. Often called a swim (or dive) platform, this feature gives you a place to don or remove gear just inches from the water and is an unbeatable addition to any boat used for extensive in-the-water activities. A freshwater shower on or near the platform is a nice plus, too, even if you do your swimming in fresh water. The shower is usually cleaner, often warmer, and will probably feel good afterward no matter where you swim.

Although it's not a consideration for swimming or even snorkeling, space to stow scuba gear becomes important if you plan to do much serious diving. It's amazing how much room even the most elementary gear requires—and how aggravating it can be if there's no proper place to put it. Racks for air tanks are particularly desirable, because loose tanks on a pitching deck can become dangerous unguided missiles. Proper stowage also leads to longer equipment life and should be a very big consideration if diving is high on your list.

Ground tackle—anchors, rode, and the facilities for handling them—is important on every boat, but particularly for swimming and diving. Arrangements that would be acceptable on other boats can prove totally inadequate when frequent anchoring is routine. A windlass or "automatic" anchor-handling system is not a luxury on a dive boat, it's nearly a must.

Cruising

Many years ago I did some extensive traveling in a 19-foot open runabout. No head, no galley, no berths. And, I must also add, no comfort. It was strictly roughing it all the way. It was fun, but I was younger then, and the adventure was part of it. Today, I want a good mattress under me when I sleep, a fully equipped galley with freezer and microwave when I get hungry, a shower with hot water to help me feel fully "civilized," and TV with VCR (and/or DVD player) to indulge my fantasies. I won't leave home without 'em. These days I live aboard a large motor yacht as a professional captain and never leave home at all. I take it with me wherever I go.

How you go is up to you. Some folks approach cruising simply as travel on water as opposed to travel on land. That is, they consider accommodations as part of the destination package and cruise from one resort complex (complete with shoreside motel) to another. If you feel that way, just about any boat will work. But many cruising folk think as I do—they don't want to be limited to destinations with shoreside accommodations, and so they take home along. This means having a boat with a cabin, sufficient berths for your crew, a proper galley and dining area, at least one head with shower, and enough total space to prevent cabin fever over a reasonable length of cruise. When you travel this way, your destinations are nearly unlimited.

Adequate space can be particularly sensitive because privacy is a fragile thing aboard most cruising boats. I steadfastly believe that anyone who needs lots of privacy is a poor cruising companion, but we all need our personal space, and the longer we stay in a confined area (and even megayachts become confined after a time), the more important it is. So give consideration to the space *arrangement* as well as total volume.

Since many areas serve double duty—convertible dinettes are a perfect example—the number of available berths is usually greater than the number of people a boat can truly accommodate. So, "How many does it sleep?" is still a lesser consideration. Stowage—for clothing, personal belongings, food, and other necessities—is perhaps more important. Its importance grows with the length of the cruise. A boat that might suit six overnight could become cramped for one couple after a week if there isn't room for the gear, provisions, and personal effects they need to feel comfortable and happy over a period of time.

Speed and range are factors to consider in all boats, but they're particularly important on cruising boats because of the influence they have on your overall activity. The two are not necessarily mutually exclusive, but as we'll discover later on, either factor can impose severe limitations on the other. If most of your cruising will be done on weekends, speed can perhaps be more important. If getting away from it all for longer periods is more to your liking, you should probably opt for range.

Waterskiing

While you can ski behind any boat with enough power to pull the skiers and enough speed to make it fun, the best ski boats are small, fast, and highly maneuverable, with a small turning radius and a flat wake. The tow rope should attach to a pylon somewhere near the boat's pivot point.

Since this combination of features isn't always desirable for many other activities, waterskiing is perhaps the one sport that begs a truly dedicated craft. Because the best ski boats tend to be smaller, however, it's often not at all impractical to have a ski boat in addition to a larger, more general-purpose family boat if a variety of activities is desired.

Wakeboarding

This activity is so similar to waterskiing in so many ways it's tempting to think they're too much alike to consider separately. But despite their similarities, they're markedly different. Just as minimal wake is desirable for skiing, wakeboarders want the wake as large as possible. Most really good ski boats just can't begin to throw the wake you need for good boarding, though some new designs do have adjustable underwater appurtenances that can be lowered to increase the wake. If you don't have a dedicated wakeboarding boat, the best alternative is often a sterndrive runabout not quite on plane. For certain, you should examine any boat's suitability for wakeboarding during sea trials if this activity is important to you.

Partying

Yes, a few pages back I did say I'd rather take rough stuff in a boat designed for it than in a cocktail barge. But I didn't intend to disparage either the idea of having parties on board or the boats designed to hold them. Rather, I mean to make the point that this, too, is a factor to be considered among the trade-offs.

Celebrating afloat has a special charm that few parties ashore can match. It's a super way to repay social obligations. As one megayacht owner put it, "People who might not attend a party at my house never refuse an invitation to my boat." The principle applies even if your boat is considerably smaller than a megayacht.

Of course, size is a factor if only to the extent that available space determines how large a party you can throw. But as with cruising, the way space is arranged is more important, except that for partying the emphasis is perhaps less on places to put things away and more on places to put things out. Likewise, there's less concern for privacy and more for open space and traffic flow. A balance of space is nice, too; the best party setups include both enclosed saloons and open deck areas.

Such amenities as wet bar, icemaker(s), and liquor and glass storage are nice, but not necessary. Their importance varies in direct proportion to total available space and their compatibility with other uses of the boat.

For pure partying, a cocktail barge doesn't need to be terribly seakindly, since some of the best parties don't require leaving the pier. If you do take a cruise, it will most likely be a short one over protected water in nice weather. Otherwise, the party is no fun. Of course, if you have other uses in mind, their needs must be considered also, and the boat must provide for them as well. (Compromise, remember?)

Since drinking and operating a boat are an even worse combination than drinking and driving a car, I'd also advise owners and skippers to hire a pro to run the boat for them while they party. This also lets you enjoy the party as host instead of being preoccupied as boat operator, so it's not a bad idea even if you don't drink. Both are excellent reasons for having a full-time professional captain on a truly dedicated party boat.

Other Considerations

Speed
Speed is a relative concept. A trawler yacht ambling along at 10 knots seems fast to the people in a 6-knot sailboat, yet the 30- to 40-knot speeds now quite common in modern family cruisers are slow to those in the 70 mph (or faster) raceboat-derived "performance" craft. The bottom line, however, is that speed on the water is a result of three factors: 1) horsepower, 2) weight, and 3) shape. The faster you want to go, the more you have to increase 1, decrease 2, and streamline 3. Since we are, at this point, still just getting our feet wet, we'll save the details for subsequent chapters. But for the moment let's note that increasing horsepower generally means using bigger engines, which need more room and burn

more fuel. Since bigger engines usually weigh more, and their greater fuel demand necessitates a concomitant greater fuel capacity, increasing horsepower will likely increase total weight far beyond the weight of the engines themselves.

Modern construction techniques and materials—including cored laminates, unidirectional fabrics, improved resins, and hollow stringers reinforced with carbon fiber—have done a lot to reduce the weight of the hull and superstructure while maintaining (or often even increasing) strength. But when you add bigger engines and greater fuel capacity, it usually works out that other things, such as amenities, have to give way to keep total weight down. And, of course, the sleeker the boat, the less room there's likely to be inside. That, too, can limit amenities. So the real bottom line is that despite technological advances that have made great strides in allowing boats to have speed and other goodies as well, speed is usually just one more item to be traded off against other desires and needs.

Range
Range is simply the amount of available fuel (usually on the order of 90 percent of total fuel carried) divided by consumption (gallons per hour) times speed (miles per hour or knots as the situation requires) at a given throttle setting. The answer will be a distance in statute miles for mph and nautical miles for knots. Deduct another 10 percent to be conservative, and you'll know how far you can go at that speed.

While it might seem that the more fuel you carry, the farther you can travel, this, too, isn't always so. What is true is that the less fuel you burn, the farther you can go, which usually means that range is gained at a sacrifice of speed. Even ultrafast megayachts with fuel capacity measured in the thousands of gallons *usually* must throttle back to gain transatlantic range.

The reason increased capacity alone won't guarantee increased range is that added fuel is added weight. So unless other factors are also changed, the additional fuel is often consumed merely in carrying itself. Most production boats are designed to carry the optimum quantity of fuel for their normal cruise speed, and when it comes to range, what you get is what you've got. It's possible to increase a boat's range beyond that of its initial design, but to do so usually entails more engineering than simply adding tankage.

Comfort

Comfort is another factor highly influenced by where you do your boating. In south Florida, totally open boats are fine, the main concern being a bimini top or other protection from the sun (Figure 1-2). Indeed, boats intended for use in this area don't need an inside control station even if they have a cabin. If they do have a cabin, air-conditioning is a must.

In New England and around Great Lakes country, dual stations are common; a flying bridge console is fine, weather permitting, but a more-protected station is needed too often to do without. In the Pacific Northwest, protection from the weather is needed so constantly that outside controls were rare until the area's builders began marketing their craft elsewhere.

Comfort is definitely a "when in Rome" situation, and you'll find there's a good reason why the majority of boats in your area are arranged and equipped as they are. Deviate at your own risk.

Seaworthiness

"As much as possible" might be your initial reaction, but the truth is that this factor, too, should be dictated by how and where you use your boat. If you plan only to putter around Lake Calmandserene in good weather, you don't need the same kind of boat you would use for serious ocean tournament fishing. The large cabin windows you'd find so desirable for cruising along protected waterways (because they allow better sightseeing and minimize cabin fever) could be downright dangerous for offshore passagemaking (Figure 1-3). Most other factors that increase seaworthiness are also gained at the loss of something you would find quite nice under less stringent conditions. Being realistic in your estimate of how you plan to use your boat is as important in this matter as it is in others. Believe it or not,

FIGURE 1-2. *The hard top over the flying bridge of this Viking 38, a convertible rigged for fishing, will fend off the sun. A canvas bimini top offers similar protection and can be folded out of the way when not needed. In either case, plastic side curtains add protection from wind and rain. (Courtesy Viking Yachts)*

you can have too much seaworthiness. The extra beef built into offshore boats is not without cost. Given that we all have a practical limit to the cost of the boat we get, if you don't need the beef, your money can go toward things you want more.

The goal is to match your boat to your needs, not to some preconceived, hypothetical "best." There is no one boat that's right for everyone, but there *is* a boat that's right for you. In subsequent chapters, we'll look at more details that will help you find it.

FIGURE 1-3. *Houseboats, such as this Harbormaster 375, combine the spaciousness of a cottage with the ability to travel. Generally designed for use on the protected waters of lakes, bays, and rivers, they provide far more living space than you'll find in sleeker craft.*

2

Boatspeak

What we have here is a failure to communicate!" That's one of my favorite movie lines. And though it's been used many times in a variety of genres, it almost always provokes a laugh. The line comes to mind just now because, after reviewing what I wrote in Chapter 1, I realize it could well sum up your feelings at this point, though I doubt you see much humor in it. As you get involved in power-boating, you'll find that it's not just this book. Dealers, boat show demonstrators, salespeople, repair technicians, and nearly everyone already involved with the sport will also tend to use words you've rarely heard before.

In the first chapter I referred to "a head with a full shower." Did this have you scratching *your* head for a moment? Well, if you're still wondering (though I think you probably figured it out), *head* is the nautical term for a toilet, and nearly everyone involved with boats seems to favor the word, even when ashore.

This use of unfamiliar expressions is not meant to confuse you—honest. The reason we do it is simple and basic. Every endeavor has its own "language," or jargon, that enables people involved in the activity to communicate more efficiently. It's almost always easier and more economical to use a single "activity-specific" term rather than the three, four, or even more "common English" words it might take to convey the same message. "Please rig a port bow line" is much simpler than "Please take this piece of rope and attach it to that metal thing up there on the foredeck. No, the one on the other side. OK, now . . ." And so on. And even when the word

count is identical, jargon usually imparts nuances that common English would not.

Of course, this works only if you know the lingo. And when you're just getting started, boating language might as well be Swahili; so many terms are so totally unfamiliar. But in time, you'll know and understand them well. In fact, one day in the not-too-distant future, I bet you'll find yourself using many of these words in your own conversations without any hesitation or even a moment's thought. But until that day arrives, you're going to need some help.

So I'll tell ya what I'm gonna do . . . For the remainder of this book, the first time I use a term I think you might find unfamiliar, I'll define it for you [right then and there in brackets] so you'll understand exactly what I mean—unless the accompanying text or illustrations so clearly suggest the meaning that there's no need for further explanation. This way you won't have to stop and consult a glossary, or worse, wonder what I'm trying to tell you. And if I repeat the term again later in the book, if enough pages have passed since I used the word initially, I just may define it again to make sure you remember.

Let me say up front that except for the occasional dockside phonies who use obscure (and often incorrect) nautical terminology to appear more knowledgeable and experienced than they are, most "salty" language serves a definite purpose. It helps us address specific concerns with as little confusion as possible—as it will for you, once you understand it.

Interestingly enough, many expressions we use in everyday speech originated on the water.

Some are obvious, such as when we speak of "taking the wind out of someone's sails." Yet whenever you say "I'm just getting my bearings" or "I'm still learning the ropes" (both of which might be apropos at this stage of your boating experience), you're also harking back to earlier times at sea. But for every one of these expressions that has crossed over to common English, there are countless others we still use only on or around boats. I won't attempt to introduce all of them here—some deserve to remain obscure. But I will try to acquaint you with the ones you need to know. And because you're just getting started, I'm going to assume you're starting from square one and define every word that isn't used in everyday English (though chances are, if you're interested enough in boats to have picked up this book, you perhaps already know a few terms, possibly more than you realize). Since the next few chapters are meant to help you understand the different types of powerboats, I'm going to use the next few pages to cover some of the common terminology that will be involved.

Critical Dimensions, Directions, and Delineations

Among the most important terms you need to understand at this point are those we use to describe the various parts of a boat as well as the relationships of those parts to one another, the boat as a whole, and our surroundings.

Let's start with the *hull*, because this is the one thing that makes a cabin cruiser different from an RV, a runabout different from a sports car. It's the part that goes in the water. Of course, not all of it goes into the water, so we further describe a hull as having a *bottom*, which is the part in the water, and *topsides*, which are the sides of the boat from the waterline up to the *gunwale* [pronounced "GUN·ul," the top edge of a topside]. The gunwale is easier to see in a small open boat, where it stands alone, than in a larger decked boat, where it's only visible as the point at which the topsides meet the deck. And on that score, a surface we can walk upon is generally a *deck* only when at gunwale level, at the top of a hull. If it's

down within the boat (and *belowdeck* or simply *below* are also expressions we sometimes use to refer to the enclosed cabin space beneath the main deck), what we'd call a floor ashore becomes a *sole*. Thus we have a *cockpit* [an open area, usually just slightly below deck level] sole, a cabin sole, and so on. Think of the sole of your shoe, and you should have no trouble remembering; it's what you walk on.

The deckhouse and everything else above deck level are known collectively as the *superstructure*. In this case, the meaning of "super" is above, as in above the hull. But just to complicate things, when a fiberglass boat is manufactured, the "deck" mold often produces some of the superstructure as well. But this is good. Having the deck and as much of the superstructure as possible molded in one piece eliminates seams and their potential for leaks. (I love the look and romance of wooden boats, but fiberglass is so much more practical!)

Perhaps a most important aspect of a hull is its LOA, which stands for *length overall*. In basic terms, this is the length of your boat on deck—as in "I have a 36-footer." Specifically, it's the exact exterior measurement, over the centerline, from the *bow* [the very front of the boat; the "pointy end"] to the *stern* [the very back] exclusive of any add-ons such as a *pulpit* [a protrusion from the bow that helps with handling and stowing anchors] or a platform, or perhaps outboard motors bolted onto the *transom* [the rear face, the very back of a squared-off or slightly curved stern; it's most common on powerboats, as opposed to the "canoe" stern seen on a few long-range, oceangoing cruising yachts and many sailboats]. Thus your "36-footer" may actually have an LOA of 36 feet 4 inches or maybe 35 feet 9 inches. Note, however, that if either the pulpit or platform (or both) happens to be molded into the hull and deck structures—not attached after molding—they are then *not* "add-ons," but rather are integral parts of the boat and must be included in the measurement of LOA (Figure 2-1). None of this is terribly important until it comes time to know what safety equipment you'll need (since many items are LOA-dependent; see Chapter 25) or to register your boat (since fees are often based on

FIGURE 2-1. *Because this pulpit is a part of the boat's molded hull and deck structures, it must be included in a measurement of LOA.*

LOA; see Chapter 27). As I'll mention again elsewhere, yard and dockage fees are also usually based on length, though in these cases you'll most likely be charged to the nearest foot rather than on your precise LOA to the inch.

Do keep in mind, however, when you start to maneuver your boat or bring it up to a pier or float, that it's not your legal LOA or even the length suggested by the builder's model name that counts, but rather how much room you actually need. So if your "36-footer" takes up 39 feet of space (due to the jutting crown of an anchor on bow rollers, a lowerable transom platform, an actual LOA several inches greater than nominal LOA, etc.), you'd better act accordingly.

LWL, the *length at the waterline*, is different from LOA primarily because of the forward *rake* [slant] of the stem. [Once the timber that defined and shaped a bow, *stem* now refers to the apex of the bow, where the port and starboard topsides meet. Similarly, while a boat's *keel* was also once a timber, the "backbone" to which all ribs were attached, it now most often refers to the centerline of the bottom, where the port and starboard sides of the bottom meet, which usually forms a V in cross section, however shallow the V may sometimes be. Some powerboats will have a slightly protruding keel molded into the bottom, a design remnant from the days when it was a timber.] LWL is usually of greater interest to sailors than powerboaters, though the term will come up again when we talk about hull speed in Chapter 3.

Another important dimension is *draft* [the depth of the boat from the waterline down to the boat's very lowest point, which is much more often the prop than the bottom of the keel]. This is directly related to *freeboard* [the height of the exposed topsides, the portion of a hull above the waterline]. Obviously, when you bring more stuff and people aboard, you increase draft and decrease freeboard.

An important question often asked by beginners is "How much depth do I need?" In calm water, I feel OK with just a couple of feet more than the boat's draft; this allows some "bounce room" if an unexpected wave comes along, plus a fudge factor because I can never know *precisely* how deep the water is. The rougher the water, the more depth I need to feel comfortable. Your main objective should be to have sufficient clearance even when you're in a *trough* [the lowest part of a wave system, between crests]. And the greater the depth, the better your odds of always having enough water under you when the waves get larger.

Vertical clearance [the height from the waterline to the highest point on the boat] is yet another important dimension. You need to know this so you can determine which bridges you can get under without requiring them to open. As with draft and freeboard, vertical clearance is not a "fixed" measurement, but rather varies with the load aboard. The deeper a boat sits in the water, the less its vertical clearance—if all other factors remain the same. (Some objects that add to vertical clearance, such as radio antennas or the fishing accessories known as *outriggers*, can be lowered to reduce the total clearance. The law requires that all such "lowerable appurtenances" be brought as low as possible before asking a bridge to open and imposes a $10,000 fine for causing an unnecessary opening.) Please note that when measuring draft, freeboard, and vertical clearance, we measure from the actual waterline at the moment, not the design waterline. The two are rarely the same.

Beam [a boat's maximum width] is also a consideration because it can determine how narrow a slip you can get into, and also how trailerable a so-called trailerable boat truly is; most states set limits on the width allowed on the highway without an "oversize load" permit and all the restrictions, complications, and limitations that come with it. Since boats are usually not rectangular objects, the maximum beam of your "baby" may exist at one point only. But you need more horizontal clearance than beam anytime you enter a slip—or anything else. Otherwise, you're sure to get stuck. You may also get "stuck" if you try to transport a "wide load" on the highway without the necessary permits.

Figures 2-2 and 2-3 show some of the basic dimensions and parts of a boat in profile and plan views, respectively. Most of the items are self-explanatory and easy to understand, perhaps with the exception of *port* and *starboard*, which I'll address below. It's also important to remember that *forward* (or *fore*, as it's sometimes expressed) and *aft* are directions and thus relative terms, while the *bow* and *stern* are specific locations. If you're standing at the peak of the bow and take one or two steps toward the stern, you've moved a bit aft, but you'll still be on the bow.

You might ask, "So why do we still use port and starboard? Wouldn't left and right be simpler?" The answer is that we use these terms to be specific. Imagine for a moment that instead of addressing you via the medium of the printed word, I'm actually there facing you as I explain things. Now, of course, my right is on your left. So if I said, "Grab the one on the right," you wouldn't know whether I meant my right or yours. But if I

asked you to pick up the one to starboard, you'd know I was referring to the *boat's* right, and there'd be no confusion.

So how do you remember which is which? There are several mnemonics, and since each seems to work better for different folks, I'll share them all. Feel free to use whichever one helps you most.

For starters, *port* and *left* are both four-letter words ending in "t." If that's not enough, how about this: Ruby Port is a red wine, and the port navigation light (see Chapter 26) is red also.

Or maybe this anecdote will help even more; I won't guarantee its historical accuracy, but I can swear it helps many people remember. In the earliest days, boats didn't have rudders. They were steered with a board or plank hung over the side and, by convention, it was always hung from the right side. Hence, the right side of the boat became known as the "steeringboard" side. Because we humans tend to be lazy tongued, *steeringboard* became *steerboard* and, eventually, *starboard* (with *board* further shortened to b'rd). Of course, with an appendage hanging off the starboard side, the other side of the boat was the one that always had to be put against a pier. Hence it came to be known as the *port* side of the boat.

We do use the terms *left rudder* and *right rudder* in reference to steering because in this case, port and starboard could be confusing. This comes from steering with a tiller, which is still used on many sailboats and small outboards that

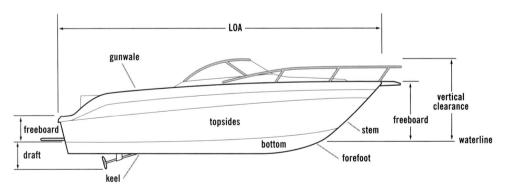

FIGURE 2-2. *This boat's LOA doesn't include either the bolted-on transom platform or the bow pulpit (used as an aid in handling the anchor) and the bow rail above it. Note that in this case, as it is most often, freeboard forward is higher than freeboard aft.*

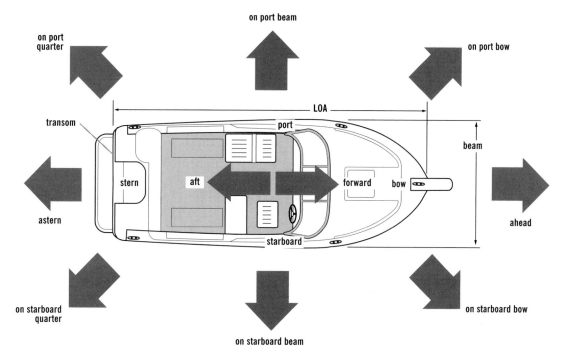

FIGURE 2-3. *Various areas, both of the boat and its surroundings, can be clearly identified for better communication among those aboard. The left side of the boat when facing forward is always the* port *side—no matter which way you're facing at the moment. Likewise, the opposite side is always the* starboard. *Note that* ahead *and* astern *can be both the location of observed objects and also the direction in which the boat is moving. Objects straight off to the side are said to be either* abeam *or* on the beam *to either port or starboard.*

don't have remote control. For a long time it was the only way to maneuver a boat—steering wheels are a relatively new development, historically speaking. The potential for confusion results because tiller action is the opposite of rudder action; you move the tiller to port to get right rudder. So steering directions were given to the *quartermaster* [the seaman whose sole job is to steer] in terms of what to do with the tiller. "Port your helm" was the command for initiating a turn to starboard.

When steering wheels were first introduced, they worked similarly because deck officers and quartermasters were so used to it. Instead of swinging a tiller to port for a turn to starboard, the wheel would be spun to port (rotated counterclockwise), and the command remained the same—"port your helm." Yes, it seems crazy to us now, but it made sense then, I'm sure. Eventu-

ally someone figured out it made more sense to spin the wheel in the direction of the intended turn, as we do today. And so mariners started to change. They also began to issue steering orders in terms of what rudder action was required rather than what to do with the helm. But this meant that for a while there was another possibility for confusion—which way should I turn the wheel on *this* boat to get the rudder action I want? Consequently, our lawmakers enacted a regulation requiring passenger-carrying steamboats in the United States to have a sign by the helm to indicate the way the wheel should be turned to get the desired rudder. Though steam had long since given way to diesel, the law was still in effect when I first went to work for a ferry line over 30 years ago. And to this day, I'm sure that many passengers who peered into the wheelhouse must have questioned the intelligence of the crew if they happened to see the sign over the wheel that read:

I mean, only idiots would need a sign to help them remember left and right, yes?

It's most important to keep in mind that only *vessels* [a general name for everything that floats, from dinghies to supertankers] have a port side and starboard side. We may use the terms in relation to other objects, as in "Keep that channel marker to starboard." Or "We're going to approach the pier port-side-to." But neither the marker nor the pier has a port or starboard side of its own.

In Figure 2-3 you'll also see descriptions for some of the common terms we may use to describe the location of an object relative to our boat. If you wonder why this is necessary, just think about it. Which helps more, telling the skipper you see a buoy "over there," or "on the port bow?"

Unconventional Conventions

While port and starboard will probably remain with us for quite a while, many nautical expressions are going by the board (another old nautical phrase that's crossed over to the mainstream) from lack of use. I have mixed emotions about this. On one hand, it's good to see some obscure terms vanish completely. We don't need "communication" that doesn't work because most people no longer understand it. On the other hand, though I have to laugh at the phonies who use "nautical talk" to appear more knowledgeable than they really are, I enjoy seeing the glimmer of recognition that occurs as another boat lover picks up on something I said unconsciously in a general conversation. Meeting kindred spirits is always a pleasure, and common language helps.

So let me offer a few more vital but perhaps dying terms in the hope you'll help keep them alive. If we can hang onto them, I honestly believe the sport will be better for it.

There are no cupboards or closets on boats; every stowage (and note that's with a "w," not an

"r"—another nautical tradition) compartment is a *locker*. If it has hooks or a rod for coat hangers (and sufficient depth, as well), it's a *hanging locker*. Walls are known as *bulkheads*, and what we call ceilings ashore are *overheads* at sea. Wooden boats do have ceilings, but this is the term for the planking applied to the inside of the ribs (usually bead board on the really "classy" boats) to hide the ribs and the rough sides of the hull's exterior planking. Ceilings are a refinement, usually found on yachts but not so often on workboats. The reason for doing this is to create a smoother finish for the interior. We often accomplish the same thing in fiberglass with a molded *hull liner*, which has its smooth *gelcoat* [the finish layer of a molded fiberglass product, the layer that was next to the mold] on what will be the interior surface. The rougher surfaces of both hull and liner face each other, totally out of sight.

If countertops have either a raised edge or an added "mini rail" to keep things from sliding off when the boat rolls in a seaway (and better boats will have one or the other), we call the slide stopper a *fiddle*.

And, just so you'll know, when we turn a boat's steering wheel as far as it will go in each direction, we're not going "lock to lock" as in a car. Instead, we say we're going "from hard over to hard over," which describes the action of the rudder(s) to which the wheel is connected—the steering action on a boat.

There will be other new terms to learn, of course, but we'll wait until they arise in context, when their meaning will be clearer and perhaps more memorable as well. How much "salty talk" should you use as you become involved in this wonderful sport? My advice is don't push it; just wait until the words come out by themselves, without effort or pretension.

There is an exception, however. When you're talking with a salesperson about a boat you're interested in, try to ask questions using the correct terminology, if you can remember it. Just imagine which question gets you a more thoughtful reply: "What kind of closet space does it have?" or "How many hanging lockers, and how deep are they?"

3

Displacement Hulls

I n Chapter 1 we looked mostly at features built onto or into the boat. Now it's time to take a closer look at the boat itself. In this chapter we'll look at *displacement* hulls, despite the truth that in the powerboating of the new century, they are a decided minority. But displacement is where it all begins.

How Does a Boat Float?

As Archimedes discovered back in ancient Greece, the weight of an object is equal to the weight of the water it displaces. Boats and other things that float do so because their volume—the space they occupy—is greater than the volume of water they displace.

Let's say you have a boat that weighs 5 tons—an even 10,000 pounds—fully loaded (that is, including engines, fuel, *stores* [food, supplies, and such], gear, and people aboard). Then let's say we have a tank large enough to hold your boat. If you were to fill that tank to the brim and then set your boat in it, you would find (let's say you have a way to do this also) that the water that would spill out of the tank when you set your boat in—the water *displaced*—would also weigh exactly 5 tons.

But putting that 10,000 pounds of water into the mold from which the hull was produced would come nowhere near to filling it. In fact, though it's not so surprising when you think about it, the water would come up to about the point in the mold where you'd find the load waterline on the hull itself.

That's why we can use materials that don't float—steel, aluminum, or fiberglass-reinforced

plastic (FRP), for example—to build boats that do float. We simply have to form the material into a shape that has a greater volume than the water it displaces. A boat needs to do more than just stay afloat, however, and the shape of the hull also has a great influence on its performance and stability.

Performance and stability are important considerations. They, too, are among the trade-offs you have to make in choosing a boat, and each hull type offers its own interpretation of both factors.

Of course, we have to note that all hulls are in a displacement mode at rest. It's when we get underway that the differences show up. In the next chapter, we'll look at boats that can get up on top of the water when they run fast enough. But for now we'll continue to examine hulls that remain in the water—the displacement mode—at all times, even at wide-open throttle (WOT).

Performance

Every coin has two sides. The downside of displacement hulls is that they're relatively slow—generally doing 12 knots or less in the size range of popular powerboating. The upside is that they can achieve this speed with little applied horsepower. Indeed, though some skippers will choose twin screws for easier maneuvering and other supposed advantages, many displacement hulls run quite nicely with only a single small engine. Needing little horsepower means operating with relatively low fuel consumption, which equates either with smaller fuel tanks and more space for accommodations, or greater range with larger tankage.

Since you don't have to concern yourself with getting up on top of the water, you can generally be less concerned about the total weight of a displacement boat. In fact, increasing a displacement hull's load can actually *increase* its speed slightly, as we'll see later in this chapter. The plus to this is that you can fill a displacement boat with all kinds of goodies—more amenities, more fuel, more water, more stowage, etc.—and not only avoid a penalty but in many cases derive a benefit. And that's only true for displacement hulls.

Stability

Displacement hulls are usually very *seakindly* [meaning that they have an easy motion and provide a comfortable ride]. High-speed hulls may be seakindly at cruising speeds but often do not perform comfortably at displacement speeds (though there are some that work well at nearly all throttle settings). Displacement hulls, on the other hand, can usually maintain their cruising speed (slow though it may be) under a greater variety of conditions, including *snotty* [nasty] weather that would make running at high speed downright uncomfortable if not totally impossible (Figure 3-1). Some displacement hulls roll more than most folks like, particularly in beam seas. But (as we'll discover in due time), this is only a matter of comfort, as the rolling is an inherent part of the vessel's true stability. It can also be easily corrected with mechanical antiroll systems, and fortunately not all displacement hulls are equally guilty. Then, too, I can't think of anything that rolls more than some planing hulls do when they're not on plane, since they achieve stability solely through a hydrodynamic action that's missing unless they're moving fast.

After these sweeping statements, it's now time to add some background as to why they're so. I hope you find the following information interesting in its own right, as details to further your appreciation of boats and their behavior. But alas, I'm afraid you'll also find some of it necessary simply to trigger the ever-important "But wait a minute, what about . . .?" question you'll have to

FIGURE 3-1. *Trawler-type boats such as this Grand Banks 46 can usually handle heavy seas that are a problem for lighter boats.*

raise from time to time when an enthusiastic salesperson carries exaggeration too far. Though the boating industry is perhaps better than some in its percentage of knowledgeable salespeople (no doubt brought about by the number of people who come into the business because they like boats in the first place), there are still those who hardly know the "pointy end" from the transom. So if *you* don't know why boats behave as they do, you could end up buying a bill of goods instead of the boat you want.

Displacement Speeds—A Closer Look

Every displacement boat has what's commonly called its *hull speed*. Unfortunately, hull speed is one of the most bandied about yet least understood terms in boating. As applied to displacement hulls, it might be defined simply as the maximum speed attainable without applying ridiculous horsepower, because *any* hull will plane if you push it hard enough. (Though there are practical limits to available power plants, and some hulls just don't have room for the horsepower it would take to get them on plane—at least not with the engines currently available.)

To put hull speed in a real-world perspective, let's see how it relates to you and the throttle lever. Say it takes 200 hp to push your boat as fast as it will go in a displacement mode. Yet let's also say the builder has given you 250 hp to play with. Once you throttle up to the 200 hp point on the power curve, you're going as fast as you can. Push the throttle all the way, and you'll only burn more fuel and make more noise. The "extra" 50 hp gives you better economy (a 250 hp engine putting out 200 is more fuel efficient than a 200 hp engine working at maximum load), longer engine life (for similar reasons), and some added thrust when you need it for maneuvering. But it won't make you go any faster. It could take 800 hp or *more* (depending on how closely the hull shape approaches a planing design and how much the boat weighs) to make that boat go faster than "hull speed."

The reasons for this speed limit lie in the way a displacement hull moves *through* the water. It makes waves. Can't help it. And waves are bound by the immutable laws of physics. Put a boat into a wave system, and not so strangely, its behavior will be strongly influenced by the same laws. But notice I said strongly, not totally.

This is not to suggest that boats aren't also bound by the laws of physics. Of course they are. In fact, by the time you finish this book you will have seen many ways in which boats are virtually living physics labs. My point is that the laws regarding free-wave motion are not the only laws influencing boat behavior. If they were, there would be far less variety in displacement hull performance.

Speed Relates to Length

Open-water wave systems move along at a speed-to-length ratio of 1.34. This means that you can determine the speed of advance of a wave by measuring *wavelength* [the distance between crests] and multiplying the square root of the wavelength by 1.34. This is one of the immutable laws. Since displacement hulls often attain their greatest speed when they generate a wave whose length equals the waterline length of the boat, it's been assumed (and too often stated as gospel) that the hull speed of a displacement boat *must be* 1.34 times the square root of its waterline length. This is *not* immutable.

The truth is that a displacement hull will achieve a maximum speed-to-length ratio of 1.34 more easily than higher speeds. It's always easier

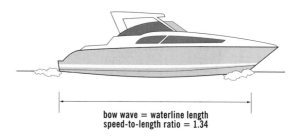

bow wave = waterline length
speed-to-length ratio = 1.34

FIGURE 3-2. *When a boat's bow wave equals its waterline length, its speed-to-length ratio is 1.34. Given enough power, displacement hulls can achieve a speed-to-length ratio of up to 2.0.*

to work *with* nature. It's certainly possible and even common for displacement hulls to be designed and powered for speed-to-length ratios higher than 1.34, but horsepower needs increase geometrically with speed at these higher ratios (Figure 3-2).

It should be obvious that shape is involved also. Wedges, needles, nails, and other pointy objects penetrate solids more easily than blunt objects do. The bows of boats are tapered for similar reasons—it's easier to cut the water than to plow through it. Similarly, the way a boat *leaves* its quarter wave is important, too, so the shape of the boat at the stern has influence as well. Indeed, breaking away from the tough grasp of the quarter wave is one of the challenges of attaining a speed-to-length ratio greater than 1.34.

The *shape* of the boat in the water is as significant in many ways as the *length* of the boat in the water, and hull efficiency comes into play for displacement hulls fully as much (though in different ways) as we'll soon find out it does for planing hulls (Figure 3-3).

To give other arguments their due, some say that any speed-to-length ratio higher than 1.34 puts the boat into the "semidisplacement" category (we'll discuss the nature of this beast a couple of chapters after this one). However, many naval architects agree that speed-to-length ratios up to 2.0 may still be considered displacement speeds. Ratios between 2.0 and 4.0 are likely to belong to semidisplacement hulls, and any boat with a ratio over 4.0 will undoubtedly be planing.

To further refute the "must be 1.34" element,

FIGURE 3-3. *Though it doesn't relate directly to pleasure boats, the bulbous bow often seen below the waterline on ships is a perfect illustration of one way in which hull shape influences speed. Without this protrusion, the ship would be slower.*

I offer as proof the boat I'm sitting on as I write this. It's steel, nearly 80 feet overall, with a 25-foot beam and a 6-foot draft. It weighs about 160 tons fully loaded. Definitely a displacement hull! But it was designed to achieve a hull speed of 13 knots, and by golly it can. With 70 feet on the waterline (square root 8.37), this equates to a speed-to-length ratio of 1.55.

Granted, it takes every bit of the 750 horses aboard to get the 13 knots. But 800, 1,000, or even 1,500 hp would push it no faster. Yet throttling back to 400 hp still gives us 10 knots and much better efficiency (about half the fuel it takes to produce 750 hp). If 1.34 were always the magic number, this boat would top out at 11.2 knots no matter what.

As a side note just to show how complex it all can be, a naval architect working on big ship design once told me about having to modify the computer program used to analyze the results of tank-testing hull models. The reason? There proved to be a slight but measurable difference in performance between hulls *pulled* through the water by external forces (as are the test models), and those *pushed* through by the action of their own propellers (as happens in the real world). You can't take any of it for granted.

Speed Also Relates to Power

Let's look at three similar displacement hulls, all of them trawler yachts with an overall length in the upper 30s and a waterline length of 32 feet. The square root of 32 is 5.66, so if boat A has a maximum speed-to-length ratio of 1.34, its maximum displacement speed will be about 7½ knots (1.34 x 5.66). If boat B has a maximum speed-to-length ratio of 1.55, we have a nearly 9-knot boat (8.8), and if boat C's S/L ratio is 2.0, the generally considered cutoff for pure displacement performance, we have a boat that can do slightly better than 11 knots.

Here's where the trade-offs come in. Although the waterline lengths are identical, their speed-to-length ratios are different, so their maximum speeds are different. This means their power requirements are different, too—but only to exceed 7½ knots. It would take roughly the same horsepower to match speeds to that point in all three boats. The difference is that boats B and C will need more power to be able to reach their full potential. A lot more. If 112 hp is enough to get the 7½ knots, boat A can be equipped with a single 125 hp diesel and do quite nicely; you'd have the reserve we discussed above. But boat C would probably need a minimum of 250 hp to get its 11 knots, which would mean either a larger single engine or two of the same engines used in boat A. Either way, boat C will inevitably cost more to buy and to operate.

The Options

We won't worry yet about the debate between singles and twins—we'll leave that to a later chapter. For now we'll just say the boats are much alike except that A has 125 hp in the engine compartment and C has 250. Let's make nearly everything else—the accommodations plans, fuel capacities, and such—identical (though, obviously, the bottom shapes are different). Given the same amount of fuel, at 7½ knots both boats would have a nearly identical range. For ease of figuring, let's make it 500 miles. On this basis, boat C's range would drop to about 330 miles if you throttled up to 11 knots. Please note that these figures are for broad comparison only. As it says on the car window stickers, actual mileage may vary.

If it's 50 miles between Bon Voyage and Laissez le Bon Temps Rouler, the trip will take 6 hours and 40 minutes at 7½ knots, but only 4½ hours at 11 knots. Not too big a difference. But if the distance between ports is 100 miles, you're looking at nearly 13½ hours on the water in boat A versus about 9 hours in boat C—a big difference when you consider daylight hours, activities on arrival, the availability of dock help, fuel dock hours, and other related factors affecting both departure and arrival times.

But you must also remember that in getting there faster, boat C will burn at least 1.5 times as much fuel as boat A. So not only does boat C cost more to buy; it costs more to run.

To complete the comparison, boat B would need about 160 hp to get its near 9 knots. Under the same guidelines as above, it would have a range of about 419 miles and would make a 50-mile trip in just over 5½ hours, burning about 1.2 times the fuel of boat A. Of course, boat C throttled back to 9 knots would do about the same.

The one constant in all this is the waterline length. Increase that, and you increase hull speed no matter what the S/L ratio—longer boats can go faster. Loading a displacement hull so it sits deeper in the water also effectively adds to the waterline length. That's why displacement hulls are used for load-carrying workboats, and it's another reason why they're so loved for long-range cruising. You can bring aboard all the fuel, water, supplies, and comforts you need and actually gain speed (however slightly) in the process.

Stability . . . Again (in Greater Detail)

Stability might be defined as a boat's ability to remain upright no matter what. This might seem an oversimplification, yet it's really what we're primarily after—a boat that won't turn turtle. Period. Of course, we complicate things by wanting to feel comfortable at the same time. And given that pleasure boats operate over a wide set of conditions with respect to load, trim, sea state, and op-

erator proficiency, we also want that to happen without much thought or work on our part.

Our main concern is *transverse* [side-to-side] stability, which is defined by engineers as a vessel's ability to resist rotation about its longitudinal axis and return to an upright position after being disturbed by an upsetting force. Whew! We call this "rotation about its longitudinal axis" *rolling*. And it bothers us because rolling can be agonizingly uncomfortable and, carried to the extreme, can lead to capsizing.

Poor *longitudinal* [fore-and-aft] stability can be a problem, too, because it leads to a wet ride, but getting wet doesn't seem to bother us nearly as much as getting queasy, so it's usually of less concern.

Fortunately, today's pleasure boats are generally very stable, and unless we do a truly horrendous job of improper loading or take the boat into much heavier seas than it was designed for, we don't have to worry about capsizing. Comfort, however, is another story. As we'll see, a certain amount of rolling is inherent in a stable hull. Unfortunately, knowing this doesn't make it feel one bit better. We humans don't like rolling at all! So we often use antiroll devices—called *stabilizers*—to make the ride smoother. But before we can fully appreciate stabilizers, we have to understand stability.

Like a lot of other things in nature, stability results from a balance of forces, which tend to keep the boat upright (static stability) or, more important in our scheme of things, return it to upright when those "upsetting forces" disturb it (dynamic stability). Many of these balancing forces have been observed, though perhaps not understood, since the first clever caveman carved a canoe.

Chances are the earliest boaters merely hitched a ride on a floating log and so discovered buoyancy. The first person who came up with the idea to cut into the log and make a dugout got a vessel that was not only better for carrying things but also more stable; cutting away part of the log lowered its center of gravity. When some distant relatives added outriggers for even greater stability, they discovered the positive effects of beam.

In Figure 3-4 we see the forces of stability diagrammed. The center of gravity (G) is the hypothetical point at which an object's weight appears to be concentrated. A boat floats because the upward force of buoyancy balances this downward force. As with gravity, we can assume a point (B) where all the buoyancy appears to be concentrated.

In normal trim (region **A** of Figure 3-4), these forces are in line and in direct opposition—B is below G. (This is true when we have "design stability," which is the case with most powerboat hulls. In deep-draft sailboats with a heavy keel, we see "weight stability," in which the forces are reversed—G will be below B. But they will still be in line and in balance.) This alignment of G and B is static stability. When the boat rolls, even a little, we are looking at dynamic stability. B moves toward the lower side, and a vertical line drawn upward from B cuts the vertical centerline at a point we call the *metacenter* (M). A boat's initial metacenter is determined when we roll the boat an infinitesimal, almost immeasurably small, amount.

Generally speaking, G does not move when the boat rolls, but B and M do. The distance from the center of gravity, G, to the metacenter, M—known as *metacentric height* (GM)—decreases as M moves down the vertical centerline.

Metacentric height is, to a degree, a measure of a boat's stability. The greater the GM, the stiffer the hull; that is, the less its tendency to roll. We don't want a boat to be too stiff, however, because in its own way a stiff vessel can be as uncomfortable as one that rolls too much, and it's potentially dangerous to boot. No matter how stiff the boat, an angry sea can throw it off an even keel; when that happens, the same design characteristics that make the boat stiff to begin with may also make it slow to recover its footing once heeled. The designer must ensure that the boat's shape and weight distribution create adequate righting moment to return the boat to an even keel. The *righting moment* is a force resulting from buoyancy working on the righting arm (see below), and a boat with healthy righting moment will roll—at least until we add antiroll devices.

In region **B** of Figure 3-4 we see that a *righting arm* (GZ) develops as the boat heels or lists. At some point, the righting arm will have sufficient leverage to push the hull back upright. Then, of course, it will roll to the other side until another righting arm develops the moment to bring it back.

Though constant rolling may be uncomfortable, it does indicate a healthily functioning system—the boat's righting moment is not letting it roll too far to either side. In this sense, perhaps, rolling is to stability as bending is to the longevity of a twig. A twig that bends can survive the strongest winds, while a stiff one may snap if the pressure becomes too great. But what's healthy for the boat may still be unhealthy (or at least un-

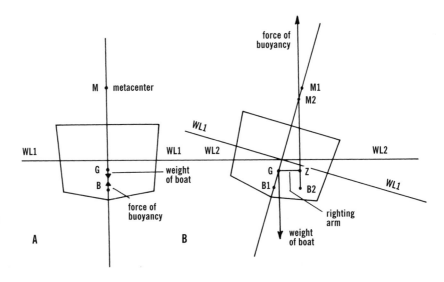

FIGURE 3-4. *In **A**, metacentric height equals GM. In **B**, it has grown shorter and now equals GM2. As the boat rolls, the righting arm GZ develops to return the hull to an even keel. In an effort to enhance stability, the designer will try to increase the magnitude of both GM and GZ in the rolling hull.*

comfortable) for its occupants, and so we look for other solutions.

Because the righting moment is essentially a matter of leverage, the resulting force can be made stronger either by pushing harder or by using a longer lever. In this case our lever is the righting arm (GZ). We've already seen that the righting arm increases as the boat rolls. But since we want to achieve stability without excessive roll, we often seek other ways to get the same result. Our choices are to make the righting arm longer by either lowering the center of gravity or increasing beam (which essentially moves B farther from the centerline as the boat rolls), or to increase the force of buoyancy. Since buoyancy is largely related to hull shape, it's possible to design a shape in which the force of buoyancy increases as the hull lays over. The result is again a greater righting moment produced from a lesser angle of roll. A perfect example of this is the traditional Grand Banks dory. It's extremely "tippy" when empty and can be laid over until a gunwale is almost in the water. But once it reaches this point, even dragging a net full of fish over the gunwale and into the boat (which is why it was designed to roll so far) can't make it roll any farther.

Truly comfortable hulls generally use all three elements—lower center of gravity, greater beam, and hull shape—in varying proportions, and a wide, low boat with a lot of reserve buoyancy will be very seakindly indeed.

Obviously, one way to lower the center of gravity is to give a boat deeper draft: the more boat in the water compared with what's above the waterline, the more stable the boat. But deep draft and pleasure boating do not truly go hand in hand because many pleasure-boat destinations can't accommodate deep-draft vessels. Fortunately draft, per se, is not the objective; balance is.

Achieving the right balance for good stability is a problem faced by naval architects no matter what type of hull we're discussing. But since displacement hulls are often derived from traditional workboat lines—in the trawler yacht (see Figure 3-1), we've even borrowed the name of the North Sea fishing boats on which they're based— the differences between the original and the derivation raise additional problems. For example,

real trawlers are designed not only to go after fish but also to bring home the catch—tons at a time. Eliminate the payload, and the boat doesn't sit or ride properly. And even if the trawler yacht were to have the same lines as a working trawler and a load of ballast to make it sit on its lines, the result would not be practical for pleasure boating. It would carry way too much draft and require more boathandling skill than most amateur boaters would possess.

So most pleasure-boat displacement hulls, regardless of what they're called, are at best *modifications* of workboat designs and thus must be cursed with a higher center of gravity. This is not to say that such boats are top-heavy but rather that they'll very likely have a less comfortable roll than the commercial craft they resemble, and some very salty-looking craft prove to be a lot less comfortable than you would imagine from their appearance.

One more note on shape. Since it's common dockside knowledge that "round-bottomed boats roll more," I think it's only right to clarify things. The statement is true without question if we're talking about a hull shape in which the whole bottom is rounded. In fact, the more closely the hull shape resembles an arc of a circle, the more roll we'll have. But a hull with round (soft) bilges will not roll appreciably more than a hard-chined hull if the lines are otherwise basically the same. (See Figure 3-5 for the difference between a hard chine and a round bilge.)

Motion Minders

Antiroll devices come in two forms, passive and active, as described by the way they work their magic. As the appellations suggest, passive antiroll devices just hang there, while active devices *do* something.

Among the most popular passive devices are *flopper stoppers* for at-rest situations and *paravanes* for use underway (Figure 3-6). Flopper stoppers may be hung just about any way, but paravanes are hung overboard from booms. The vanes add to the vessel's rolling inertia and tend to reduce uncomfortable motion simply by making it physically harder to produce a roll in either

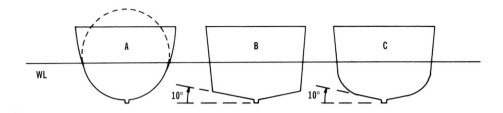

FIGURE 3-5. *Hull A will roll easily because its shape is nearly circular. Hull B, with its hard* chine *[the "corner" between the side and bottom of the hull as seen in cross section], will roll less than A. But what is perhaps less intuitively evident is that hull C will roll little more than B despite its rounded bilges, because both have 10-degree-deadrise shallow-V bottoms of equal beam and draft.*

direction. That the vanes must be set and retrieved as conditions require (for example, they're in the way coming into a marina) is but one of their drawbacks. Another is that they don't work as effectively as active devices. On the plus side, they *do* work; being relatively simple, they're less expensive than active devices; and because they're "mechanical" only in the simplest sense and have no sophisticated parts or need for electric power, they'll continue to work, free of breakdown, with little maintenance. The need for booms, and masts from which to suspend the booms, does limit their use to boats that have room for such appurtenances, but then again, this category includes many types of displacement craft. There are several types of active antiroll devices, including such things as weights on tracks

that slide hydraulically in the opposite direction whenever a roll begins, and supersized trim tabs that work under the stern. But by far the most common are fin stabilizers, which control the rolling of a boat in much the same way that ailerons on an airplane wing cause the plane to bank in turns. Using a gyroscope to sense the slightest deviation from upright, the system angles the fins to produce an immediate counterroll. Because the hull doesn't have to use its designed-in righting moment (which would eventually develop, but not until the boat had rolled farther), the difference in comfort level is almost unbelievable. Of course, no device can completely eliminate rolling, but a good fin system can go a long way toward that objective, often reducing roll by 90 percent.

FIGURE 3-6. *A paravane is a passive stabilizer and in use is hung over the side on a cable suspended from a boom. The cylindrical weight forces the paravane underwater, while the horizontal "wing" tends to resist lift and keep it there. With one of these devices hanging off each side of a boat, its tendency to roll is greatly reduced. (Illustration by Rob Groves)*

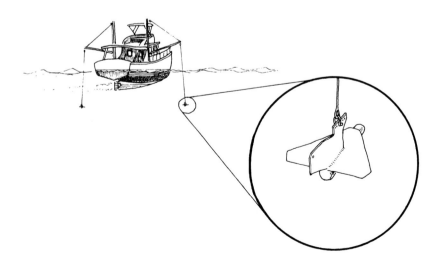

Decisions, Decisions, Decisions

Even after you've decided to add fins, there are still some choices to be made, though the vagaries of the marketplace have narrowed them considerably by eliminating some former manufacturers.

First, there's the matter of control. One of the oldest system designs, and one that is still in considerable use, is mechanical (or actually hydromechanical) all the way. That's what we see in Figure 3-7. In this system, the gyroscope's control of the actuators is purely hydraulic. One of the principal advantages of these systems is simplicity. There's little to go wrong and no sensitive electronic components to be ravaged by salt air. And although proponents of electronic control boast that electrons move at the speed of light whereas hydraulic pressure does not, the truth is that for the distances involved in the systems on pleasure craft, hydraulic response is nearly as instantaneous. And if hydromechanical systems didn't work very well, Naiad (their manufacturer) would have replaced them rather than augmenting them with electronically controlled systems.

The main advantage of electronically controlled systems (most of which still use hydraulic actuators to rotate the fins even if they're now directed by electrical impulses) is that they can be programmed to be more than simple antiroll devices. For example, some feature rate and angle adjustments at the operator panel to permit fine-tuning the system response while underway, which can be especially helpful in following or quartering seas where the rolling is more complex. And as for being "ravaged" by salt air? Well, engineers now have enough experience with bringing electronic circuitry aboard that this is really not a consideration.

There's another choice. Do you want hydraulic or pneumatic activation of the fins? I've always questioned using pneumatics to work against a variable resistance such as the sea. After all, compressed air can be further compressed when resistance increases, whereas fluids are not compressible. That's why we usually use hydraulic steering even if the boat is equipped with pneumatic controls for the throttles and clutches; rudders must work against a variable resistance. But there are enough pneumatic antiroll systems currently in use, including many that were chosen and installed by engineers whose judgment I respect, for me to conclude that my prejudice may have been ill founded. Ask around the waterfront before

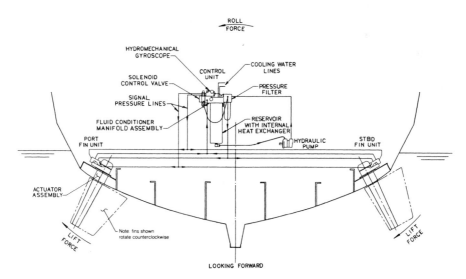

FIGURE 3-7. *This is an example of an* active *stabilizing system. Working similarly to the ailerons on an airplane, the fins can actually make a boat roll to either side, much as an airplane banks. A gyroscope senses true vertical and directs the fins to produce a counterroll opposing the natural roll induced by the hull's reaction to wave motion. The result is near-level cruising. (Courtesy Naiad Marine)*

you decide for yourself. Be particularly inquisitive of people who have your make and model of boat. What works for them should work for you.

Actually, the integrity of installation is perhaps more important than the make and type of system, so you should pay far more attention to installing correctly sized fins in the correct location than to selecting a particular brand or type. The vessel's speed and displacement—not LOA—are the primary factors used to calculate the best fin size. Others include waterline beam and transverse metacentric height (GM). For modest hull speeds, the fins are positioned within the middle one-third of the waterline length. If the vessel exceeds 20 knots, this region is limited to the middle one-fifth. The fin and corresponding fin actuator assembly should be installed perpendicular to the hull bottom (to assure full range of motion) and as far from the keel as practical (to achieve the best possible leverage). The fin should also be located to assure that its tip stays within the envelope of the beam and keel.

With a new boat, simply have the builder install the system during the initial construction. If you're retrofitting, make sure the yard knows what it's doing. In either case, going with system types and fin sizes they have used successfully on similar hulls in the past should produce like results for you.

Maintenance

No onboard system works forever without proper maintenance, and allowance for it should be a part of the decision when it comes to adding any gear to your boat. But stabilizer systems aren't terribly demanding. For its systems, Naiad Marine recommends you change the oil in the reservoir and replace the lower seals every 3 years or 4,000 hours. They further suggest that you replace the oil filter element when the "Dirt Alarm" approaches the yellow arc with the system operating in either the "Center" or "On" mode. And periodically you should check the cooling-water pump for impeller wear and verify adequate flow. That's all. It's really very little work for the degree of comfort derived.

Here's a final note regarding the positive effects of active stabilization. In addition to enhancing comfort, a properly installed system can also increase fuel efficiency and, particularly in displacement boats, even add to your speed. They do this despite the inevitable *drag* [resistance to forward motion] the fins create, because a boat that rolls less will usually run a straighter track. That translates to a better speed made good; you spend less time wandering, and that, of course, means you burn less fuel.

A well-balanced, stable displacement boat can take you nearly anywhere because it will make its speed no matter what, and given the lack of weight restrictions (both statements must be modified by "within reason"), you can also go in considerable comfort. All of which is a pretty strong argument in favor of displacement hulls. But still, to a lot of people, displacement boats are no good because "they can't get out of their own way." So in the next chapter, we'll look at boats that *can!*

4

Planing Hulls

Displacement hulls, while desirable for many purposes, just don't go fast enough for most modern recreational boatowners. It seems we're in a hurry to relax. That's why the majority of today's pleasure craft are designed to *plane* [to get up and move across the water rather than through it]. There are many approaches to the task of making a boat get up and go, and in this chapter we'll cover some of the advantages and disadvantages of each. Though by now it shouldn't be a surprise, there are trade-offs to be made in the choice of hull form even within the category of planing hulls.

As I pointed out in the last chapter, any hull can plane if you apply enough power (in theory, at least; in reality, finding large-enough engines to get an ultraheavy hull to plane might be an overwhelming challenge). One of the objectives in designing a planing boat, however, is to get the boat on plane with as little horsepower as possible. And while the power required for a planing hull will always be greater than that needed by a displacement boat of similar size, it will never approach the power that would be necessary to plane a hull not designed for the purpose. However, just as we ask of all hulls that they do more than simply stay afloat, we also ask that planing hulls do more than simply plane. So we often sacrifice a degree of planing efficiency in an effort to gain other attributes.

Deep-V, Modified-V, and Other Arcane Shapes

As Figure 4-1 shows, a flat surface will plane with little difficulty—even if it isn't a boat! The photo is from the early 1950s. In those days, my father,

FIGURE 4-1. *Any flat surface will plane when it's trimmed properly. A proper planing hull, however, has more to it than a flat bottom. (Courtesy Mercury Marine)*

who knew this fact well and gave me much of my basic boating education, constantly amazed (and often embarrassed) the owners of sleeker, supposedly faster boats by racing them in a tubby, flat-bottomed, solid-wood skiff powered by a 5-horse outboard kicker. He'd just lock down the tiller so he didn't have to sit back by the motor and move his considerable weight forward until the boat reached optimum trim, and then he'd let her rip. It was quite a sight. The skiff didn't look fast, particularly with a rather rotund gentleman sitting in it, but given the right sea conditions, Dad could pass nearly everyone around.

The required condition is a slight chop, just enough to make it easy for the boat to break loose from the bonds of surface tension (which tends to cancel lift and keep a hull from planing) but not enough to cause the flat surface to pound. Pounding is the main drawback to a flat bottom and the reason you're more apt to see a planing table than a totally flat-bottomed planing boat larger than a skiff. Once the seas build up, a flat bottom will slam, pound, and otherwise bang into the water in a quite obnoxious manner. At first it's merely uncomfortable, but when the seas get high enough, the pounding counteracts forward motion sufficiently to take the boat off plane. So while they rate high on initial planing efficiency, flat bottoms rate low on total practicality.

Just the opposite might be said for the form known as the *deep-V*. Deep-Vs generally require more horsepower than other planing hulls because the form produces less purely upward lift (Figure 4-2), but a deep-V will continue to perform on plane and at speed under conditions that force other shapes to slow down. This is why offshore racers still often turn to the deep-V for rough water, as they have since Dick Bertram's *Moppie*,

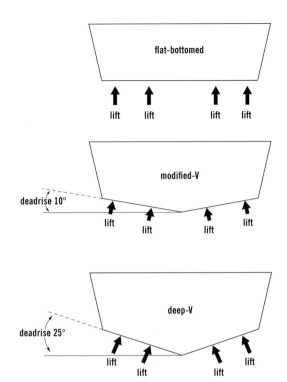

FIGURE 4-2. *A flat-bottomed hull will plane easily because hydrodynamic lift tends to be perpendicular to the hull surface. In this case, the lift is all straight up. The farther from horizontal the bottom, the less vertical the hydrodynamic lift; so a deep-V hull requires more power to get it up on plane.*

designed by C. Raymond Hunt, first showed her mettle by whipping everyone handily back in 1961. Also known as *constant deadrise* hulls because the deadrise doesn't change from bow to stern (Figure 4-3), the sharply angled bottom of a deep-V simply behaves toward the water beneath as the sharply angled bow of any boat does to the water

FIGURE 4-3. *In this computer-generated model of a Mach 1 Sovereign, note that the hull's 25-degree deadrise extends all the way to the transom. Deep-Vs are also known as* constant deadrise *hulls. (Courtesy Mach 1)*

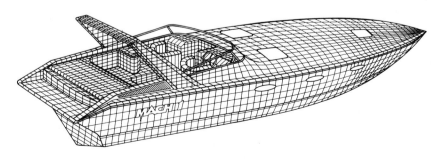

ahead: cuts it like a knife. Since the cutting edge carries all the way aft, a deep-V can run with very little wetted surface (wetted surface equals friction, which equals reduced speed) and still cut into heavy seas by keeping only the extreme after-portions of the hull in contact with them. Indeed, offshore racers often seem to have nothing but their drive units in the water.

Of course, deep-Vs aren't perfect. In addition to needing more horsepower than other planing forms, they have a few other drawbacks. None is insurmountable, however, and many builders use deep-V hulls for boats that will be subjected to far less rigorous conditions than rough-water offshore racing.

Deep-Vs have one particular performance penchant that can be either a blessing or curse, depending on circumstances: they run as straight as if they were on rails. When you *want* to go straight, it's wonderful. You can take a deep-V through surging following seas—the kind that constantly tend to push most other boats off course—or through a nasty inlet with ease. Hands off! The boat will hold itself true. But when you want to turn, it can be a different story. Then you often have a fight on your hands. A deep-V *will* turn, of course, but usually not as easily as other hull forms. If you have a deep-V, you definitely want power steering.

Given that a flat surface will plane more easily, it's not surprising that deep-Vs can also have a tendency to lay over and run on one of the V's flats instead of on the apex. With every wave or so, the boat may flip from side to side in an action that undermines stability and makes control difficult. This action, logically called *chine walking*, can be corrected to a large degree with modifications of the simple V form. Not so strangely, some of these modifications also alleviate other deep-V drawbacks as well.

Running strakes and chine flats (Figure 4-4) are the two principal additions. Running strakes are often considered to have cosmetic value only, but anyone who has ever suffered through the tribulations of conducting sea trials on a prototype deep-V (particularly in the early days) will tell you that repositioning the strakes to their most effective location is a part of the drill. I'll

FIGURE 4-4. *The underbody shape of deep-V hulls usually includes running strakes and chine flats to increase lift and add lateral stability. (Courtesy Dag Pike*, Fast Powerboat Seamanship*)*

grant that their effect is minimal, but the small flats of the running strakes do *help* prevent chine walking. Chine flats help more. When the boat starts to heel, the lift provided by the flat surface at the extreme outboard edge will counter the heel and bring the boat back into proper trim. Chine flats also help deep-Vs with their transverse stability under low-speed or at-rest conditions. While the locations of the center of gravity, beam, and other factors also have some influence (as we saw with displacement hulls), the added lift at the extreme outboard edges helps considerably in keeping the boat upright in the displacement mode, though not as much as it does when the boat is moving fast. Indeed, deep-Vs are often not the most stable boats at rest even with chine flats. However, many anglers use deep-V sportfishermen anyway, because they feel the boats' other attributes (particularly the ability to go fast in heavy seas) outweigh this minor drawback.

Steps Planing hulls, particularly deep-Vs, are sometimes *stepped* (Figure 4-5). As the term implies, this introduces an abrupt change in the bottom's horizontal lines, which (in a greatly simplified explanation) allows the part of the hull *abaft* [aft of] the step to "surf" on the wave created by the portion ahead of it. It's not uncommon to see high-speed hulls with two steps. I find it interesting that racing-boat hulls were often stepped way back in the earliest days of powerboat racing. Stepped hulls never vanished, but they did go out of fashion when other shapes, such as the deep-V,

FIGURE 4-5. *Steps allow the hull to ride on two or (in this case) three shorter surfaces, which reduces total wetted area, lessens drag, and improves longitudinal stability. Because steps also introduce air under the hull (which also seems to improve efficiency), designers have to be careful to create steps that will continue to work similarly when the boat banks in turns in order to maintain stability and consistency of handling whether going straight or turning. (Courtesy David Clark/Fountain Powerboats)*

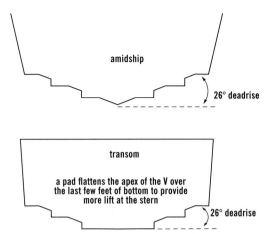

FIGURE 4-6. *While the conventional deep-V hull carries its constant deadrise all the way to the transom, hull designs employing a* pad *gradually flatten the V over the last few feet to create greater lift in the part of the hull that is usually in the water at all running attitudes.*

came in. In recent years the value of a step (or two) on a planing hull has been rediscovered with a vengeance. The feature is nowhere near universal, but you'll see it often in a wide variety of hull forms (and with an equally wide variety of modifying names).

Pads Another modification sometimes made to deep-V hulls is to flatten the extreme after-end of the V—the part normally expected to be in contact with the water at all times. Usually called a *pad* (Figure 4-6), this modification reflects the better planing efficiency of a flatter surface while allowing all the other attributes of a constant deadrise, since the hull still presents the cutting edge of the V forward of the pad. Pads are generally seen only on "performance" hulls.

Modified-Vs Perhaps the ultimate departure is the so-called *modified-V*. Unlike the constant deadrise of a deep-V, the deadrise of a modified-V changes, starting out in the neighborhood of a deep-V at the bow (26 degrees or more) and flattening out to 18 to 14 degrees (or less) at the transom (Figure 4-7). For this reason, modified-Vs are also known as *variable deadrise* or *warped plane* hulls. The object is to retain cutting action forward and gain greater lift aft, which results in a more-efficient hull that is easier to get on plane than a deep-V but less capable of handling the

rough stuff at top speed. It's a practical compromise, so you'll find that a lot of boats, from small open fishermen to large motor yachts, do indeed sport warped plane bottoms. There are probably as many variations on the theme as there are builders and designers, and they all try to keep their designs proprietary. Differences are usually minor, however, and the truth is they often have better luck in getting a trademark for the *name* of the design than they do in claiming something exclusive, and therefore patentable, about the design itself.

Note that in recent years boat companies have been able to register their designs in an attempt to stop the *splashing* [unlawful copying] that occurs when people make a mold from someone else's existing hull and then start producing apparently identical, but actually quite different, boats under their own brand. So far, hull registration has helped ease the problem, but it hasn't totally eliminated splashing. So beware: a boat that *looks* like the one you want may not be the one you *really* want. It's best to buy a known brand from an established, reputable dealer.

One design that's been patented (which is a more stringent process than trademark registration) is the Delta Conic hull developed by Harry

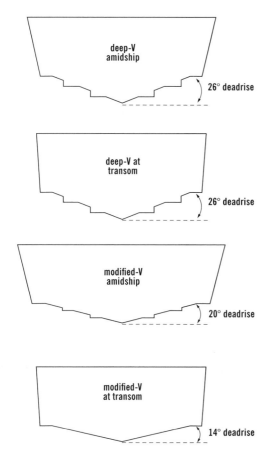

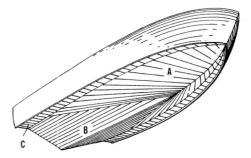

FIGURE 4-8. *The forward portions (A) of the Delta Conic hull are of varying deadrise but take their form from sections of a cone. The after part (B) is the delta, a 12½-degree constant deadrise. The chine flats (C) angle slightly downward at the outboard edge. (Courtesy Schoell Marine)*

FIGURE 4-7. *Also known as a* warped plane *hull, the modified-V starts with a sharp entry similar to a deep-V but has a varying deadrise that flattens out to something on the order of 14 degrees or less at the transom.*

Schoell, an engineer and designer who lives and works in Fort Lauderdale, Florida. The Delta Conic hull is not, technically, a warped plane. The forward portions are of varying deadrise but take their form from sections of a cone. The after part

is the delta, a 12½-degree constant deadrise (Figure 4-8). The sections blend smoothly, and there are no compound curves involved (as there may be with some modified-V designs). The Delta Conic hull uses chine flats (actually angled slightly downward at the outboard edge) to provide some of its running stability, but it gains stability at rest by having different rolling periods for the delta sections and the conic sections, which tend to cancel each other out. Delta Conic hulls are quite efficient and seakindly at just about any speed. Their major drawback, in my opinion, is that to work properly, all dimensions have to expand when the hull increases in length. Operationally, that's no problem; the form works at all sizes. But when you extend the length over 40 feet, the beam begins to exceed the width of many marina slips (though the increasing popularity of larger boats is changing marina design).

With the introduction of his Duo Delta Conic hull (essentially a stepped version) Schoell overcame the problem. This arrangement allows improved Delta Conic performance (which was excellent to begin with) in greater lengths without increasing the beam. The design isn't limited to large boats, however, and is being used on some family cruisers in the 30-foot range.

Cathedrals and Catamarans In Figure 4-9 we see a planing hull form quite common in smaller boats. Sometimes known as the *cathedral* hull, it's also

FIGURE 4-9. *The cathedral hull form offers considerable stability to a narrow-beamed small boat by increasing the buoyancy at the chines. This design is also often called* gull wing. *(Courtesy Chaparral)*

(for obvious reasons) often called the *gull wing*. Its main attributes are a performance similar to the deep-V and slightly better lateral stability—the outer wings give essentially the same aid to a planing hull as do the outriggers on a Polynesian dugout canoe.

Catamarans (Figure 4-10) work somewhat similarly, but in effect eliminate the center portion and work on the "outriggers" alone. This gives the advantages of greater beam with less draft and, often, less total wetted surface, which

FIGURE 4-10. *Twin-hulled craft gain added lift and higher speeds as a result of the tunnel between the hulls. They also present less wave-making resistance (WMR) for a softer, drier ride. Catamarans are no longer just for racing; as you can see by the rods in the rod holders, this Sea Cat 25 is meant for serious fishing. (Courtesy North American Fiberglass Corporation)*

adds up to greater speed. Catamarans win many of today's offshore races, though they don't always work as well in heavy seas, so racers frequently revert to the deep-V when the going gets rough.

Previously seen only in these still-narrow "racing machine" hulls, the catamaran concept has started to show up more in beamier fishing and cruising boat versions. Interestingly enough, several of these cats originate in New Zealand, where cruising catamarans have been quite common for a number of years. And at cruising speeds, these beamier catamarans seem to handle the "rough stuff" rather well.

Planing Hull Performance

Since we choose a planing hull because we want to go faster, going faster often becomes the quest itself. If you recall our discussion in Chapter 1, you'll remember that speed on the water is a result of three factors: horsepower, weight, and shape. Since we're discussing planing hulls, we'll consider shape a constant for any particular boat and look at horsepower and weight as variables.

Horsepower

What happens when we up the power? Generally, we'll gain speed. But this isn't always the answer. Aside from limitations on the horsepower standard engines can deliver, there are other reasons why adding more power may not be the best alternative for increasing speed. As we've already seen, when you increase engine power, you usually increase engine weight (though there also have been recent gains in this area, with new engines offering more horsepower per pound than formerly available). And, of course, the added horsepower means burning more fuel, which means carrying more fuel (read: more weight—this hasn't changed) in order to maintain any kind of practical range. Sometimes the results are disappointing in that the added load cancels out the added horsepower for no net gain in performance. Even when it works, increasing horsepower may not be the answer. After all, you just might want your boat to be something more than engines and fuel tanks. So let's look for a better solution.

Weight

Planing results from hydrodynamic lift. And whether we're talking about a boat or a sack of groceries, the lighter the object, the easier it is to lift. So if we make the boat lighter, we'll get more lift and thus more speed from the same horses.

Yet, as logical as that statement seems, getting lighter boats has not been easy either. When we first started building with fiberglass, boats were usually heavier than they had to be. There were a number of reasons for this, ranging from seat-of-the-pants engineering, which tended to "add a little, just in case," to be sure the boat was strong enough, to consumers who wanted a plastic hull to thump as soundly and seem as thick as the wooden ones they were used to. So most boats of quality were way overbuilt, which further bolstered consumer opinion that this is what a fiberglass boat should be. Because boatbuilders ultimately have to sell their product to the consumer, this belief made it difficult for engineers to sell better construction methods to the builders' marketing departments. And so it went. Though many current state-of-the-art techniques have been known since the mid-1970s, they were rarely used until a decade later except by racers and performance enthusiasts for whom the quest for speed overrides *everything*. These days, many planing (and even some semidisplacement) hulls take full advantage of the latest weight-saving technology, though the practice is by no means universal. In fact, though I've long believed we'd soon be able to say "most" rather than "many," the transformation to fully engineered hulls is still progressing rather slowly. A lot of boats are still built heavier than they need to be, though they're fine in most every other respect. Unless performance is of the highest priority, a lighter boat may not be a huge concern for you. But since the use of weight-saving technology can be an indication of progressive thinking in general, builders who look to make lighter boats that hold up under tough conditions often produce boats that are better in other ways as well.

Hull Construction

One of the most significant changes has been the evolution from solid FRP (fiberglass-reinforced plastic) construction to cored laminates. There's no question that a lot of hull strength comes from hull thickness regardless of the material used—¾-inch plywood can take a greater load than ½-inch. But there's no need for a plastic hull to be solid FRP. Look at an I-beam; its strength comes from the distance between the flanges. It will bear the same load as a solid piece of steel of like dimensions. The web need only be thick enough to keep the flanges apart under load. Similarly, a 1-inch-thick hull will have the same strength and rigidity whether it is solid FRP or has some other, lighter material, or core, sandwiched between inner and outer FRP skins (Figure 4-11). Rigidity interests us more than anything else. Since planing performance can depend so greatly on hull shape, a hull's ability to maintain that shape under stress is critical. The more rigid it is, the less a hull will be deformed by the stresses induced by water pressure and other forces acting on it underway at speed.

There are four generally used core materials: Baltek's end-grain balsa wood, and three plastic foams—Airex, Divinycell, and Klegecell. Naturally the makers of each product tout their own as being the "best," but they're all good. Each has

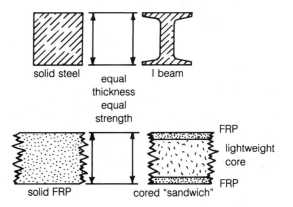

FIGURE 4-11. *Just as an I-beam can possess the same strength as a similarly sized piece of solid steel, cored "sandwich" hulls can be as stiff as a similar thickness of solid fiberglass-reinforced plastic (FRP).*

strengths and weaknesses compared with the others (surprised?), and the main consideration is less which core is used than how well the core is bonded to the inner and outer skins. The entire laminate—the inner and outer skins and the core—must remain a cohesive unit in order to have the desired strength. The technical and production difficulties involved in getting a good core-to-skin bond are among the reasons many builders have been reluctant to change from solid to cored hulls despite their obvious advantages. Solutions are available, however, and I think it's reasonable to conclude that conscientious builders will find ways to embrace them before releasing cored construction to the marketplace. That some still haven't changed to cored construction is, I believe, evidence of the validity of this conclusion. But the change is happening. Even those builders who are reluctant to use cored construction in high-stress areas, such as below the waterline, will often core topsides, superstructures, and interior bulkheads. And all builders seem willing to use some of the so-called exotics wherever feasible to improve their boats' strength-to-weight ratios.

Incidentally, in addition to the core materials listed above, there are a couple of honeycomb cores that, in powerboats, are used primarily for interior components such as bulkheads and built-in furnishings (though they're seen more often in sailboat hulls). Nomex is a paperlike material that's actually related to Kevlar and is also used for electrical insulation, and Nydacore is a tough polyester.

Cores of all types are often vacuum-bagged to their surface (skin) materials for better structural unity, which is critical to all laminates whether they are essential to the hull or superstructure or merely non-load-bearing interior components (Figure 4-12).

A Closer Look at Fiberglass

In the beginning, the fiberglass in FRP boats came in two forms, fabric and chopped strand. Fabric, in turn, could be either *cloth*—a warp-and-weft woven material similar to any other kind of cloth but made of fiberglass strands rather than cotton,

FIGURE 4-12. *Vacuum-bagging is one way of assuring a perfect core-to-skin bond. All the air is removed from the transparent vinyl bag so that atmospheric pressure will hold the balsa core tightly against the skin until the bonding resin is fully set up. (Forest Johnson photo courtesy Baltek and Bertram Yachts)*

nylon, or other fiber—or *woven roving*, which is simply a coarser weave with thicker yarns that contain more glass fibers. Chopped strand, as its name suggests, comprises random pieces of chopped-up fiberglass filament. Because of its randomness and lack of any real interlocking connection between individual strands of glass fiber, chopped strand contributes the least strength to the laminate. It's often used as the outer layer, next to the gelcoat, to avoid *print-through* [the transfer of a woven fabric's texture to the gelcoat surface]. It's also a good filler, helping to maintain a good glass-to-resin ratio (too high a proportion of either reduces a laminate's strength) while building the total thickness faster than is possible with fabric alone.

Using cored construction lessens the need for chopped strand, but there will most likely always be some in every FRP boat. So please let me burst another balloon.

Chopped strand gets into a laminate by either of two methods. In the hand-layup method, the strands are first lightly bound into sheets of mat, which can be handled much like fabric. The binder merely holds the strands together in workable form until the layers of mat (and cloth or roving) can be wetted out by application of resin and hand-rolling. The other method is called *chopper gun* because the "gun" that sprays on the resin also chops continuous filaments of glass into strands, which get blown into the laminate along with the resin.

Hand-layup proponents often try to sell that method as the best, and imply that chopper-gun construction is a shoddy substitute. The truth is that once they're included in a good laminate with a proper balance of resin to glass (usually 65-35), the chopped strands don't care how they got there. And neither should you, although it's good to know which method was used on a boat you're considering, because it helps in following up on the builder's quality control. When either method is handled properly, the result is the same—a sound laminate. However, the opportunities for fouling up are different and unique to each. Hence, each requires its own type of quality control.

With hand-layup, the main problem is improper wet-out—that is, not getting a thorough penetration of resin. This leads to resin-poor sections that may delaminate easily under stress. This can usually be detected during layup, and conscientious builders watch each mold carefully to avoid the problem.

Chopper guns are faster and, when properly adjusted, eliminate inadequate wet-out. But maladjustment can lead to either too little or too much glass for the amount of resin applied. This can't be as easily judged during application, because the result will look much the same no matter what. Good chopper-gun builders will lab-test the plugs cut out of the hulls for such purposes as cooling-water intakes or ports. By weighing the plugs before and after baking them in a high-temperature oven, they can easily determine the glass-to-resin ratio because the resin burns out in baking. The best builders check plugs frequently enough to correct chopper-gun adjustment before the resulting laminates get beyond tolerance. That means every hull will be within acceptable standards.

In addition to basic cloth, woven roving, and chopped strand, we now have nonwoven biaxials (including some that are knitted), triaxials, and a multitude of unidirectional fabrics, which have their greatest strength in specific directions.

We also have CorMat, Fabmat, and various other materials that were unknown only a few years ago. By taking advantage of each material's particular attributes, engineers can now design laminates that gain their strength by use of the *right* material rather than by using *more* material. This, too, has contributed to great gains in the strength-to-weight department.

In some cases, we've actually gotten away from using fiberglass in "fiberglass" boats and use Kevlar for the reinforcing fabric (KRP?), while other boats use a Kevlar-fiberglass mixture. If you consider that one version of Kevlar is the material of flak jackets and bulletproof vests, you'll understand how it can add strength without weight by reducing the need for more layers of a weaker fabric. Kevlar's main drawback is that it costs more than glass, and since it must be cut with special tools and techniques and can be used in a "drier" laminate (which requires more careful handwork), the layup labor costs are higher, too.

Carbon fiber rods, which have a tensile strength five times greater than steel, are often used to reinforce high-stress areas such as stringers, chines, and gunwales, providing considerably more stiffness with little added weight.

We've also seen changes in resin. Epoxy has long been known to be stronger than the traditional polyester resin but has often been bypassed because of its greater cost. In recent years we've seen wider use of such new materials as vinylester resin, which wets out more easily (especially with some of the more exotic fabrics) and remains more flexible than polyester. When used with Kevlar, for example, vinylester permits a 50-50 resin-to-fabric ratio rather than the 65-35 ratio generally used in standard glass construction. Vinylester resin is also more resistant to water absorption than polyester, which makes it a natural for boat construction by eliminating the problem of osmotic blistering. But it, too, costs more.

Of course, *all* weight-saving technology generally costs more than plain old solid FRP, which means that a lighter boat will probably be a more-expensive boat to buy (which could be another reason weight loss has been a slow process). Since the lighter boat will gain the same performance from lower horsepower, however, it should burn less fuel, which means it will inevitably be a less-expensive boat to run. If you use your boat a lot, the higher initial cost could add up to a lower ultimate cost.

New Technology

Even when hulls are cored and made with "exotic" fabrics, the construction process usually remains as it has since the beginning of fiberglass boats. The materials are still placed, one layer at a time, inside a female mold, where they sit until the resin cures and the individual layers meld into a cohesive unit. It's a labor-intensive process whether hand-layup is involved or not. Even when chopper guns play a huge role, it takes a lot of manual labor to build a powerboat hull by traditional methods.

The traditional layup process is also somewhat unfriendly to the environment because the curing resin releases styrene into the atmosphere. "Clean air" requirements imposed by legislation have led to many boat companies being unable to expand or build new manufacturing facilities, which can adversely affect their bottom line as well as hinder the development of new construction techniques. Clearly, we not only need to consider the "new" materials employed in boatbuilding; we need to come up with some new methods all around. Well, it's happening, albeit rather slowly.

One of the reasons change is slow in coming is that many boatbuilding companies are quite small (despite being well known and having a lengthy history) and thus lack the capital to embrace new methodology, even when they might very much like to. Their integrity won't allow them to do it wrong, and they can't afford to do it right, so they just don't do it. It's to their credit that many of these independent companies are employing any new technology at all—progress can be expensive!

But there are signs of change. One of the trends we've seen in the late 20th and early 21st centuries is independent boatbuilders being purchased to become divisions of larger corporations. The jury is still out as to whether this is to-

tally good. Only time will tell. In the past, on some of the boating industry's upswings, many financially diverse conglomerates bought boatbuilders simply to further diversify their portfolios. When money became tight and the boat business swung back down, these companies were sold or, too often, merely closed, and the brands disappeared. Today, the leading owners of multiple boatbuilding companies (Brunswick Corporation and Genmar Holdings) appear to be in the boat business because they like the boat business, so the prognosis seems much better. But we still have to wait and see.

But one benefit that's immediately apparent is that these larger organizations can afford to invest in new technology. And they have. We see an example at Genmar Holdings, a Minneapolis-based company that currently encompasses sixteen brands and is thus one of the world's largest manufacturers of recreational boats.

Genmar has developed the Virtual Engineered Composites fiberglass molding system, better known as the VEC process (Figure 4-13). The VEC system is unlike traditional labor-intensive fiberglass open molding; rather, it's a computer-controlled, automated closed-mold process. Production takes place in a self-contained cell, and according to the company, the completed hulls, which incorporate the entire stringer system and inner sole, are so precise in material portions, bonding, and thickness that they're both stronger and lighter than conventional versions. The company also claims the VEC process is four times faster than open molding and, perhaps more important, reduces styrene emissions during lamination by more than 90 percent.

Since this process is relatively new, we'll have to wait a while to judge its effect on boatbuilding as a whole. But anything that impacts favorably on both quality control and the environment has to be considered a positive change.

Trim and Stability

The one thing that can be said about all planing hulls is that they're sensitive to trim. The table in Figure 4-1 and my dad's tubby skiff were able to plane only because of the way they were trimmed.

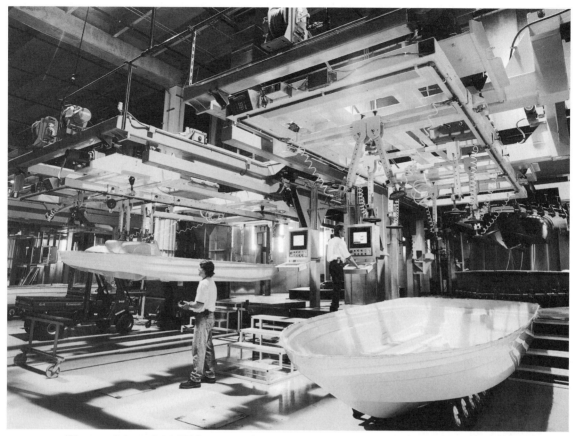

FIGURE 4-13. *The precision of the VEC process (computers monitor more than 500 variables) results in hulls the builder claims to be more consistent in weight, density, and thickness. (Courtesy Genmar Holdings, Inc.)*

But all planing hulls deliver better performance when they're trimmed correctly; you can see an increase in speed and engine rpm without touching the throttles when you reach optimum trim. In fact, the throttleman in an offshore racer is actually controlling trim as much as engine speed to keep the boat at its highest performance level.

The reason is simple. The hydrodynamic lift that results in planing is due, to a large degree, to the angle at which the hull meets the water. Change the angle, and you change performance.

Well-balanced planing hulls seem to rise on plane and settle back down with little change in running angle. Others need to climb out of the "hole" before they attain a planing attitude and tend to squat again when you back off on the throttles. This is not necessarily bad. In fact, it

often can't be helped. Aft-cabin cruisers and small boats in which engine weight is a disproportionate amount of the total weight are prime examples; the only way they could be balanced would be to carry some compensating but otherwise unnecessary weight forward, which would be detrimental to top-end performance.

It is, however, wise to equip such hulls with trimmable drive systems such as outboards or sterndrives when possible; conventional underwater running gear just doesn't work as well. It's also a reason to use adjustable electrohydraulic trim tabs no matter what kind of drive system you have. Some boats can perform adequately without such aids, and their designers often adamantly resist adding them. But this is true only when the boat is properly balanced—a condition not always easy to attain under real-world conditions. Tabs give you the option of maintaining trim underway even if other factors are working to disrupt the delicate balance. They're particularly valuable in keeping a deep-V upright when it wants to lean a bit—and they do have a tendency to lean into the wind. In short, there are very few planing hulls that won't benefit from some trim-tab action at some time or other, even if that action isn't needed all the time (Figure 4-14). That's why I'm pleased to report that although some builders still offer trim tabs as optional accessories, most now recognize the wisdom of making them available even if you don't always need them, and include tabs as standard equipment.

There are other devices that can also contribute to proper trim. But because this is so critical to planing hull performance, I've written a whole new chapter on these tools and techniques. Since how you use them can be even more important than which tools you select, I've put the chapter on trim—Chapter 30, The Tools and Techniques of Trim—with the other "operational" elements in Part Four. For now, just know that proper trim is an essential element of planing hull performance.

Planing hull stability is similar to displacement hull stability except that in the planing mode we have other forces at work. The hydrodynamic lift that makes the hull plane also tends, to a large degree, to offset external forces that might lead to rolling. That's the good news. The bad news is that the lift is there only at planing speeds. Slow down, and there goes your stability. There's worse news. In our quest for lightness to provide higher speeds with less horsepower, we may develop boats that are so light they bob like a cork unless they're moving fast. And the worst news: antiroll devices, which will help displacement and even semidisplacement hulls, tend to get in the way on fast-moving planing hulls. So we're left with different approaches to low-speed stability in fast-moving boats.

A very common approach is to forget the

FIGURE 4-14. *Although trim tabs are not always needed, they are a welcome addition to almost every planing hull because proper trim is so important to planing performance and efficiency. For more on trim and all its aspects, see Chapter 30. (Courtesy Bennett Marine)*

problem and develop a boat that just goes fast! Nice work if you can get it, but unless you're racing, you often can't, which means being very uncomfortable when you can't throttle up. Other builders and designers try to take a more pragmatic approach and work out a hull form with a degree of at-rest and low-speed stability built in. Some succeed better than others, but on the whole we have to face the truth that fast boats usually ride better going fast. When you go for a sea trial in a planing boat, don't get carried away with seeing how fast it will go and how quickly it gets on plane. These points are important, of course, but be sure to include some slow running and a stop or two to see if you can live with the boat under those conditions as well. Although no boat will ever be 100 percent comfortable 100 percent of the time, you want one that approaches this goal as closely as possible, or you won't be happy with it. Remember, comfort is subjective, and with stability as with other aspects, you and your family must be the final judges of what's comfortable for you.

Now that we've seen the advantages and disadvantages of slow and fast boats, let's turn our attention to those that fall somewhere in between.

5

Semidisplacement Hulls

The first thing to say about semidisplacement hulls is that some people claim there's no such animal. This school of thought maintains that a hull either planes or it doesn't. Simple as that. I think these people also see the world in black and white. Not only do they miss the colors, but they don't even recognize gray!

Another group maintains that semidisplacement boats are really displacement boats that manage to trick Mother Nature into believing they have a longer waterline. This, of course, creates a speed-to-length ratio higher than 2.0, though the boat is still in the displacement mode (Figure 5-1).

And yet another group maintains that these boats should be called *semiplaning* rather than semidisplacement, because they "sort of" plane, though not to the degree we observe in pure planing hulls.

To me, the determining (and defining) element is bow action. If the forefoot remains in the water, it's a displacement hull. If it gets clear, and the bow wave begins abaft the forefoot, the hull is planing. If it's *almost* clear, the hull is semidisplacement. To give the either/or crowd their due, perhaps a semidisplacement hull is actually an underpowered (or overweight) planing hull. I would buy that except that semidisplacement hulls seem to run better in the displacement mode than do most pure planing hulls. Perhaps that's part of the answer, too; maybe the underwater lines that contribute to better displacement performance somehow detract from pure planing performance. The whole question is probably

FIGURE 5-1. *With this semidisplacement hull, the bow wave doesn't crest again until it's well behind the transom, yet the forefoot is indeed still in the water, a clear indication that the boat is moving through the water rather than over it.*

academic and best reserved for those endless, never resolved discussions we boaters often have over a cool one or two at a dockside bar. The bottom line is that if the boat exceeds pure displacement hull speed yet doesn't show a speed-to-length ratio greater than 4.0, it must be, by definition, *semidisplacement*. And since we're looking for the pluses and minuses inherent in every possibility, it's really only these aspects of performance that concern us. So let's not bother with the whys and hows; let's just look at the whats.

Many years ago, Johnny Mercer wrote a song called "Ac-Cent-Tchu-Ate the Positive" in which he cautioned us to "Eliminate the negative" and "Don't mess with Mister In-Between." When it comes to semidisplacement hulls, the positive is that they *are* in between. Not as slow as pure displacement hulls, they can still carry more of a payload than a pure planing hull. Whether this is the best or the least of both worlds depends on your objectives. For many, the ability to have a decent cabin, room for the whole family, enough stowage for a practical cruise (two weeks, for example), and still not be limited to displacement speeds is all the argument they need. To others, the "semi" prefix means the boat is either not fast enough or doesn't have enough load capacity to suit them.

The semidisplacement compromise makes sense for a lot of applications, and that's the reason many large family cruisers and motor yachts have this type of hull. It isn't perfect, and it can't be all things to all people, but it *is* a very reasonable general-purpose hull, delivering acceptable performance at displacement speeds and faster.

One thing you'll notice about many semis is that they're much like pure displacement hulls and stern-heavy planing hulls through a certain portion of the power curve. Throttle up to maxi-

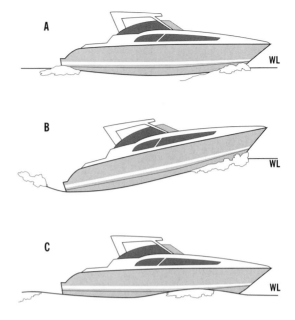

FIGURE 5-2. *A semidisplacement boat will often exhibit relatively inefficient performance as it moves out of pure displacement mode (**A**). The stern digs in, the bow wave gets deeper but not longer, and you simply burn more fuel and make more noise as you try to climb out of the "hole" (**B**), until you can lift the boat over the "hump" and begin to semiplane (**C**).*

mum displacement speed, and from then until you have enough power to get out of the hole and over the "hump" you only burn more fuel and make more noise. Once you apply enough power, however, the stern lifts and the semiplaning activity begins (Figure 5-2). Needless to say, running the boat at any throttle setting between "max displacement" and "over the hump" is just wasting fuel. It also should be obvious that trim tabs can help here, too, making the stern lift a little more easily and quickly.

6

Comparing the Three Hull Types

Now that we've had an opportunity to look at the three major hull forms, it's time to go further and look at some of their similarities and differences.

One of the big factors affecting hull performance is at-rest draft. Displacement hulls will sit deep in the water because they can and should. As we saw in Chapter 3, this gives them their load-carrying abilities and a big part of their low-speed stability. Planing hulls, on the other hand, should be shallow draft (relatively speaking) so that there's less distance to go in lifting the hull up onto the surface to plane. As you'd expect, semis fall in between and never do quite get up onto a full plane even at wide-open throttle (though they generally leave pure displacement performance far behind). Since there's more boat in the water than with pure planing hulls, semidisplacement boats can usually benefit from stabilizers as much as displacement hulls do.

Unfortunately, many builders seem reluctant to include stabilizers as standard equipment. A colleague of mine, Charles Nichols, and I have often been on a soapbox trying to get them more generally accepted by builders. Given the draft limitations placed on all pleasure craft (especially those we want to move faster than displacement speeds) coupled with our desire for all sorts of creature comforts, which can only add weight aloft, it's not an admission of "poor design" to include an antiroll device any more than it is to include trim tabs. Both systems add to the enjoyment of boating, and in my opinion it's wrong to make the consumer have to choose them as extras. They belong aboard and should be included

in the initial construction and in the base price. I believe it's best for all concerned.

Locating the waterline is one of the many calculations that naval architects must make in designing a hull. To do this, they use a figure termed "pounds-per-inch immersion." This figure, which is simply the weight it takes to sink the boat an inch lower into the water, is directly related to its cross-sectional area at the waterline. (Cross-sectional area at the waterline is also known as *waterline plane*—remember this term because we'll see it again shortly.) While pounds-per-inch immersion is primarily a concern of the designer and builder, it can also be important to the operator in that it helps you determine how much gear and provisions you can bring aboard without adversely affecting performance and stability.

In Figure 6-1 we see athwartships cross-sectional views of three boats that have similarities above the waterline. Beam, freeboard, and overall length are nearly identical. Boat A is simply more boat (remember that it takes more weight to sit deeper in the water)! Boat A will inevitably have a greater fuel and potable water capacity, heavier construction, and probably more living space and creature comforts aboard, or it wouldn't sit as deep. On the other hand, boats B and C *can't* have as much aboard, or they couldn't sit as high. If we were to load either B or C to the point where they would weigh the same as boat A, we would reduce freeboard to a dangerous point in B and to a critical point in C (there would be so little freeboard that the slightest wave could flood it). A is a displacement hull; B, semidisplacement; and C, planing. It should be no

FIGURE 6-1. *Although all three hulls show similar freeboard and beam at their midsections, their underbodies reveal three quite different boats. Boat A is a displacement hull; boat B, semi-displacement; and boat C, planing.*

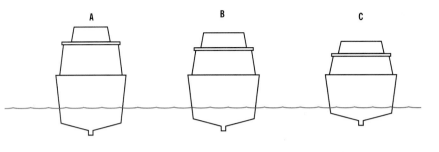

surprise that boat A will have the greatest initial stability, and boat C will have the highest speed.

Now let's see what I mean by "more boat." In Figure 6-2 we see profile views of the boats we've just discussed. Boat A sits deep enough in the water to carry considerable weight aloft. It can have an open upper deck, or bridge deck, that includes a spacious flying bridge with lots of usable guest seating at its forward end, and probably a wet bar, a fair-sized dinghy, and maybe even a motor scooter and Jet Ski or two.

Boat A can carry this load aloft because of the weight it carries below. This hull depth permits full standing headroom in the space belowdeck. This in turn means a walk-in engine room(s), and if the overall length is in the 50-foot-plus range, probably three staterooms plus crew quarters with private heads for each.

The main deck can house a *saloon* [the traditional and still commonly used name for the "living room" of a cabin cruiser or motor yacht], dining area, galley, wet bar, and, if desired, an inside console—again all on one continuous deck. Because of the hull depth and weight required to attain the design draft, fuel and water capacity will be substantially greater than in boats B and C.

Boat B will have to be what we would call a "split-level" if we were discussing houses. There isn't room for a continuous deck at any level. There would likely be a raised aft deck to allow headroom in the stateroom (or two) beneath it. From there you could go up to a flying bridge or down to the saloon. The walkaround portion of the foredeck would probably be at a different level from either the aft deck or the saloon sole.

The bridge would have to be smaller than on boat A simply because this boat can't carry as

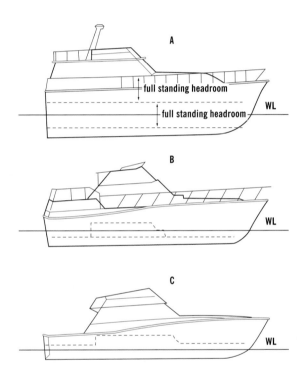

FIGURE 6-2. *These are the same boats as in Figure 6-1. All are about 55 feet long overall, 50 feet on the waterline. Boat A, the displacement hull, permits the most variety in accommodation plans. Two full-length decks, both with full standing headroom, grant considerable flexibility. Even the engine room can be located anywhere from fully astern to amidships. Boats B and C offer less flexibility and less room for accommodations but will inevitably be faster.*

much weight that high. With the bridge above the saloon, headroom requirements in the saloon would push the saloon sole low enough to reduce the engine compartment beneath it to a crawl space.

Traditionally styled hulls are deeper forward, so we would probably find a galley and dinette down and forward from the saloon, and another stateroom in the bow.

This arrangement is practical, and you'll find it (or a variation of the theme) in many motor yachts from 35 to 60 feet. It is a fine compromise but doesn't offer the total comfort or space we saw in the similarly sized displacement boat A.

Boat C will have to have a lot less in the way of living space to keep total weight down. In this case we're probably looking at a "convertible," which will have a saloon with galley up and two staterooms and a single shared head down and forward. I have drawn it with little weight aloft—mostly in a small but functional flying bridge. If you were to use it as a sportfisherman, it could probably stand to carry an aluminum tuna tower as long as other weight is kept low in the boat.

The greater hull depth of boat A offers a couple of other advantages I should also mention. Because the lower and main deck living spaces are both full length and full height, you're less restricted in the placement of bulkheads and other interior design features. The accommodations plans of both B and C are somewhat dictated by the "split-levels" inherent in the designs. Perhaps more important, boat A can have watertight bulkheads below deck because every bulkhead can be a *full* bulkhead, vertically as well as horizontally. The arrangements of B and C require more openness and often allow only partial bulkheads, since there are no "lower decks" per se. The locations of stairways (which are always called "ladders" if you stick to nautical tradition, though most pleasure boaters do not) are also dictated by the requirements of the levels, and they, too, often preclude dividing the hull into watertight compartments. Boats B and C could have watertight engine compartments but probably no further subdivisions.

As I said, the waterline and stability of a boat as built are the designer and builder's responsibilities; after that it's up to you. Unfortunately, some skippers ignore these factors, and the sad truth is that overloading and improper loading are among the leading causes of small-boat mishaps.

Say you have a 26-foot center-console fisherman and decide to add a tower for better visibility. You can, provided you don't go too high. But once you have the tower, it doesn't mean you can invite all your fishing buddies to come up there with you! Whatever you do with any boat, you have to keep the weight relatively low to keep the center of gravity low. You might wonder who would be so foolish as to let everybody ride on the tower of a small boat, but should you ignore the advice to keep weight low, you wouldn't be the first to do so.

And what about overloading? Well, it's perhaps more of a *very* small boat problem, related to those who would rather ignore their dinghy's capacity plate than make an extra trip. But overloading bigger boats can have its drawbacks, too, even if the potential for danger is less. A few years ago I was involved in the management of a 58-foot motor yacht with a semidisplacement hull. It had belonged to the same owner for 10 years. When we had the bottom redone to eliminate the "dead" antifouling paint that had built up over the decade and remove the blisters that had formed, we decided we should raise the waterline a couple of inches to effect a better exposure of antifouling action—the original waterline had been underwater for some time. About a year after that, the owner sold the boat and unloaded 11 years' worth of accumulated personal belongings. When I delivered the boat to its new owner, the painted waterline was 3 inches above the water, and the boat cruised 2 knots faster than it did before the owner removed his gear!

Bottoms, Topsides, and Fine Points of Form

One factor affecting performance in all hull types is the cleanliness of the bottom. Bottom paint is usually an option, and the choice of brands and types is left to the buyer and dealer. There's a good reason for this. The bottom paint you should use depends not only on what sort of boat you have (fast boats need a slicker finish), but also on where you do your boating. If you operate your boat on fresh water or store it on a trailer, you may not need bottom paint at all. The builder can't possibly put the same paint on every boat, which means applying the paint is often left to the dealer (though many builders will apply the paint of your choice—as an option—before initial launching). A word of advice: Antifouling paint is probably the most expensive paint you'll ever buy. Even the least costly options are dear. But this isn't the place to cut corners. If you love your boat, use the best paint you can. For your particular boat and boating area, it may turn out that you don't need the most expensive paint available, but heed your dealer's advice. I repeat: Use the best bottom paint you can get. It will pay for itself in the long run in better performance and lower operating costs. Then, too, many paints that cost more initially deliver better performance for a longer time, and thus actually cost less when you consider the expense of hauling and repainting.

There are a few features you should consider in every hull type except the deep-V, which is a different bird and can get away with breaking the rules. Some of these features may be seen in deep-Vs, and if so, OK. For the most part they won't do any harm. But the benefits they give to other hulls just aren't generally needed by deep-Vs.

Fine Entry

The sharper the knife, the swifter the cut. The same holds true for the bows of boats. A fine, sharp entry cuts the water better and allows the boat to slice through oncoming waves rather than pound into them (Figure 6-3). The result in a displacement boat is a steadier, smoother forward progression, and the same is true in semidisplacement boats. In planing boats, the fine entry should carry back abaft the forefoot, because this area, too, will be cutting the water when the boat gets on plane.

A very fine entry can make for a wet boat because the water cut by the bow will fly upward rather than out (a blunt bow pushes the water away rather than up). There are remedies for this, however. One of the simplest is to install spray rails just above the waterline. They will knock the

FIGURE 6-3. *A sharp angle at the forefoot—a fine entry—as in this Symbol 44 MKII, almost guarantees a smooth ride by cutting the seas like a knife. (Courtesy Symbol Yachts)*

water back down and away from the boat before the wind can catch it and bring it aboard as spray.

Flare

A bow with a lot of flare will also tend to keep spray in its place. More important, however, is the reserve buoyancy it provides. Buoyancy is influenced by shape in that pounds-per-inch immersion is directly related to the area of waterline plane. If the hull angles out rapidly (flares), the waterline plane expands rapidly with increasing height above the design waterline, and the deeper the hull is immersed the more it resists still-deeper immersion. This is particularly important forward, though a slight outward angle can be good all along the topsides. A flaring bow tends to keep the bow in an "up" attitude, which is good for longitudinal stability and for a smoother ride (Figure 6-4). Deep-Vs do not need much flare, because at high speed they are wont to run on surfaces so far abaft the bow it doesn't matter. And since a deep-V bow tends to lift anyway, flare can actually be detrimental to control by providing too much wind lift. That's one good reason racing hulls and their derivatives usually have a reverse-sheer "needle-nosed" bow. Another is visibility. If the foredeck didn't curve downward from the windshield forward, the operator wouldn't be able to see much ahead of the bow as it lifts while getting on plane.

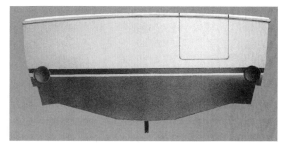

FIGURE 6-5. *Having two sets of chines can be beneficial to deep-V hulls and, as this drawing shows, modified-Vs as well. The upper (outer) chines are in play only at rest and displacement speeds, when they add lateral stability by increasing effective beam. The lower chine flats are, in this case, angled slightly downward to provide added lift and better spray deflection when the boat comes up on plane. (Stephen Davis drawing, courtesy Viking Yachts)*

FIGURE 6-4. *The shadow under the gunwales at the bow of this Jersey 42 sportfisherman is a result of flare. This shape (traditional along the Jersey shore) assures more than adequate reserve buoyancy and, usually, a dry ride. (Courtesy Jersey Yachts)*

Freeboard

Remember, freeboard is the term for the height from the waterline to the gunwales. The more the better, generally speaking, because it gives you room to play with in loading and trimming your boat. As we saw earlier, overloading causes a boat to sink below its design waterline. Whether this is merely a detriment to optimum performance or a serious threat to safety depends, to a great degree, on how much freeboard remains. The more freeboard you start with, the more reserve you have.

Beam

In Chapter 3 we saw how greater beam helps increase stability in displacement hulls. It does the same for semidisplacement and planing hulls. Furthermore, because spreading a similar weight over a greater area increases buoyancy (it's that waterline plane again), a wider boat can actually plane more easily because it will likely have a

shallower draft to begin with. Again, the exception is the deep-V, which usually works better in narrower hulls. The deep-V's beam is partly dictated by the points at which the bottom of a 24- to 26-degree-deadrise hull will cut the plane formed by the topsides, although a designer can gain a little beam by working with the chine flats. Some deep-Vs employ a double chine (Figure 6-5), bringing one set of flats into play at rest and at displacement speeds, while the second kicks in at speed. This allows a deep-V to be beamier than the basic lines might indicate.

By the way, beamier boats offer another advantage, too. They give you more boat for the money in marinas and boatyards. Most facilities charge by the foot of length overall. A 27-foot boat with a 10-foot beam permits you more amenities than a 27-footer with an 8-foot beam, but either boat will incur the same fees at most marinas and yards.

Higher Math and Other Nonsense

There are formulas you can use to determine a lot of things about a boat's performance simply by considering its dimensions against other factors such as displacement weight or volume. The result is generally a coefficient that, when applied to another of the figures involved, will give you a performance indicator. But you really don't have to know about waterplane coefficient, prismatic coefficient, block coefficient, or any other such esoteric factors to determine the right boat for you. For one thing, most salespeople would be totally unable to answer a question regarding any of the above, and I daresay that after as brief an explanation as I'd have room for here, you would be as hard-pressed to understand the answer if it could be given. Naval architects and engineers must work with these factors to develop a boat that will do what we want, but for our purposes, all we need to see is what it will do on the water. To hell with theory! If it rides the way we like and has the speed and other features we want, it's right. If it doesn't, it isn't. Keep looking. It's as simple as that.

Certification

Of course, when we find a boat we like, it would be nice to be able to judge whether it's suitable in *every* way. That is, it would be nice to have a way of being sure the boat of our dreams has the level of quality we want before we make such a major investment. Well, we do. One way is to look for a boat that has been certified by the National Marine Manufacturers Association (NMMA; www.nmma.org) as meeting its certification standards, which in turn are based on the *Standards and Recommended Practices for Small Craft* published by the American Boat and Yacht Council (ABYC; www.abyc.com). NMMA certification, which will appear on the capacity plate of boats under 26 feet and on Yacht Certification placards of larger vessels, assures you that the boat meets U.S. Coast Guard requirements (which, unfortunately, are minimal) and the further guidelines of the ABYC standards as well.

It's also wise to hire the services of an accredited marine surveyor. Often your lender or insurance company will require a survey anyway, so you might as well have one done to protect your interests also. If you make your purchase agreement subject to a successful survey, you'll be ahead of the game. I used to think that only used boats needed a survey, to be sure they had been properly maintained. But over the years I've learned that the objective eye of a qualified surveyor can be an important ingredient in the purchase of any boat, even one straight out of the factory. Though certification and a thorough survey should be a part of every boat purchase, you can narrow the choices before you get that far by making careful inspections on your own. There are ways anyone can determine a boat's basic quality, and Charles Nichols once summed them up quite nicely in a "Ship's Systems" column in *Power and Motoryacht* magazine. Since I can't think of a better way to put it myself, with his kind permission, I include them here.

Ten Clues to Quality

In each of the following ten checkpoints, what you're really looking for is *care* in one of several phases of the construction process.

1. The first place to check is the finish itself. Here, you're looking for care in the development of the tooling—the plug and mold from which the hull is made—and care in this particular boat's layup. Study the hull surface obliquely, and you can tell a lot. We used to look for *print-through* [the pattern of the woven roving or cloth showing through the gelcoat]. The better the hull, the less you'd see. Since most builders now use a layer of mat or another patternless material immediately beneath the gelcoat, this problem has been essentially eliminated, but there are still things you can spot.

Fortunately, shiny surfaces aren't forgiving of imperfections that lie beneath. When you look down along the hull surface you'll see something ranging from absolute perfection—a totally smooth, flawless shine no matter what the angle of view—to disaster, where you can spot the location of every interior bulkhead by its telltale bulge, and "flat" places are anything but. Most production boats will lie somewhere in between. Look closely at reflections of straight lines (fluorescent tubes overhead can be a big help). The better the hull, the straighter and sharper they'll be. A little waviness is acceptable, but shy away from a hull that shows too much.

I don't know if Charles has ever experienced this, but I've found that sighting down the side of a hull will often prompt salespeople to reveal any flaws they know about, even if I don't spot them, because they understand the procedure and offer the information as a preemptive strike to try to stop me from spotting more!

2. Next, look at the electrical system. True, most of it is hidden. But what you can see—if you look closely—speaks volumes about the system (and the boat) as a whole.

Check out the distribution panels (Figure 6-6). Look for an ample number of circuits (including

blank spares). When several items must share the same fuse or breaker, trouble in one means the potential loss of all. And give points for using breakers only. Fuses are OK, of course, but they add some drawbacks: you have to stock spares on board, and there's the possibility of creating further problems by replacing a blown fuse with one of the wrong amperage.

Look for ample metering on the panels. Voltmeters for both AC and DC are the minimum. Ammeters help you avoid overload. If you have a genset, a frequency meter is immensely valuable because some equipment is frequency sensitive. With 120-volt AC dockpower, a reverse-polarity indicator is also essential.

If you can, take a peek behind the panel. Color-coded wiring and identifying markers at each terminal are good signs (Figure 6-7).

3. Plumbing systems are also good quality checks, though there are fewer places to look. Among the signs of better quality: seacocks or ball valves rather than gate valves on throughhulls, double clamps on critical hose connections (all those below the waterline and anywhere else a broken connection would be more than an

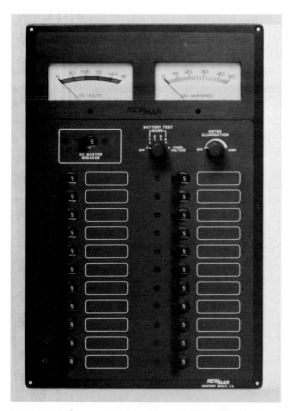

FIGURE 6-6. *One good sign of overall quality is the use of good components. For example, a good electrical panel will feature ample circuits (including spares), circuit breakers rather than fuses, and metering for both voltage and current. (Courtesy Newmar)*

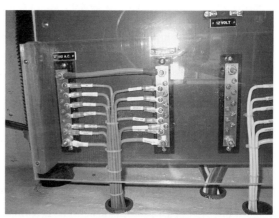

FIGURE 6-7. *This is an example of good wiring practice on several counts. For starters, the holes for the wires to pass through the deck are all lined with rubber grommets to prevent chafing. The labels on the wire ends help eliminate guesswork. The neatly executed turns and ample ties around bundled wires are also indications of a well-executed electrical installation. (Courtesy Nordhavn)*

FIGURE 6-8. *The seacocks and double clamps show that these hoses have been installed with care. What doesn't show quite as well, but happens to be true in this case, is that the seacocks are all mounted on a sea chest, which means only one hole in the hull rather than several. This, in itself, is an excellent indicator of quality engineering in the yacht as a whole. (Courtesy Davis Yachts)*

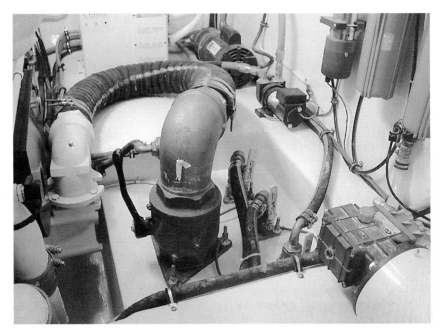

inconvenience), and reinforced hose on suction lines (Figure 6-8).

4. Look again at the electrical and plumbing systems as a whole, with an eye for neatness. The neater the workmanship, the better the boat. Look for straight runs with definite turns at each change of direction and solid support along the way. Better wiring will be bundled, or run in chases or flexible conduit.

A neat installation suggests good materials. It's no guarantee, but because the greater cost will be in the labor, a builder will rarely pay someone to do a proper job of installing inferior stuff.

Look for labels on switches, valves, junction boxes, pipes, and wires. The more the better, because they can tell you more than just what's written on them. Not only will they make it easier to learn your way around your new boat, but they also show the builder's care in helping you do so.

5. See how things fit. Back when boats were all wood inside and out, interior joinerwork was an indicator of unseen workmanship. It still is to a degree, in that good woodwork reflects overall care in building. Even in a boat that substitutes molded interior components for joinery, you can get a hint of the level of engineering and quality

control involved by studying how the modular units fit together. Sloppy fits, if present, will be readily apparent. The better the quality of things where you can see them, the better the chances of the quality being fine where you can't.

6. Check for watertight integrity. In hull lengths up to 25 feet or so, one compartment is OK, but unless you have an open outboard-powered runabout, a bigger boat should have at least two independent, watertight compartments. I'm pleased to report that many builders today are isolating the engine compartment and making all the through-hull penetrations there. This reduces the chances of water intrusion into the cabin area.

Needless to say, there should be at least one bilge pump for each watertight compartment. Ideally, there will be a manual backup for the engine compartment and some means of extending its suction to other areas.

7. Ask about the hardware. It all shines when new. But chrome-plated Zamak (a zinc alloy) will not stand up to salt nearly as well as chrome-plated bronze or stainless steel. Many builders are opting for the lesser shine of Marinium hardware. This anodized aluminum alloy isn't quite as tough

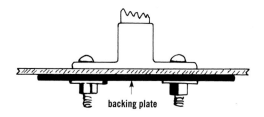

FIGURE 6-9. *Fiberglass doesn't hold screws very well. Be sure that handrail stanchions and other load-bearing elements are through-bolted with adequate backing plates. (Courtesy* Power and Motoryacht *magazine)*

as stainless but seems to stand up nearly as well.

In handrails, welded one-piece units are better than separate sections held together by yet more pieces of connecting hardware. Welded rails are more solid to begin with and will stay that way.

Look for ample cleats, chocks, and fairleads, and make sure that there are no sharp or rough edges that can damage your lines.

8. Look into the way the hardware is attached. Fiberglass doesn't hold screws well (Figure 6-9). It's better if hardware is through-bolted using a backing plate of hardwood, stainless steel, or aluminum. Hardwood backing plates are comparatively bulky and require large washers on the bolts; aluminum plates are good if well constructed; stainless steel is probably the best alternative other than bronze, which is rarely seen anymore. Another good method replaces the core

of a deck sandwich locally with aluminum, the hardware then being held by machine screws threaded into the aluminum. Not so good is a hardwood backing plate with wood screws to hold the hardware, though it's slightly better than screws into plain fiberglass.

9. Look for built-ins (electronics, galley appliances, etc.). Many boats today are offered as a complete package. For those that aren't, there should still be ample room to add the extras, preferably as built-ins. This means blank spaces on or around the console, and easy access to run the wiring they'll need.

10. Ask to see a hull cutout plug. Few hull penetrations are molded in; they are cut. This means there is a piece of scrap (or plug) for each hole. Many builders destroy one plug in quality control, but some plugs should still be available, especially when yet more hull penetrations are made by the dealer. Lack of available plugs for inspection does not mean poor quality, but obviously the more pride the builder and dealer have in the quality of layup, the more likely they'll be anxious to show you a piece of cross section.

If you recall the adage about free lunches, you'll realize that each of these quality indicators has its price. The better the boat, the more you'll probably have to pay. But using them can be a big help in understanding why two outwardly similar boats can have such different price tags. Quality costs initially, but it pays in the long run.

7

Drive Systems

Just when you think you have all the options under control, you get hit with the question "What kind of power?" Gas or diesel, single or twin screw, conventional drive, V-drive, sterndrive, inboard, outboard, surface piercing, jet, raw- or freshwater cooling . . . whew! Your choice of power train components involves perhaps even more options than type and style of boat. Again, each offers advantages and, of course, drawbacks. Just as you can work through the maze of boats to find the best one for you, you can do it with power systems, too.

Conventional Inboard Drive

Since we have to start somewhere, let's begin with the conventional inboard drive system; that is, an engine or engines inside the boat and shaft(s), prop(s), and rudder(s) beneath it. There's a historical precedent for this, because in the early days of powerboats, it was all there was.

In conventional drives these days, our choices generally come down to gasoline or diesel, and single or twin screw. We'll also try to put the drive system itself into perspective, so you can see how conventional underwater running gear stacks up against other choices.

Gas or Diesel?

Gas engines cost less. All inboard engines adapted for marine use are derived from standard car, truck, or industrial engines. Because there are more gasoline-burning cars than other vehicles on the road, engines designed for this appli-

cation are more plentiful and thus less expensive to begin with—greater volume of production equals lower cost per unit. (Most marine engines these days are built on General Motors blocks.) True, the cost of marinization is similar for all engines and depends more on size than type, but when there's a lower cost for the block and those other components that are identical whether the engine will be used on the road or off, the final product has to cost less, too.

Gasoline engines are lighter. Great strides have been made in this department, and some new diesels offer astounding horsepower-to-weight ratios. But on the whole, if you're trying to keep the weight of the boat down, gas engines will help.

Gas engine parts are often more readily available and less expensive. Because the engines themselves are more common on both highways and waterways, their parts tend to be around in greater abundance also. Please note, however, that in most cases, though automotive equivalents will usually fit marinized engines, safety dictates using certified marine components, because automobiles don't require the ignition protection under the hood that is mandatory in marine engine compartments.

This brings us to gasoline's biggest drawback: its ability to explode easily (which makes it such a good fuel inside the engine) makes it potentially dangerous to have aboard. I say "potentially," because although gasoline can be very dangerous indeed, it doesn't have to be. Gasoline does require a greater degree of care in handling and certain precautions in all areas—care and precautions that quite simply can be forgotten if you use diesel oil for fuel. However, a properly built boat (as are most of those on the market today) that is properly maintained and operated (which is up to you) will be safe no matter what its fuel.

Realistically, this means that although using diesel allows you to let your guard down in some areas, you can't be totally complacent. Diesel won't explode like gasoline, but even diesel fuel calls for certain maintenance and operational procedures to keep your boat fire-safe; gasoline just calls for a few more.

The big thing to keep in mind is that hydrocarbon vapors are heavier than air. In a car this isn't a problem; any gasoline vapor present outside the engine sinks to the ground, where it dissipates in the open air. In a boat, what goes down collects in the bilges, and unless you take precautions to keep the bilges scoured with plenty of fresh air, the collected vapors can reach the lower explosive limit (LEL) and go "boom" at the first spark. Experienced boaters are well aware of this and make keeping their bilges clean—*in every way*—a number-one priority.

Gas engines have one other major drawback: their exhaust tends to contain significantly more carbon monoxide (CO), and this colorless, odorless gas is a killer! CO reacts with the red blood cells and actually prevents them from absorbing oxygen. The mild effects of CO poisoning include eye irritation, fatigue, and an inability to think clearly, which are certainly not the best conditions for operating a boat! More severe exposure can lead to collapse and, eventually, death.

CO can get into the cabin from leaking exhaust fittings in the engine compartment, which is another good reason to keep *all* of your boat's systems in good repair. But even a well-maintained boat can get CO inside via the "station wagon effect," in which a partial vacuum that develops abaft the superstructure underway attracts a disproportionate amount of exhaust gases into the cabin by the back door.

It's also possible to have exhaust enter a cabin through open ports, even if it originates on the boat "next door." Because exhaust from gasoline-powered generators can be a big problem for people staying onboard overnight, the Westerbeke

Corporation, which makes small propulsion engines and gensets of many sizes, has introduced a new line of generators whose CO emissions are 99 percent less than those from old-style engines. In my opinion, this is a good move that I hope will be emulated. But I do suggest that if you opt for gasoline power (or moor where others do—which will be most everywhere!), you install a CO monitor or two in your cabin. They are not expensive, and because CO is otherwise undetectable (remember, it is colorless and odorless), the advance warning one of these devices can give could be priceless. It could save your life.

A final thought on gas engines in boats. Once upon a time they were simpler than the engines in our cars. Long after we had fuel injection and computer-controlled functions on the highway, marine power plants remained mostly the old carbureted variety with breaker points and a condenser in the distributor. These days, however, marine engines are usually as advanced as their automotive counterparts, and in many ways, this is good. They are now more reliable, more efficient, and their emissions are cleaner. But this progress is not without a cost. The more complicated the equipment in your engine compartment, the greater the need for professional help (and specialized tools) to maintain it. Boating still offers a lot of opportunity for do-it-yourself involvement, if that's your choice, but engines are rapidly disappearing from this category.

Though they cost more initially, diesels can cost less in the long run. The drastic differences in fuel prices of 35 or 40 years ago, when diesel was only about half the cost of gas, are unlikely to return, but diesel is still usually at least several cents less per gallon than gas, even at marinas. Diesel engines also turn out more usable power per gallon, so the fuel stretches a little farther. But the big difference shows up if you put a lot of hours on your boat. Diesel engines last longer than gas engines. They usually come from the truck and industrial world and are built tougher, which is another reason they cost more initially. They also run at lower rpms (though today's models run at higher revs than diesels of old), which equates to less wear on internal components, and this also leads to longer life. All this means you can run diesel engines harder and longer before you have to consider major overhaul or replacement.

Not too many years ago I would have had to say that diesel engines are not only generally heavier, they are physically bigger, too. This is no longer universally true. There are now a number of diesels on the market that will fit the same space (and often the same mounts) as the more popular large gas engines.

In recent years we've also seen another change in diesels. As has happened with gas engines, the simple mechanisms of old are rapidly vanishing. Many of today's diesels have electronic systems controlling the fuel injectors and include built-in diagnostics (courtesy of computers, naturally) that reduce offensive emissions and make for easier troubleshooting when something goes wrong. But these improvements also make diesels just a tad more delicate than they used to be. Given clean fuel, clean air, and enough oil in the crankcase, an old-style diesel can run forever. The new engines are a bit more finicky. But on the whole, I have to believe the results are still more positive than not.

When you get into maxi-engines for mega-yachts, the field is almost exclusively diesel, but for boats up to about 50 feet LOA, the bottom line is probably whether you would rather pay more initially but less in the long run (diesel) or have a lower purchase price but potentially greater operating and maintenance costs (gas). Some boats come only one way or the other, but with the proliferation of smaller, lighter diesels you'll undoubtedly be faced with an even greater variety of choices in the future.

Single or Twins?

If single-screw boats didn't work, a majority of the world's commercial fishing fleets would never leave port. For many boats in most situations, a single screw is fine (Figure 7-1). Granted, single-screw boats aren't quite as maneuverable, but speaking as someone who spent a number of years operating large, single-screw commercial vessels, I can honestly say that in the hands of an experienced skipper, a single-screw boat can do almost anything a twin-screw boat can do. However, that "almost" is important. We'll get into boathandling later in the book; for now, suffice it to say that the one thing a single-screw boat cannot do as well as twin screws is handle going astern easily. If total maneuverability in all directions at all times is important—as it is, for example, with a sportfisherman—you *need* twins. Otherwise you have a choice.

"What about safety and dependability?" you

FIGURE 7-1. *The propeller provides the push, the rudder gives direction. Note the shaft angle and the under-propeller protection possible when you use a single screw. (Keel Drive photo courtesy Shamrock Marine)*

might ask. "Isn't it better to have two engines so you have one to get home on if one of them quits?" I'd have to answer "Possibly," but the notion of twin-screw superiority for greater safety is largely hogwash. One well-maintained engine is far more reliable than two inadequately maintained engines, and given the time constraints we all face, it can be far more practical to keep up a single engine.

Even if you have all the time in the world, squeezing two engines into the limited space available in many pleasure-boat engine compartments can make some components extremely difficult to reach. Human nature being what it is, you'll be less inclined to give those hard-to-reach components the attention they deserve, regardless of their importance. Having two engines *can*, in some situations, mean you have *less* reliable power than you would with a single.

And even if you maintain both engines faithfully, one of the prime causes of engine failure is contaminated fuel, which will usually affect *all* engines aboard, even your genset. So again, having twins is not necessarily going to help prevent your being stranded by a lack of propulsion.

Then, too, some twin-screw boats simply won't go well on one screw. Many will (and incidentally, behavior with a single engine is a good thing to check when you go for a sea trial in a twin-screw boat), but there's no guarantee. Since some will only run in circles on one engine no matter what you do with the rudders, twin screws are *not* an automatic guarantee of standby power. It depends on the boat.

Twin engines are a good way to double horsepower while keeping the individual engines within the popular (and thus relatively less expensive) size range (Figure 7-2). This is also a practical way of fitting the desired horsepower into available space. True, two engines will take up more room athwartships, but inevitably they'll fit the engine compartments of pleasure boats—where there's usually more width than height—better than a single engine of equivalent horsepower. Fortunately, the exception to this occurs in the very boats that can best use a large single: deep-draft displacement hulls.

FIGURE 7-2. *Twin-engine installations allow easier handling than singles and, usually, more horsepower than would be available from a single engine that would fit the same vertical space.*

A Final Word on Conventional Drives

The conventional drive system is what it is, and whether any particular attribute is a plus or minus depends on what you're looking for. Here's the prime "for instance": conventional drives are under the boat. This is great when you want a clean transom—say, for less interference with fishing or to moor stern-to or simply to have a larger area on which to paint the boat's name. But when you want to take your boat on and off a trailer or cruise shallow waters, underwater running gear can be a hindrance (though it doesn't totally eliminate either trailering or shallow-water maneuvering). Likewise, there are some operational trade-offs. Many of these are best left for greater in-depth discussion in the chapters on handling techniques, but the main point can be simply stated here. Conventional running gear is the least flexible system of all. Most other drive systems allow you to change their trim (the angle at which the propeller meets the water). This creates a number of possibilities ranging from changing the trim of the boat itself (in many, but not all, cases) to changing the load on the engine (in every case). Though these features are desirable, they aren't absolutely necessary, and if the conventional system didn't work basically well, it would have been replaced rather than augmented by other systems.

FIGURE 7-3. *This V-drive has been directly coupled to a "standard" reverse/reduction gear at the point where a straight shaft would be coupled were there no need for the "bend." Other models may incorporate the V into the basic transmission. (Courtesy BorgWarner)*

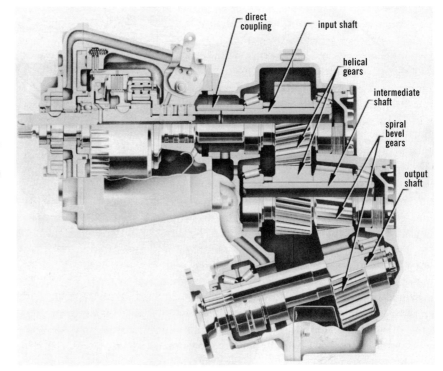

V-Drives

These are simply conventional drives with a "kink" in them. As the name implies, the drive train makes a V, leading forward from the engine to the V gear, then turning back beneath itself to exit the hull sternward as in conventional drives (Figure 7-3). The V-drive's main function is to allow engines to be placed farther aft than they could be with conventional drives, thus allowing a larger uninterrupted cabin area forward of the engines. The drawbacks include the additional set of gears, which adds more friction to the drive train and thus reduces efficiency, and the potential balance problems that result from locating the engines aft. The former problem is very slight and not a major drawback; the latter can usually be overcome with trim tabs, and realistically, it can be better in some boats to have the engines in V-drive position rather than all the way back at the transom, as sterndrives would probably require. I would neither choose nor reject a boat because of V-drives.

Outboards

Ask any old-timer about outboards, and you're sure to get a tale of woe. In the early years, and even in fairly recent history, outboards were notorious for being cranky, cantankerous, smelly, and unreliable power plants. But that *is* history. Today's outboards are generally as reliable as any power plant can be. The only engines made exclusively for boats, they're most assuredly a viable option.

Given that outboard motors have changed so much in less than ten full decades of use, maybe we should examine that history before we take a closer look at the outboards of today. Knowing where we've been may better enable us to understand where we're headed.

In the Beginning

The outboard era actually began in 1906 when a Danish immigrant in Wisconsin, one Ole Evinrude, came up with the idea, though it took him 3 years to make it workable. Legend has it that he and a young lady had gone by rowboat to an island in a lake for a picnic. It was a hot summer day, and she wanted ice cream, so being a dutiful suitor, the young Ole (he was twenty-nine at the time), rowed back to the mainland, bought her some, and returned to the island—only to discover the ice cream had melted before he could get it there.

Now, the story is plausible and could well be true. But if you've ever done any rowing under a hot summer sun, you can easily understand that Mr. Evinrude may not have needed a melting frozen treat to convince him there had to be better means than oars to propel a small boat.

By 1909 he had built the $1\frac{1}{2}$ hp outboard motor that started it all. In 1910 he founded Evinrude Motors to produce them commercially. In 1936 Evinrude merged with Johnson Motors (run by the Johnson brothers, who had also started building outboards in the early 1920s) and formed what eventually became Outboard Marine Corporation (OMC), one of the real powerhouses (no pun intended) in the marine industry for much of the late 20th century.

The Race Begins

In 1939 racing great Karl Kiekhaefer started the Kiekhaefer Corporation (also in Wisconsin), which later became Mercury Marine. The first Mercury outboard came on the scene in 1940, and for nearly five decades, Evinrude, Johnson, and Mercury fought for market dominance. It was a lopsided three-way race; Evinrude and Johnson motors were identical, just with different paint (and different dealers), but Mercury more than held its own. There were a few other trial balloons lofted over the years, including a four-stroke model or two, but no one could shake the dominance of Mercury and OMC, and none of these upstarts caught on. In fact, nothing really threatened the OMC/Mercury grasp on the marketplace until the Japanese started making inroads in the late 1970s and early 1980s. Then, just as we'd seen previously with automobiles, there was a strong Japanese incursion, and within little more than a decade, outboards bearing names such as Honda, Suzuki, and Yamaha became as common in marinas as Evinrude, Johnson, and Mercury.

Along the way, Mercury Marine was purchased by the Brunswick Corporation, a company that was, at the time, more noted for making bowling balls and pool tables than anything marine, though it already owned a few boatbuilders. That soon changed, however, and before long the Brunswick Corporation had become well established in the marine industry. It now also owns several of the most popular boat marques including Bayliner, Boston Whaler, Hatteras, and Sea Ray.

The Only Constant Is Change

Though we've seen some rather drastic changes in outboards recently, they've actually been undergoing nearly constant change since their introduction. The first outboards hid nothing; all external machinery was totally exposed. After a few years, a streamlined cowling was added to improve appearance, to reduce noise, and even more to help keep hands and clothing away from critical and moving parts. This new sleek look was further enhanced when the addition of recoil starters eliminated the need to wrap a rope around the flywheel, so the flywheel, too, could be enclosed. This not only improved outboards' looks, but it also made starting them less of a chore.

Some of the concurrent changes in outboards were less visible though probably even more important. For example, loop charging helped the motors to be more efficient in their exchange of exhaust for the incoming fuel-air mixture while operating within the two-stroke cycle, which led to improved performance all around. And the automatic choke proved to be as big a help as the recoil starter when it came to reducing the potential frustration inherent in trying to start a recalcitrant motor.

As boating became more popular in the postwar boom of the 1950s and early 1960s, the demand for small boats having a steering wheel and console forward (which thus seemed more like their larger, inboard-powered cousins) brought us remote control, electric starting, and the addition of a clutch and shift; outboard-powered craft could now operate astern or sit at a pier in neutral. Again, this made outboard-powered boats more like larger craft in every way but available power; 50 hp was still big in the outboard world well into the 1960s.

The addition of power trim and tilt has to rank as one of the most important improvements ever, because an outboard motor's trimmability is one of the prime features that makes outboards so perfect for planing hulls.

But my personal favorite (which also came along with the move to remote control) has to be the external portable fuel tank. I'm sure anyone who has also suffered through repeatedly stopping to fill a tiny motor-mounted tank from a 5-gallon reserve can while balancing on a small boat that was bouncing in a seaway would have to agree.

At the same time, the amount of oil we had to mix with the gas for internal lubrication kept decreasing as outboard engineering continued to improve. Ultimately, a tiny can of oil (about the size of a Red Bull can) was enough for 6 gallons of gas, the standard size of a portable tank. But then it got even better. VRO, which stands for variable ratio oiling, allowed the oil and gas to be carried in separate tanks to be mixed inside the engine in exactly the correct ratio for the power demand at the time, thus reducing even further the oil consumed in running an outboard. And outboards continued to get bigger and bigger, eventually topping out in the neighborhood of 300 hp.

But outboards remained predominantly two-stroke engines, which meant they still burned some oil, and that in turn meant more pollutants in their exhaust than equivalent four-stroke engines. And since the exhaust first has to bubble up through the water (outboards mostly exhaust through the propeller hub), it meant more pollutants there as well.

So as the 20th century drew to a close, the proverbial handwriting was on the proverbial wall. Outboards *had* to change drastically to be able to meet the emissions standards being imposed for the early 21st century (2006 for the EPA, 2008 for CARB—the California Air Resources Board). This upheaval, in which OMC became enamored of a new two-stroke technology that never did live up to expectations, combined with a growing influx of the Japanese outboards that were,

truthfully, better than American motors in many ways, and the expensive (often *too*-expensive) purchase of an increasing number of boatbuilding companies proved to be too much for OMC, which filed for bankruptcy in 2000. (Brunswick Marine, the parent company of Mercury and Mariner outboards and MerCruiser sterndrives, was also heavily involved in buying boatbuilders at this time, but with greater success.)

OMC's boat brands were ultimately bought (mostly by Genmar Holdings, which already owned a number of popular lines including Carver and Wellcraft), while Bombardier, the Canadian maker of Ski-Doo snowmobiles and Sea-Doo watercraft, bought the engine side of the business, promising to retain the Evinrude and Johnson brand names. In late 2003, however, Bombardier spun off its entire recreational division as Bombardier Recreational Products (BRP), an independent company. As of this writing, BRP seemed quite confident of making the new Evinrudes and Johnsons as popular as they once were, and for the first time since Ole Evinrude merged his company with the Johnson brothers in 1936, Evinrude and Johnson outboards were being developed as truly separate brands, with Evinrude concentrating on its new E-tec two-stroke technology that, according to company claims, blends the best of two- and four-stroke engines while eliminating the worst. These new Evinrude engines are direct-injection two-stroke outboards, available in models ranging from 40 to 250 hp, while Johnson outboards as of 2004 came in both two-stroke carbureted (3.5 to 175 hp) and four-stroke (4 to 225 hp) models.

Not to be outdone, in early 2004 Mercury unveiled its new four-stroke Verado, the first supercharged production outboard ever (Figure 7-4). A result of four years and more than $100 million spent in development, this impressive design dropped a lot of jaws with its raw power (up to 275 hp, so far). At the other end of the spectrum, Mercury also introduced a couple of smaller (8.8 and 9 hp) four-strokes with many big-engine features such as optional electric starting and remote steering.

Just to complete the picture, I should note that as of 2004, the Japanese brands Honda, Nis-

FIGURE 7-5. *A Yamaha two-stroke outboard. (Courtesy Yamaha Marine Group)*

FIGURE 7-4. *Introduced in 2004, the Mercury Verado is the world's first supercharged four-stroke outboard. (Courtesy Mercury)*

san/Tohatsu, and Suzuki are all four-stroke, while Yamaha still produces both two-stroke and four-stroke models (Figures 7-5 and 7-6).

A New Day Dawns

Just as Oldsmobile declared a few years ago, "It's not your father's Oldsmobile" (alas, it's no longer anybody's!), today's outboards are a far cry from what our fathers and grandfathers knew, or even what we knew just a few years ago. *All* outboards—whether you're considering a four-stroke or one of the few remaining, but also mostly radically new, two-strokes—are more fuel efficient (thanks largely to fuel injection, which makes many of the new two-strokes in many ways more similar to the four-strokes than to

FIGURE 7-6. *A Yamaha four-stroke outboard. (Courtesy Yamaha Marine Group)*

their counterparts of old), quieter, much less the "stinkpot," and thus far kinder to the environment than anything that ever came before. In outboard motors, it's a whole new world.

Yet outboards remain the only power plants designed and manufactured exclusively and especially for marine use. And that's true from that

FIGURE 7-7. *Outboard engines provide relatively lightweight power that doesn't intrude into usable cockpit space. (Courtesy Boston Whaler)*

first blank sheet on the drawing board (of course, these days it's a blank screen in a CADD system) to final assembly, which is now more automated than ever before. Outboards are truly *boat* motors, and for planing craft up to about 35 feet LOA, they would often be my first choice.

Not everyone is unreservedly happy with the "new" outboards. I've heard quite a few folks say they miss the sound (which others would call "noise," I'm sure) of the older motors. And since most four-stroke outboards are slightly heavier than two-strokes of similar horsepower (they have more inside, including oil), some boatbuilders have felt it necessary to redesign some popular hulls to account for the increased weight on the transom. The other side of this coin, of course, is that outboards, even four-strokes, will probably still prove to be much lighter than in-boards of equivalent horsepower. And for a planing hull, where minimal total weight is so important, this can still amount to a huge advantage for outboard power.

Another advantage outboards offer is that they're usually mounted outside the boat, which leaves more interior room for people and gear (Figure 7-7) and also keeps all potential gasoline-vapor problems outside the boat. There's an associated repair or upgrade advantage, too: changing an outboard, even one of the largest ones, is a job measured in hours, while changing or replacing an inboard engine is a job measured in days.

These blessings are not without their drawbacks, however. The old problem of requiring a cut-down transom or long-shaft lower unit (or both) has been eliminated in recent years by the development of the outboard bracket. This allows a full transom—nice for keeping the boat dry inside in following seas or when backing down on a fish—and the bracket truly puts the whole works outside the boat. That leaves as the main drawback a cluttered transom, which for many boats (and their owners) is a small price to pay for the added interior space and safety the arrangement allows.

As we'll see in greater detail later in the chapters on handling techniques, the ability to aim all of a propeller's thrust enables outboards to offer better cruising maneuverability than conventional drives, in which only part of the thrust is deflected by the rudder. The other side of this coin is that without the propeller thrust—as when the motor is in neutral—you have limited rudder action. And at low speeds, say in docking situations, directing the thrust can lead to oversteering.

As mentioned, outboards offer you the ability to adjust engine trim for maximum efficiency, though with the older and smaller sizes, adjustments can't be made underway. This allows you to eliminate, or at least drastically reduce, some of the problems inherent in moving a relatively large object (your boat) horizontally by spinning a small object (the propeller) vertically beneath it. But some problems remain. And until near the end of the 20th century, the problems were compounded with twin outboards because both props rotated in the same direction (with conventional inboards, counterrotating props are the norm), and the effects of torque were doubled. Now outboards in the horsepower range of twins come almost exclusively in matched sets with counterrotating props.

This is only one more example of the ways in which the manufacturers of outboard motors have been chipping away at the entrenched objections of yesteryear.

Sterndrives

If today's outboard technology had been available in the late 1950s, the sterndrive might never have come about. But it wasn't, so it did. The idea was to couple the familiar and reliable inboard engine to the trimmability and steerability of the outboard's lower unit. Theoretically it's the

best of both worlds: a familiar (read: four-cycle automotive-type as opposed to the unknowns, such as reed valves inside the two-stroke outboard), reliable (as opposed to the sometimes-it-starts, sometimes-it-doesn't outboard of the day), and more powerful (big-block Chevy V8s, for example) engine combined with all the advantages of transom power. It isn't a bad idea, and obviously, since there are still a lot of sterndrive boats being built and sold, it works. But I'm not totally convinced it's always the *best* solution. In many boats, placing a large engine or two just inside the transom is so detrimental to overall trim and balance that it takes every bit of trimmability in the drive(s) *plus* the help of tabs to get the boat on plane. A pair of lighter outboards might be better. Yet, once on plane the boats work OK, so the arrangement can't be totally wrong either.

Sterndrives were initially similar to outboards in that the twins rarely offered counterrotating props. This has been corrected in recent years, and some sterndrives now come in matched pairs, with a left-handed prop on the port drive and a right-handed one to starboard, though the practice is not yet widespread.

One particular advantage of sterndrives over outboards is a greater flexibility in the engines themselves. For example, it's now possible to couple a high-speed diesel to a heavy-duty drive unit and gain the advantages of diesel power plus trimmability. Since power trim with its ability to fine-tune the drive every moment you're underway is now a standard part of all sterndrives, the combination of high power and trimmability is a very inviting package for those seeking ultimate performance.

At cruising speeds and above, sterndrives exhibit the same improved steering control (as compared with conventional drives) seen in outboards. They also usually exhibit the same tendency to oversteer at low speeds, an idiosyncrasy that will often be exaggerated in boats that are particularly sensitive to the added weight in the stern (and even more so with twins if both props have the same rotation). But sterndrive makers haven't been complacent, and when Volvo introduced the Duo Prop drive, which has contra-rotating props on a single drive—that's right, two

FIGURE 7-8. *Using two contrarotating props on the same lower unit, the Duo Prop sterndrive from Volvo Penta eliminates many of the torque-related problems involved in moving a large object (the boat) through the water by rotating a small object (the prop) behind it. (Courtesy Volvo Penta)*

props, just like a torpedo—they presented us with a solution to several problems (Figure 7-8). The concept works well enough that MerCruiser (Mercury Marine's sterndrive division) has adopted it in its Bravo III drives. From what I've seen, having two props on one sterndrive shaft is an excellent arrangement. It retains high-speed maneuverability yet seems to lose the tendency to oversteer at slow speeds. Plus, it allows much straighter operation astern than any other single sterndrive I've ever run.

Surface-Piercing Drives

Surface-piercing drives were to the 1980s what sterndrives were to the 1960s: the new kid on the block, the nautical equivalent of a better mousetrap. Yet only the execution was new; the concept goes back to the early 1900s, but it took nearly 80 years for metallurgy and other technology to catch up with the principle involved and allow a practical application.

Early in the 20th century, with the advent of internal-combustion engines for boats, engineers began experimenting with propellers. Among their discoveries were that much of the applied power is lost to water friction on the shaft, strut,

and propeller hub. And perhaps more important, the prop doesn't develop full thrust throughout the entire 360 degrees of its rotation but rather produces the bulk of it in the arc from 30 to 150 degrees past top dead center.

Among the first to attempt to put this knowledge to use was Albert Hickman of South Boston, Massachusetts, who tried running shafts straight out from the transom of his experimental Sea Sleds—a forerunner of the hull design seen these days in the smaller Boston Whalers. The idea worked, sort of. By allowing the propeller to break the surface (hence the name "surface piercing") he reduced friction and gained thrust. But the water surface wasn't the only thing broken; Hickman kept breaking shafts, too. So the idea was abandoned until Howard Arneson revived it, with important modifications, in 1980.

Arneson took the basic concept and added flexibility. The external segment of the drive is connected to the internal with a constant-velocity joint and can be moved both vertically and horizontally by hydraulic rams similar to those on sterndrives. This adds steerability and trimmability to the equation. Offshore racers soon found that Arneson drives allowed them higher top speeds, and the drives are now widely accepted on high-performance pleasure craft as well (Figure 7-9).

Another historical note: soon after he introduced the drive, Arneson sold the rights to gear manufacturer BorgWarner. Not too long after that, the late Betty Cook (who didn't even begin

FIGURE 7-9. *An Arneson surface-piercing drive increases thrust and reduces drag by taking the prop out of the water through the least-efficient portion of its rotational circle. Note the two hydraulic rams: one for steering, and one for trim. (Courtesy Arneson Marine, Inc.)*

racing until she was fifty and a grandmother, and then quickly proved you needn't be either young or male to be a champion) introduced a similar (but sufficiently different to avoid patent infringement) system under the marque of her race-equipment team, Kaama Engineering. By 1985, BorgWarner had ceased production of the Arneson drives, leaving the field to Kaama. In the late 1980s, the Kaama drive was acquired by Volvo, but it sort of dropped out of the picture as the company concentrated on other things (such as the Duo Prop), and Arneson was once more an independent company. Then it was bought again in the early 1990s by gear-maker Twin Disc, where it remains. The future is always subject to change, of course. But Twin Disc recently bought Rolla, the Swiss propeller company that makes, among other things, props for Arneson drives, so I would guess there are no plans to change anything soon.

Not being one to shun controversy, I have to add a few personal opinions regarding surface-piercing drives. First, a lot of what I've seen has impressed me. For example, I've witnessed speeds of 50 mph and higher in a couple of 70-foot Magnum motor yachts. I'm not sure the same speeds could have been reached with conventional drives. Further, had the boats been set up conventionally, they would have drawn 6 feet. With the Arnesons, they drew only 3!

But I'm not sure surface-piercing drives are for everyone. Back in 1983, I had the opportunity to compare two nearly identical boats. The only difference between them was that one had sterndrives, the other had Kaama drives. With radar gun and stopwatch, I compared performance between them on the same day on the same waterway with the same driver. Simply stated, we did as much as we could to make the drives the only difference between the boats. What I saw was a higher top end from the surface-piercing drives, but better all-around performance—tighter turning radius, better acceleration (shorter time to plane), and generally easier, more-responsive handling, particularly in low-speed, tight-quarters situations—from the sterndrives. So I have to think that while surface-piercing drives have their place, they're probably not for the beginner.

For the record, though Arneson drives are by far the best-known surface drives, they aren't the only ones. The principle has merit, and from time to time other boat companies and engine makers produce their own versions. Though I have no firsthand knowledge of most other brands, I certainly wouldn't reject them out of hand. If the company that makes them has a good history and good prospects for continuing in business, I'd consider any make of surface-piercing drives with one significant caveat: as I noted above, I don't think this means of propulsion is the best option for beginners. But that's just my opinion; it isn't a decree from Mount Olympus.

Jet Drives

Except for a number of regional builders in the Pacific Northwest who use jet drives because their boats will most likely be run in shallow, rock-strewn rivers, jets have mostly shown up on either very small or very large watercraft. The waterborne scooters often called wet-bikes or Jet Skis (which is actually Kawasaki's trade name, not a generic), use jets to eliminate the danger of a propeller (Figure 7-10). It's easy to fall off one of these "personal watercraft" (PWC), and the last thing you need is to be cut up by a propeller when you do. At the other end of the spectrum, in recent years many 100-foot-plus megayachts have been powered by large diesel engines turning jet drives rather than propellers. The reasons are similar to those that caused jets to replace props in large airplanes—jets are more efficient than props when it comes to moving an object rapidly through a fluid medium, whether the medium is air or water (Figure 7-11). Jets are not without their drawbacks, however, and several megayacht builders still won't use them.

Jet drives have rarely been used in boats of the size range we're covering in this book (roughly 14 to 65 feet), but such boats do exist. Several small jet-driven boats entered the marketplace in the mid-1990s. Though these new craft were in many ways an outgrowth of wet-bikes, they were nonetheless real boats. But just as jets have never totally replaced props in aircraft, I seriously doubt we will ever see jets totally

FIGURE 7-10. *Kawasaki's version of jet-driven personal watercraft has become so popular that the name Jet Ski is nearly generic. Jet propulsion is also often seen on much larger craft—megayachts of 90 feet and up. (Courtesy Kawasaki)*

replacing props on the water. In fact, many of the makes and models of jet boats that were quite popular when introduced roughly a decade ago didn't stand the test of time and are no longer in production. For small craft (other than PWC), it seems people still prefer props, though BRP is still producing several models of jet boat under the Sea-Doo marque (Figure 7-12).

FIGURE 7-11. *The twin water jets on this megayacht clearly illustrate the principle—you can see the rapidly flowing water coming out of the jets. The units employed on boats of the size we're discussing in this book will be considerably smaller, but they work the same. (Courtesy Dag Pike,* Fast Powerboat Seamanship)

Volvo Penta Inboard Performance System

While all propulsion systems seem to undergo a rather constant but gradual change through evolution (the new outboards and electronically controlled diesels being perfect examples), every 20 years or so we are treated to something totally new and *revolutionary*. Sterndrives in the 1960s and surface-piercing drives in the 1980s are prime illustrations. By 2005 we were more than due again, and sure enough, early in the year we saw the introduction of yet another radically new drive: Volvo Penta's IPS propulsion system.

This system is "different" on several fronts. For one, it is used only in twin-engine installations and only on planing hulls designed for speeds from 25 to 45 knots (Figure 7-13). For another, though at first glance each unit resembles a Duo Prop sterndrive, these drives go *under* the boat and the props face forward!

As we go to press, I have yet to operate an IPS-equipped boat, so I can't offer any firsthand observations on their characteristics. But I have to admit I'm impressed with the design parameters—and some early reports from fellow boating journalists who were lucky enough to witness some pre-introduction sea trials. (I'll really have

FIGURE 7-12. *Though jet-propelled small* boats *are nowhere near as abundant as they were in the mid-1990s, BRP still produces a complete line under the Sea-Doo brand. (Courtesy BRP)*

to let more people know when I'm working on a new edition!)

All underwater components are either stainless steel or *nibral* [a nickel-bronze-aluminum alloy most often used in props]. The cooling-water intake and engine exhaust are also directed through the unit, which should accomplish several goals: it reduces the number of holes in the hull; and it helps eliminate the "station wagon effect" by releasing the exhaust gases underwater and into the discharge screw current so they shouldn't reach the air until well abaft the boat itself, which should also make for quieter operation underway.

Another design goal was improved efficiency, and reports from Volvo Penta suggest they've achieved it. In a comparison test with identical boats and identical engines, the company says the IPS-equipped boat showed a 6-knot higher top speed, better fuel economy (25 gallons per hour at 30 knots versus 37 gph on the non-IPS boat) and 15 percent better acceleration (time to plane). As an added plus, sound levels aboard the IPS boat were reported to be about 50 percent lower.

As I write this, I've seen reports on two installations—a Fairlane Phantom 40 and a Tiara

Sovran 4000. One of the more frequent comments I've heard was, "It handles and responds like a smaller boat!" This would most likely be because the drives are also part of the steering system, turning to direct *all* of the thrust rather than deflecting part of it with a rudder. (The importance of this will become clearer after you've read more of the book, but as I wrote earlier in this chapter concerning outboards and sterndrives, being able to aim a prop's entire discharge current can equate to infinitely better control.) Each drive's counter-rotating props also eliminate side thrust, the significance of which will also become clearer when you read the chapters on handling. But at this point let me say this is important enough that I can easily believe the reports of easier handling in both close-quarters situations and also at speed.

I should note that as of now, this drive system is available with only two versions of the Volvo Penta D6 diesel engine. The IPS 400 is coupled to the 310 (shaft) horsepower, turbocharged, and aftercooled model while the engine in the IPS 500 also has a compressor, which ups the shaft horsepower to 370.

I'm really looking forward to operating a boat or two that has the IPS system and anticipate that should I still be around and have the opportunity

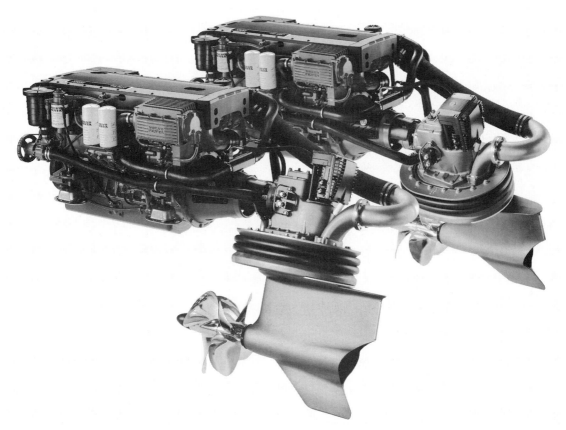

FIGURE 7-13. *The brand-new IPS drive system (introduced in 2005), which is only available in pairs and only for planing hulls, features several innovations. It places the greater control of directed thrust—as we get with outboards and sterndrives—under the boat rather than abaft the transom. Note also that the counterrotating props face forward so they operate in less-disturbed water, which makes them more efficient. (Courtesy Volvo Penta)*

to write a fourth edition of this book a few years from now, the Volvo Penta IPS drive system will still be around also, and I'll have a lot more to say about it.

In today's highly packaged marketplace, you'll often find that a particular model boat comes only one or two ways—with sterndrives but with a choice of a couple of different horsepower packages, for example. That means your choice of power plant is limited. However, you should still consider the ways in which different power plants and drive systems fit into your boating plans. Even if a particular boat offers limited choice, similar boats might offer different drive systems. It's not at all unlikely that one of the de-

ciding factors in choosing one boat over another will be the way it's powered.

Last (and quite possibly least), before we leave the subject of power plants, I should tell you about one more choice you might have to make.

Raw- or Freshwater Cooling?

Raw-water systems cool by circulating through the engine some of the same water you boat in, whether it's lake, river, bay, or ocean water. They're simpler and less expensive, and they're used in all outboards as well as in many gas inboards, both conventional and sterndrive. If used in salt water, they need frequent flushing with clean fresh water to reduce internal corrosion or the blockage caused by salt buildup, because blockage can lead to "hot spots" with resulting long-term damage.

Freshwater systems recirculate a water-antifreeze mixture (generally 50-50) through a closed system—engine block, oil and transmission coolers, and a heat exchanger that releases heat to a through-flow of raw water. This means two pumps, and two separate circulating systems that only interact through heat exchangers and coolers.

On slower boats, heat exchange can also be via keel coolers—tubing that runs along the bottom and exchanges heat via contact with water in which the boat floats. In the closed part of the system, antifreeze aids heat transfer and helps keep the entire cooling system cleaner while it reduces internal corrosion. Freshwater systems are more expensive initially—they need that additional pump and more plumbing as well as more labor in manufacture—but they add greatly to engine longevity. Freshwater systems are used in many larger gas inboards and nearly all diesels because they provide a more even cooling and hold the system at a rather constant temperature. They also help maintain the minimum operating temperature (140°F) necessary for best diesel performance.

Again, this choice will have been made for you if the object of your desire comes only one way or the other. But if the decision is up to you, as it often will be if you're considering a small- to mid-sized gas-powered boat, give freshwater cooling careful thought. Builders usually make the raw-water version standard to keep the base price low, and yes, a freshwater or "closed" system will cost more, but you stand a better chance of recovering the cost when you sell or trade your

boat; the engines on older boats with raw-water cooling are always suspect, and this will be reflected in the price you can get as well as the ease of sale. As with other systems (though closed cooling is probably easier to retrofit than many), installing closed cooling during initial construction is usually the least expensive way to go.

If you use your boat in fresh water or flush your engines religiously, raw-water cooling is fine. And if you're interested in maximum speed, raw-water cooling does weigh less; there's not as much plumbing, and you don't have to carry the weight of the circulating coolant. But remember the value of freshwater flushing. There are devices, often called "earmuffs" because of the way they clamp onto the lower unit, that make for easy flushing of outboards after each use.

As for inboards, one of the best arrangements I've ever seen was on a go-fast I once tested. The boat was powered by three V12 Lamborghini engines turning Arneson drives, so you know the raw-water cooling was to save ounces, not pennies. But a part of what impressed me was the hose connection and manifold in the engine compartment that made it easy to flush the engines thoroughly with fresh water after each use.

Remember, raw-water cooling is not necessarily bad. It just means you have to give the engines a bit more care to be sure there's no internal cooling system blockage from salt deposits if you do your boating in salt water.

Your boat has to be right for you in every way. Make sure every aspect of the drive system fits your needs, too, or the boat as a whole may be less than totally satisfactory. Making every aspect suitable includes using the right propeller(s) for the boating you plan to do. But we'd better save that discussion for another chapter.

8

Picking the Proper Prop

The whole "propeller story" cannot be told in a few pages. So this chapter can't begin to be everything you need to know about choosing the right prop(s) for your boat. Dave Gerr has covered the subject thoroughly in his book *The Propeller Handbook: The Complete Reference for Choosing, Installing, and Understanding Boat Propellers*. If you want to know *all* about props, I suggest you find a copy and read it, though I suspect the book might be more technical than you need at this stage of your boating involvement. When you're just getting started, all that information could be overwhelming.

But you shouldn't be totally in the dark either, so please allow me to offer a simplified view of some of the mysteries and quirks involved in propeller selection so you can better understand the props that will be chosen for you. I also hope I can help you recognize the importance of communicating thoroughly with the person or persons who will prescribe your propeller(s) based on the specifics of your boat, its power plant(s), and your intended plans for its use. And that last element is *so* important; identical sister ships, even those with identical power plants, often should have quite different props because their owners load and use their boats so differently. I should also acknowledge that prop selection is another of those processes that can be as much art as science. There are tables, graphs, formulas, and even computer programs that can help. But all of the superior prop specifiers I've ever known personally seem to rely as much on their instincts and experience as they do on technical principles and math.

So Ubiquitous, So Little Understood

Propellers, unfortunately, are among those common objects whose function we too often take for granted, like the tires on our cars. But just as the correct tires can make a huge difference in automobile performance—including fuel economy—because they are "where the rubber meets the road," a boat's props must be exactly right because they're also the ultimate link between engine output and "traction," as it applies on the water (Figure 8-1).

Let me illustrate with a story. Back in the late 1970s I had the pleasure of riding with Reggie

FIGURE 8-1. *Most outboard motors vent their exhaust through the propeller, hence the three slots around the central hub. (Courtesy Michigan Wheel Company)*

Fountain in his prototype, the very first Fountain sportboat ever. I was writing for *Motorboat* magazine at the time and had come down from Boston to attend the Fort Lauderdale Boat Show. Reggie was there also, introducing his boat to the public for the first time. Although the magazine had already reviewed his boat, he clearly wanted every boating writer he could corral to experience it firsthand.

It was the day after the show closed, and as soon as I climbed aboard, we cruised down to Port Everglades and the straight strip of the ICW (Intracoastal Waterway) that leads south from there. Reggie knew that many other sportboat builders had facilities in North Miami Beach and would be heading that way to take their boats home.

In a manner reminiscent of high school days on otherwise quiet streets (I guess I can admit it now; the statute of limitations has long since run out), he was quite obviously interested in drag racing other sportboats. As each would approach, Reggie would signal his intentions and give "the other guys" a head start to let them take a slight lead. Then he'd pour it on and, in every case, catch and quickly pass them. (All the skippers were experienced boathandlers. Even so, this stretch of waterway now has speed limits and is more congested, so we couldn't do that sort of thing there today.) One time he even said, "I should have given him a bigger lead, Bobby. We caught him way too soon!"

On the way back to drop me off and take on some more fuel (that's one thing about sportboats, they can be awfully thirsty!), Reggie apologized for not having been able to show me a higher top speed. "I have her propped for acceleration today, Bobby. I knew we wouldn't be involved in anything where maximum speed would count. She's capable of going a lot faster than anything you saw today, believe me. But not with these props. Today I was looking to jump ahead as quick as possible, not reach top speed. Props make a big difference in a boat's performance, you know. You have to choose the right ones for what you want to do."

Of course, he isn't the only one to know this,

though more often than not, maximum top speed is the desired goal. You wouldn't believe the number of times I've heard during a boat test, "We know she can go faster, Bob, but we're still experimenting with props."

I learned an important lesson from all this: having the right prop(s) for what you want your boat to do is critical. And so I pass it on, along with the suggestion that when you're choosing the type, size, accommodations arrangement, power plant(s), and other equipment for your dreamboat, carry the discussion one step further and talk with the salesperson about props as well—not necessarily in propeller specifics, but with regard to the performance you're looking for and how you plan to use the boat. Better to put it all on the table while you're still discussing options than to be dissatisfied with your boat's performance later. Changes are usually less expensive when you're still negotiating. Always make your final decision subject to a satisfactory sea trial, and don't commit to purchase until you're actually satisfied.

Prop Basics

We describe props by their dimensions—there are just two—and a few other aspects. The first dimension is the prop's *diameter*, which, as you might guess, is the size of the circle described by the blade tips as they revolve (Figure 8-2).

The second dimension is pitch, which is a bit more esoteric because it's purely theoretical. *Pitch* is the distance the prop would advance in one revolution if it were a real screw being turned into a solid rather than something we metaphorically call a "screw" advancing through a liquid (Figure 8-3). A prop with a 24-inch pitch would advance 24 inches through the water with every revolution if it weren't for a very important element called *slip*. We'll take a closer look at slip a bit further on.

A *28" x 26" prop* has a diameter of 28 inches with a 26-inch pitch. A prop whose diameter and pitch are identical, say 28" x 28", is known as a "square" prop, though it still spins a circle. In practice we'd refer to this prop as 28 inches

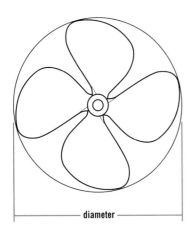

FIGURE 8-2. *The propeller's diameter is the size of the circle described by the blade tips as they revolve.*

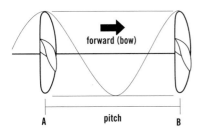

FIGURE 8-3. Pitch *is the distance the prop would advance in one revolution if it were a real screw moving through a solid. Because the propeller is moving through a liquid, the actual advance is less. The difference is the* slip *(see text).*

square. Incidentally, there's nothing special or magical about a square prop. It just happens that sometimes the ideal pitch for a given application will be identical to the prop's diameter.

We also describe a particular prop by the number of blades it has. Props can have as few as two, though these are usually seen only on sailboats. Most powerboats use three- or four-bladed props, though in some applications, such as boats with very large engines, it's not unusual to see five blades or even more, and this trend seems to be growing.

One reason for multiple blades is that *blade area* [the total amount of blade surface available to work], has a direct relationship to the amount

of energy that can be transformed from *torque* [the rotational force in the shaft] into *thrust* to push the boat. The greater the blade area, the more power a prop can handle effectively, and, naturally, more blades equal more total blade area as the individual blades overlap.

Of course, the more blades, the less efficient each of them can be because all must work in more-disturbed water. The turbulence is created by the blade before it, which becomes more of a factor as the number of blades increases and each overlaps the other to a greater degree. But multiple blades are often used to gain smoothness despite this minor problem. A three-bladed prop produces its thrust in three pulses per revolution (each blade doing its share of the job). And just as more cylinders make for a smoother-running engine, more blades make for smoother thrust. Exactly how many blades will be right for the prop(s) on your boat is another variable to consider. The right combination of diameter, rotational speed at cruise, and number of blades can have a huge influence on eliminating vibration (or at least reducing it drastically).

In addition to a prop's diameter, pitch, and number of blades, we also have to consider whether we need it to be left- or right-handed. Right-handed props turn clockwise when viewed from astern (for a boat going ahead). Obviously, left-handed props spin counterclockwise under the same circumstances. For single-screw vessels, the lone prop can be either—it depends on which way the shaft rotates when the clutch is engaged ahead—but most are right-handed. With twin screws, the standard procedure is to have a right-handed prop on the starboard and a left-handed prop to port.

The shape and arrangement of the blades are also factors in prop behavior, so the specifics of a particular prop can also include the type of blade by shape, such as the "cleavers" used on many sportboats, and whether the blades are cupped or raked (explanations to follow).

Finally, we must consider which material will be best for our installation. Props can be made of stainless steel, aluminum, bronze, nibral [a nickel-bronze-aluminum alloy], and even composite plastics. As you might guess, there are advantages and disadvantages to each, and we'll discuss them all in good time.

The Relationship of Prop Specifications

Each aspect of a prop is at least somewhat related to all the others, and changing one element often prompts other changes as well. But we can still look at the prime contribution of each in an attempt to understand its major influence on a boat's performance.

Pitch

The primary effect of pitch is comparable to the transmission in your car. Greater pitch relates to the higher gears: more speed but less acceleration. Smaller pitches are like lower gears and provide more acceleration but a lower top speed. For every installation there's a maximum practical pitch. If pitch is too great, the prop literally tries to bite off more than it can chew and overloads the engine. So instead of producing more speed, too much pitch can actually slow a boat by preventing the engine(s) from developing full power. Too little pitch isn't good either, especially if you've chosen gasoline power. If a gas engine isn't loaded enough, it can over-rev (diesels can't; they're controlled by governors), so not only will too little pitch rob you of maximum top speed, but it can also wear out your power plant(s) prematurely. Note that pitch can be constant or progressive. *Constant-pitch* propellers have the same pitch across the entire *pressure face* [the aft face, the one that pushes water back, thus creating thrust]. *Progressive-pitch* propellers have a lower pitch at the leading edge, which then increases across the blade face. This type of propeller typically provides superior planing performance.

How you use your boat can influence desired pitch also, in that you may not want the maximum speed a particular engine can deliver, but rather maximum efficiency at cruise. In this case, your best props would have a pitch quite different from the props that would allow your engine(s) to reach maximum rpms, which is so often the goal. In your case, the prop specifier would choose a pitch that would allow the maximum transfer of *power* at a specified rpm below WOT, your designated cruise speed. This is why it's so important to communicate fully about your intended operation with those who will pick your prop.

Incidentally, though the vast majority of props have but one overall pitch (even those with progressive pitch), there are props that essentially shift gears by actually changing pitch. Starting with a lesser pitch to provide better acceleration initially, they then shift to a greater pitch when the prop reaches a certain rpm; the shift is mechanical and activated by centrifugal force. They are mostly used on bass boats by anglers who want the best of both worlds: maximum acceleration and highest top speed. But their mere availability shows just how complex prop selection can be—and what a wide variety of choices there are!

Diameter

Diameter can also influence the speed you get, but it has its greatest effect on acceleration and thrust. Using a larger diameter is like putting bigger tires on your car: you get more traction—or in our case, less slip. Larger diameters put more load on an engine because they move more water, so there are limits as to how big you can go, depending on available horsepower. There are other limits, too. One is the clearance between the blade tips and what's above them (either the hull or the antiventilation plate of an outboard or sterndrive), which must be sufficient to allow a good solid flow of water and also to help prevent the small bubbles that spin off the prop from wearing away any structural or operational material above them.

Tip velocity is another determining factor. If too great, it can cause *cavitation* [a similar bubble-induced erosion of the blades themselves], which results from the lack of good firm contact with the water. Though rotational speed remains the same as shaft speed regardless of prop diameter, the linear speed of a blade increases rapidly with distance from the center of rotation. Thus the blade tips of larger-diameter props move through the water much faster than the tips of smaller props at the same rpm. When we were propping the trawler yacht on which I lived and worked when I first wrote this book, I had to settle for much smaller diameter props than I would have preferred—large, slow-turning props are perfect for maneuvering large, slow, heavy boats. Unfortunately, the only reduction gears available for the moderately fast-turning engines we had chosen would have resulted in large, very fast turning props that would not have worked well at all. So I settled for the largest practical diameter for reasonable tip speed despite having the physical clearance to swing much bigger props. And there's an important key here: generally (and unless you have a very fast boat) you want the largest diameter that meets all other requirements. Larger-diameter props are more efficient.

A blade moving through the water does encounter resistance (drag). Can't help it. But the less blade there is (either less diameter, fewer blades, or less blade thickness), the less the resistance. If you have a fast-moving boat, your speed should increase slightly when you decrease diameter because there will be less drag. This only works, of course, if you still get enough thrust with the smaller prop. This is another of the considerations that go toward determining the correct diameter. And what makes it a decision for experts is that there are always factors favoring a larger diameter (more thrust, greater efficiency) and also those suggesting smaller (the need for less drag, less engine load, or greater tip clearance). The right balance of all factors, and hence the right diameter for your boat, is rarely a simple choice unless you have an outboard or sterndrive for which diameter is pretty much standardized (for each size of power plant), and prop selection usually involves pitch or other factors only.

OK, I can almost read your mind. You're thinking, "I can understand selecting diameter, pitch, and number of blades, but isn't blade thickness beyond our control? I mean, how do you decrease blade thickness without sacrificing necessary strength?" It's fairly simple. For one thing, increasing the number of blades decreases the load on each, since they all share the engine power

equally. This means each blade can be thinner. Or we can use a stronger material. This is why stainless steel is so popular for performance props; stainless steel blades can be much thinner than aluminum or bronze.

Cupping

A *cupped* propeller is one on which the trailing edges of the blades are curved aft toward the pressure face (Figure 8-4). Cupping increases a prop's effective pitch, so a cupped prop will produce the same performance as an uncupped prop with greater pitch while actually biting less water with each revolution, which increases its efficiency and lessens the load on the engine. The result is usually higher speeds at the same rpm. Cupping is so beneficial that these days nearly all high-performance recreational or racing propellers have at least a little cup.

Rake

Rake refers to the angle of the blades when you view a prop from the side (Figure 8-5). On a prop with zero rake, the blade tips are centered on the hub. With positive rake, the blades lean aft. Negative rake has the blades leaning forward.

Negative rake can offer several advantages. On outboards or sterndrives, it allows a prop to be trimmed out to run nearer the surface without

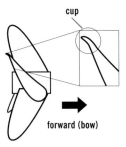

FIGURE 8-4. Cupping *gives the trailing edges of the blades a slight curve aft. Cupping increases the prop's efficiency and reduces engine load, which means a higher speed at the same rpm or the same speed at lower rpm, either of which can be so beneficial that these days nearly all planing-hull propellers have at least a little cup.*

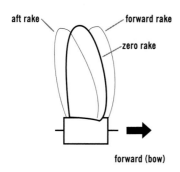

FIGURE 8-5. Rake *is the angle of the blades relative to the hub when viewed from the side. A great majority of propellers have zero rake, meaning that the blades are perfectly perpendicular, with their tips centered on the hub. Slanting the blades, either back toward the stern* (positive rake) *or forward* (negative rake), *can be helpful in certain applications (see text), which is why you will see raked blades on some props.*

incurring excessive ventilation, which is what we call the process of drawing air down into the prop stream. As you might guess, ventilation isn't desirable; you want the prop to work in "solid" water, as it was meant to do. Rake can also contribute to bow lift, which can be good for planing hulls, though it can also be a detriment if there's too much lift up forward. I'll have more to say on this in Chapter 30.

On inboard installations, props with positive rake are often used on boats whose bottoms slope upward as they approach the transom (as do most), since positive rake moves the blade tips back. And, of course, the farther aft the tips are, the larger the diameter that can be accommodated while still allowing adequate clearance. The main drawback to positive rake is that the thrust when going astern is usually much less than the thrust when going ahead, which can be a disadvantage to maneuvering on many boats.

Slip

Slip isn't a specification, but it's an inevitable element of every prop nonetheless. Since *slip* is the difference between the advance per revolution that would theoretically occur if the prop were

working in a solid and what actually happens in water, it is often confused with lack of efficiency. And so it's easy to think that if we could eliminate slip we'd have 100 percent efficiency. Well, slip and efficiency certainly are interdependent, but if you could eliminate slip, you'd get a nonworking prop.

Slip, which is related to a blade's angle of attack, is essential to the prop advancing through the water, creating thrust as it does. Granted, we want a minimum of slip—and the faster the boat, the less we want—but we always need some. The only "zero slip" situation I can think of involves a freewheeling prop spinning beneath a boat as it is towed, which is certainly not the epitome of propulsion!

Slip is also an important element of our ability to operate a boat with such a simple transmission; no series of changing gear ratios as we have in autos, but rather just ahead, neutral, and astern with one gear ratio that reduces shaft speed for more practical rpms at the prop. Slip is higher and efficiency low until the prop "gets a grip" on the water, and the boat attains our intended cruise speed. Then slip diminishes to whatever percentage the choice of prop allows, and the whole engine-gear-prop system reaches its maximum efficiency for that installation. Through it all, the more perfect the choice of prop, the better the system works.

A Matter of Material

Before we conclude this discussion of propeller attributes, let's look at what props are made of. I've already stated that stainless steel allows thinner blades. SS props are available in what sometimes seems an infinite variety of sizes and variations for just about every make and model of outboard and sterndrive, though I've never seen them on an inboard installation. But is stainless the best material for props? I wouldn't say so. That's not because I have anything against stainless steel, but rather that I'm not sure there can be a single "best" material.

Stainless steel is tough, and that's good. But it can also be bad. If you have a penchant for venturing into shallow water and hitting the bottom on occasion, you might find SS props very costly. For starters, they are more expensive to buy. And although they can take a lot of punishment without needing repair, they are not invincible. And when you do damage them, SS props cost more to repair. Further, since the props are so tough, hitting something very hard (a rock, perhaps) while going very fast can not only damage the prop itself, but can also send shock waves up the drive train with sufficient force to damage gears and other internal components. Lesser materials would break on contact.

For outboards and sterndrives, the basic aluminum prop is often the more practical all-around choice. It may not deliver quite as much as a stainless prop if you're looking only at pure "performance," but when you also consider other aspects, they look fine in the balance.

Nibral (nickel-bronze-aluminum) is often the choice for inboard installations. The alloy is strong, easy to machine and "fine-tune" for perfect pitch, and stands up well in use. Repair costs, if you do damage one, are not cheap, but they are reasonable. Good old bronze works well too, though the material isn't quite as tough as nibral and is also a bit heavier.

So far, we've discussed metal props only. Well, for many, many years, props were only metal. In recent years, however, we've seen the introduction of composite plastics. Plastic props? Yes. And they can be good. One of the disadvantages of using cast metal for precision parts is that metals generally cannot be cast as a finished product. Shrinkage and distortion on cooling require most metal parts to be cast oversize and then machined down to finish specifications. Composite plastic props cost less not only because the raw materials are cheaper (though often not by that much these days) but also because most plastics can be injection molded as finished pieces. When they come out of the mold, the parts are nearly ready to go to work. Injection molding can be that precise. Composite plastic props cost less because they are way less labor intensive than metal props.

On the downside, composite props cannot be repaired. The blades tend to break rather than bend out of pitch. Of course, metal blades can break also. But while a damaged stainless steel, aluminum, bronze, or nibral blade can have new metal added (by welding or brazing), which can then be machined to match what was there before the damage, a plastic blade, once broken, is lost forever (currently, at least; who knows what the future holds?). Of course, buying a new composite prop can often cost less than repairing a metal one. Besides, with one brand of composites (Piranha), the hubs and blades are separate units, so you can replace a single broken blade instead of replacing the whole prop, which makes their repair even faster, easier, and less expensive than metal. (You can also change pitch by changing the blades rather than the whole prop.)

I like composite props, but I've observed that the blades do tend to flex more than stainless or bronze (despite manufacturers' assertions that the composites are as stiff as metal, which is sort of true—they don't seem to flex appreciably more than aluminum) and so can't deliver quite the same performance under extreme loads. But for "average" use, in my experience, composites and aluminum are about on a par all around.

Parsing Propeller Premises to Predict Performance Particulars

As Yogi Berra once said, "In theory, there's no difference between theory and practice. In practice there is." And I have to admit the "practice" aspect of propellers can be even more complicated than the theory we've looked at so far. Because "off the shelf" props of the same nominal size have rarely been exactly alike. And I'm not suggesting packaging error; the dimensions of a prop are usually stamped into the hub, so there can be no confusion. Since actual performance depends on many factors, including the cross-sectional shape of the blades, it shouldn't be too surprising that nominally identical props from different manufacturers might perform differently when installed. What may be a huge surprise, however, is that props with identical markings may not produce identical results when they're from the same maker!

A part of the problem is pitch. As noted, it's a theoretical dimension and thus difficult to measure, though determining the face pitch of the blades has long been the common approach. A bigger element is that here in the United States, we don't have a standard for propellers. That is, we have nothing that specifies acceptable "tolerances," which are what would tell us how close to its nominal dimensions a prop must actually be.

Instead, many boatbuilders keep a set of carefully calibrated props of differing diameter and pitch, which they use for sea trials of new models. They know that if a particular prop doesn't produce the desired results, it's the specifications that are wrong, not the prop itself. Unfortunately, when production models start rolling out the door, they are equipped with off-the-shelf props, and thus the performance of any particular hull may or may not match the test results of the prototype.

Fortunately, the rest of the world does have prescribed tolerances, established by the International Standards Organization (ISO; www.iso.org). ISO 484 describes the manufacturing tolerances for marine propellers:

ISO 484

CLASS	MANUFACTURING ACCURACY
S	very high accuracy
I	high accuracy
II	medium accuracy
III	wide tolerances

As clear as these descriptions may be, we can get a better understanding of the different ISO 484 classes by examining the tolerances numerically, as the percentage of error allowed when a propeller is actually measured, plus or minus the nominal pitch stamped on a propeller's hub.

Incredible as it may seem, until very recently a great percentage of props manufactured in the United States failed to meet the minimum ISO Class III standard. This is really pitiful, and the failure to meet any standard at all, even one this loose, has been the cause of many otherwise unexplained engine and vibration woes.

Fortunately, this miserable situation is changing. One of the benefits of more and more U.S. companies selling their products internationally has been the application of ISO standards to U.S.-manufactured boats and all their components.

And it gets even better. Using Prop Scan (see below), a technician can even get a prop to exceed the ISO S-Class standard. Such props are considered to be of optimum enhanced accuracy, or S-Plus Class propellers, where allowable deviation from nominal is less than 1 percent in every measurement.

ENHANCED TOLERANCES FOR PITCH (S-PLUS CLASS)

MEASUREMENT	DEFINITION	TOLERANCE
local pitch	one portion of one blade	±0.75%
section pitch	one radius of one blade	±0.5%
blade pitch	mean pitch of one blade	±0.38%
propeller pitch	mean pitch of all blades	±0.25%

As you can see, the acceptable tolerances are small, indeed. So what is this Prop Scan that helps us acquire such accuracy? Developed in Australia, Prop Scan is a computerized measuring assembly that, when combined with its proprietary software, enables propellers of any type to be measured and remanufactured with the highest possible accuracy (Figure 8-6).

ISO TOLERANCES FOR PITCH

MEASUREMENT	DEFINITION	TOLERANCE BY CLASS			
		S	I	II	III
local pitch	pitch of one portion of one blade	±1.5%	±2%	±3%	—
section pitch	mean pitch of one radius of one blade	±1%	±1.5%	±2%	±5%
blade pitch	mean pitch of one blade	±0.75%	±1%	±0.5%	±4%
propeller pitch	mean pitch of all blades	±0.5%	±0.75%	±1%	±3%

FIGURE 8-6. *Using computerized measurement and proprietary software, Prop Scan allows technicians to determine pitch more accurately and tune propeller specifications to much closer tolerances than previously possible. (Courtesy Propeller Dynamics Pty. Ltd.)*

Additionally, and perhaps more important, the Prop Scan computer system keeps a record of all repairs, which allows the shop to reproduce a propeller to the same specifications every time. This means that when you get a prop that works beautifully, you can have it again if you somehow manage to bollix up the first one.

Here in the United States, you'll currently find Prop Scan–equipped shops along the Atlantic, Gulf, and Pacific coasts, and on Lakes Michigan and Erie.

If I seem excited by this system, it's because I am. For years our apparent lack of concern about accurate prop specifications has frustrated me to no end. I'm immensely relieved this situation is changing.

Other Faults?

I'd like to conclude this chapter with one important thought. It's not *always* the prop(s)! Yes, it's true that in many cases, changing (or correcting) the prop(s) will make things better when a boat isn't performing quite up to snuff. Often, much better! For a majority of the boats I tested and heard the comment about "still experimenting with the props," the results did improve with time and (often considerable) effort in narrowing the choices (Figure 8-7). But this wasn't 100 percent true. Sometimes the boat never did quite reach expectations. I mention this only because it's all too easy to say, "OK!" when a salesperson suggests that a prop change will make a boat perform better. It could be true and often will be. But don't take anyone's word for it. Always insist on the change being made and then having another sea trial before you agree to buy. In short, never accept a boat until its sea-trial performance is the performance you desire. Otherwise, you'll only be disappointed. And although it's quite probable you'll become disappointed with your "wonderful" new boat in time—that's one reason we often keep moving to bigger and bigger (or merely differently styled) boats—you never want to be disappointed as soon as you take delivery.

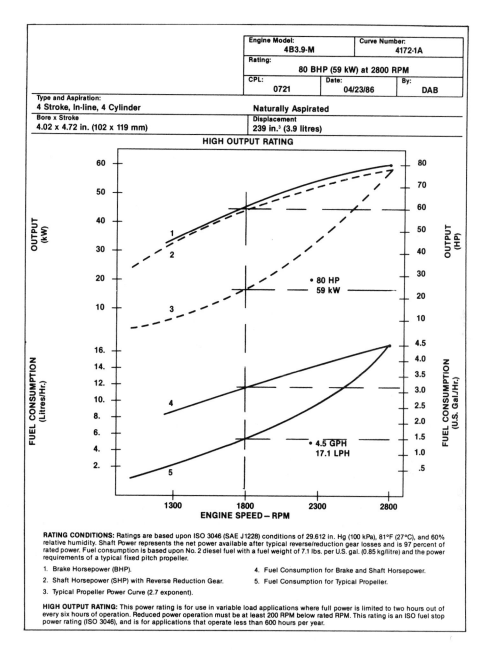

Engine Model:			Curve Number:	
4B3.9-M			4172-1A	
Rating:				
80 BHP (59 kW) at 2800 RPM				
CPL:		Date:		By:
0721		04/23/86		DAB

Type and Aspiration:
4 Stroke, In-line, 4 Cylinder   **Naturally Aspirated**

Bore x Stroke
4.02 x 4.72 in. (102 x 119 mm)   **Displacement**
239 in.³ (3.9 litres)

HIGH OUTPUT RATING

RATING CONDITIONS: Ratings are based upon ISO 3046 (SAE J1228) conditions of 29.612 in. Hg (100 kPa), 81°F (27°C), and 60% relative humidity. Shaft Power represents the net power available after typical reverse/reduction gear losses and is 97 percent of rated power. Fuel consumption is based upon No. 2 diesel fuel with a fuel weight of 7.1 lbs. per U.S. gal. (0.85 kg/litre) and the power requirements of a typical fixed pitch propeller.

1. Brake Horsepower (BHP).
2. Shaft Horsepower (SHP) with Reverse Reduction Gear.
3. Typical Propeller Power Curve (2.7 exponent).

4. Fuel Consumption for Brake and Shaft Horsepower.
5. Fuel Consumption for Typical Propeller.

HIGH OUTPUT RATING: This power rating is for use in variable load applications where full power is limited to two hours out of every six hours of operation. Reduced power operation must be at least 200 RPM below rated RPM. This rating is an ISO fuel stop power rating (ISO 3046), and is for applications that operate less than 600 hours per year.

FIGURE 8-7. *A typical performance curve for a small marine diesel engine. The top curve (1) represents brake horsepower. The dotted curve (2) is shaft horsepower, the power delivered to the shaft just abaft the reverse/reduction gear. The middle dotted curve (3) is a typical propeller power curve. Fuel consumption is shown in curves 4 and 5; 5 is the propeller fuel consumption. These curves are provided by the engine maker and are based on dynamometer tests. When checking a new hull's performance, boatbuilders try to mirror (or at least come very close to) these curves in sea trials. When they achieve this, they know the selected prop is "right" because it is loading the engine correctly. (Courtesy Cummins Engine Company)*

9

How to Read Boat Reviews and Tests

Potential boat buyers often look to the reports published in magazines as a source of information on production powerboats. Since I've written so many of them, I think I can offer some practical advice on how to read—and interpret—such articles.

First, though it has ruffled a few feathers when I've said this in the past, I have to restate emphatically that I don't believe we should call them "tests." In a scientific or engineering sense, the word *test* implies a degree of control and repeatability that is impossible with boats. You can make a hundred different landings with the same boat at the same pier and face a hundred different sets of conditions. Wind, current, and, more important, their interaction create a nearly infinite range of variables that defies absolute repeatability.

Further, no hull is identical to the next. Even sister ships from the same mold will usually show discernible differences. And as I stated in the previous chapter, so will any two propellers. Even if they're stamped as having the same diameter and pitch, a lack of established tolerances precludes precise performance comparisons unless they're specifically calibrated (and those you buy off the shelf still usually aren't). So testing a boat is not like running a car on a test track, using known tires inflated to a known pressure on a surface of known quality and double-checking results by dragging a "fifth wheel." We simply can't test boats as we do cars! By that, do I mean to imply that the reports have no value? Not at all. They can be extremely beneficial. It's just that you should understand what boat reports *are not* before you can appreciate what they *are;* you have to know what not to look for before you can see what's there.

Don't look for data chiseled in stone. Although some magazines (including those I have written for) make a big deal out of the thoroughness of their testing, it's really a matter of smoke and mirrors. Performance figures, speed curves, fuel consumption, and the other hard data that articles often contain should be accepted as valid—for the subject boat, under the conditions prevailing at the time of the "test" (Figure 9-1). They shouldn't be taken as absolutes and definitely shouldn't be projected as such onto a boat you're considering unless *that particular boat* (not merely the same model) was the one tested. Though "test" figures should be close to what you might experience with a similar boat, you can't expect to duplicate them exactly. If you read that the Zipper 425 hits 35 mph at wide-open throttle, and the one you just bought tops out at 33, you shouldn't feel shortchanged. Neither should you feel terribly special if yours shows 36. Just remember that we can only give ballpark figures, and you'll be OK.

Don't look for comparisons. Apples and oranges are more alike than many outwardly similar boats. Once in a while a story will concentrate on the similarities and differences of a certain type of craft as produced by different builders, but for the most part each report is about a particular boat and that boat only. How it may or may not compare with others is beyond the scope of a reasonable article.

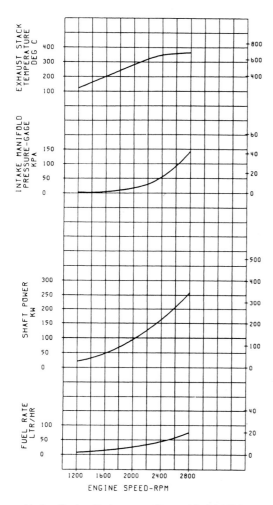

Marine Engine Performance Curve, Model 3208

FIGURE 9-1. *Boating magazines often go to great lengths to "test" a boat's performance, but the truth is that a properly powered boat with the right components in its drive train will nearly mirror the engine manufacturer's dynamometer-derived performance curves. (Courtesy Caterpillar Inc.)*

Filling a Need

When I first began to write boat reviews, my editor gave me this advice: "Discover the niche the boat was designed to fill, then concentrate on how well the boat does what it was intended to." To this day, I try to follow that advice, and I still believe that the only valid comparison to use in a boat report is the real-world boat against the boat's intentions. Anything else is speculation.

Don't look for major negatives. There are reasons for this. I can only speak for myself, but the biggest reason for me is (to paraphrase Will Rogers) that I've never met a boat I didn't like. Well, let me amend that. In over 20 years of writing boat reports, I only saw two boats that didn't have far more positive attributes than negative. In both instances I was aboard a prototype, and the truth is, all parties involved were guilty of one-upmanship. The builders (two different companies were involved) let us examine not-yet-finished prototypes in the hope of getting early publicity, and the magazine was out to scoop the competition. In both cases, I felt the only fair thing to do was write nothing, and I told the builders why there would be no story. In both instances the builders ultimately agreed that the boat had more negative than positive characteristics and decided that to try to correct the situation would involve throwing good money after bad. Neither boat was ever released as a production model.

No boat is perfect, and I always try to find places where improvement is warranted and point them out to the reader. Such a search is never impossible, but it's becoming more difficult. These days, builders seem to wait until all the developmental problems are solved before they'll let us aboard, and many smart builders willingly sacrifice early press coverage while they work out most of the production problems as well, which means waiting until they've launched hull number 4 or 5. With all of the bugs thus eliminated, the boats we review come as close to being perfect as anything produced by human hands can be.

There's another big reason review writers don't dwell on negatives: we can't spend enough time with a boat to discover all of them, and there isn't space in the magazine to go into the extensive detail that would be required to give a truly in-depth report.

Back in the 1970s, I was with the late and lamented *Motorboat* magazine (a name that has since been revived and then allowed to die again) and had the responsibility of developing the structure for its report program. Based on my experience as a surveyor, I worked up a list of over 150 individual items that we rated on a scale of one to ten whenever we examined a boat. The items were grouped under electrical system, mechanical systems, hull and superstructure, living space, and so on, and each group received a combined rating. Our inspection was as close to a survey as we could get. Further, to reduce subjectivity to a minimum, each boat was inspected by two of us working independently. We then compared and averaged our results for the final report. But most important, we also spent three or four days actually using the boat as it was intended to be used. We'd get a few couples together and take cruising boats on a cruise. We went fishing with fishing boats. In short, we got familiar enough with each boat to learn what worked and what didn't. The reports reflected this.

However, when the *Power and Motoryacht* editor asked me about developing a similar boat-test program for that magazine when it was new in the mid-1980s, I had to advise against it. Quite honestly, it simply was not cost effective; two people tied up for four to six days on one article isn't practical. Nor would it be space effective in print, since the information thus generated would require more pages than could realistically be devoted to a single boat, especially in the publishing world as it exists today. When I started writing boat reports they were about 2,500 words. A few years later we cut back to 2,000, and now most run 1,500 or fewer (though the pictures are bigger!). You can see the trend.

Finally, we have to admit that boat reports are, to a degree, for the dreamer in all of us and as such tend more toward "show biz" than pure journalism. For every reader who gleans a report for facts about a boat he or she is considering, many more read it to enjoy vicariously a boat they'll never own. Because no boat can be everything we want, and few of us can afford a different boat for every need, we buy the boat that suits us best and merely read about the rest. This reality precludes a *Consumer Reports*–type of coverage, which would presume that every report is for a potential buyer.

So what is a boat report? I believe its objective is to reflect upon the unique qualities of each boat and evaluate them as fairly and honestly as possible. In the final analysis, every boat report is generated by a human being writing on a topic that by its very nature involves a lot of emotion, so inevitably there will be personal bias. We boat reviewers try to be objective, but we can't help but be influenced by our own likes and dislikes. To counter this, you should read a lot of reviews and compare what you read with what you see at marinas, in dealers' showrooms, and at boat shows. You'll learn which writers have views similar to your own. Just as you might rush to see a movie panned by a critic whose opinion is generally opposite yours, you can interpret boat reviewers' reports in the same light.

At the same time, you should develop your own standards and be honest about your own likes and dislikes. If, for instance, you can't stand spinach, a restaurant review raving about chicken Florentine won't impress you at all. With experience, you'll interpret boat reports in the same fashion.

Boat reports are a great way for all of us to enjoy boats we would otherwise never see, and they're a fine way to become initially acquainted with some boats we *may* eventually know quite well. In this respect, they're an excellent vehicle to use in the early stages of shopping. But don't let the printed word influence you too much. When you're shopping for a boat, you're looking for the boat that's right for you. The pictures may be pretty, the words may ring with praise, but it's the real boat in the real world that has to suit you. Learn to be your own reviewer.

10

Twenty Questions to Codify Boat Selection

Let's make the process of boat selection simpler by encapsulating it in twenty questions you should ask yourself before or as you look. Write down the answers so you'll be sure not to overlook anything.

1. **How will I most often use the boat?** Be realistic. Don't talk yourself into an impractical boat simply because it has desirable features. Remember boat-buying rule number two: "Your boat should make your favorite on-the-water activities easy." And, I might also add, fun. Look for the boat that will suit your intended uses, and don't settle for anything else. And remember, you can't find the boat best suited to your needs until you define your needs (Figure 10-1).

2. **Where will I use it?** The answer will influence many things about your boat: its size, power plant(s) (remember, outboards and sterndrives are generally better for trailered boats), the amount of beef in its construction, the amount and type of shelter aboard, and more. Be realistic at the outset, and you'll be happier down the line.

3. **How much time do I have to use it?** It's easy to overestimate available time when you're excited about buying a boat. Time shrinks in the real world, and there's nothing worse than having a boat that needs more time and attention than you can give it.

   All boats need attention, mostly in the form of simple routine maintenance, but some need more than others. Likewise, some boats

FIGURE 10-1. *Trailerable boats offer many practical advantages, not least of which are that you can keep your boat at home and have an almost unlimited choice of boating areas. (Courtesy Calkins)*

FIGURE 10-2. *In today's world of plastic boats, a bit of teak—such as the step and handrail on this Maxum—can add a touch of natural warmth. Just remember that wood, even as forgiving a variety as teak, demands more maintenance than plastic.*

need more attention before you leave the dock and when you get back. The less time you have, the more important it is to have a simple, no-frills boat. Do you think oiled teak *covering boards* [narrow walkways found atop the gunwales along the sides of a fishing cockpit and also across the stern just inside the transom] are the saltiest-looking cosmetic treatment a boat can have? Get them . . . if you have time to keep them oiled (Figure 10-2). If your time is limited, you'll be better off with surfaces that only require washing.

Back before I got my priorities straight and decided it was better to work all the time on other people's boats than to work five days ashore to get two on a boat of my own, I made it a rule never to accept an invitation that would keep me ashore on a weekend during the boating season. Friends often felt snubbed until they experienced one weekend of cruising themselves. Then, usually, they would envy me for spending every weekend on my boat. It worked for me, but I'm not so sure it would for everyone. Be serious in your estimates of available time, and plan your boat accordingly.

4. **Where will I keep it when I'm not using it?** If you are new to boating, this question might seem irrelevant. But it won't be long before you realize that slip space is often as scarce as a parking space in Times Square, and when you find space, you'll discover it can be as precious as platinum. Space is available, even if you have to suffer through a few years on a waiting list to get it. My point is, don't go out and buy a 40-foot cabin cruiser, even if it suits all your other needs perfectly, unless you have a place to park a 40-footer when you're not using it. If it's going to have to sit in your driveway, it's going to have to fit in your driveway (and be trailerable to boot).

5. **Will it be my boat or a family boat?** Since boating is a perfect sport for the whole family to enjoy together, maybe the question needn't be asked. But boating isn't always for everyone, and it just may be that what you need is the perfect boat for occasional use by you and some fishing buddies rather than a larger, more luxurious vessel your spouse and kids could enjoy on a regular basis. If you plan to include your family, however, make sure the boat is meant for a family. Comfort can be subjective; let your family help judge what's comfortable.

6. **Is the answer to question 1 in accord with question 5?** Could be you've already covered this one. But it won't hurt to double-check. In listing needs by use, have you thought of everyone who will regularly be using the boat with you? Some compromise may be necessary here; the boat that best fills most of your criteria may not suit everyone in the family equally well. Better to consider all needs and compromise accordingly than to spoil the fun for other family members.

7. **How much can I spend to buy it?** A wag once described a boat as "a hole in the water surrounded by fiberglass into which one pours money." As with many jests, there's an element of truth in it. The purchase is just the beginning, so don't blow your budget up front. Like all rules, this one can be bent slightly, but don't bend it too far or you'll break yourself rather than the rule.

8. **How much can I spend on operation?** Most operational expenses are directly related to

the size and type of boat you buy. Marina and yard charges, for example, are usually based on overall length. While many costs are fixed—dockage, insurance, hauling, and winter storage if you're a seasonal boater, for example—fuel and some maintenance costs will vary with use. Obviously, the more you use your boat, the more hours the fixed costs are spread over and the less the cost per hour. Still, your choice of boat will influence operational costs; a gas-guzzler will burn more fuel per hour than the more economical low-horsepower single-screw trawler. This doesn't make the trawler better; it only means that you have to face and plan for long-term expenses. Check with marinas and yards to determine current costs and figure accordingly (Figure 10-3). This may help you determine how large a boat you can afford. Find out about insurance—different types of boats carry different rates. In short, be sure to include a realistic appraisal of all operating costs when you make up your boating budget.

9. **How much can I spend on maintenance?** Maintenance costs depend to a degree on the size of the boat but even more on its simplicity. The more fancy stuff you have aboard, the more time and money it will take to keep everything shipshape and working properly. If you want to spend your time and money enjoying the boat rather than taking care of it, keep it simple. One way to save on maintenance is to spend time instead of money—do the work yourself. And that brings up the next question.

10. **Is do-it-yourself maintenance practical for me?** If you resent the hours spent on maintenance, be prepared to pay others to work on your boat when you can't be there. But perhaps you'll find, as many have, that

FIGURE 10-3. *Though boats commonly stay in the water at all times, marinas in many parts of the country now offer dry-stack stowage (background) to get more boats into a given area. Usually, it only takes an advance phone call to have your boat in the water and waiting for you when you arrive.*

maintaining your boat can be a big part of the enjoyment. If this is the case, you may even discover that when other engagements prevent you from taking the whole day to go boating, you can still spend a morning or afternoon on needed maintenance.

The more work you do yourself, the better you'll know your boat and its systems, and the less you'll be upset should something go awry underway. Of course, this presupposes that you have the requisite knowledge, but as your boating experience grows, there's no reason why your maintenance knowledge can't grow with it.

11. **How big a boat do I need?** Bigger is not necessarily better, but you do need a boat large enough to be comfortable for all concerned. A boat that's too small won't be fun. When you examine all the elements—purchase price, operational costs, and so forth, plus the needs of your family—you may decide that a larger, simple boat will fit your needs better than a smaller, fancy one at the same bottom line.

12. **How big a boat can I handle?** Generally speaking, the bigger the boat, the more knowledge and experience you need to handle it properly. The reason is simple: larger boats react more slowly. That means more planning ahead on the part of the skipper. The less experience you have, the tougher it is to plan ahead.

The 80-foot boat I'm currently skippering takes about 40 seconds to react to a change of controls. Not only do I have to know what I want to happen, but I have to decide what adjustment will achieve the desired result nearly a minute ahead of time so as to initiate the proper action at the proper time. I don't think I could do it if I hadn't been running big boats for a number of years. You can learn with the boat no matter what its size, but you'll have an easier time of it if you don't bite off too much too soon.

13. **What's the biggest boat that suits all of the above?** This is your upper limit. You don't have to get one that big, and you might find something smaller that meets all your needs best, but you do have to set limits. Decide what you can accept as your biggest boat at this time, and then live with your decision no matter how appealing some larger boat might be.

14. **What's the smallest boat that suits all of the above?** Again, you may well buy something larger, but you have to define your limits in order to narrow your choices. Just as you might pass by the exciting two-seater sports car when you're really in the market for a station wagon or SUV, you have to bypass boats too small for your current purposes if you want to make your search realistic and practical.

15. **What features are most important?** Remember boat-buying rule number one: "Every boat is a compromise." You have to know which features are least negotiable before you can begin making deals with yourself. The best way to handle this is simply to list everything you're looking for in a boat and then arrange the items in order of descending importance.

16. **What features are least important?** This should be fairly easy. Just don't be hasty. It's entirely possible that some of these least important features are attainable, but you can't count on it; so don't list anything that isn't truly expendable.

17. **What features are absolutely necessary?** This again is simply a matter of choosing—in this case between those things you really need and those you only want very much. Though the principle of compromise is to give up what you want least in order to gain what you want most, sometimes in the real world you have to give up what you would want *more* to gain what you want *most*. Be very clear in your own mind as to which features are positively not negotiable.

18. **What features are absolutely unnecessary?** The point in even including these items (since they most likely won't be a part of your boat) is simply to help you get priorities completely straight in your mind. If it isn't on your list, you won't know where it fits into your priorities.

Here's a suggestion. After you've made

your initial list of desirable features, assign each item to a category from 1 to 5. Use 5 for things you must have, 4 for those you would like very much, 3 for those that would be nice, 2 for those that are expendable, and 1 for those you can definitely do without. Then rearrange your list by category and start shopping with the full confidence that you know exactly what you're looking for.

Again, if there are too many 5s on your list, it just won't work. That's not to say the list must be perfectly balanced, but if everything on your list is a "must have," you leave yourself no room to compromise.

19. **Have I found the best dealer?** This question can be far more important than you might imagine. In fact, finding the right dealer can be more critical than finding the right boat.

Because nothing made by humans is perfect, you have to face the truth that your wonderful new boat is going to give you some problems. It will when it's new; it will after you've owned it awhile. It will, period. The pleasures of owning a powerboat far outweigh the problems, however, and this is especially true if you have a cooperative and understanding dealer. A good dealer will do everything possible to minimize your problems and maximize your fun. But you must also be a good customer. The customer-dealer relationship is often a matter of chemistry, which means the right dealer for you is not necessarily the right dealer for your next-door neighbor.

There are some general guidelines, however. The best dealer will have a strong service department with the tools, parts, and knowledgeable (preferably certified) mechanics it takes to get your service work done quickly and correctly, handling everything from warranty work to routine maintenance. But a good service department will be busy, so smart dealers pay attention to their own customers first—one good reason not to look only at the purchase bottom line. If you shop entirely by sales price, expecting to get another dealer to do the service work, be prepared to stand in line behind the dealer's regular customers every time. For similar reasons, the best dealer will be close to your boating area even if you can get a seemingly better deal farther down the road (or on the Internet).

The best dealer will be more concerned with helping you find the right boat than in merely making a sale. The dealer wants to sell you a lot of boats, not just one, because chances are that if you enjoy boating, you won't stop with one boat. After a few years you'll want something else—most likely something bigger. (That's why in question 13 I made the point about determining the biggest boat that suits you *at this time;* eventually you'll answer the question differently.) Boatbuilders recognize the probability of this progression and keep adding to the top of their line. In the late 1970s, for instance, the largest Sea Ray was a 36-footer, and the biggest factory Hatteras was 77 feet (though some dealers specialize in making customized stretch models that are longer than standard). As of the early 21st century Sea Ray has gotten up to 68 feet and Hatteras to over 100!

A truly smart dealer knows that you won't want to move up to something bigger unless you like nearly everything about the boat you have now except its size. If the dealer steers you wrong in the beginning, that first boat may be the only one you ever get. Some dealers are happy with that single sale; the good ones look ahead and cultivate long-term customer relationships.

20. **Have I found the best deal?** Unless the boat meets the criteria you have outlined for yourself, the answer to this question is "No." No matter what incentives a dealer may offer, you don't have a good deal if the boat isn't right to begin with. But let's assume for the moment that the boat is essentially ideal, and then take a look at what makes a good deal better and what you can do to make it best.

Shop around. Sure, I said the dealer with the lowest price is not necessarily the best place to buy your boat, and I'll stand by that advice. But until you see what the marketplace has to offer, you can't begin to negotiate.

And you should negotiate, provided you're realistic. The dealer with the great service department and in-depth parts inventory will probably have a higher overhead than the dealer who sells but doesn't service boats. Don't expect to get the same price from both. But by knowing what the lowest price may be, you'll have a better idea of what an acceptable price should be from the dealer you'd rather do business with. Even the best dealers will usually start out asking more than they expect, just so they have room to come down a bit. It's the nature of the business.

Consider the cost of money along with the cost of the boat. A boat is a major purchase, so you'll probably be financing it with a consumer loan. Lenders appreciate boat buyers, who, for the most part, are good customers. Using the boat as collateral, you can borrow a large chunk of the purchase price.

Though pleasure boating has long since ceased to be the sole province of the very rich, it's still a luxury. If you have the discretionary income to be able to afford boating, you probably have the savvy to shop for your boat loan as carefully as you shop for the boat itself. So I'll just add the reminder.

Popular production boats are much like automobiles in that they depreciate quickly when new. This has been aggravated in recent years by an excess of demand over supply of popular new boats (which keeps their prices up), coupled with excess supply in the used-boat market (which holds their value down). (One reason there are so many used boats on the market is that these days boats tend to remain functional and seaworthy for a long, long time. People most often get rid of boats because they want a bigger boat or maybe just a different model, not because the old one is no longer working.) You should make sure—if possible—that you owe no more on your boat than you could get if you were to sell it tomorrow. A dealer may be reluctant to let you in on how much you're going to lose to initial depreciation, but you should try to ascertain it nevertheless. Otherwise, when you prepare to trade up to something bigger in a year or two, you'll discover that not only does your boat not have any trade-in value, you might actually have to add cash just to pay off the note and satisfy the lien, particularly if you made little or no down payment to begin with.

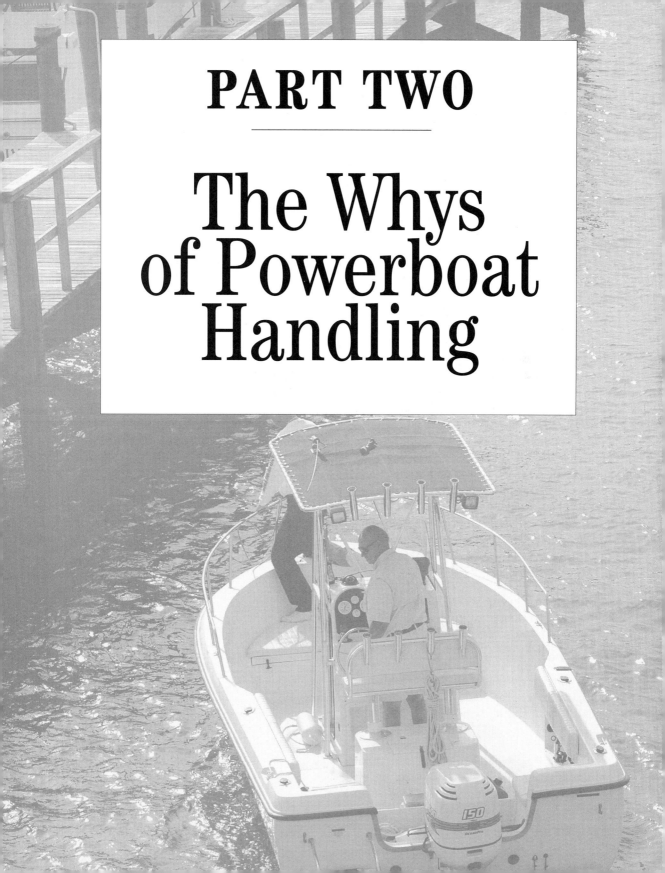

PART TWO

The Whys of Powerboat Handling

11

Why Boats Don't Behave Like Cars

It happens to nearly every boating neophyte. You're sitting alongside a pier or float. When the lines have been cast off and you're ready to get underway, you do as you would with a car at a curb: turn the steering wheel away from the pier, put the boat in gear, and advance the throttle gently. You expect your boat to glide away from the pier as smoothly as your car glides away from the curb. But it doesn't. Instead of the bow swinging gracefully away from the pier, the stern swings *into* it with a thump. Surprise! You've just learned lesson number one in boat-handling: Despite having a motor, throttle, and steering wheel, powerboats do not behave like cars. Let's see *why* they don't, and perhaps more important, let's find out how boats *do* behave.

In a car, your steering action is in the front wheels. (These days, the drive power more often is, too.) Aim the front, and the rear end follows. In a boat, your motive power *and* steering control are both in the stern. Remember this if you remember nothing else: When you steer a boat, nothing happens until the stern swings. Nothing! That's the *what*. But let's examine the *whys*, because it's usually easier to understand actions if we know what causes them.

We'll begin with single screw. One engine, one propeller, one rudder. And since it offers a good basis of understanding as well as a standard against which we can later compare other systems, we'll start with conventional underwater gear. In the following examples, I'll be talking about the actions of a *right-handed* propeller— one that spins clockwise (as viewed from astern) when the boat goes ahead. In all cases the actions

of a left-handed wheel would be opposite. We'll also pretend for the moment that outside forces such as wind and current don't exist, and we'll look only at the actions of the boat itself.

How a Boat Is Steered

As a powerboat moves ahead, a stream of water, called the *discharge screw current*, is forced aft by the propeller (Figure 11-1). We steer the boat by deflecting this current (as well as the apparent current created by the boat's movement through the water) with a rudder (Figure 11-2). If there's no flow across the rudder, there's no control, which is why you can't steer a boat that's drifting.

Most modern powerboats use a balanced rud-

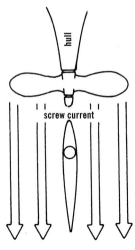

FIGURE 11-1. *Discharge screw current.*

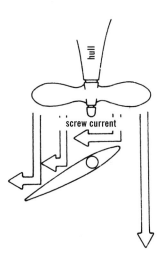

FIGURE 11-2. *Steering forces.*

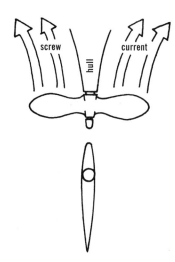

FIGURE 11-3. *Absence of steering control going astern.*

der—that is, one with part of its blade forward of the rudderpost—so that more of the screw current can be deflected when the rudder is turned. Even with a balanced rudder, however, some of the screw current misses the turned blade and isn't deflected. This undeflected thrust tends to push a boat straight ahead despite the angled rudder and is another reason your boat won't behave quite the way your car does when you turn the steering wheel.

The ease with which a boat turns depends on the location and size of its rudder in relation to the location and size of its propeller. It also depends on engine speed; rudder action increases with an increase in engine rpm because the screw current increases.

A boat going astern has no screw current passing over the rudder (Figure 11-3). The rudder's movement through the water must supply what turning power there is. Thus it can be extremely difficult, if not impossible, to steer a single-screw boat going astern.

The Forces at Work

One of the first things we discover about single-screw boats is that with the rudder amidships [centered], a boat with a right-handed screw will have a tendency to veer slightly to port when

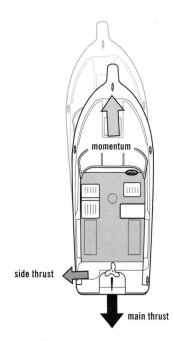

FIGURE 11-4. *The forces at work: with headway, rudder amidships.*

moving ahead. In Figure 11-4 we see why. In addition to the main thrust provided by the discharge screw current, another force, usually called *side thrust*, comes into play. Discussions about the causes of side thrust will probably keep dockside sea lawyers busy for years; every experienced boater has a pet theory. It may be that the propeller blades swing in a denser fluid and with greater efficiency in the bottom hemisphere (moving starboard to port) than the top hemisphere (moving port to starboard) of each revolution. This induces the stern to "claw" to starboard and thus the bow to fall off to port. We know also, as stated back in Chapter 7, that the bulk of a propeller's thrust occurs in the sector from 30 to 150 degrees from top dead center, which in a right-handed propeller puts most of the thrust on the starboard side. Another important factor is that the propeller shaft is inclined from the horizontal plane as it leaves the hull, and thus the propeller is not square to the water surface, a condition we'll reexamine in Chapter 13 in the Transom Power section. Regardless of its causes (and, as you can see, there are several), side thrust is real and one of the forces we must always deal with in handling a powerboat.

Momentum is another. Boats don't have brakes, and even after you back off on the throttle and put the gear lever in neutral, momentum will keep a boat moving ahead. We'll deal with this in greater detail later; for now let's just affirm that in boathandling, "no brakes!" is almost as important as "nothing happens until the stern swings."

Momentum also affects the way a boat turns. Since it's not following its front wheels as a car does, a boat continues to move ahead at least slightly before initiating its turn. This phenomenon is known as *advance*, and the importance of allowing for it increases with the vessel's size and displacement. Large ships carry tables that allow bridge officers to know the distance before the desired turning point they must apply "standard rudder" (usually 15 degrees) for different course changes at various speeds.

Couple this with the stern swing, and you can see that putting a boat precisely where you want it takes a different approach from putting a car where you want it. If all this seems a bit daunting, let me assure you that eventually you'll allow for your boat's "different" behavior without any conscious thought. And if it's any consolation

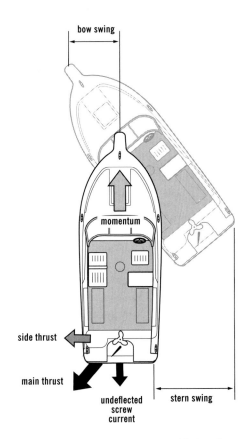

FIGURE 11-5. *The forces at work: with headway, left rudder.*

while you get used to the differences, let me confess that whenever I've been at sea for a while, the first time I get behind the wheel of a car and pull out of the parking lot, I find myself allowing for stern swing!

Figure 11-5 shows what happens in a left turn underway. The stern swings to starboard (stern swing is always the initial action), and from a combination of forces—momentum and undeflected screw current—the boat advances slightly as it turns. Note also that stern swing is greater than the resulting bow swing; in effect, the boat pivots around a point that's about one-third of a boat length abaft the bow. Even though you're turning left, you need ample clearance on your right.

The exact location of the pivot point depends on hull design and varies from boat to boat. It also

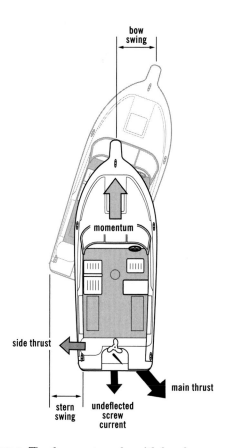

FIGURE 11-6. *The forces at work: with headway, right rudder.*

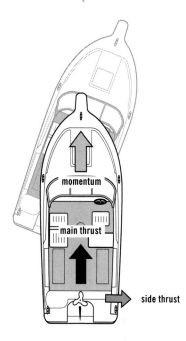

FIGURE 11-7. *The forces at work: with headway, rudder amidships, engine astern.*

depends somewhat on speed, and in a given boat will change slightly with throttle setting. With practice and experience, you'll learn where your boat's pivot point is and just how it moves when you advance or retard the throttle. Viewed from a different perspective, you'll learn the clearances you need to swing the boat around without hitting anything in the process.

Another thing you'll learn in a single-screw boat is that right turns are different from left turns. In Figure 11-6 we see that turning right— against the side thrust—lessens stern swing and as a result causes a broader turn.

How to Stop without Brakes

Because boats don't have brakes, to stop you must create an opposing force to arrest your for-

ward motion. The solution is to apply some power astern. In Figure 11-7 we see what happens when you do. The boat stops after some advance, the extent of which depends on several factors including the weight of the boat, its speed at the time, and how much power you apply.

When you use power astern to stop, you'll discover another phenomenon. Side thrust when power is applied astern is not only the opposite of side thrust when going ahead, but it's also stronger! Again, the reasons are too numerous and complex for discussion here, but the result is worth emphasizing: Side thrust when going astern will always be stronger (at equivalent rpm) than side thrust going ahead. The stern will most likely swing to port as you come to a halt, and, in fact, it's very difficult to hold a single-screw boat straight at such times.

Whatever problems side thrust may cause when you're trying to stop pale in comparison with what happens when you try to back up. In Figure 11-8 we see the actions of a right-handed single-screw boat when you apply power astern while dead in the water. First, the stern swings

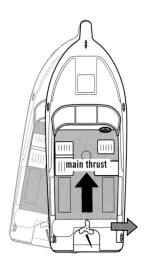

FIGURE 11-8. *The forces at work: dead in the water, power applied astern, right rudder.*

to port—often markedly. Then sternway develops. One thing is certain: The rudder has little effect until considerable sternway develops. The reason, of course, is that lacking screw current across it, the rudder can't do much until sternway creates a boat-motion current across it. That's why steerageway astern usually requires a much higher speed than steerageway ahead.

Later we'll see how we can make these inevitable actions work for us. But in the meantime, let's see what we can do to eliminate them.

12

The Twin-Screw Advantage

There are several ways to overcome the drawbacks inherent in single-screw conventional drive, and before we're through, we'll examine them all. But first, let's see what happens when we stick with conventional drives and add a second screw.

Though it's by no means the only way, the most common twin-screw practice uses counterrotating props with a left-handed screw on the port side and a right-handed screw to starboard. What we get from this is, in effect, an absence of side thrust. It's still there, of course, but because one of the causes of side thrust is the *torque* [rotational force] from a spinning propeller, counterrotating props cancel each other's side thrust. Figure 12-1 shows counterrotating twin screws in gear, going ahead. In the absence of other forces (that is, disregarding wind and current), a twin-screw boat with both props engaged for going

ahead will go *straight ahead* when you put the rudders amidships. Gone is the single-screw tendency to veer to one side. Also gone is the difference between left and right turns.

However pleasant this may be, the big difference is seen when going astern. Side thrust is still greater when a prop is set astern—you can't change that. But with *both* props astern, the canceling effect of counterrotation allows the boat to back straight (Figure 12-2). (Remember, for the moment we're disregarding wind and current. But as we'll see in Chapter 14, boats will always tend to back into the wind regardless of what type of power they have.) And since the overpowering side thrust we saw in the single-screw situation is now tamed by the countering side thrust from the other prop, a twin-screw boat will usually follow its rudders much sooner than will a single-screw boat when going astern.

By utilizing the power of side thrust, it's possible to work some twin-screw maneuvers

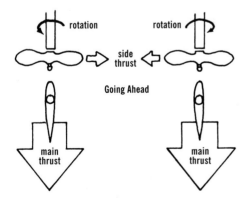

FIGURE 12-1. *The forces at work: twin screw, both engines ahead, rudders amidships.*

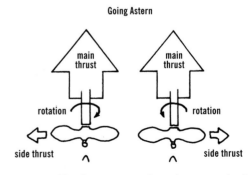

FIGURE 12-2. *The forces at work: twin screw, both engines astern.*

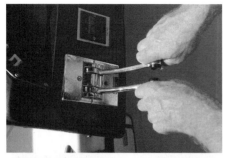

FIGURE 12-3. *1. With both engines astern (rudders amidships for least drag), the boat backs straight. Unless there's influence from outside forces, the boat will back as straight as you wish for as long as you wish.*

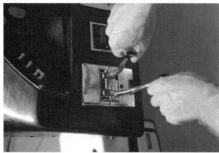

2. Turns are best accomplished without touching the steering wheel by simply taking one engine out of gear. The offset main thrust will swing the stern toward the out-of-gear side.

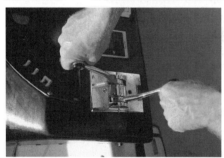

3. To tighten the turn, put the out-of-gear engine ahead. Then, before the boat is lined up on the intended course, put the engine back in neutral. As the boat nearly approaches the course, put the engine astern, and your turn will be completed as you once again back straight. Just how soon to shift is a variable, and developing the proper timing is a part of learning your own boat's responses. In time, you'll feel that the boat is an extension of your hands, as it moves ahead or astern or turns in any direction forward or backward simply by your moving the clutch controls.

without even considering rudder action (Figure 12-3). Indeed, when we get to specific boat-handling situations later in the book, I'll suggest that you initially forget the steering wheel and work only with the clutches; propeller forces alone are that strong (Figure 12-4). When maneuvering with clutches and throttles, it helps to think of a big X superimposed on your boat with the base at the console and the top at the bow (Figure 12-5). This will help remind you that putting either engine ahead swings the bow toward the opposite side (to port with the starboard engine, for example) and the stern toward the same side.

Throttle and clutch maneuvering can produce some neat results. For example, you can spin a twin-screw boat around quite nicely by "splitting" the clutches; that is, by putting one prop ahead

and the other astern (Figure 12-6). If you also bring the rudders into play—for example, using right rudder along with port engine ahead and starboard astern—many boats will turn in a much tighter circle (Figure 12-7) and often within their own length.

However, when you set the rudders *opposite* the split clutches—in this case left rudder with port engine ahead—an amazing thing can happen: the boat slides sideways (Figure 12-8). I say "can" rather than "will" because the ultimate action depends on a number of factors including the relative placement of the rudders within the discharge screw current and the proportionate force of side thrust for a particular boat. Basically the propeller forces tend to push the bow to starboard while the angled rudders tend to push the stern to starboard.

If the forces balance, both ends go to starboard; that is, the boat slides. In actual practice, engine speeds may have to be adjusted for optimum effect; sometimes one engine or the other (usually the one astern, since side thrust astern is stronger) has to go in and out of gear to balance the thrusts, and often the boat "walks" rather than slides sideways. But unless you're trying to move the boat directly into an opposing wind (which can range from merely difficult to downright impossible, depending on its strength), the boat usually *will move sideways* with little movement ahead or astern.

We'll look at specific twin-screw handling techniques in a later chapter, but now let's examine other ways of overcoming the problems of the single screw.

FIGURE 12-4. *Turning completely around in little more than its own length is a classic twin-screw maneuver. Although this move has some practical applications in itself, we are more concerned with the factors that make it possible, because they lead to the greater general maneuverability of a twin-screw boat.*

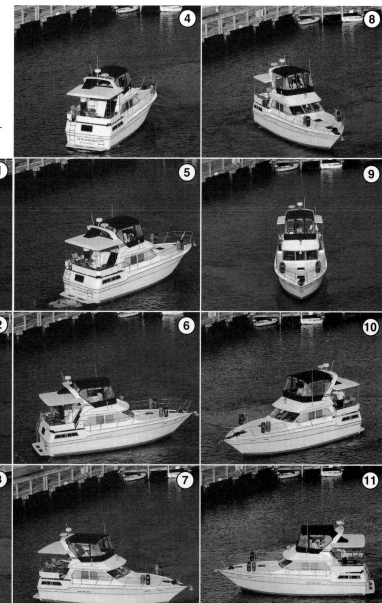

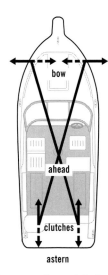

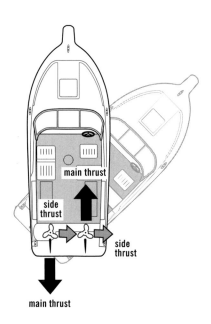

FIGURE 12-5. *When steering with the clutches, imagine a huge X superimposed on your boat to remind you that moving either clutch control ahead induces the bow to turn toward the opposite side. Putting the starboard engine ahead, for example, induces a turn to the left.*

FIGURE 12-6. *The forces at work: one engine ahead, one astern.*

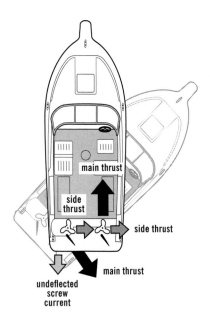

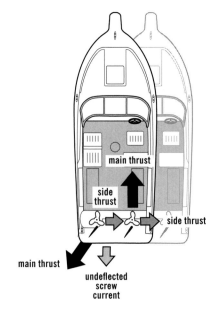

FIGURE 12-7. *The forces at work: one engine ahead, one astern, rudders set "with" the turn.*

FIGURE 12-8. *The forces at work: one engine ahead, one astern, rudders set "against" the turn.*

13

Transom Power

We just saw one way to overcome the problems associated with single-screw conventional drives: add a second, counterrotating prop. Another solution is to move the motive power out from under the boat and hang it off the transom. Since outboards and sterndrives are more common, we'll concentrate on their behavior. Surface-piercing drives are also "transom power" in a technical sense. However, except for their trimmability, they behave more like conventional inboards. Outboards and sterndrives aren't *exactly* alike, either. But they're so similar that the following discussion can apply to both.

In some ways, transom power offers a *big* advantage over conventional drive systems. A single, properly trimmed *outdrive* [a synonym for sterndrive] or outboard lower unit exhibits much less of the side thrust behavior of single-screw conventional drive (though it will usually exhibit some). Better still, turning the steering wheel redirects the entire discharge screw current, thus eliminating the problems that result from the undeflected screw current of conventional drives (Figures 13-1 and 13-2). The result is much better maneuverability—tighter turns, less tendency to veer, straighter stops, easy steering when going astern, etc. However, we see much of this improvement only at cruising speeds. The downside is that lacking a true rudder, a transom-powered boat gliding along under momentum alone is not as easy to steer as a conventional inboard. Yet when you apply power at low speed, the totally directed discharge current has a bigger effect, and that can lead to *over*steering. To compound

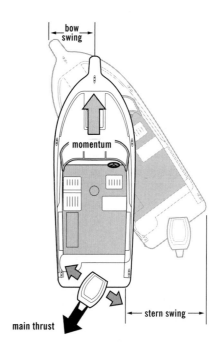

FIGURE 13-1. *Because the whole drive unit turns with transom power, there's no undeflected screw current, and therefore all the thrust serves to turn the boat.*

the problem, most transom-powered boats have planing hulls that aren't always on their best behavior in the low-speed displacement mode; they perform better when going fast. Transom-powered boats can be very touchy at low speeds as you alternate between too little steering action when the propeller is not engaged and too much when you put it in gear. You must learn by experience exactly how gentle you have to be with the

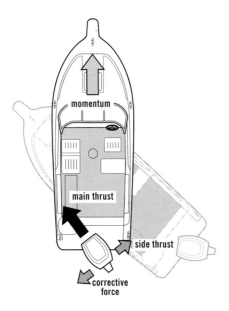

FIGURE 13-2. *Going astern with transom power is much easier than with a single-screw inboard because side thrust is manageable, and the screw current is fully directable. Backing with right rudder against forward momentum produces the result shown here.*

throttle and steering wheel to get the actions you want during low-speed maneuvers.

These drawbacks can be relatively insignificant in light of the positive control you have at cruising speeds. And the ability to adjust transom drive(s) to optimum trim is a *huge* advantage over conventional drives with a planing hull.

Keeping Trim

One of the causes of side thrust in conventional drives is the angle at which the propeller meets the water (caused in turn by the angle at which the shaft leaves the hull). This changes the effective pitch of the blades so their ability to convert torque [rotary force] into forward propulsion is not constant throughout the circle of rotation. The imbalances contribute to side thrust. Because you can adjust (trim) a transom-mounted drive unit so that the plane of the prop revolutions is exactly perpendicular to the line of forward motion, some of this problem can be eliminated.

Though some side thrust remains (a product of torque and the fact that most main thrust occurs in the arc from 30 to 150 degrees from top dead center), it can be counteracted to a large degree by adjusting the fin, or mini-rudder, usually found beneath the antiventilation plate just above the prop (Figure 13-3). When set correctly, this small fin lets you go straight with the main "rudder" (i.e., the drive unit) set amidships. The adjustment of this fin is somewhat counterintuitive and requires trial and error. As you'll soon see, an improperly trimmed drive unit tends to swing so as to produce some "right rudder," the result of greater push from the starboard side of the prop. Instinct would suggest adjusting this trim tab to create some "left rudder" to counter it. But by angling the fin toward the starboard, in effect creating more "right rudder," we actually create additional drag on that side, which helps keep the unit aimed straight ("rudder" amidships).

The drawback here is that the fin works best at just one speed, providing more corrective action when you go faster or less when going slower. You have to decide what speed you want that to be (the usual choice is normal cruising speed) and adjust the fin accordingly.

Although the results are less readily apparent in higher-powered outboards or sterndrives with power-assisted steering, outboards with simple rope-and-pulley steering systems will quickly tell you if you have the trim set right. A properly trimmed drive system will hold its course quite well even if you take your hands off the steering wheel. If the boat veers to starboard or if you have to fight the wheel, you may need to adjust the trim. You can also see the effects of improper trim in boats with power steering: starboard turns will be easier to hold. It's just not quite as obvious as it is with a looser steering system.

Adjusting the mini-rudder on the antiventilation plate is one of two ways you can affect trim. The other is by setting the vertical angle of the drive unit, and while I don't wish to diminish the importance of the former, the latter is perhaps more critical. Although improper adjustment of the trim fin can make a boat harder to steer straight, improper vertical trim can adversely affect everything from the way the boat rides to fuel

FIGURE 13-3. *Located under the antiventilation plate of most transom drive units, the mini-rudder helps counterbalance side thrust. It's adjustable, because side thrust is a result of both propeller forces and hull forces and thus changes from boat to boat. When the tab is set at the proper angle, an otherwise properly trimmed boat will maintain a steady course by itself.*

economy and even its speed. As I indicated in Chapter 4, *all* planing hulls deliver noticeably better performance when they're trimmed correctly.

Sterndrives and modern large outboards offer the advantage of continuous power trim. This means you can adjust the angle of trim in nearly infinite increments throughout the available range and at any time to respond to changing conditions. Smaller outboards (as well as most older ones of any horsepower) can be trimmed also but only through a "pin-in-hole" arrangement that lacks the range of angles and the ability to make adjustments underway. In this configuration you have to put the pin through the set of holes that offers optimum trim for the way you use the boat most of the time. Any drastic change in load or basic operating speed will call for a change in setting. Because you can't make constant adjust-

ments underway, you must resort to other methods (shifting the load within the boat, for example) or stop the motor to move the pin. We'll take a closer look at all the ways to achieve proper trim (and for all boats, not just transom-powered ones) in Chapter 30.

Note that planing hulls with transom power rarely need the added lift of trim tabs to get on plane, because tucking the drive(s) under will usually do the trick (though some particularly stern-heavy boats need all the help they can get). However, trim tabs are desirable on any planing boat to aid in lateral trim (when sitting on one side rather than in center). Whether you use them all the time or only occasionally, you will use them. If the boat you're considering doesn't have trim tabs as standard equipment, be sure to include them among the extras.

What about Twins?

Most new outboards offer counterrotating props for twin installations, thus eliminating torque-induced side-thrust problems, as do counterrotating under-the-boat props. But many older outboards and most sterndrives do *not* allow counterrotation. When twin drives have the same rotation, torque problems can be multiplied, though proper adjustment of the trim fin on both units should reduce them to manageable proportions. Then there are the Volvo Duo Prop and MerCruiser Bravo III we saw back in Chapter 7. Contrarotating props may not be the total answer, but in my limited experience with Duo Props and Bravo IIIs, the absence of torque-induced side thrust is amazing, and the effect this has on boathandling is beautiful. I'll have more to say on specific twin-transom power techniques in Chapter 21; for now I'll merely suggest that although many newer outboard-powered boats with dual drives may respond to some twin-screw handling techniques, most older ones do not.

That pretty much covers the forces working on and within the boat itself—the ones we can adjust through manipulation of steering wheel, throttle, and trim. Now it's time to move on to outside forces—ones we can't control, though we have to live with them just the same.

14

The Influence of Wind

So far we've been dealing with the idyllic, hypothetical condition of no wind and no current. Were it only that way in real life, boathandling would be much easier. But, of course, we have to deal with nature, too. Wind and current exert their influence on our every move—often with tremendous impact. In this chapter, we'll take a look at wind alone, since it's often the more influential.

Powerboats are usually affected by wind more than current because of their relatively shallow drafts and high superstructures. To appreciate this, you have only to look at boats on moorings in a tidal basin; keel sailboats will inevitably swing with the tide, while powerboats will more often swing with the wind (Figure 14-1). For this reason, rather than snobbishness, harbormasters usually keep them segregated.

It might seem that we can do little but enjoy fair winds and suffer the foul. Actually, although the wind itself is beyond our control, how it *affects* us isn't. The overall effect depends on a number of factors, and it changes with the speed of the boat, the velocity of the wind (a 20-knot wind has four times the force of a 10-knot wind), and the direction from which the wind is blowing relative to the boat's heading. The accompanying diagrams show the effects of wind from different relative bearings.

In studying the illustrations, remember that another factor in the wind equation is the shape of the boat. Since every boat is different, experience will be the best teacher when it comes to learning how your boat behaves. I can, however, present some basics to build on.

A boat's shape, both above and below the

FIGURE 14-1. *Generally speaking, moored powerboats swing with the wind, while keeled sailboats swing with the current. This truth is not always easy to prove, however, because for reasons quite unfathomable, there are always more sailboats than powerboats on moorings.*

waterline, is not merely a factor in the equation; it is a *huge* factor. Obviously, the more there is sticking up, particularly as compared with how much is sticking down, the more surface—"sail area," if you will—is available for the wind to act upon.

Since powerboats often have less draft forward and less superstructure aft, wind most often has more influence on the bow. The exceptions are aft-cabin cruisers and motor yachts having considerable "house" all the way back. How wind affects such boats depends largely on the surface area of the superstructure relative to that of the underbody; if there's enough boat in the water, the large "sail area" in the stern may have less influence.

In Figure 14-2, we see the effects of wind on a

boat that is making headway. We'll look first at what happens with a right-handed single-screw conventional drive and then consider how different power options alter the response.

Boat A has the wind dead ahead. This will slow the boat somewhat and magnify steering action. The latter response is the result of two factors: 1) Screw current will likely be greater for a given boat speed because of the added throttle you'll use to overcome the wind, and 2) with every slight turn away from your initial heading straight into the wind, the bow gets an added push from the wind.

Wind on the port bow (boat B) tends to push the bow to starboard. Usually, a little left rudder is all you need to counter the wind and keep the boat on track. If the wind is slight and the boat

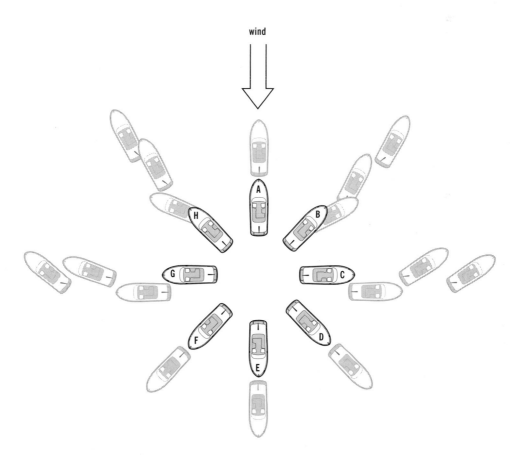

FIGURE 14-2. *The effects of wind on a boat going ahead.*

has a natural tendency to veer to port, you may find that you can run straight with the rudder amidships.

The effect of wind abeam from the port side (boat C) depends on the superstructure. As mentioned above, however, most boats will see more push against the bow. A beam wind from the port side will move the boat to the right of its intended track and will require an answering left rudder.

Wind on the port quarter (boat D) generally has little effect other than to add to the natural tendency of a right-handed single-screw boat to veer to port.

A wind dead astern (boat E) probably has the least effect on steering, although at higher velocities it can create steering problems indirectly by putting you in following seas, which tend to kick the stern around. Its main influence is to increase your speed over the ground.

Wind on the starboard quarter (boat F) has little effect unless it's of great velocity.

Wind on the starboard beam (boat G) is similar to wind on the port beam with the added effect of increasing any tendency to veer to port; the same is true of wind on the starboard bow (boat H). In either case, answering with slight right rudder should hold you on your intended track.

Except for those instances in which wind exaggerates the tendency of a right-handed single-screw boat to veer to port, the wind's effect on twin-screw and transom-powered boats that are making headway will conform to the single-screw examples; relative above- and below-water "sail areas" and their fore-and-aft distributions are more important than drive systems.

Things change, however, for a boat moving astern (Figure 14-3). Most boats, most of the time, exhibit what is commonly called the *weathervane effect*. Simply stated, boats generally like to *back straight into the wind*. A drifting boat will often swing around until its stern faces the wind, and the application of power astern usually does little to change this attitude. For this reason, most boats will back directly into the wind (boat I) even if their no-wind behavior displays a marked swing to port. Indeed, even boats having such strong single-screw side-thrust behavior that they will back only to port in the absence of wind will

often back to starboard if the wind is on the starboard quarter (boat J).

With wind on the starboard beam (boat K), you can probably back straight, though with a considerable side-set to port. You can also probably back to starboard, as you can when the wind is on the starboard bow (boat L), simply by letting the bow fall off the wind. In the latter case you can probably back straight, again with considerable side-set.

So far we've seen that as long as the wind is astern or at least over the starboard side, we can use it to overcome a right-handed single-screw boat's tendency to back to port. If the wind comes from ahead or over the port side, however, it reinforces the boat's normal swing to port. Regardless of rudder angle, the stern swing resulting from side thrust usually combines with the wind action on the bow to cause the boat to fall more and more off the wind. This means that the apparent wind will move gradually around from dead ahead (boat M) to the port bow (boat N) to the port beam (boat O) to the port quarter (boat P) and finally to dead astern.

Because we're dealing with a balance of forces, the wind velocity required to overcome side thrust in boats I, J, K, and L will depend on the force of the side thrust, the boat, and the throttle setting. You'll have to learn about your own boat on the water—unfortunately there are no shortcuts.

In the absence of strong side thrust—as on boats with counterrotating twin screws or properly trimmed transom power—the behavior exhibited by boats M, N, and O will be absent. The behavior of boats P, I, and J, however, is not exclusive to single-screw drives. The weathervane effect is nearly universal. No matter how your boat is powered, most of the time it will be easiest to back straight into the wind, and whenever the wind is nearly dead astern, backing any other way but straight into it will be tough.

Although wind is usually the predominant force of nature affecting powerboats, it's by no means the only one. In the next chapter we'll see what current does. And since neither wind nor current works alone, we'll also take a look at how they interact.

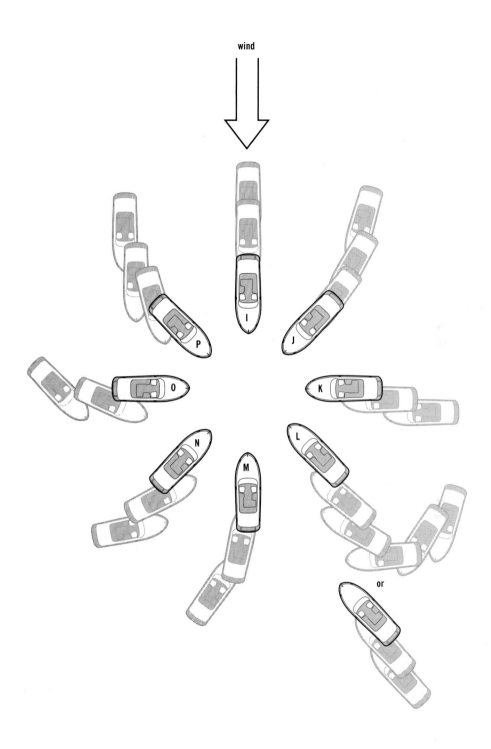

FIGURE 14-3. *The effects of wind on a boat going astern.*

15

What Current Does

As does wind, current can complicate maneuvers by pushing you off your intended track. Also as with wind, the manner in which current affects your boat depends on its strength and on how your boat reacts to it. Current can be a big factor in your boat's behavior in any situation, but because powerboats generally present less surface area to the water than to the wind, wind is often the bigger factor. So, at times, we can forget about current. But always? *No!*

If the current is strong enough and the wind gentle enough, current becomes the dominant force, even with a boat of very shallow draft. This is particularly evident in rivers and in areas of strong tidal current. Thus, we must consider current along with wind in the operating equation, though here we can't be quite as broad in our approach to the problem. No convenient diagrams here!

Yet there are generalities to consider, and though each boat's reactions to current must ultimately be learned by experience, the learning will be easier if you have knowledge of the generalities beforehand.

Draft and Speed

The current's effect on a boat is directly related to surface area of the underbody, yet draft is not the only consideration. The boat's speed through the water is also important, particularly for a planing boat, whose draft decreases with an increase in speed.

The faster you go (even in a slow displacement boat, where "fast" is definitely a relative term), the less effect current will have as its speed becomes proportionately smaller. The other side of this coin is that in close-quarters maneuvers, every boat is in a displacement mode and going slowly (or should be!) so that the effect of current, if any, will be at its greatest just when it can upset you the most.

Pressure Points

Just as wind usually has its greatest effect on the bow because the boat's draft is less there, current generally does most of its work on the stern, where draft can be greatest (and you also have things such as rudders, struts, and maybe even a bit of keel hanging down). In fact, in the absence of wind, there's a similar though opposite weathervane effect in which the bow swings to face the current. The operative phrase here is "in the absence of wind," something we rarely see.

A current from directly ahead will retard your progress and lower your speed over the ground for any given speed through the water. Likewise, a current from directly astern will move you ahead faster than your speed through the water would indicate. Currents from abeam will push you off your intended course, currents at 45 degrees on either bow will push you off course and retard progress, and similar currents from astern will advance you as they move you off course. Yet we can't put these elementary generalities into diagrams as we did with wind because current will take a backseat to wind in many situations, and its total effect is usually a result of its interaction with the wind.

When wind and current move in the same direction, their forces are generally additive. That is, a 15-knot wind and a 5-knot current from the same direction will act upon your boat much like a 20-knot wind from that direction. When wind opposes current, however, the net result is rarely a direct subtraction. A 5-knot current opposing a 15-knot wind will *not* reduce the wind's influence to that of a 10-knot blow; rather, the wind's effect will be slightly diminished but still dominant. If the current is stronger than the wind—for example, a 5-knot current and a 3-knot wind—the current may dominate, though the ultimate interaction depends on your boat.

When wind and current are neither in opposition nor in the same direction, the net effect depends on their relative strengths and your boat's particular behavior, which is difficult if not impossible to predict, though it can be learned be-

cause it will usually be repetitive. In the next chapter I'll offer some advice on how to learn quickly under the circumstances of the moment.

Because current usually has a stronger effect on the stern, and thus your boat can tend to swing into it, single-screw boats (and low-powered vessels of any configuration) are usually most maneuverable when the bow is headed into the current. With twin screws, however, you have more options, thanks to their high degree of maneuverability when operating astern. For this reason, you can often maintain the best control over the situation by backing a twin-screw boat into the current, especially if wind and current are working together. A slight increase or decrease in engine speed will advance you faster (astern) or slower as conditions demand; alternating clutches in and out of gear will let you steer. You can stop by taking both engines out of gear, but be aware that it will be a brief stop because the current will soon start moving you ahead. On the other hand, in all but the strongest currents, you can hold in place

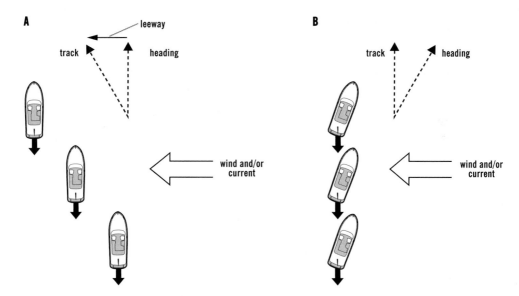

FIGURE 15-1. *Wind and current tend to push us off our intended course and prevent a boat from going directly where pointed, whether we're steering by eyeball or compass (A). To travel in a desired direction (B), we most often have to head the boat slightly into the weather and "crab" our way toward our objective. In this case it often helps to identify your boat's "point of forward progress" and aim it, rather than the point of the bow, toward your desired goal.*

quite nicely by alternately shifting both engines astern until you just start to move and then returning to neutral until the current starts to move you.

So Is It Wind? Or Current?

A few years ago, I was on the flying bridge of a 50-foot motor yacht, heading back to the marina after a boat test. With me were a company delivery captain and the builder's marketing director. The test finished, and we were talking about boats and boating in general. The discussion turned to dealing with nature, and the marketing director asked, "So which is the greater influence, wind or current?" In nearly perfect unison, almost as if we'd rehearsed it, the delivery captain and I replied, "It all depends!" Of course, if we'd thought of it, we could have added, "But it often doesn't matter." A skipper's main concern should be Ma Nature as a whole; what the combined forces of wind and current together are doing to your boat *at the moment.*

The main thing you have to remember is that it's almost certain that your actual forward progress will *not* be the same as your *heading* [the direction in which your bow is pointed]. Figure 15-1 part **A** shows us what can happen if you don't allow for Ma Nature, while part **B** shows us what happens when you do.

The term "leeway" comes from sailing and derives from the boat's making way to the lee, the direction away from the wind. But in our world of powerboats the offset could just as easily be from current, though we usually call it leeway regardless.

As I indicated above, ultimately you should be most concerned with your boat's overall reaction to the combined influences of wind and current. And in the next chapters, I'll tell you how to determine quickly just what that reaction is.

PART THREE

The Hows of Powerboat Handling

FL 2669 MJ

16

Know Your Boat

Learning exactly how your boat behaves in every situation is—or ought to be—a never-ending process. The learning is rarely a chore, and it's deeply satisfying to know intimately a particular boat's every nuance of behavior. Long before that day is reached, however, you need at least a general idea of what will happen under given circumstances. Indeed, you should have this knowledge before you attempt your first close-quarters maneuver in an unfamiliar boat.

Because my career path has led me to spend a great deal of time aboard boats that are new to me, I've had to develop a drill to acquaint me with a boat's responses as quickly as possible, and I'd like to share it here. Naturally, the drill varies with the type of boat, and I'll cover each in due time. With any boat, however, it's best to approximate initially (as closely as you can in the real world) the "no-wind, no-current, boat-behavior-only" situation covered in Chapters 11, 12, and 13. Look for an area with little current, adequate shelter from the prevailing wind, sufficient depth, and ample maneuvering room. And though you're looking for a fairly unrestricted open area, look also for landmarks to help you gauge direction and distance. This testing ground may sound difficult to find, but every boating area I've ever known has several such places nearby.

Single Screw

Let's begin our real-world approach as we did the theoretical—with single-screw conventional drive. First, you want to learn how big a problem side thrust will be. Since side thrust is greater when going astern, we'll check it out first. With the boat dead in the water, set the rudder amidships. (If there's no rudder angle indicator, and with most pleasure boats there won't be, count the number of turns of the steering wheel from hard over right to hard over left and then come back half the total.) Put the clutch astern and increase the throttle. You'll be able to see how much the stern swings and how steerable the boat is. You'll see how much sternway is required for the rudder action to overtake side thrust (if, indeed, it will—some single-screw boats cannot be steered when backing, no matter what!), and you'll learn whether you have a right-handed or left-handed wheel. (The stern will swing to port with a right-handed wheel, to starboard with a left.)

With the rudder back amidships, put the clutch ahead and ease the throttle up to cruising speed. Using landmarks, see how much you veer to port (with a right-handed prop) and how much right rudder it takes to go straight. Then come back to idle speed, and put the clutch astern to stop. How far do you advance before stopping, and how much stern swing do you get in the process? You should also see how long it takes the boat to come to a stop without applying more power than idle astern, and how much rudder action you have in the absence of screw current.

Next, try going ahead again at cruising speed and observe the differences between port and starboard turns and between stern swing and bow swing. In short, you want to determine how closely your boat's behavior matches the typical single-screw behavior outlined in Chapter 11. You also want to discover how much room you need to execute the different maneuvers.

Twin Screws

Twin screws give you a few other things to test. For example, in stopping with both screws astern, you shouldn't see any stern swing, but it's still a good idea to find out how much effect momentum has; that is, how long it takes to come to a stop from various speeds ahead with varying degrees of throttle astern.

You also need to find out how much rudder action you get at maneuvering speeds both ahead and astern—and be sure to check the difference in rudder action with and without screw current (engines in or out of gear). This determines how much attention you should pay to rudder angle when you're executing a maneuver or, put another way, how much help you'll get from changing the rudder angle. As I pointed out back in Chapter 11, the effectiveness of a rudder is primarily dependent on the screw current across it. Because rudders are often located so that screw current is a lesser factor than side thrust until the throttles are advanced considerably, side thrust is often far more influential on boat behavior than rudder angle—especially in negotiating typical twin-screw maneuvers at idle speed.

Try putting the rudders amidships and splitting the clutches; that is, put one ahead, the other astern. The boat should start to spin around. Now turn the steering wheel in the direction you're spinning. If you've put the port gear ahead and the starboard gear astern, turn the wheel for full right rudder. Look for a change in the radius of your turning circle. If the turn gets considerably tighter with an increase in rudder angle, the rudders are helping a lot. If they make little or no difference, you should be able to forget them in most maneuvering situations.

Now bring the clutches to neutral and wait for the boat to stop spinning. When it's settled down, leave the steering at full right rudder and split the clutches the opposite way—starboard ahead, port astern. If you didn't see much effect from the rudders before, you won't now; the boat will start to

spin the other way. But if the rudders aided the turn before, the boat will now slide to port instead of spinning. If you see even the slightest indication of this, try playing with the throttles to see whether running one engine or the other a little faster makes a difference. Then try taking each engine alternately in and out of gear (but don't disengage the clutch of an engine you've revved up until you first bring the throttle back to idle). You'll get a good indication of whether this boat can be walked sideways or not, how difficult a process it is, and what you have to do to make it happen, all of which can be extremely valuable information.

In Chapter 7, I suggested that twin screws do not automatically provide get-home power when one engine fails because some twin-screw boats simply won't operate properly on a single screw. Now's the time to find out whether this boat will.

Put the rudders amidships, and then put one engine in gear and advance its throttle. Initially, you'll probably see a turn toward the opposite side. That is, if you've put the starboard engine in gear, you'll see a turn to port. If the boat is operable on one engine, however, it'll begin to straighten out, and at some point you should be able to steer the boat—even to starboard. If the boat just keeps turning to port, forget running on one engine.

Even if you observe near-total control when going ahead, you should still find out what happens going astern. Remember the single-screw tendency to back only one way, and consider the ramifications of moving that screw off the centerline. Even if they behave well on one engine when going ahead, most twin-screw boats show exaggerated single-screw behavior when forced to *back* on one. It's better to find out before you need to know.

Finally, you need to find out how easily the two engines can be brought into synchronization at cruising speed. Many twin-screw boats have mechanical synchronizers, and when these work they can be a big help. Unfortunately, synchronizers seem to be among the first accessories to fail, and you want to discover this quickly. If the sync system doesn't work, no matter; I've found it easier in many ways to do it by ear. Yes, by ear. Getting the two engines in sync is akin to tuning a musical instrument. You listen for the beat frequency, the very low frequency pulses that occur when the rumbles from both engines are nearly, but not exactly, at the same frequency. Then you adjust one engine until the low, slow throbbing either disappears completely (the ideal, which will happen when both are running at identical rpm) or beats so slowly as to be almost nonexistent, which happens when you have the two engines very, very close. You can also often sense this by feeling the vibrations through your feet. As with other skills, synchronization becomes easier with practice. But even the first time you do it, the point of perfect sync will make itself known. It just takes longer at first.

Transom Power

If you have an outboard or sterndrive boat, the first thing you want to find out is what happens when you change trim: how much you must trim in to get on plane, and how much you can trim out before the boat begins to porpoise.

Next, you need to try some low-speed maneuvers to determine how sensitive the steering is at idle speed and how much steering ability remains when you take the engine(s) out of gear.

Though backing a transom-powered boat is generally easier than backing a single-screw inboard, you should still try going astern to see exactly how steerable this boat is when backing. You should also determine how much side thrust remains (remember, transom power can reduce but rarely eliminate it) and thus how much initial stern swing you get when you put the engine(s) astern. This knowledge can come in handy when you begin docking practice. Since the angle at which the prop attacks the water is one of the factors influencing side thrust, be sure to assess the changes that occur as you change trim at maneuvering speed.

If you have twins, are the props counterrotating? Look at the propeller blades. If both blades are pitched in the same direction, they must rotate in the same direction. If they are opposite, you have counterrotation. (Since manufacturers are still rather proud of having counterrotating

props on outboards, the units will probably say so—boldly, I might add—often right on the cowling, but certainly in the specs.)

You don't *need* to know whether you have counterrotating props, but the knowledge will help explain the behavior you're about to evaluate. If you lack them, the odds are you won't see typical twin-screw behavior with twin transom power. However, the spacing between the drives can often be as much (or more) of a factor; if they're very close you won't get much "twin-screw" behavior from any outboard installation.

You need to determine whether you have twin-screw action or merely a single screw doubled up. Put the "rudders" (drives) amidships and split the clutches. See how tight a circle you turn. Then put the rudders hard over one way or the other and put only the outside engine (starboard, for a left-hand turn) ahead, leaving the other in neutral. If the twin-screw action gave you a tighter turn, use it; you have the capability. If the rudder-action turn was tighter, you can almost forget you have twins when it comes to maneuvering. We won't try mixing clutch and rudder action as we did with twin inboards because with transom power the thrust of the engine astern is fully directed, unlike the screw current from an inboard astern, which doesn't flow over the rudder. This means that trying to split the clutches and use the steering wheel at the same time usually will result in a looser turn than you get just from splitting the clutches. For similar reasons, it's rarely possible to walk a twin-screw transom-powered boat sideways. Thanks to greater maneuverability in general, however, it's no great loss.

Adding Nature

Since we've done the above exercises in a location that's as free from nature's influences as we could possibly find, it's now time to move. Seek out wind and current and do the drill all over from the top, observing the changes nature adds as you go along. If you move around to different locations, you can find quite a variety of combinations. Time alone will offer you the rest. You'll get an *infinite* variety if you stay with it long enough.

17

Boathandling in Wind and Current

In the following chapters, you'll see a "by-the-numbers" approach to typical boathandling situations. The caveat is that boathandling can't be done strictly by the numbers; every experience is unique. Each time you make a landing or set your anchor or do any of the myriad maneuvers I'm about to outline, you'll be doing it for the first time *under that particular set of conditions*. Wind varies in both velocity and direction, as does current, and their interaction varies further by the relative strengths and directions of the component forces and their respective influences on your boat. Add the changing load and trim conditions aboard your vessel, and you're faced with an infinite set of variables.

In any boathandling situation you have to modify the basic procedures (which hold true in principle in all situations for any size vessel from toy to tanker) to suit the specific conditions you face at the time. While this may sound ominous, in actual practice it isn't difficult at all. The main thing you have to remember is this: *Don't try to fight Mother Nature!*

Let me put it another way. In past chapters we've seen that there are certain things your boat, if left to its own devices, will do by itself. Wind and current will do other things to it. If you plan your maneuvers to work with these tendencies, boathandling will be simpler than if you fight them. In truth, if you fight them, you may win sometimes, but most often you won't. In the long run, it's not only smarter but also much, much easier to get nature to work with you, and that means working with nature.

Gauging Wind and Current

First, you need to determine, to the best of your ability, what wind and current are doing. Your eyes are excellent tools. To gauge the wind, look at flags and pennants on other boats or ashore (Figure 17-1). If you're about to make a landing, you care less whether the wind is from the north, south, or some other point of the compass than whether it's blowing onto, away from, or parallel to the pier, or from points in between. You also need to know, in simple terms, how hard it's blowing, and thus whether it will be a major or minor influence. Are the flags really flapping, barely moving, or hanging limp? Lacking flags, look for smoke, trees, or even birds, which usually sit facing the wind.

You can gauge current similarly, though the signs are not always as numerous nor as obvious. Tethered floating objects such as buoys usually give you a hint. Whether they're aids to navigation, mooring devices, or the visible markers of crustacean corrals doesn't matter at all. Anchored boats can help, too; just remember that most powerboats will swing with the wind, and look at deep-draft vessels such as keel sailboats for signs of current. Even fixed objects such as pilings or bridge piers and fender systems will show telltale signs of current in the ripples that form on both the up- and downstream sides (Figure 17-2). The stronger the current (that is, the more trouble it can give you), the more visible the signs. If you can't see its signs (providing there are objects there to help you), you probably don't have to worry about current.

FIGURE 17-1. *A flag waving in the breeze is a perfect clue to which way the wind is blowing. In this situation you'd use a "wind off the pier" approach.*

FIGURE 17-2. *Look closely at the ripples around the piling, and you can quickly tell which way the current is flowing—and often, how strong it is.*

Looking for these signs takes conscious effort initially, but with a little practice you'll find yourself processing clues constantly without a bit of thought.

It doesn't matter whether the predominant force is wind or current, since it's inevitably the interaction of forces that produces the observed effect on your boat. The good news is that determining the combined effect of outside forces is easy. You need only bring the throttle(s) back to idle, take the clutch or clutches out of gear, and wait until the boat settles dead in the water. Then wait a few seconds more, and you'll see—or more important, feel—the effect. Is the boat still sliding forward? Have you begun to move backward? Sideways? Are you swinging? How fast and which way? To plan your maneuver, you need only factor in these natural movements with your boat's known behavior under power, and you can fairly well predict the ultimate behavior and make your moves accordingly.

To learn more about your boat's behavior under the conditions of the moment, make a dry run in open water before you try the real thing in tight quarters. If you miscalculate the first time, try again. Some dockside wiseguys may wonder why you stay out there fooling around, but taking time to fully appreciate the conditions of the moment can help you avoid the day when they wonder why you hit the pier so hard.

Even after you've become adept enough to skip the dry runs, you can benefit from taking a moment to stop and check out wind and current before you commit to a maneuver. I still do.

18

Docking a Single-Screw Inboard

Before tackling this chapter you might read Chapters 11 through 17, if you haven't already done so. It will make the explanation of docking more meaningful and a lot easier to grasp.

Note that in the following explanations I often use the word *wind* to simplify things. Most of the time you can read that to mean the combined force of wind and current.

Docking can be a traumatic experience. Usually the last event of the day, your return to the marina can set the tone for your memories of the entire outing. When the landing goes well, you may breathe a sigh of relief. When it doesn't, you may curse. Either way, you're usually glad when it's over because chances are you're tired and ready to head home. Your crew is probably even more tired and may be less help than you'd hope for, so you're left somewhat to your own devices. To make matters worse, there's usually a crowd watching to see how well you do (and offering plenty of free, though conflicting, advice). That's the stuff trauma is built of. I can't guarantee perfect landings, but if you have an idea what to do before you actually have to do it, you should be able to take some of the hard knocks out of the process. Look at the diagrams, think about the process involved, temper the approach each time as suggested in Chapter 17, and you should be OK.

Single-Screw Stern Swing

Exaggerated stern swing when power is applied astern, the action that can so often be a curse, can be a blessing when bringing a boat alongside a float or pier. If you approach the landing with the side to which the stern will swing when you apply power astern—port side for a right-handed screw, starboard for a left—the swing you can't avoid will bring the stern in smartly as you come to a stop.

Let's take it by the numbers. Look at Figure 18-1. In this illustration we're assuming a right-handed wheel, so we're coming into land port-side-to. The initial approach (1) should be at an angle of 20 degrees or so, the exact angle being determined by the force and direction of wind and current, as we'll discuss in a moment. When you get closer to the dock (2), ease the throttle to minimum steerageway and make final adjustments in your approach angle to allow for wind and current. As you near the pier (3), put the clutch in neutral and give full right rudder. This will start bringing the boat parallel to the pier. Finally, as your bow *almost* touches, put the clutch astern and apply just enough throttle to stop the boat and swing the stern in (4).

If all conditions are ideal, and your approach speed isn't too great, idle speed will be sufficient; merely putting the clutch astern will be enough to bring you to a stop. But if you've had to approach a little fast, it will take more thrust to stop so you'll need some throttle, too. You sometimes see hotshots come roaring in, and then stop quickly with a burst of power astern. This may look flashy, but one day their reverse gear may not work. Ouch! It's much better to take it as easy as possible every time.

Now let's introduce some wind and current.

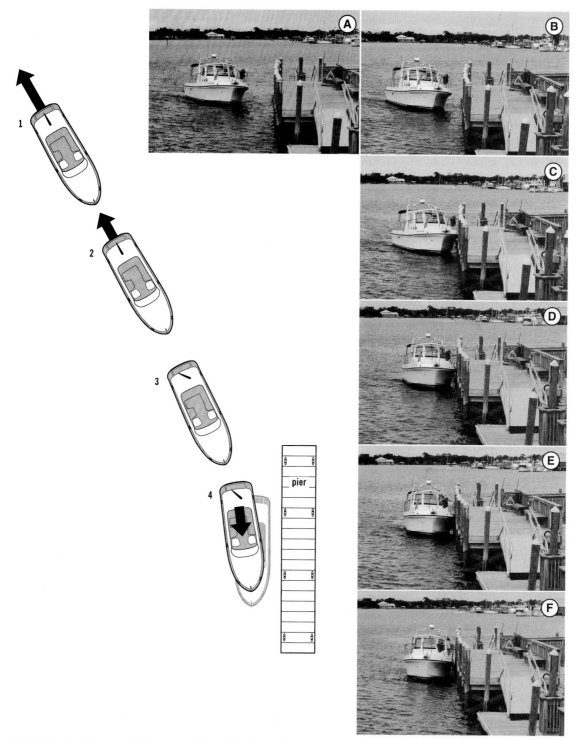

FIGURE 18-1. *Docking a single-screw inboard—the basic approach. Arrows indicate direction of thrust. For clarity, only the main thrust is shown.*

When docking on rivers or places with a strong tidal current, you should always try to make your approach into the current—it will help you stop. The direction of the wind should be of secondary importance, though you cannot ignore it. If the wind is behind you (thus pushing you forward), throttle back sooner and (probably) apply power astern sooner than you would in an absence of wind. If the wind is from ahead, you need to stay under power longer to get to your desired berth, since the wind will be pushing you back.

If the wind is pushing you toward or away from the pier, you must modify the approach angle and your rudder action to account for it. Let's check it out.

Wind Blowing On the Pier

A wind pushing you toward the pier presents at once the easiest and perhaps the most difficult landing situation. It's the easiest because you'll end up against the pier even if you do nothing! It's difficult because your object is to make *gentle* landings, and with nature forcing you against the pier, it's not so easy to land softly.

Figure 18-2 shows a wind-on situation. The secret is to come in at a flatter angle and to start the approach farther away. It may help to imagine that you're landing at a pier that's closer to you than the real one, since you'll probably move toward the actual pier faster than you'd prefer.

Note that in this case you'll probably have to use slight right rudder to keep the bow out. Here's another tip to help soften the landing: Instead of continuing to slide in sideways—as you'll be doing through much of the approach— let the bow come in when you get close, and then roll onto the pier on the curve of the bow. This rolling action will usually be softer than hitting flat. Use a fender or two to soften the landing even more.

If the wind is really strong, you may want to take yet another approach. In Figure 18-3, we come in with the wind dead astern. Remember the weathervane effect? Let it work for you. By applying power astern (1), you can counter the force of the wind, and the weathervane effect will

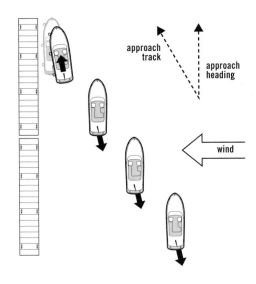

FIGURE 18-2. *Docking a single-screw inboard— wind blowing onto the pier.*

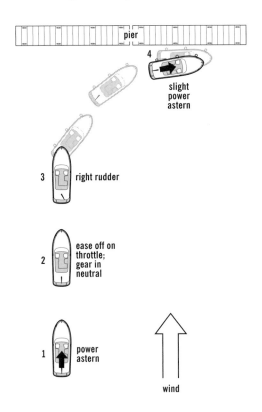

FIGURE 18-3. *Docking a single-screw inboard— strong wind on pier.*

keep the stern from swinging. As you ease off on the throttle (2), the wind will push you in until you're close enough (about 1½ boat lengths off) to put the clutch in neutral and the rudder hard right (3), which will start you swinging parallel to the pier. When you're nearly in place (4), another short application of power astern should be enough to stop you and complete the procedure. Since the wind will aid in making the stern swing in, it's best to emphasize "short"; too much power astern will most likely result in a bump and bang.

Wind Blowing Off the Pier

When Mother Nature seems to be doing her best to keep you away from your intended landing spot, you may be tempted to curse her loudly. But in truth, you should be somewhat thankful, because, though it can sometimes be the most work, landing with the wind off the dock almost assures you of coming in gently.

The key here is a broader approach angle—say 30 degrees or perhaps more, depending on the wind (Figure 18-4). You'll probably need left rudder and a bit more throttle to keep the bow from

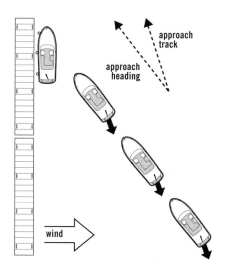

FIGURE 18-4. *Docking a single-screw inboard—wind blowing off the pier.*

being pushed away. When you're almost touching the pier, take the engine out of gear, give hard right rudder, and finally apply a short burst of power astern to stop your forward motion and bring the stern in. As I said, this should result in a very gentle landing. The nice part is that if you react too soon, the wind will merely take you out, and you can try again.

If the wind is very strong, your moment at dockside will be brief, so it's essential that you get a line ashore and *made fast* [tied down] immediately. As we'll see in Chapter 22, you may even need that line to complete the maneuver.

Against the Thrust

All other things being equal, the added help stern thrust can provide makes it worth landing "right side" to the pier (port for right-handed screws, starboard for left-handed). All other things are not always equal, however, and at times we have no choice but to land "wrong side" to—maneuvering into the current can be that important. The problem then is that the last-minute burst of power astern swings us away from the pier as we stop, definitely not the desired action. We have to allow for it by getting the stern closer to the pier before we finish the maneuver. Figure 18-5 illustrates the routine. The initial approach is similar to landing port-side-to (again using a right-handed wheel). Set an approach angle of about 20 degrees (1), and ease off on the throttle as you get close (2). When you're nearly there, put the clutch in neutral and give left rudder (3). Then comes the big difference. Before you reach the stopping point, give an additional short burst of power ahead to set the stern swinging to starboard (4). Then quickly come to neutral, put the clutch astern, and give a short burst of power to stop (5). If you set up just enough starboard stern swing from the burst of power ahead to cancel the stern swing resulting from the application of power astern, you'll come to a stop just where you want to be. Too much power ahead can swing the stern in too far too soon. Too little, and the stern will still swing away when you apply power astern. This move will improve with practice as you get to know just what it takes to achieve the desired balance with your boat.

The downside of docking "wrong side" to is that much of the time you won't have to, so this maneuver gets less practice than others. Practice it once in a while just to keep your touch.

The upside is that most of the time you'll have a choice. Though single-screw boats are not as maneuverable as boats with twin screws, you can often put yourself in a position to dock the desired way despite prevailing circumstances. In the next chapter, we'll find out how.

FIGURE 18-5. *Docking a single-screw inboard—against the thrust.*

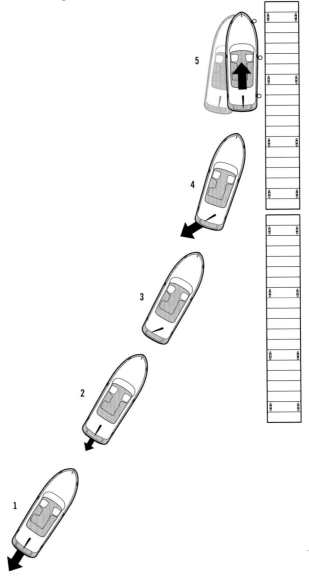

19

The "Impossible" Moves with a Single-Screw Boat

Without question, twin-screw boats are much more maneuverable than single-screw, particularly when it comes to backing or turning in tight quarters. Merely because these moves are easier for twins, however, doesn't mean we can't do them with singles. This chapter will show you how to turn obstacles into advantages.

The following descriptions are for a right-handed screw. All the actions should be reversed for a left-handed screw.

And Baaack We Go!

As we've seen, when you apply power astern, side thrust tends to overcome sternway in degrees ranging from mere nuisance to major obstruction. Couple this with rather poor steering action astern (at best), and backing can be a real chore.

Chore though it may be, you *can* do it. A little right rudder (Figure 19-1, 1) will sometimes suffice to counter stern swing and let you back straight (or nearly so). If your boat will behave this way, consider yourself lucky. Most will not. Be careful with the right rudder (2), and don't use too much because it can be tough on the steering gear to back *against* a turned rudder.

If your boat is like most, it won't back straight and will veer to port of your intended track. This calls for a little shuffle with your hands. Use one hand to turn the steering wheel quickly for hard left rudder and the other to go from astern to ahead (with a short pause in neutral to be kind to your gearbox). If you apply a short but strong burst of power ahead (3), the stern will swing

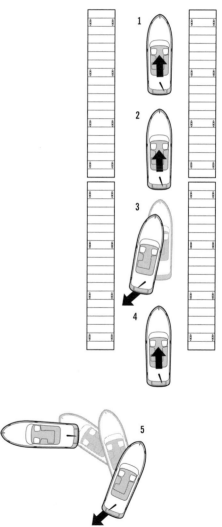

FIGURE 19-1. *Taking a single-screw boat straight back. For clarity, only the main thrust is shown.*

back to starboard without losing much sternway in the process.

As the stern swings to starboard of your intended course, put the rudder back to slightly right of amidships and again ease the power astern (4). You may have to repeat this procedure several times if you want to back very far. On the other hand, once you get the boat straightened out after its initial swing to port, you may find that the steering ability you gain as your speed astern increases will be enough to keep you going the way you want by rudder action alone. If you can steer when backing after you gain sufficient sternway, you can also try kicking the stern to starboard *before* you begin backing up. Just be sure your boat will respond this way before you try it in close quarters.

How you finish the procedure depends on how steerable your boat is going astern and which way you plan to go after you finish backing. If you plan to head to starboard, you can let the stern swing to port as soon as you clear the obstructions you're backing out of. If you plan to head to port, you'll need to back far enough to allow turning room (5).

Restricted Turning

Ah, turning room. If you have a single-screw boat, undoubtedly there will be many times you'll wish you could spin it in scarcely more than its own length—as the twin-screw skippers do. Well, you can't, and that's something you have to learn to live with. But you can come close. Very close. Again, use the boat's natural tendencies to help you out.

The secret in this case is to couple the boat's inevitable stern swing when you apply power astern with the stern swing you can create from short bursts of power ahead with full rudder. Thanks to most boats' tendency to spin around their pivot point once you get them started, you can turn easily to starboard (if you have a right-handed screw) in little more than a boat length by working the throttle and clutch. Short but strong bursts are the key.

Figure 19-2 shows what happens. With the clutch in neutral, put the rudder over hard right. Then give a strong, *short* burst of power ahead.

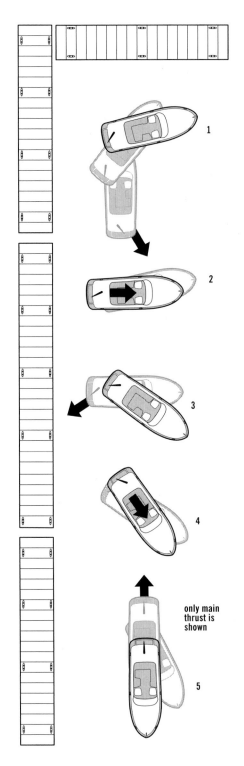

FIGURE 19-2. *Turning a single-screw inboard boat in tight quarters.*

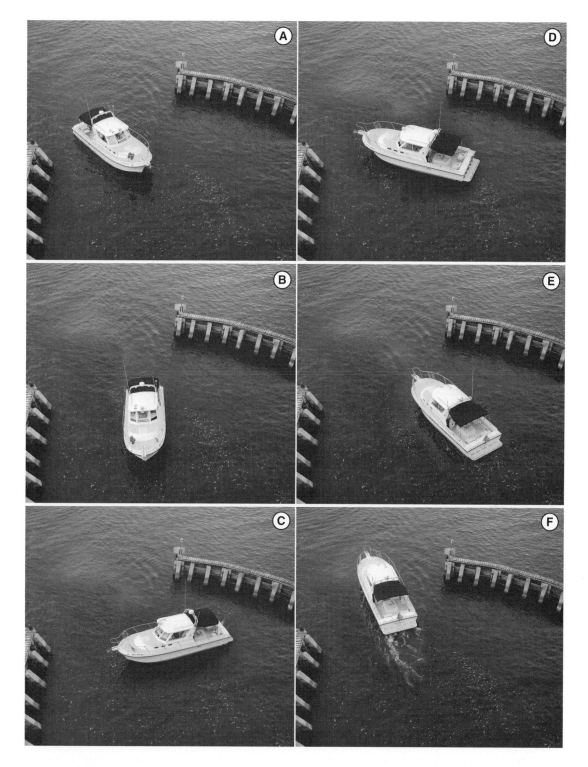

FIGURE 19-2. *Turning a single-screw inboard boat (continued).*

Before the boat can advance very far, it will start to swing to starboard as the stern swings to port (1). If you were to leave it ahead, you would begin to see some advance. But you don't. Instead, you quickly bring the throttle back to idle, shift the clutch to neutral, pause a brief moment, then put the clutch astern and give another burst of power (2). The initial stern swing you get from the side thrust astern coupled with the swing you started with the burst of power ahead will continue the spin without causing any sternway. Then, before sternway has the chance to develop, another shift through neutral into ahead and a short burst of power will add yet more swing (3). Again, if you were to allow the thrust ahead to take over, you would begin to straighten out and see some forward motion. But since you apply the power in a burst and then again shift to apply power in a short burst astern (4), you'll see yet more stern swing without movement either ahead or astern.

Repeat the procedure one or two more times, and you'll be turned around (5). Remember, you have to keep the power bursts short so as to accentuate stern swing without producing headway or sternway. Leave the engine in gear too long in either direction and you'll defeat your purpose. If you make the bursts short but strong, you can almost duplicate a twin-screw pirouette.

20

Docking a Twin-Screw Inboard

Wait a minute! Just because you have a twin-screw boat doesn't mean the details of single-screw handling aren't important to you. They are. If you're jumping in here to get what you need to know without wasting time on the unnecessary, please go back and read Chapters 18 and 19 first. They will help.

The Twin-Screw Approach

One of the reasons for reading the chapter on docking a single-screw boat is that when coming alongside a float or pier, you do essentially the same things with a twin screw that you do with a single. For example, the suggestions regarding the changes you should make in your angle of approach to allow for nature apply equally to singles and twins, so I'm not going to repeat them. The main difference is that you no longer have a "right side" and "wrong side" for easy landings. With twin screws, you can put either side to the pier with equal ease. And this means you can almost always approach into the current.

Rudders versus Clutches

Another difference is that you can ignore the rudders and maneuver the twin-screw boat with clutches and throttles alone. Whether you use the rudders or leave them amidships depends greatly on how much rudder action you get when the engines are out of gear or at idle. If rudders are a significant factor in handling your boat, by all means use them—every little bit helps. But if you've found that rudder angle makes little difference at maneuvering speeds (see Chapters 12 and 16), why go to the trouble of messing with the steering wheel in addition to the clutches and throttles?

We might as well recognize the truth that the first time you face the console of a twin-screw boat you can't help but wonder how you're going to do it all with just two hands (Figure 20-1). Even

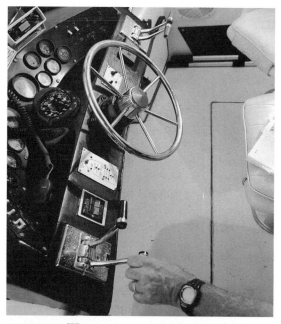

FIGURE 20-1. *When twin-screw boats have dual-lever controls (two throttles, two clutches), the console can be intimidating. After all, you only have two hands. But that's all you need. Single-lever controls do make it easier, but you can manage quite nicely without them.*

119

with single-lever controls (clutch and throttle in the same handle), you seem to need one hand for each engine and another for steering. If the throttle and clutch levers are separate, the thought of handling twin screws can be even more intimidating! But it needn't be. Fortunately, two hands are plenty, even when you have two throttles and two clutches (though single-lever controls are much easier to use).

The Docking Drill

Let's come alongside a float. Since we did most of our single-screw landings port-side-to, let's come in starboard-side-to this time, simply because *we can*. In fact, let's do it twice, once without rudders and once with, just to see the differences.

In Figure 20-2 we see a typical landing. As with the single screw, approach angle is about 20 degrees off the face of the pier. (Remember, you have to adjust this angle to accommodate wind and current, just as with the single screw.) Since you're steering only with the engines, it may be necessary to take one or the other out of gear to swing the bow slightly. At position 2, let's say you're being pushed onto the dock faster than you'd like. Simply take the outboard engine (the one *away* from the pier—in this case the port) out of gear, and the bow will swing slightly away. When you get close to your desired dock space (3), take the other engine out of gear and coast toward the pier. In fact, this may be a good time to remind you that neutral is a part of your control—you can use it often to keep your speed down. Just so long as you have enough headway to maintain control, you'll be OK.

When the bow is about to touch (4), put the outboard engine (the one away from the pier) astern to reduce headway and swing the stern in. Since a twin-screw prop going astern is essentially an exaggerated single screw—a result of its being off center—sometimes the stern will swing too much when you use the outboard engine alone. In this case, put the other engine astern also (5) to cancel the swing. If putting both engines astern should go beyond stopping and begin

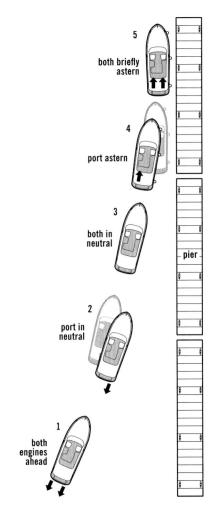

FIGURE 20-2. *Twin-screw docking—the basics. For clarity, only the main thrust is shown.*

to produce sternway, you can cancel it with a quick application of power ahead on both engines and still remain parallel to the pier.

For the sake of brevity, I just simplified the steering actions involved at position 2. In the real world, you might have to put the port engine back in gear if the bow swings out farther than you want, and you may have to take the starboard engine out of gear to help swing it back. You might even have to repeat these actions a few times to keep the boat going the way you want. This is one of those maneuvers that can only be described in broad terms, since every boat and situation will be different. Just remember that if you're steering with the engines, it may take several shifts of either or *both* clutches to fine-tune your final approach.

With the Rudders' Help

The technique I just described will work with any twin-screw inboard boat. You can use it without reservation even if you're unsure whether the boat responds well to its rudder at maneuvering speeds. "So," you may wonder, "why bother to do it any other way?" The answer is that if your boat *will* respond to its rudders, the variety of movements you can get from different combinations of clutch, throttle, and rudders makes the extra effort well worth it.

Let's try the same landing again, this time adding rudder action. Figure 20-3 shows the basic approach—roughly 20 degrees off the pier. Turn the steering wheel at (2) to fine-tune the approach angle for ambient wind and current. When you get close to your desired dock space (3), take the

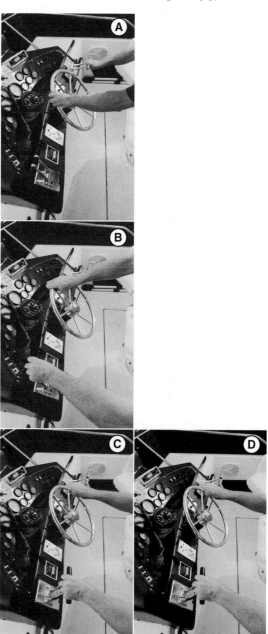

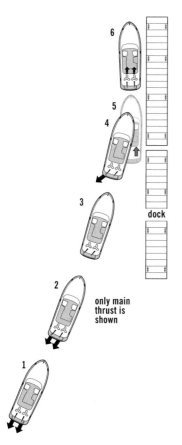

FIGURE 20-3. *Twin-screw docking—adding rudder action.*

engines out of gear and coast toward the pier, applying left rudder to begin swinging the stern. Here's the exciting part. If the boat will slide sideways (see Chapter 12), you can essentially parallel park by using a lot of left rudder with the port clutch ahead (4) and perhaps the starboard astern (5). When you're just about in place, put both engines briefly astern, then out of gear (6).

Using the rudders to steer frees the throttles and clutches to control speed. If leaving both engines in gear causes an overly rapid approach even at idle speed, you can take one engine out of gear to cut your thrust in half and keep the boat pointed in the right direction with adjustments to rudder angle. Because side thrust can be a potent factor even when you apply rudder action, you may have to alternate engines to keep precise directional control. That is, rudder action might not be enough to keep the thrust of a single engine from swinging the stern (and thus the opposite bow) more than you'd like.

Even if your boat won't "slide" sideways, you may be able to walk it in sideways with left rudder by putting the port engine alternately ahead and astern (Figure 20-4), thus swinging first the bow and then the stern closer to the pier. In this case, most likely you won't need to do anything with the starboard engine until you're almost at the float or pier, at which point putting it ahead will stop the bow from swinging in too much, and putting it astern will do the same thing for the other end.

Once again, remember that we landed star-board-side-to in this illustration to contrast it with the one-sided approach preferred with a single screw. You could come in port-side-to just as easily simply by swapping the starboard and port actions described above.

Backing

As we've seen in previous chapters, a major advantage of twin-screw power is better handling when going astern. This makes it much easier to back your boat into a slip, as is preferred by many dockmasters and virtually required for sportfishermen (Figure 20-5).

Docking stern-to is common in Europe; so common it's called a Mediterranean moor. In North America it's usual to simplify matters by sinking outer pilings off the ends of the slips and inserting finger piers between slips. Let's see how to use twin screws for a typical American-style stern-to docking maneuver.

The maneuver itself is easy in its basic form. As Figure 20-6 shows, it's a matter of splitting the clutches to initiate the turn (2), then putting both astern to back in (3), and finally putting both ahead long enough to stop (4).

The variations (or complications, if you wish) are introduced because, despite the superior maneuverability of a twin-screw boat, you have to take nature into consideration, or the move won't go as smoothly as you'd like.

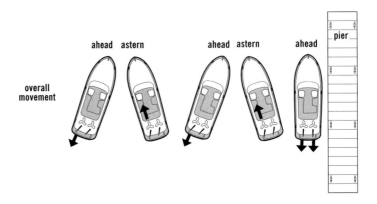

FIGURE 20-4. *"Walking" sideways with twins. Swing is exaggerated for emphasis.*

FIGURE 20-5. *Because sportfishermen are easy to maneuver, and because having the cockpit next to the pier makes it easier to unload the catch, sportfishermen skippers almost always back into their slips.*

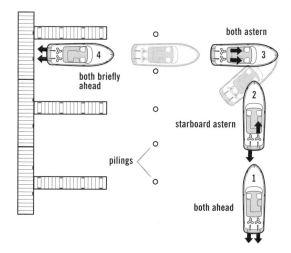

FIGURE 20-6. *Backing in—the technique.*

Effects of Wind

In Figure 20-7 three boats are backing into their respective slips. Boat A, with the wind on its stern, will initiate its turn before arriving at its slip because the wind will keep moving it as it turns. Since wind usually works more on the bow, the bow should point slightly into the wind before backing (2). The wind will then help straighten it out.

Boat B, approaching into the wind, will run beyond its slip and begin backing sooner because, again, the wind will help swing the bow.

The skipper of boat C didn't allow for the wind and is in an awkward position because of it.

If the wind is really strong, it sometimes pays to first put the boat into a position where you have to back into the wind to get into the slip. In this case, you'd follow the suggestions below, which, though initially suggested for handling current, will work for a strong wind as well.

Effects of Current

Because current works more on the stern, it's often easier to maneuver with the current behind you. In Figure 20-8, boat A proceeds just as it would with the wind behind—with one important exception. If current is the major force, you don't need to swing as far around before backing. In fact, with a strong current behind you, you should begin backing *before* you're lined up with the slip, because your stern will continue to swing down-current as you back.

A boat approaching into the current, as boat B is, will be better off turning completely around before getting to the slip and executing the final

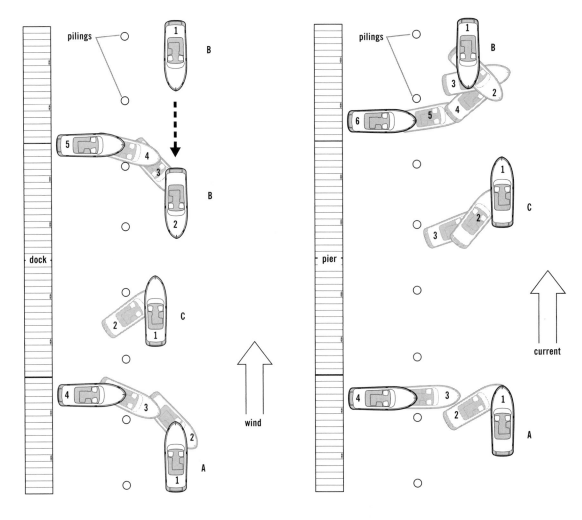

FIGURE 20-7. *Backing in—allowing for wind.*

FIGURE 20-8. *Backing in—allowing for current.*

portions of the maneuver going astern. Here it's usually advisable to back slightly beyond the slip so that when the current sets you down, you'll be in the right position.

Again, failure to allow for nature has put boat C in difficulty.

You've probably noticed that we didn't bother with the rudders this time. That's because, as I mentioned above, twin-screw maneuvers can always be done without them. If rudder action is a big factor on your boat, you can use the steering wheel to help counter the forces of nature. In the above examples, for instance, slight right rudder might have helped slow the bow swing when wind was the major force, and slight left rudder might help keep the stern into the current as you back up. However, this depends greatly on your boat's responses and your ability to find the rudder angle that will help the most. These factors take time to learn, and you'll probably find it much easier initially to ignore your rudders.

21

Docking Transom-Powered Boats

Transom-powered boats, whether outboard or sterndrive, don't handle quite the same as inboards, for reasons examined in Chapter 13. Yet our objectives remain the same when putting a boat into its berth at a pier, which means that many of the suggestions made previously still apply. Indeed, the handling of transom-powered boats is most easily described in terms of differences and similarities relative to conventional drives.

Side Thrust

We've already covered this, but it's so important that I feel compelled to bring it up again. One of the big differences between conventional drives and transom power (perhaps the *major* one) is that outboards and sterndrives can often drastically reduce, if not eliminate completely, the side thrust of inboard-drive systems. Whether this is a blessing or a curse depends on your point of view and the situation at hand. It surely is nice to see the stern of a conventional inboard swing neatly into place alongside the pier when you apply power astern to stop. On the other hand, not being able to back a single-screw inboard the way you might desire is a good example of the downside.

In handling transom power you need to consider the magnitude of side thrust *at maneuvering speeds*, particularly when power is applied astern. If it's considerable, you can handle the boat much as you would a conventional inboard. If side thrust is negligible, as it often will be, different techniques are required.

Single Drive

Let's begin our discussion with a single-drive unit sans side thrust. For clarity, we'll illustrate with an outboard, but the operational differences between an outboard and a sterndrive are minor.

In Figures 21-1A and 21-B we approach a float for a routine landing. We're coming in port-side-to in order to emphasize the differences between transom power and a single-screw inboard. The initial approach is essentially the same for all boats—20 degrees or so off the face of the pier. How we handle the fine-tuning at (2) depends on the boat. If your boat answers the drive-unit "rudder" when you take it out of gear, you can turn the wheel as necessary to correct your heading. Chances are, however, you'll need prop thrust to exercise any appreciable steering control. The secret here is to avoid oversteering and to use no more prop thrust than is required. Your immediate reaction will most likely be to turn the wheel yet further if the boat doesn't respond to its rudder initially, but it's better to use less steering-wheel action and to nudge the throttle in and out of gear to produce the desired result. I can't overemphasize this point. Transom-powered boats tend to understeer in neutral and oversteer in gear, and one of the biggest challenges in handling them is learning the balance of "rudder" and throttle necessary to produce the desired speed and heading without constant weaving. The knowledge will come with practice, and once again I must emphasize that neutral is most definitely a part of your control.

When you get close to the pier (3), put the

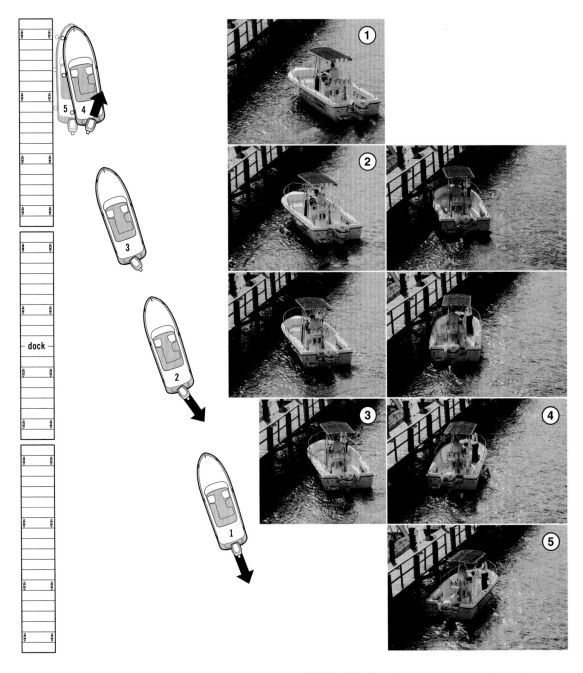

FIGURE 21-1A. *Docking with transom power.*

FIGURE 21-1B. *The docking sequence in photographic detail. The numbered photos relate directly to the text and illustration; the unnumbered photos show what happens in between. The steeper approach angle reflects a proper wind off the pier approach (see page 113).*

"rudder" hard away (in this case, right) to swing the stern in and bring the boat parallel to the pier. Ideally, you'll take the engine out of gear at this point and coast in; considering your lack of rudder action, however, some power may be necessary to effect the steering you desire. Here again, a delicate hand on the throttle with short intervals in and out of gear will allow you to steer as you wish without coming in too fast. As you come alongside (4, 5), use power astern to stop motion ahead as in the situations discussed in previous chapters. The difference here is that you lack significant side thrust and thus have to turn the propeller toward the pier (left rudder) to help pull the stern in as you stop. Note that this is true even if your boat exhibits quite a bit of side thrust because, at the very least, you'll have to get the "rudder" back amidships, and that will require at least a slight turn toward the pier before applying power astern to stop. Since turning the steering wheel toward the pier is counterintuitive (no one wants to crash!), you may have to almost "force" yourself to remember to do it. But, as you'll all too quickly discover if you don't, it's absolutely necessary. Exactly how much of a turn (how much left rudder) is required depends on the degree of side thrust in the unit. Too much rudder causes too much stern swing, and vice versa. You'll have to experiment with your boat to learn how much it takes.

Since we may be using directed main thrust to bring the stern in where we want it (rather than relying totally on side thrust as we did with inboards), landing starboard-side-to would be almost as easy. All you'd have to do is swing the steering wheel the opposite way (and perhaps a bit more, to make up for the lack of side thrust).

Twin Drives

Now let's see what happens with two-drive units. There's no diagram for this one because most dual-drive installations are simply single units used in pairs. Counterrotation, the main ingredient in twin-screw responses, is still quite new in outboards, though it's becoming more common (much more so than with sterndrives to date). Then, too, most outboards, and even some sterndrives, are still usually mounted too close together to make effective use of the "twin-screw" techniques that work so well with inboards. This means you can usually handle twin transom power as if it were single. In fact, I've found it's usually easier to almost forget that you have a dual installation and do your docking maneuvers on one engine alone. This gives you enough power for control, and that's really all you need; the thrust from one motor at idle is enough to provide steerageway, but not enough to move you too fast. Note that maneuvering with the engine on the side away from the pier usually gives you a slight advantage, which is why I suggest you only *almost* forget you have twins.

Backing In

Because transom-powered boats are quite steerable when going astern, they can usually be backed into a slip with ease. The difference is that most turns must be aided with the steering wheel even if you have two units, since dual-drive installations seldom exhibit enough twin-screw action to be handled with throttles and clutches alone. You may also discover that transom-power side thrust will increase or diminish with a change in drive trim angle. If this is so with your boat, minimize side thrust before backing—it will make the job easier.

Figure 21-2 shows a typical maneuver with a single-drive unit. One of a pair would produce basically the same results. If you have a dual installation, you might want to experiment with coming in twin-screw style, but I'll bet ultimately you'll stick with transom-power techniques, because they work better.

Remember that the advice in Chapter 20 regarding allowance for wind and current applies here as well.

Trailering Techniques

They're not exactly docking techniques, but handling a trailer and getting your boat on and off it are often part of transom-powered boating, so let's look at these aspects also.

If your vehicle is suited to the task, towing a trailer is easy. You mainly have to remember that

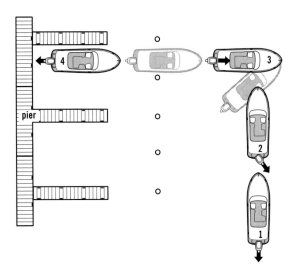

FIGURE 21-2. *Backing with transom power.*

your vehicle is, in effect, a lot longer with a trailer in tow, and it bends in the middle. This means taking wider turns and watching your clearance when you do turn. The fun comes when you back up (Figure 21-3). That bend in the middle can get

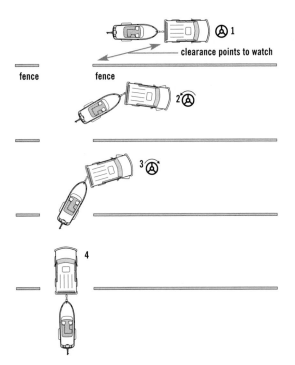

FIGURE 21-3. *Backing a trailer.*

you every time. To make the trailer back the way you want, you have to start backing your towing vehicle the other way (2). Until that gets to be a habit, you'll have problems.

Figure 21-4 shows a tip I learned years ago from a fellow boater whose vocation was driving 18-wheelers. When going ahead, put your hand on the top of the steering wheel and move it in the direction of the desired turn. When backing, put your hand on the bottom of the wheel and do the same. It works.

Once you have the trailer turning the way you want it (Figure 21-3), turn the wheel the other way and follow the trailer back (3), straightening out when you're lined up on the ramp (4).

Before you back all the way, stop and get the trailer and boat ready for the launch. Disconnect the trailer taillights, make sure docklines are made fast on the boat and ready to use, and *make sure the drain plug has been put in* (you might want to double-check this point!). Then back the trailer as far as you need to, keeping in mind that you don't want your drive wheels to get onto the really slippery part of the ramp. When you're in position, chock your vehicle's rear wheels so they can't move back any farther, turn off the engine, and release the winch line from the boat's bow eye.

Depending on the angle of the ramp, the depth of the water (which is influenced by stage of tide in many areas), and the design of your boat and trailer, getting the boat off and floating can be as easy as a gentle shove or as difficult as backing it off with its own power. You'll probably run into every variation sooner or later. If you're able to push it off, you or a companion should have the bow line in hand, ready to secure to a pier as soon as the boat clears the trailer. If you have to power off, you can maneuver the boat back for an easy landing. All that remains then is to park the rig and get aboard!

Hauling the boat is equally easy. Again, you'll want to back in the trailer as far as you can without compromising the traction needed to pull it up the ramp. Many trailer boaters make sure the trailer's bunks are thoroughly wet before hauling, even if it requires backing farther—the boat slides better on wet bunks. Just be sure your towing ve-

22

Using Springlines for Maneuvering

Several years ago I had to "parallel park" a 58-foot yachtfisherman into a tight berth on a nasty day. It was a hairy predicament with the wind blowing about 35 knots off the pier, very shallow water not far from its face, and just room enough (about 60 feet) to squeeze between two other boats. Definitely a get-it-right-the-first-try situation. In fact, if I'd had a choice, I wouldn't have tried it at all! But it was the last available space in the marina, and the weather, bad as it was already, was deteriorating so rapidly that we didn't want to travel on. When we got settled and secured, I thanked the dockmaster for her help—and for letting us have the space. She commented that she had been "turning people away all morning. But I let you come in because I saw you had a hand ready with a springline and were obviously prepared to make it OK."

I can't guarantee that proper use of springlines will get you dock space, but I can promise that it will help you get into—and out of—spaces with greater ease.

A Springline Taxonomy

Before we go through the techniques involved in using springlines, we should get together on what to call them. First, the matter of "lines" in general. It may be "rope" when it's in the store, but once you bring it aboard and put it to work, it becomes a "line." Just what term prefaces the word "line" depends on where and how it's employed; that is, whether it's a bow line, stern line, breast line, or springline, which may be collectively known as

docklines. By convention, springlines get a two-part name. The first part refers to the direction in which the line leaves the boat; the second refers to where it's made fast on the boat (Figure 22-1). That means a *forward-bow spring* leads forward from a cleat at or near the bow, while an *after-bow spring* runs aft from the same cleat. The same applies to *forward-* or *after-quarter* (or *stern*) *springs*. Larger boats have more possibilities, but in the size range of concern in this book, bow and quarter springs are probably all we need.

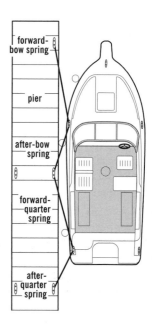

FIGURE 22-1. *Springlines.*

131

Who's On First?

Over the years I've heard many discussions (arguments, even) as to whether you should make one end of the line fast to the boat and handle the free end on the pier or first secure the pier end and do your line handling on the boat. Which is it? At the risk of seeming wishy-washy, I have to say, "It all depends."

On ships, tugs, ferries, and large yachts, the pier end is usually made fast initially (often by dropping the loop of the eye over a bollard or piling), and the line handling is done by the crew aboard ship. This has created the impression among some observers that it's the only correct way. Nonsense. Rather, it's the better way for these situations because the vessels have the crew and working space to make it feasible. As we'll soon see, there are definite advantages to keeping full control of your lines in your own crew's hands.

Many small boats, on the other hand, barely have deck space for the cleat, to say nothing of room for a line handler. Then, too, in many situations you have more available help (in both number and ability) from the dockhands than from your deckhands. In these cases, why not attach the line to the boat and do the handling on the pier? It not only makes sense, but it's often the only option. Not as shippy, perhaps, but practical nonetheless.

Docking

The After-Bow Spring

An after-bow spring is the first line I put ashore 99.9 percent of the time when coming alongside a pier or float. This one line can act as the "poor man's bow thruster" and can help you get alongside and, more important, stay alongside the dock even if wind and current are doing their best to push you away. Figure 22-2 shows how it works. When you go ahead against an after-bow spring, the line keeps the bow from going much ahead or (in this case) swinging to starboard despite the propeller thrust and right rudder. This sets up a parallelogram of forces: Since the stern is swinging in and the bow can't swing away, the boat moves sideways.

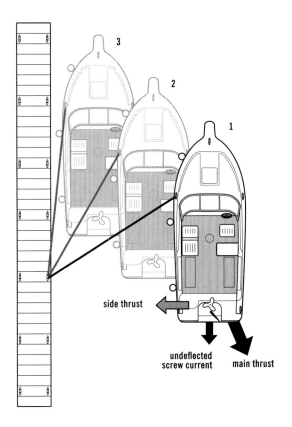

FIGURE 22-2. *Using an after-bow spring to come alongside.*

A nice attribute of a well-placed after-bow spring is that you can nestle stationary against the pier on that one line as long as you leave the engine in gear with the rudder away from the pier. This means that for short stops, such as to let someone run ashore for groceries or cold drinks, it's the only line you need. If you plan to stay awhile and thus will put out other lines, this spring will keep you snugly in place until the other lines are secured.

Essentially two factors control the way in which a boat moves sideways on an after-bow spring. One is the location of the cleat—the point on the boat to which it's made fast. Ideally, it will be nearly straight abeam from the pivot point, which is usually about one-third of the boat's length aft of the bow. The other is the length of the line. Generally speaking, the longer the line, the more the stern swings in; the shorter the line, the more the bow comes in. If cleat location and line length are perfect, you'll slide almost exactly sideways and stay neatly in place, parallel to the pier, on one line alone.

Of course, if the spring is too long, you might run into the boat in front of you; the line has to be properly adjusted for safety even if doing so compromises its performance. Simply changing the point at which the line is made fast ashore can often make it "right" again, but you won't always have this option.

This brings us to the very-strong-wind-off-the-dock landing maneuver. The basic problem is that no matter how close you get to the pier before you stop, a very strong wind will begin to set you away almost immediately. You can *get* there, but *staying* there is another matter. However, if you can get that springline ashore and made fast at both ends, you can't be set off any farther than the length of the line. The only problem is that the springline will often be too long for the available space because of the distance you drift before the line can be made fast at both ends. If you then use the spring to come all the way in, you'll hit the boat lying ahead of you.

The answer is to shorten the line in stages, a simple procedure though not an easy one (Figure 22-3). You must work your way in under power ahead just as far as you dare, then ease slightly astern to create slack in the line. As soon as the slack appears, the line handler lets loose the working end, removes the slack, and then secures the line so you can once again go ahead on it. Most important, you have to do this very, very quickly before you drift out too far, or you won't gain an inch. Naturally, if the line is being handled aboard the boat, communicating with the line handler is easier, and you can give better warning of your intended throttle and clutch actions. That's a prime reason for making the boat end the working end whenever you can.

You may have to repeat the process many times to shorten the line enough to let you bring the boat alongside and into the available space. The more slack you remove each time, the quicker you'll get there, but you can't rush it. If you try to grab too much slack at once, you'll only drift farther away before you can retie the line,

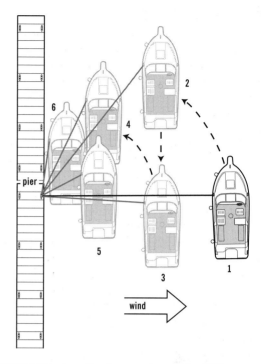

FIGURE 22-3. *An after-bow spring and a little patience can work near miracles in getting a boat against the pier when a strong wind is blowing you away.*

and you'll lose as much or perhaps more than you gained.

The After-Bow Spring with Twin Screws

Using twins in conjunction with an after-bow spring gives you even more control over the boat's sideways movement. For example, the outboard engine (the one away from the pier) will tend to move the bow in faster, while the engine closer to the pier tends to bring the stern in first (Figure 22-4). When lying alongside, the inboard engine will usually hold you close and parallel to the pier, though if the line is too long, the bow will tend to swing out.

The Forward-Bow Spring

This one isn't quite so useful for getting to the pier, but it can help you stay there if for some rea-

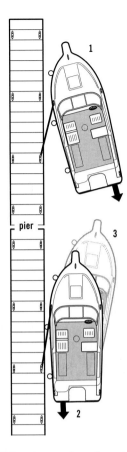

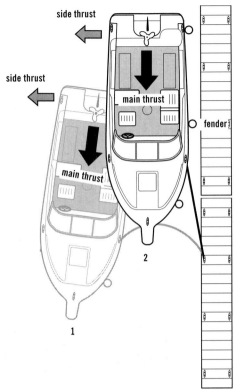

FIGURE 22-4. *With the starboard engine ahead and the port engine in neutral, the stern swings out (1). With just the port engine ahead, the boat will remain at station and parallel to the pier (2) provided the spring is not too long, in which case the bow will swing out (3).*

son (such as not having located something ashore to make fast to) you can't use an after-bow spring. Since you use power astern to make it work (Figure 22-5), the forward-bow spring can also be useful in preventing you from going too far when you have to back into the berth or slip.

You can use a forward-bow spring and power to hold your boat in place without other lines in a manner similar to the after-bow spring (Figure 22-6). It doesn't work quite as well, however, for two reasons. First, the length of a forward-bow spring is even more critical than that of an after-bow spring. The longer it is, the more the bow tends to swing out. This can be countered slightly

FIGURE 22-5. *Backing in against the forward-bow spring.*

FIGURE 22-5. *Backing in against the forward-bow spring (continued).*

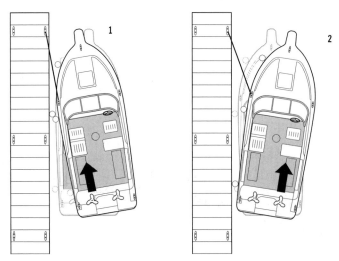

FIGURE 22-6. *When backing against the spring, the inside engine will hold the boat in place but allow the stern to swing slightly out; the outside engine will allow the bow to drift out.*

in a twin screw by using only the inboard engine. There's no solution to the second problem. Propellers running astern aren't as well protected as those running ahead, so they're more prone to damage from flotsam and other debris.

Most of the time, a bow spring is all you need to come into a pier. Chapter 11 showed that control begins at the stern. If you can keep the bow from going where you don't want it to, you can usually get the stern to cooperate with little difficulty. Sometimes a quarter spring will help, but usually it's best not to restrain the stern while you still need control. Remember, if the stern can't swing, you can't do much to make the bow move either. The exception arises when a strong current makes swinging the stern especially difficult, at which point you may need springs at both ends to keep close to the pier. Once you have experimented a few times and have a working grasp of the principles, you'll be able to use a combination of springs whenever conditions require.

So much for using springlines to get in. Now let's see how they can help us get out.

Getting Away

There are a number of ways to use springlines when leaving a berth, but we'll concern ourselves with the two primary techniques. One involves a bow spring and the other a quarter spring, and both work well. The choice depends primarily on whether you're going ahead or astern immediately after leaving the pier. Needless to say, one technique swings the stern clear first while the other moves the bow.

The After-Bow Spring

Figure 22-7 shows that the line that's so handy for getting in can be equally handy for getting out. Many times, all you have to do is swing the rudder toward the pier, and the stern will start moving away. If this isn't enough, and under some conditions it won't be, shortening the line will usually take care of things. Once the stern is far enough out, straighten the rudder, apply power astern, and back away.

With twin screws (Figure 22-8), go ahead on the outboard engine and, if necessary, back on the inboard. When the stern is angled sufficiently to clear the berth, put both engines astern and back away.

The after-bow spring will also work if you want to clear the berth by going ahead. The limiting factor is initial maneuvering room astern. As long as you can back up even a little, the spring will usually let you get the stern far enough out to then swing it back in as you go ahead, pointing the bow away from the pier (Figure 22-9). If the after-bow spring was your first line ashore, making it the last line you cast off is usually easiest.

If you have no room astern, however, and the

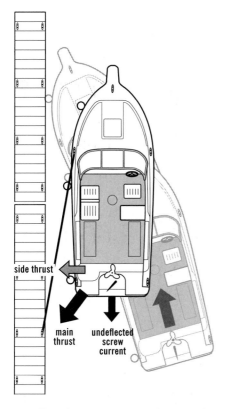

FIGURE 22-7. *Leaving your berth with an after-bow spring—single-screw boat.*

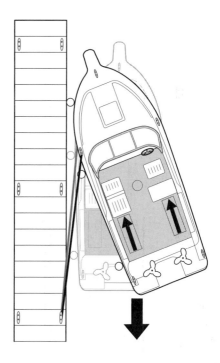

FIGURE 22-8. *Leaving your berth with an after-bow spring—twin-screw boat. Initiate your swing away from the pier by running the outside engine ahead against the spring. When you have the stern sufficiently clear, put the outside engine in neutral, cast off the spring, put both engines astern, and back away from the pier.*

wind is making it difficult to get away, you may want to swing the bow out first. "How can I do that," you ask, "when nothing happens until the stern swings, and the stern *can't* swing through the pier?"

It's easy. Use a forward-quarter springline to create a new combination of forces that will *make* the bow swing out.

The Forward-Quarter Spring

When you apply power astern against a forward-quarter spring, you keep the pier side of the boat from moving back while the screw current tries its best to move the whole boat. Since it can't, it will move the free side, and since the pier prevents the stern from swinging inward as it does, the bow has to swing out (Figure 22-10). Leave the rudder amidships as you do this so that you'll be all set to go straight ahead when you apply power

ahead, which you should do as soon as the bow has swung out enough for a clean getaway.

With twin screws, you'll usually use just the outboard engine astern and then both ahead when it's time to go forward.

Mind Your Ps and Qs

Here we're talking about *protection* and *quickness*. When you use springlines to move away from a pier, the portion of your hull that is held to the pier by line tension will be subjected to considerable compression, especially when you use a forward-quarter spring. In both cases, but especially at the stern, be sure to use a substantial fender or two at the point of contact to protect your topsides.

Because springs are most useful when nature

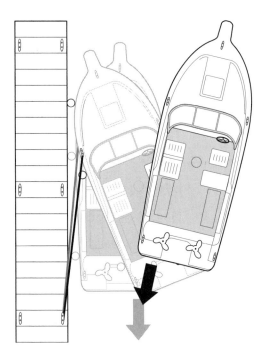

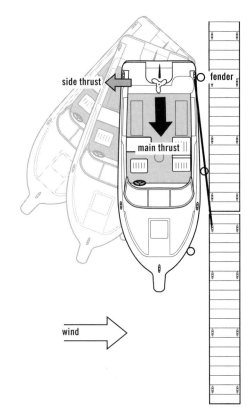

FIGURE 22-9. *Moving ahead on an after-bow spring. If there's room to back up (even just a little) before you move ahead, the same initial actions as in Figure 12-8 will also allow you to get clear of the pier and any boat in front of you. Start as in Figure 12-8 by going ahead on the outside engine. When your stern is out far enough to have some room to swing back toward the pier as you turn, put the outside engine in neutral and cast off the spring. Put both engines astern for just a moment. When you've moved back a bit, put the inside engine ahead, stopping briefly in neutral, of course. (You can leave the outside engine astern, if necessary, to sharpen the swing; otherwise put it in neutral and use only the inside ahead.) When you have cleared the boat in front of you, put both engines ahead and proceed.*

is trying to hold you against the pier (otherwise you could probably get away without them), you must make a quick transition from swinging out to moving away. That means shifting the clutch(es), engaging the throttle(s), and casting off the line with dispatch. Here are a couple of tricks to make things easier.

If you're working with a cleat on a pier or float, hook the eye of your springline over one

FIGURE 22-10. *Leaving your berth with a forward-quarter spring.*

horn of the cleat (Figure 22-11). Tension on the line will hold it in place while you're using it, yet it will come free (often automatically) as soon as the boat starts moving the other way.

If you're working with a piling, secure the springline to the boat, then run it around the piling and back to the boat (Figure 22-12), where

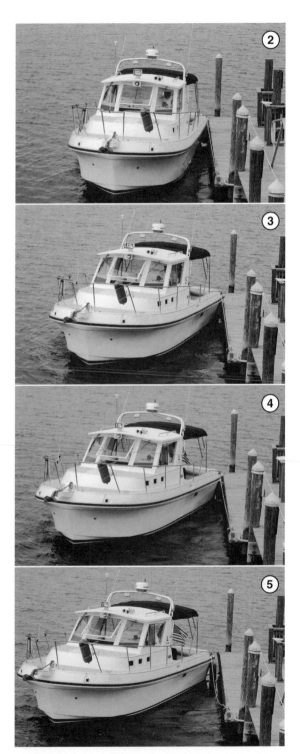

you secure it again. When the time comes to cast it off, you need only undo the second set of hitches to be clear, and you can pull the line aboard as you leave.

This chapter has really only scratched the surface of maneuvering with springlines. The more you work with them, the more you become aware of the kind of help you can expect from different lines as well as when and how to use them.

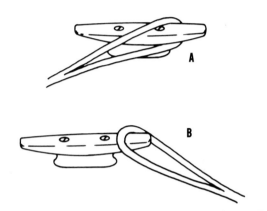

FIGURE 22-11. *With the eye looped over one horn of the cleat, the springline will hold well under strain while the boat pivots (**A**), yet release easily when tension is relaxed (**B**).*

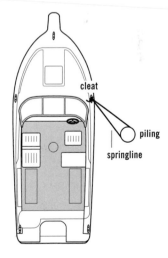

FIGURE 22-12. *When you secure both ends of a springline at the boat, releasing one end will free the line from the piling even when it's out of reach.*

FIGURE 22-10. *Leaving your berth with a forward-quarter spring (continued).*

23

Using Thrusters for Maneuvering?

I put a question mark in the title because I somehow wonder if this chapter is really necessary. Bow (and stern) thrusters are still uncommon on entry-level boats, so I've hesitated to include them among the things you really must know about in order to get started. But there seems to be a trend underway that could change this. Bow thrusters are being installed these days on smaller and smaller boats; even on those we might consider "beginner" size (and the concept of what constitutes beginner size is extending upward also!).

Not long ago, I saw a neat little craft up on a lift along the seawall behind a house. It was a deep-V that appeared to be roughly 30 feet long or slightly less, with clean lines, a nice open cockpit, and a hardtop to cover the helm area forward. It was a very attractive boat. But what really caught my eye were the three outboards on the transom and a thruster tunnel in the bow. Imagine, outboard maneuverability and a bow thruster, too. Amazing! Especially on a boat of that size.

Since it's now apparently quite possible that you can get started in powerboating aboard a thruster-equipped vessel (though I still believe you'll be decidedly in the minority), I'd say it's time to address the issue.

A Helpful Push

Thrusters themselves are far from new; they've been on the scene for decades now. A friend of mine skippered one of the Coast Guard's first thruster-equipped cutters back in the early 1960s, and they weren't new then. Thrusters have been

with us all these years because, in many cases, they serve a constructive purpose. Their use on large ships has eliminated or greatly reduced the need for harbor tugs in docking and undocking, which saves the shipping companies considerable money. Thus, in commercial service, thrusters quickly pay for themselves. So nowadays it's rare to see a large vessel built without at least one bow thruster and, quite often, two or three of them, plus a thruster or more at the stern, as well (Figure 23-1).

Not surprisingly, in a pattern we see in marine equipment of all sorts—that of being initially developed for ships and eventually becoming common on pleasure boats—in recent years thrusters have been made in smaller and smaller sizes to be installed on smaller and smaller boats. They are no longer just for ships and megayachts. And though I personally believe that using thrusters on any vessel smaller than one that would otherwise require the aid of tugs is "cheating" (and usually quite unnecessary), I must confess that they can be a godsend *at times* for the skipper of any vessel.

Personal Experience

When we built the 80-foot trawler yacht on which I was living and working when I wrote the first edition of this book, one of the many compromises we made was to forgo a bow thruster in favor of other things the owner and I thought would be more universally desirable and thus a better use of his money. After all, the boat had a 25-foot beam, and the shafts would be 11 feet apart on

FIGURE 23-1. *The "blades in a circle" symbol on the bow of this container ship tells us the vessel is thruster-equipped. On ships and other large vessels, bow thrusters eliminate or greatly reduce the need for harbor tugs, thus saving their owners considerable money. On any vessel that never needs the aid of a tug, a bow thruster falls in the "nice, but* definitely not necessary" *category.*

center. I figured an 11-foot spread would make for some pretty good leverage when maneuvering with the twin screws. Of course, I neglected to consider the results of wind against a high bow that was nearly 80 feet in front of the screws. That made a pretty good lever, too. Fortunately, over the 3-plus years that I ran that boat, there were only three times I really wished we had included a bow thruster. So on the whole, it was a minor issue; just three times in over 3 years is insignificant. But on each of those occasions, a bow thruster would have made a major difference. A thruster could have shifted the situation from one that was largely in the hands of Mother Nature to one that was merely difficult (or better) but at least somewhat under my control. As it was, lacking direct movement of the bow and not wanting to exacerbate an already sticky situation by adding powered movement to the stern, all I could do was hold my breath and pray. A thruster would have been sooo nice.

Fortunately, no serious harm resulted on any of those occasions, and everything turned out OK. But I do believe they each grayed my hair a bit more. Yet I still have to believe that in the whole scope of things, a bow thruster on an 80-foot yacht is an unnecessary luxury. Nice to have at times, for sure, but certainly not required. And, of course, that applies in spades to boats of less

than 80 feet. But I'm beginning to think I don't have a whale of a lot of company in this belief.

Size Doesn't Matter

At least as it now seems to apply to how small a vessel can be thruster equipped. Then again, in many ways, size *is* relevant. Thrusters must be proportionate to a boat's LOA, draft, displacement, and windage and must fit the hull perfectly in both diameter and available thrust. But these days, bow thrusters come in a wide variety of sizes and horsepower and are often included routinely, at least as planned-for options, on boats well under 50 feet LOA.

For that matter, my first experience with a stern thruster was aboard a 36-footer. It was a single-screw trawler, and the thruster was a self-contained stainless steel unit designed to be bolted on a transom just below the waterline with minimal yard time and nearly zero alteration of the hull's watertight integrity. It was a retrofitter's dream.

I had been hired by the thruster's inventor to write copy for a brochure, and we agreed some firsthand experience would help. I have to admit that although I had long seen ample evidence of what a bow thruster could do for the handling of ships and large yachts, I had serious reservations about the value of adding a stern thruster to a single-screw boat. After all, I thought, control of the stern is already there; the problems, should any arise, will be way up forward.

Was I wrong! If you recall what I wrote about the typical single-screw tendency to resist backing straight, you'll understand my reaction when I was able to back that trawler into a slip as smoothly and directly as any twin-screw sportfisherman. Yes! The key, of course, was to counter the screw-induced side thrust that would normally prevent backing straight with opposing side thrusts from the device on the transom. It worked.

In truth, this push straight to the side is the main advantage of thrusters. Though the bow and stern of any boat (and especially a twin-screw) can be moved sideways as a result of prop and rudder action, there's also inevitably at least some movement ahead or astern also. With thrusters, all movement is straight sideways. Plus, with a bow thruster you have direct control of the bow, while without it, any bow movement can come only after some stern swing, which *always* comes first.

A friend once told me about the stares (and a bit of applause) he received after sliding a 150-foot megayacht straight sideways into an alongside berth that was only slightly longer than the yacht. "I just came in parallel to the pier and stopped her with the mains when we were off the berth," he said, "and then I used the bow and stern thrusters alone to finish the job and slide straight in. I raised a few eyebrows because I don't think anyone ashore had ever seen a boat handled that way before. They were astonished."

I mention that incident because it brings up an important point: Docking with thrusters usually demands a different technique from the one you would use to dock without them. So you have to realize that instead of being a simple answer to potential docking problems, as these devices are so often advertised, a thruster can really mean you have more to learn. And practice! Because repeated practice remains the one and only way to get good at docking. You have to just do it. And do it. And do it. 'Til you get it right. And that truth

holds whether you have single or twin screws, and thrusters at one end of the boat or both. To repeat: There's no substitute for practice to become competent at docking; adding a thruster to the mix only adds another element of handling to learn and another variable to practice with. It also involves learning (and practicing) two techniques for nearly every situation—one for when you use the thruster; one for when you don't. And you definitely still need to practice docking without the thruster if only to cover yourself on that day when, for whatever reason, you no longer have a *working* thruster. As you can see, the cost of having a thruster aboard is not entirely monetary.

Learning the Routine

Let's examine a couple of typical situations. First, to refresh your memory as to what you'd do without a thruster, please review the procedure for docking a twin-screw boat alongside a pier as outlined in Chapter 20. Then come back here, and we'll examine the differences.

With Thruster Power

When we use a bow thruster, the approach changes. This time we aim the bow straight toward a spot on the pier that's just a tiny bit behind where we want it to end up. When we're almost there, we again use power astern to stop, but this time on the outboard main only, which also swings the stern in toward the pier as it halts forward progress. We prevent the bow from swinging away from the pier with short bursts from the bow thruster (Figure 23-2).

If necessary, a short bump or two of power ahead (at dead idle) on the inboard main will keep us from sliding back. But most often, the stern swing that results from putting the outboard engine astern will be enough to bring it in without making much sternway because any force that would tend to pull the boat backward is balanced by the momentum of approach, which still wants to take it forward.

Similarly, if you're stopped parallel to your desired alongside berth, instead of "walking" the boat sideways with alternate thrusts ahead and astern from your outboard engine (as described in Chapter 20), just put it astern and use the thruster to push the bow. This will require a bit more use of the thruster than if you had first put the bow nearer the pier (just remember to use it in short bursts only), and maybe a bit more push ahead from the inboard main (to keep from sliding backward), but otherwise it's essentially the same as described above. The main difference is that in this situation you use the thruster to move the bow toward the pier, rather than merely to hold it there (Figure 23-3).

So yes, a thruster can help you with alongside docking. But as we saw in the previous chapter, so can an after-bow spring. And lines cost a lot less than thrusters. Plus, they don't require

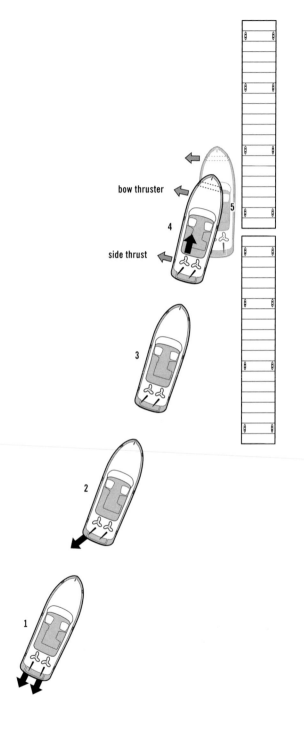

bow thruster

side thrust

FIGURE 23-2. *Docking alongside with the aid of a bow thruster.*

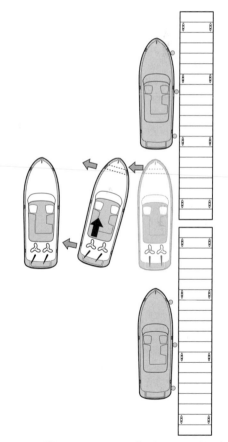

FIGURE 23-3. *"Parallel parking" with the aid of a bow thruster.*

anywhere near the maintenance, and their effects are more predictable.

Backing Into a Slip

This is where a thruster can really shine. If the wind and current are from any direction other than dead astern, the bow will tend to swing a bit to one side or the other, even if the general overall movement of the boat is straight back. While you can compensate for this bow swing with minor adjustment of the throttles or clutches, whatever you do with them will also affect the stern as well, even if only slightly.

But when you use some thruster action to offset bow swing, the general behavior of your boat can be as if there were no wind or current.

Of course, you can accomplish this without the thruster. If, instead of trying to back straight in, you start with the boat angled slightly into the wind or current, or back into the wind (as I described in Chapter 20), you'll back around and end up straight. The forces of nature will assist rather then hinder your maneuver. Yes, this will require a judgment call on your part in order to get the correct angle, and if you misjudge it won't work exactly as planned. But again, with practice, your judgment will improve along with your other abilities. So even here, a thruster can be considered nice, but not necessary.

Shifting Winds

This is when a thruster can be invaluable. It's impossible to align the boat to allow for what Mother Nature will do when the wind refuses to blow at a constant speed from a single direction! Each of those three times I regretted not having a thruster on the trawler yacht involved swirling or shifting winds. (I've always known them as *williwaws*, though I understand that technically the term applies only to whirlwinds in the Strait of Magellan.)

Fortunately, these unpredictable winds don't crop up all the time. But when they do, they can really complicate maneuvering. A bow thruster is nice because you can hold the bow against the wind no matter which way it blows—even if it changes direction midmaneuver, which can really throw off advance planning! I must caution you, though, that you should never shift the thrust immediately from one side to the other; you must always allow time for the thruster's prop(s) and motor to come to a complete stop before reversing their direction for thrust the other way.

Lacking a bow thruster, you have only a few options in a whirling or shifting wind. One of them is to wait, as these conditions don't always last very long. But they can! Sometimes, all day. So waiting isn't always a *practical* option, though a short wait to see what's really happening is never a bad idea.

During that time, you should try to assess which wind direction seems to predominate. If you're lucky, there will be one direction, and you can use it in planning your maneuver. Of course, there's no guarantee it will remain the same when you finally attempt your move, so don't count on it too heavily.

Another possibility is to go somewhere else where the weather might be more cooperative. I'd suggest taking this option unless you absolutely *have to* dock right there.

In that case, your only real option is to take a deep breath, pray to whichever higher power you believe in, cross your fingers, and hope that you get through it OK.

The Bottom Line

Given that a bow thruster can be the only solution to boathandling in shifting winds, you might be inclined to think having one is a must. But think again. Realistically, we can't always afford to equip our boats with everything we may need just once in a while. And shifting winds are definitely a "once in a while" condition in most places. But even if you can afford to buy it, you have to look at the complete picture. Every piece of gear you put aboard not only has its purchase price, but you generally have to consider maintenance as well. Some require a little care; others need more. I'd put thrusters in the latter category, which suggests having one aboard will mean more work for you to do, or hire someone else to do if you don't have the knowledge or time to do the maintenance yourself. Because it's not just the thruster itself that needs attention, but all the ancillary equipment, too.

Remember also, unlike your main engines, which you can leave in gear and have "working" for you for essentially unlimited stretches, you can only apply a thruster in short spurts—usually 4 seconds or less. Exactly how long those thrusts can be will depend on the size and power of your unit (be sure to read your owner's manual thoroughly!), but all electric thrusters—which is what you'll find on most small-boat installations—have a time limit both as to the length of continuous operation and also to total running time per hour. This is partly because of the battery power that continuous running would use up, but also because the motor can overheat if it's run any longer than recommended. Hence, your use of a thruster must be rationed, which is another aspect you have to learn so you don't waste it prematurely.

Another consideration is the increased weight forward. In addition to the thruster and its tunnel, you might also need to place the thruster's dedicated battery (and perhaps a dedicated battery charger) up there too, to save having to run heavy cables from the engine compartment (thruster motors draw a huge current). That extra weight can quickly add up. Then there are the holes the tunnel puts in your hull—one on each side of the bow. You have to consider what these factors will do to your boat's performance when you're not concerned with docking; in other words, most of the time.

Neither the added weight nor interruption of hull surface should be a major problem if the thruster is properly sized, but no act can be without consequence. And when you make changes to the total weight aboard and its distribution, as well as doing something that will affect the flow of water across the bottom, you can't help but change your boat's performance in some way, even if ever so slightly. Most of the time, the difference will be negligible. But you still have to consider it in your plans. In short, you should carefully analyze and evaluate *all* aspects of the installation before you add a thruster to your boat.

Final Thoughts

If you get the impression I'm anti-thruster, I apologize. This is not the case at all. I actually like bow thrusters! And if available, I'll happily use thruster power whenever appropriate on any size boat. And though I've so far written mainly about using a thruster as a docking aid, a bow thruster can be very helpful in *un*docking also; especially when the wind is blowing onto the pier, or when you want to swing the bow out into an oncoming current. But I still have to classify a bow thruster as unnecessary on any vessel that wouldn't otherwise require the aid of tugs, and on most boats that have a thruster, I use it sparingly. A thruster is definitely *not* a magic "silver bullet" that will somehow make maneuvering easy in every situation. It can help, of course, but only to assist in offsetting the effects of wind on the bow during an otherwise sound maneuver. And the only way you're going to make sound maneuvers every time is to practice, practice, practice. There simply is no hardware you can buy, thrusters included, that can do more to help your boat-handling than the "software" of improved awareness and function you build in your mind and body through repeated practice.

Now, I realize I can consider thrusters "nice but not necessary" for docking because I've been doing it for so long; you simply can't beat years of experience for making a job easier. But I also have to acknowledge that in my case it's not longevity alone, it's the *kind* of experience I was fortunate enough to gain early in my career. Way back when I first started out as a professional, I had two jobs that, together, covered over 5 years. And on each of them, I had to make twenty to twenty-two landings a day, six days a week, for fifty weeks a year. That meant I was docking in all kinds of weather, in all sorts of sea conditions, and doing it repeatedly. This kind of docking activity could produce only two possible results: either I would get to be quite good at it, or I'd become frustrated and decide to find another line of work. Of course, I'm still running boats, so I'm pleased to say it was the former.

I know there's no way a typical pleasure-boat skipper can acquire that kind of experience; if you spent that much time aboard, you might have a hard time coming up with the money to afford it. Plus, you'd probably get bored doing that many landings and departures just for the sake of practice. But it does show the value of repetition, and I hope you'll try to emulate it to a degree, though I do suggest you apply some moderation. In truth, these days I typically do only about three or four landings a day myself, and I'm rarely on the water every day. Plus, because I'm mostly doing day or evening charters for people who are out to have a good time, it's generally only in fair weather,

too. So these days my docking activity is more like a typical pleasure-boat owner. But this limited activity is enough to keep me from getting rusty because the skills I acquired years ago from that enforced practice have stood me well over time. And so I suggest again that if you want to reduce whatever problems you may encounter with docking and undocking, you just go out and practice, practice, practice. The effort should pay off. And then, if you desire to add a bow thruster to your boat—and if you can afford it in all respects, including the increased maintenance demands it brings—go ahead. A thruster can be very nice to have on board. Just never even *think* you can't live without one.

24

Using Docklines

To me, one of the saddest sights is a beautiful boat tied up with a rat's nest of docklines. Not only does this look terrible, but it can be hazardous—improperly secured docklines may not be secure at all. And it's such a shame, because doing it right is usually easier than doing it wrong.

A correct dockline configuration consists of the proper number of adequately sized lines deployed in directions that will best hold the boat in place despite nature's attempts to move it. The exact arrangement will vary with the circumstances, but the basics are universal. As you'll discover, rigging proper mooring lines for your boat involves only a few simple principles and knowledge of how and when to apply them. The better you know the "how," the less trouble you'll have with the "when."

In the Slip

Five or six lines are usually all you need to hold a boat securely in a slip. In Figure 24-1 we see that the lines from the bow (A) prevent side-to-side movement forward, and if the pilings are far enough ahead of the boat, they also prevent it from moving very far back. When the pilings are closer to the bow, a forward-bow spring (B) prevents backward movement. The crossed stern lines (C) hold the after section laterally but won't stop forward movement totally because they scissor. However, an after spring (D or D1; you would seldom need both) will do that job.

Since the load is spread rather evenly over five

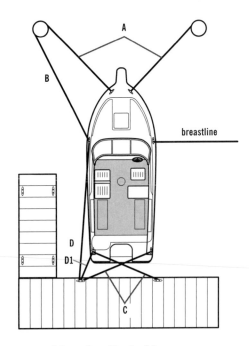

FIGURE 24-1. *Lines for slip docking.*

or six working lines, you'll rarely have to add more or double up. In a strong blow from starboard, a breastline straight out to a dock, piling, or even an anchor would take some of the strain off the starboard bow and stern lines. If you do double up for security, be sure to equalize the length of the lines to balance the load, or the added lines won't help much. The shorter line will overload before the longer line takes much strain.

Alongside

Three or four lines will hold a boat alongside a
float or pier (Figure 24-2). As mentioned in Chapter 22, we generally put out the after-bow spring
(A) first because it can help us come alongside
and hold us there until we get the other lines set.
Since we want to maintain control until we no
longer need it, leave the stern free to swing and
put out the bow line (B) second. When that is set,
add the stern line (C). Please note that to hold
best, it should go ashore from the outboard cleat.

If the bow line is long enough (thus making an
acute angle with the dock), it will keep you from
sliding back. A shorter bow line calls for a forward-quarter spring (D).

If you feel the need for greater security, you
can spread the load to six lines by adding another
bow line (E), which is preferably rigged to a cleat
not used by the first bow line, and another stern
line (F). As in Figure 24-1, a strong blow from
starboard would suggest another line or two in
that direction.

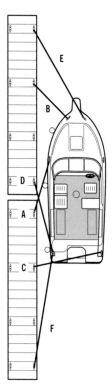

FIGURE 24-2. *Lines for lying alongside a float or
pier.*

Considering Tide

If your docklines are long enough and cut a good
angle, they will usually work for either fixed or
floating piers, at least in the most commonly encountered tidal ranges. One huge difference is
that when tying up to a floating pier, all lines can
be brought up as short and snug as possible, and
you don't need to worry about angles—the boat
and float will rise and fall together. If the lines are
going to pilings or a fixed pier, you'll need to leave
some slack to allow for tide unless they're long
and cut a good angle. If you should venture to an
area of extreme range, just pay attention to what
local boaters are doing. Amply long docklines
coupled with a single breastline to the pier may
do the trick. The breastline is kept snug and adjusted periodically with the tide to keep the boat
close alongside while the other lines are slack.

One way to simplify dockline handling is with
a permanent set at your home berth. You can cut
them to the exact length you need for that location, with eyes on the boat ends. When you come
in you need only pick up the lines, slip the eyes
over your cleats, and you're all set. It's quick and
easy. You then keep your other lines stowed to
use only when you visit marinas, waterfront
restaurants, and other locations. Permanent lines
add expense, but the time and effort they save
can be well worth it.

Now that we've seen how to deploy docklines,
let's take a closer look at the gear involved. When
it comes to the lines themselves, there are two
criteria for "big enough." One is working strength
(Figure 24-3), which will generally put you in the
ballpark. However, modern synthetics are very
strong for their size, so you can have sufficient
strength in a line that's otherwise too small. For
example, in mooring lines you have to consider
abrasion and comfort in handling. A smaller line
will wear down more quickly than a larger one because there's less bearing surface. And because
the line has less diameter to begin with, nicks,
scrapes, and general wear take a proportionately
greater toll than they do on thicker line. A $1/16$-inch
deep cut leaves about 90 percent strength in a $5/8$-
inch line but only 80 percent in a $3/8$-inch line. If
the $5/8$-inch line was oversized to begin with, 90
percent working strength is probably adequate,

SIZE		MANILA		POLYPROPYLENE (MONOFILAMENT)		NYLON	
Diameter (in.)	Circumference (in.)	Breaking test (lbs.)	Weight (lbs. per 100 ft.)	Breaking test (lbs.)	Weight (lbs. per 100 ft.)	Breaking test (lbs.)	Weight (lbs. per 100 ft.)
1/4	3/4	600	2.0	1,250	1.2	1,650	1.5
5/16	1	1,000	2.9	1,900	1.8	2,550	2.5
3/8	1 1/8	1,350	4.1	2,700	2.8	3,700	3.5
7/16	1 1/4	1,750	5.25	3,500	3.8	5,000	5.0
1/2	1 1/2	2,650	7.5	4,200	4.7	6,400	6.5
5/8	2	4,400	13.3	6,200	7.5	10,400	10.5
3/4	2 1/4	5,400	16.7	8,500	10.7	14,200	14.5
13/16	2 1/2	6,500	19.5	9,900	12.7	17,000	17.0
7/8	2 3/4	7,700	22.5	11,500	15.0	20,000	20.0
1	3	9,000	27.0	14,000	18.0	25,000	26.0
1 1/16	3 1/4	10,500	31.3	16,000	20.4	28,800	29.0
1 1/8	3 1/2	12,000	36.0	18,300	23.7	33,000	34.0
1 1/4	3 3/4	13,500	41.8	21,000	27.0	37,500	40.0
1 5/16	4	15,000	48.0	23,500	30.5	43,000	45.0
1 1/2	4 1/2	18,500	60.0	29,700	38.5	53,000	55.0
1 5/8	5	22,500	74.4	36,000	47.5	65,000	68.0
1 3/4	5 1/2	26,500	89.5	43,000	57.0	78,000	83.0
2	6	31,000	108.0	52,000	69.0	92,000	95.0
	Recommended Working Loads:	20% of breaking test		17% of breaking test		11% of breaking test	

FIGURE 24-3. *The tensile strength of new, unused rope is determined according to Cordage Institute standard test methods. The working loads recommended in the table are based on rope in good condition with appropriate splices and should not be exceeded without expert knowledge of conditions and a professional assessment of the risks. The working loads shown are for twisted rope; recommended working loads for braided rope are 15 to 20 percent of tensile strength. (Courtesy Cordage Institute)*

but if the 3/8-inch line was just right, 80 percent won't be enough. Then, too, larger line is easier on the hands. Smaller sizes tend to cut into human flesh if there's much strain involved, and there can be under many conditions. Within practical limits, the larger the line, the better the grip you can get. One of the most unfortunate practical limits is your deck hardware. Boatbuilders tend to choose sizes that will look good on the boat, and this means that smaller boats get short-changed. Too often, you cannot use the most appropriate size of line because it's too big for the hardware. Do the best you can.

What about length? For bow lines, I generally

recommend the distance from the bow cleat to just ahead of the prop(s) measured through the water. This is the length you'll end up with if you drop the line overboard, so why not start this way? Stern lines can be a bit shorter, but you might make them as long as the bow lines for interchangeability. Springlines should be longer, but exactly how long depends on such variables as tidal range, whether you'll moor to fixed or floating piers, etc. Twice the length of your boat will not be far out of line except for a few unusual circumstances (a very small boat in a great tidal range on a fixed pier would require longer, for example). If you mark the bitter ends, you can tell at a glance which line is which. I put one turn of whipping twine on the ends of the shortest lines, two turns on the medium, and three on the long. Tightly bound turns of electrical tape will work as well.

Although line stowage can be a problem, carrying two for each cleat will allow you to double up in severe weather. The added safety factor justifies the effort.

As for fiber, there's only one practical choice—nylon. Natural fibers rot too quickly if not cared for properly. Dacron doesn't stretch enough, and polypropylene suffers from exposure to ultraviolet rays. Commercial boats often use polypro for large-diameter line where the added weight of nylon could make a difference in handling. They also subject their lines to so much wear that replacement is usually necessary before ultraviolet damage can take its toll. Chances are you won't have the same conditions, so stick with nylon.

There's also a choice between ordinary three-stranded twisted construction and braided line. I confess to straddling, though I like braided more and more as time goes by. Three-strand costs less, but braided is stronger size for size. Braided is more flexible and easier to handle, though it doesn't wear quite as well since the outer braid

is more susceptible to damage from rough surfaces. Braided has slightly less stretch, but the difference is negligible; it's still nylon and still offers the shock-absorber effect. Braided line also seems harder to splice, though once you learn how it really isn't. Ultimately the choice is one of personal preference.

All lines will last longer if you use chafing gear (Figure 24-4), including hardware in the form of chocks, hawsepipes, or fairleads wherever line must change direction. If a line doesn't lead directly from boat cleat to shore, you need one of the above. Make sure hardware surfaces are completely smooth inside and out (some have hidden sharp edges and can do more harm than good) and that the radius is compatible with both the diameter of the line and the bend it must make around the device. The sharper the bend, the larger the radius. If you have a sportfisherman or other boat in which the stern cleats are recessed in the cockpit, pay particular attention to how the stern lines will lead as they exit the boat. If the fairleads are in the aft ends of the *covering boards* [the sportfisherman's equivalent of narrow side decks between cockpit coaming and rail], a single stern cleat to port and one to starboard will work fine. If the fairleads are in the sides of the boat, it's better to have two on each side—one in the tran-

FIGURE 24-4. *Chafing gear can be as simple as a piece of hose slid over the line and tied, stitched, or otherwise seized in place.*

som and one on the topside quarter (possibly with an accompanying cleat for each). This will allow you to run stern lines in any fashion and use forward-quarter springs without having to go around the corner of the transom.

Your lines will last longer if you add chafing gear at every point of potential wear. You can use store-bought devices such as guards and tape or the less attractive, equally effective, and less expensive alternative, lengths of split hose.

Don't forget chafing gear, otherwise known as fenders (Figure 24-5), for the boat itself. The determining factors for size are the weight and windage of your boat. Select fenders with sufficient diameter to provide reserve protection after they have compressed under the load of your boat and whatever is pushing it against the pier or piling. Depending on the berth, you may need from two to four to provide adequate protection for a boat more than 22 feet long. This means carrying a minimum of four fenders (leaving your other side to the other guy if necessary) to a maximum of eight. Six should cover you well most of the time.

If you often have pilings between you and the pier, consider carrying fender boards (Figure 24-6) in addition to fenders, especially if there's much range to the tide. Hang one fender board (which may or may not have some padding of its own) between the piling and a pair of fenders, and you'll be thoroughly protected as the tide

FIGURE 24-6. *A fender board will protect a hull against pilings better than a single fender. As the tide goes up and down, and the boat moves forward and back in its slip, some portion of the board will always remain between hull and piling.*

rises and falls, even if the boat shifts slightly forward or aft in the process.

Finally, consider protection for the fenders. Most of them are made of a soft white plastic that soils with use. While there are fender cleaners on the market, it's easier to use washable cloth covers to keep your fenders pristine.

Getting Attached

Now that we've discussed the principles and the gear, let's look at the details—the little points to consider in doing a truly professional job of securing a boat.

The cleat is the most common object you'll find for attaching a line, yet it's amazing how often the task is done incorrectly. Usually you have only to drop the eye over the cleat. If you suspect that the eye may pop free, however, a couple of precautions will make sure it won't. The first (Figure 24-7) is more difficult to undo, but it holds well even when there's no strain on the line. I recommend it especially for those times when you attach the line to the boat and work the shore end. Just push the whole eye through the space between the mounting bolts and drop it back over the horns.

The second precaution (Figure 24-8) is better

FIGURE 24-5. *Fenders are a bit like pocket change—you can almost never have too much of a good thing.*

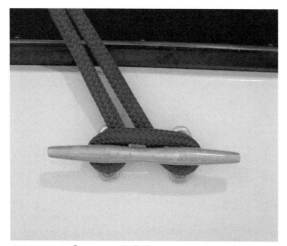

FIGURE 24-7. *One way to belay an eye to a cleat.*

FIGURE 24-8. *Another way to make fast an eye to a cleat.*

for eye-ashore handling. Simply loop the eye around the cleat twice before putting any strain on the line. This way, a slack line can be flipped off the cleat from on deck, yet a line under strain cannot come undone accidentally.

Now for the belaying of a working end with no eye (Figure 24-9). Remember, always put one turn around the base first. This ensures that *both* sides of the cleat (horns and mounting bolts) share the load. Then take two or three crisscross (figure-eight) turns—the exact number depending on the relationship of line size to cleat size—and finish with a half hitch that follows the same pattern as

FIGURE 24-9. *Proper belaying of a line that does not terminate in an eye. Always apply a round turn first; finish with a half hitch.*

the crisscross windings. This allows a relatively easy release even if the line has been under abnormal strain. If you need to shorten the line, simply undo the hitch, back off the riding turns, take up the slack, and then belay it again. Any other cleat belay will one day force you to cut a jammed line to get it free.

Piling It Up

Pilings are also easy to attach to. If the eyes of your docklines are big enough, you can drop them over the pilings and work the other ends on your boat. However, the eyes of many commercially available docklines are too small to do this. You can fashion a bigger loop by passing the standing part of the line through the eye or by tying a bowline (Figure 24-10) in one end of the line. Passing the end through the eye to form a loop may seem easier, but it will snug up under tension and probably leave you more firmly attached than you would prefer. The bowline loop can be flipped off with ease.

If there's already another line on the piling, be sure to dip your line's eye through the eye of the other line (Figure 24-11). This way, either line can be removed without disturbing the other.

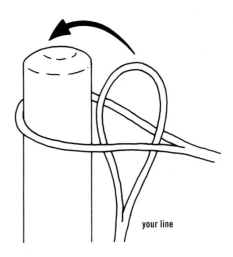

FIGURE 24-11. *Putting the eye of your line up through the eye of a line that's already on the piling allows either line to be removed without disturbing the other.*

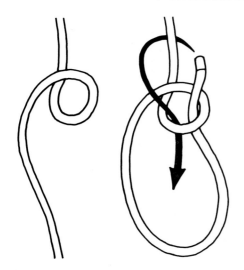

FIGURE 24-10. *The bowline is as near to all-purpose as a knot can be.*

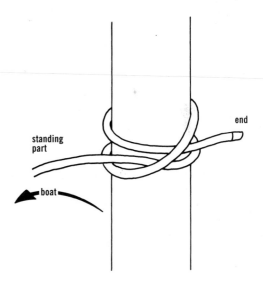

FIGURE 24-12. *To make a clove hitch, pass the end of the line around the piling and under the standing part. Then pass it around again, over the first turn, tucking the end under the start of the second turn.*

When putting a line *over* a piling is impossible, you'll have to use one of two other methods to make the line fast after you pass it *around* the piling. One is a clove hitch on the piling (Figure 24-12). Pass the end under the standing part, then around the piling again. The free end then goes *under* the most recent turn. The clove hitch is fine for short layovers, but it has two drawbacks. First, it must be under constant tension, or it can come undone by itself. Second, if it comes under too much tension, a clove hitch can be nearly impossible to undo. Supplementing the clove hitch with a half hitch around the standing part alleviates the first drawback but not the second. A better method is to take a couple of turns around the piling and then a couple of half hitches or a clove hitch around the standing part (Figure 24-13). Incidentally, either of these methods is also good for hanging fenders from your rails.

There are hundreds of knots you can learn if you wish, but all you need are the bowline, the clove hitch, the half hitch, and the cleat belay. If you learn these techniques well, you'll have no trouble securing your boat at any pier.

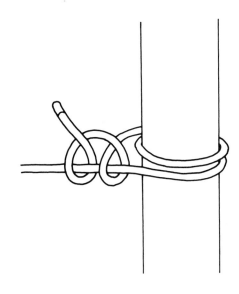

FIGURE 24-13. *Sometimes putting a clove hitch on a piling is not such a good idea. Another option is to take a couple of turns around the piling, then tie a clove hitch on the standing part. This is also called a "round turn and two half hitches."*

PART FOUR

Enjoying Your Boat

25

A Matter of Safety

Now that you've learned how to choose the right boat and what it takes to handle it, you're *almost* ready to go boating. But there a few other things to consider before you ever cast off a line or touch a throttle. The most important is basic boating safety.

Please understand that this subject is not presented out of fear, either actual or implied. Accident statistics show us that going out in your new boat is probably safer than stepping into your bathtub at home. In fact, you're *much* better off in the boat—that tub can really hurt you!

However, boating is statistically safe primarily because the great majority of skippers prudently take steps to keep it that way. Admittedly, sometimes this is because the safety measures are mandated by law and carry stiff penalties for failure to comply. But many are strictly voluntary. Yet people also comply with these "laws" because they know not doing so could carry a potentially stiffer penalty—their life, or the lives of loved ones. Boating safely is not difficult, and it should become second nature as you gain experience (if you develop good habits), but initially you'll probably have to give the matter some conscious thought. This chapter is meant to help you by getting those thoughts—and good habits—started.

The first thing to remember (and remember, and remember) is that the fuel all powerboats must have aboard to run their engines does its job by exploding within the cylinders. Which means it also has the potential to burn or explode *outside* your engines' cylinders. And that we want to avoid.

Back in Chapter 7, I wrote that diesel fuel is safer than gasoline because it's less explosive. Well, it *is* safer, but it still burns. And in reality a fire aboard is a potential disaster whether it starts slowly or with a boom; gasoline just requires greater care. Whether you have gas or diesel, your number-one safety rule should be: TREAT FUEL AND FUEL SYSTEMS WITH THE UTMOST CARE AND RESPECT AT ALL TIMES.

You might initially respond, "Wait a minute, my car burns gas, and I don't have to give it a second thought. Why make a big thing out of the fuel on my boat?"

You saw the reason back in Chapter 7 also. But since it was mentioned then more or less in passing, it might not have made a lasting impression. So I repeat it here for emphasis. Fuel vapors are heavier than air. Because your car's engine compartment is open to the atmosphere, the vapors will dissipate as they fall toward the ground. Because they go away, they aren't a problem.

Not so aboard your boat. There, when fuel vapors sink to the lowest parts of your boat they have nowhere else to go, so they can accumulate. If you allow it, the concentration will eventually reach the *lower explosive limit* (LEL) and *BOOM!* Consequently, aboard boats we have to be extra careful to prevent that accumulation.

Federal law helps us with this. Since the late 1970s, gasoline-powered boats have had to have a natural ventilation system for all enclosed compartments that contain either engine(s) or fuel tank(s). (Fuel tanks that are built in with no air

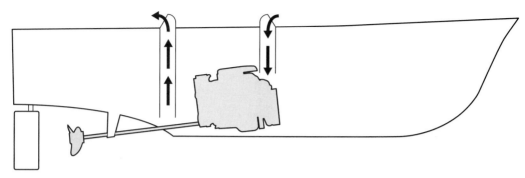

FIGURE 25-1. *A natural ventilation system consists of at least two ducts fitted with cowls or their equivalent. Exhaust duct(s) must extend from the open atmosphere to the lower portion of the bilge. Intake duct(s) must extend to a point midway to the bilge or at least below the level of the carburetor air intake.*

space around them—that is, those foamed in place under a cockpit sole—are not considered to be in "enclosed" compartments requiring ventilation. Since there's no open space around the tanks, there's nothing to ventilate.) A natural ventilation system consists of at least two ducts (one intake, one exhaust) fitted with cowls or their equivalent. Exhaust ducts must be installed so as to extend from the open atmosphere to the lower portion of the bilge (but not so low as to be covered by normal bilge water), and intake ducts must be installed so as to extend to a point midway to the bilge or at least below the level of the carburetor air intake (Figure 25-1). There are published standards regarding the size of ductwork required to protect different compartment volumes (a 2-inch diameter is the minimum), and builders are pretty good about installing adequate systems, though sometimes just barely.

Topping Up

Fuel can present its biggest problems when it first comes aboard simply because the fueling process unavoidably creates excess vapors. The truth is, failure to adhere religiously to proper procedures around the fuel dock is the leading cause of boat explosions and fires. That accidents of this type are relatively few in the total scope of things should be some consolation. Just make sure you

avoid being among the statistics. If it happens to you once, it's way too often.

Before you pick up the fuel hose, make sure the boat is ready: all engines shut down, all ports and hatches closed, all smoking materials extinguished, and everyone else off the boat. Then, and only then, should you start pumping fuel. If you have an outboard-powered boat with portable tanks, simplify matters by filling them on the dock rather than in the boat.

Flowing fuel creates static electricity, and that can mean sparks—something you don't want considering the high level of fuel vapors produced in the process. Always touch the nozzle to the metal fuel fill before you start the flow, and maintain contact until you've finished. This grounds the nozzle and prevents sparks.

To avoid spills and the damage they can do to the environment, keep an eye on the fuel tank vent—which should be located close to the fill—and stop the flow as soon as the first sputters come out. Your goal is to *stop* pumping *before* liquid fuel spurts out of the vent (or back up through the fill itself). This will be easier if you accept that your tank is effectively "full" at 95 percent of its total capacity and figure your safe range accordingly. There are devices you can buy to temporarily attach to the hull with suction cups that will sit just below the vents and catch any spillage before it hits the water. They're not expensive, and if you have a problem detecting the "sputters" before they become liquid, you might consider getting one.

After the flow stops completely, remove the nozzle from the fill tube, put the hose back on the dock, and screw the fill cap back in place. You're finished with the fueling. But you are *not yet* ready to hit the starter!

First, you must open all the ports and hatches and run the bilge blower(s) for 4 (or, better yet, 5) minutes. Don't touch the start switch until you're sure that any accumulated vapor has been cleared out. Needless to say, if you have a totally open boat, you can skip most of this. But in every case, make sure there's no trapped fuel vapor anywhere aboard before you ever go to start an engine. By the way, your nose can be a big help in this department—it remains the *best vapor detector* known to mankind. Always sniff the bilges before you start. And be aware that after airing a boat and running the blowers for 4 or 5 minutes you shouldn't smell a thing. If you still smell gasoline after a thorough venting process, you have a problem that needs immediate attention. *DO NOT START* your boat until you find and correct whatever is wrong. A former student once reported back to me that he started following this advice after hearing it in class. Then one day he did smell gas after airing his boat and running the blower for 5 minutes. So he called a service company. The technician found minute pinholes in his fuel lines (he'd bought an older boat) that were as yet too small to leak liquid but that were leaking vapor. The repair cost him a few bucks, but his nose had saved him from perhaps a greater expense. And he still had the boat.

On a busy day with other boaters impatiently waiting for space at the fuel dock, those few minutes you need to play it safe can seem like forever. And it can be tempting to consider bypassing the proper routine "just this once." *Don't!* Make it a habit to clear your boat of possible accumulated fuel vapors *every time* you take on fresh fuel. As a matter of fact, running the blower(s) and sniffing the bilges before you touch the key is a good habit to develop as general practice for *every* start-up, not just after refueling.

To remind us of this, boats built after July 31, 1980, with power exhaust blowers in gasoline engine compartments must have this sticker near the instrument panel:

> **WARNING**
> **GASOLINE VAPORS CAN EXPLODE.**
> **BEFORE STARTING ENGINE**
> **OPERATE BLOWER FOR 4 MINUTES**
> **AND CHECK ENGINE COMPARTMENT**
> **FOR GASOLINE VAPORS.**

Cleanliness Is . . .

Keeping the bilges absolutely clean and as dry as possible is another safe habit to get into. If the inside of the bottom of your boat is normally clean and relatively dry, the potential hazard of spilled fuel or lube oil is much easier to spot before it can cause trouble. Conversely, if you normally have oily water sloshing around, how can you tell when there's too much?

It's also a good idea to regularly wipe down *all* surfaces of your engine compartment(s), including the power plant(s). That way not only will you have a cleaner-looking boat, but you'll have a safer one as well. Incidentally, I recommend that you repaint inboard engines with a heat-resistant gloss white if they didn't come that way. White surfaces make it much easier for you to spot leaks at their source—and usually while they're still insignificant and thus easier to fix and clean up after.

Legal Requirements (Plus)

If cleanliness and respect for fuel form the first line of defense against boating fires, adequate firefighting ability is the second. Unless your boat is totally open and outboard powered, U.S. Coast Guard regulations call for having one or more fire extinguishers aboard, depending on the size of the boat (see table). I recommend having at least *two* on *any* boat and at least a couple more than the legal minimum on all boats. The reason is that if a fire should start (despite your precautions), you stand a better chance of stopping it in its tracks if you can extinguish it quickly *and completely*. Since the extinguishers we carry aboard small boats are limited, having "extras" greatly increases your odds of success. If one extinguisher *almost* does the job, without the backup you're back to square one, and the fire wins. On the other hand, there are few fires that won't succumb to a "double dose" of extinguishing agent as long as you respond quickly enough and catch the fire while it's still small. Firefighting isn't like either horseshoes, where "close" can count, or hockey, where games can end in a tie. In this case, you beat the fire or the fire beats you, and the former is infinitely more desirable.

Once a year you should hire a professional to inspect your refillable extinguishers and fixed systems. The technician will either attach dated tags that indicate they're OK for another year or service them as needed and then tag them. Look in the Yellow Pages under "Fire Extinguishers" or "Fire Equipment." Better extinguishers can be refilled after discharge to be ready to use again. The less-expensive types, though totally reliable (if they are UL [Underwriters Laboratories] and USCG approved), are "throwaway" devices you can use only once.

You need to inspect all of your extinguishers weekly (or thereabouts) to make sure the pressure gauges remain "in the green." On a monthly basis you should remove dry-chemical extinguishers from their mounting brackets, turn them upside down, and give them a good whack on the bottom with the heel of your hand. This keeps the powder loose enough to disperse easily when you need to discharge it on a fire. By the way, never discharge a fire extinguisher "just a little" to see if it works. Once opened, the valve may not reseat

properly, which can result in a gradual release of the propellant—effectively rendering the extinguisher inoperable and useless.

Another point to remember is that extinguishers are far more effective if you discharge them in spurts, rather than in one steady spray. Even the largest portable extinguisher you can bring aboard won't last long if you release the agent all at once. There's an acronym to help remember the procedure for employing fire extinguishers—PASS—which stands for the following:

Pull the locking pin that prevents an extinguisher from being discharged accidentally. Until you pull it out, you can't squeeze the handle to release the agent.

Aim the extinguisher (or hose) at the base of the flames—this is where the fire is actually taking place.

Sweep the nozzle back and forth across the base of the flames.

Squeeze the handle to release the agent in spurts, one per sweep.

Keep doing this until the fire is out. When that extinguisher is empty, grab a backup so you can keep spraying until the fire is out.

It's a good idea to practice this technique on a controlled fire ashore to get the feel of it. (Always use a fireproof container such as a cutoff 55-gallon drum, a steel wheelbarrow, or a barbecue pit. You want the fire to be big enough to give you a realistic sense of what it's like to fight a fire and put it out, but don't get carried away; this *is* your first time.) If you follow the safe-boatkeeping practices outlined at the end of this chapter, you'll probably never have to use an extinguisher on

FIRE EXTINGUISHER REQUIREMENTS

	EXTINGUISHER CLASS (BASED ON LOA)			
	A (less than 16 ft.)	I (16 to less than 26 ft.)	II (26 to less than 40 ft.)	III (40 to 65 ft.)
No fixed system		1 B-I	2 B-Is or 1 B-II	3 B-Is or 1 B-II and 1 B-I
With approved fixed system		0	1 B-I	2 B-Is or 1 B-II

Note: This table should make it easy to remember two things: 1) The number of B-I extinguishers required is the same as the boat's class—I, II or III, and 2) Although this number is the minimum needed to be "legal," it is also inadequate in the real world. Three B-I extinguishers are simply not enough for a boat of 40 feet or more! Cabin boats should have one for each cabin, plus one in the galley, one by each helm, one in the cockpit, and at least one *plus* a fixed system in the engine compartment.

FIRE EXTINGUISHER SIZES (IN POUNDS OF AGENT)

	EXTINGUISHER CLASS	
	B-I	B-II
CO_2	4	15
dry chemical	2	10
Halon*	10	10

Note: One B-II holds much more agent than two B-Is; so B-IIs are better if you have the space, though they're not quite as portable because they weigh more and are physically bigger.

*The production of new Halon has been banned since January 1, 1994, by EPA edict. However, fixed systems employing Halon are still around because they were either charged with recycled Halon or were installed prior to the ban, although they are becoming more and more rare with the passage of time. New agents have been certified, and so far they are proving to be almost as efficient as Halon but not quite. Thus they require a slightly larger container than Halon for equivalent firefighting capabilities, though these systems still tend to be smaller than those using CO_2. A fixed system of any type offers the advantage of instantaneous response. It can often detect *and extinguish* a fire in the engine compartment before you even know the fire exists.

your boat. So practice sessions may be your only opportunity to know how it's done. Aren't you glad?

Please note that we're most concerned with B-rated extinguishers, because Class B fires involve burning oil, which is the biggest potential problem aboard boats. But we must also be prepared to fight Class A fires (those that involve common combustibles—think things that leave an ash) and Class C fires (those involving electrical items—think C for "current"). Water is the best agent for fighting Class A fires, and on boats we're surrounded by it. But to work best, water must be sprayed on a fire in as fine a mist as possible, something we can't always do aboard pleasure boats. We also have to consider the problem of getting too much water inside the boat, which can lead to sinking or capsizing. Some dry-chemical extinguishers are rated for A, B, and C fires, but most often they are least effective on Class A fires.

If you follow all the precautions outlined above, all this should be entirely theoretical. Prevention is the best firefighting agent of all.

Safety in Numbers Means Keeping Them In Line with Reality

Read your boat's capacity plate and know how many people and how much gear your boat can carry. Never give in to the temptation to carry more of either. "Just one more" could prove to be like the proverbial last straw on the camel. Overloading (particularly of small boats) is a major cause of boating fatalities.

"Just one more" also applies to drinking alcohol aboard—another huge factor in boating accidents. Sunshine, heat, reflections off the water, and physical reactions to vibration and motion underway all tend to increase alcohol's effects on your body and mind. The result is that "a couple of beers" can be far more intoxicating aboard your boat than they are when you're ashore.

You must be totally alert at all times when you're running a boat, so limit your indulging. Or, better yet, follow the practice recommended for the highway and be an abstaining "designated driver" for as long as you're apt to be underway. No matter what your guests are doing, you'll have more fun if you curtail your own partying until the boat is safely secured for the day *(and is going to stay that way)*. Believe me, you'll enjoy it more when you know that your good time won't result in a bad time for anyone else.

Alphabet Soup

Personal Flotation Devices (PFDs)

Most of the other legally required safety elements shown in the table on page 166 are pretty straightforward, with the exception of life jackets—personal flotation devices (PFDs) as they're called by the Coast Guard. The law requires one wearable PFD for each person on board (POB). Coast Guard Auxiliary examiners look for that number when conducting a Vessel Safety Check (VSC). By the way, having a VSC is a great way to make doubly sure your boat is "legal" and then some. A VSC decal, awarded upon satisfactory completion of the vessel check, is a sign of a properly equipped boat, and you can display it with pride. It can also help stave off being boarded (see Chapter 27), because it clearly shows your boat has all the required safety equipment and your papers are in order.

I say PFDs are not straightforward in concept because of two factors. The biggest is that the number of PFDs aboard is meaningless by itself—a PFD does you no good unless you're wearing it. In Chapter 33 I suggest that you and everyone else aboard should don one as soon as it looks like the going may get rough. Some other writers whose judgment I respect even go as far as suggesting that, in small boats, one should be worn at *all* times.

I don't go that far—though I should emphasize that PFDs are a *must* when the seas get lumpy. But I do say that since proper fit is essential to both comfort and safety, everyone should be given a *truly* "personal" flotation device the moment they come aboard. They should try their PFD on immediately, adjust the straps for proper fit, and stow the PFD until it's needed. Since everyone does their own stowing (with perhaps some guidance from the skipper), no one should ever have to wonder where to find his or her very own PFD.

That's for adults. Because small children and small boats have a big thing in common—they can make erratic, sudden, and unexpected movements—the safest practice for youngsters 12 and under is to wear a PFD anytime they are not within the safe confines of a cabin. This means on the decks, in the cockpit, on the flying bridge—even on the marina docks until they're safely back on dry land—*anywhere* there is the potential to fall in.

I say "12 and under" rather arbitrarily. More important than age is the individual child's maturity, size and strength, agility, and experience—sea sense, if you will. When kids have truly learned "one hand for the boat, one hand for me" and are able to keep their balance when a boat is rocking and rolling, they may be ready to go on deck without the protection of a PFD. If you start your kids boating at a very early age, they'll possibly be able to outgrow the guideline sooner; they'll have good "sea legs" well before age 12. But until they know for sure how to keep from

falling overboard if they or the boat should make a sudden lurch, get 'em in the habit of wearing one. In fact, if you carry the children's PFDs in the car, it's easy for the kids to wear them coming and going as well as on the boat, and it's a good way to develop the habit.

Having kids under 13 wear PFDs at all times they aren't within the protection of a cabin isn't just a good idea; it's now federal law. The only hitch is that it applies only in the nineteen states (as of this writing) that don't have their own PFD regulations for kids. Since state law prevails in this case, your local requirements may be less stringent. For example, here in my adopted home state of Florida, PFDs are currently required only on kids 6 and under and then only on boats 26 feet or less. But law or no, having youngsters under 13 wear a PFD at all times they're outside the cabin remains a very good idea!

Small boats usually lack the luxury of having dedicated compartments for PFDs. But if they must share space with other things, make sure the PFDs are always on top and easy to grab.

The other factor that keeps PFDs from being straightforward is the variety of available styles. Given the plethora of choices, you may well wonder which ones you should buy for your boat. Price should not be a major consideration—this is one place you want the very best. And though all approved PFDs are adequate, they're not all equal. Durability is important, so inspect for quality of workmanship before you commit your dollars (and perhaps, your life) to any particular brand or type. Which brings us to another important consideration. Type I, the full "life jacket," is by far the tops in terms of flotation. A full jacket will support the most weight (at least 22.5 pounds buoyancy is required for Coast Guard approval) and is designed to make sure you'll float faceup even if you're unconscious. For these reasons, Type Is are the only kind allowed on boats that carry paying passengers. So they're the best, right? Theoretically, yes, by a wide margin.

But, in reality, Type Is can require more stowage space than some small boats have available. They also come in only two sizes: adult and child; and one size rarely fits all—at least not well, and especially for kids, who come in such a wide variety of sizes. They can also be cumbersome to wear, though I personally find the secure feeling they provide to be more of a comfort than an annoyance. Others don't agree and will use the lack of comfort as an excuse to delay wearing the device. These aspects, of course, can negate much of the theoretical merit of Type Is.

So you may be better off with Type II vests (most of which will also turn an unconscious person upright, though this isn't necessary to gain approval) or Type III "ski" jackets, which will be far more comfortable than the Type IIs, by the way. In cooler climes, you can also consider Type III "float coats." One advantage of a float coat is that it's very comfortable and is thus more likely to be worn. Since it doubles as a windbreaker, it's a practical purchase on several counts. On the other hand, Type IIIs provide less flotation and won't flip you faceup if you should get knocked out as you're knocked overboard. Base your pick on all considerations and make the best compromise.

To keep PFDs in "good and serviceable condition" (as required by law and common sense), always let them dry before stowing; wet PFDs can mildew or rot. And let them dry naturally—heat or forced drying will shorten a PFD's life. Never launder or dry-clean a PFD, either; that would also shorten its useful life.

You should inspect your PFDs frequently for rot, tears, or failed stitching (thread will usually rot before fabric; failed stitching can also cause straps to part from the rest of the PFD), and replace them when flotation or serviceability appears to be anything less than perfect. If you can't trust it absolutely to work when you need it, a PFD is worthless. When in doubt, throw it out!

One more thought regarding PFDs, and then we'll move on. Every boat over 16 feet must have at least one Type IV (throwable) aboard. In my opinion, once you get a boat over 35 feet LOA, you probably need more than that if you're going to have one handy in each location you're apt to need it. I also believe that though a properly rated cushion will satisfy the legal requirements, anyone unfortunate enough to wind up in the water will appreciate being tossed a ring buoy rather than a cushion. It's easier to hang onto and more substantial (a great psychological boost) all

around. Granted, stowage can be a determining factor here also. But if you can, find room to hang at least one ring.

Backfire Flame Arrestors (BFAs)
The need for much of the listed safety equipment was recognized by the U.S. Congress way back in the late 1930s, which resulted in the Motorboat Act of April 1940, our first attempt to regulate boating and the first time boats were classified by length for the purpose of determining the equipment required. This early legislation overlooked a lot of things, however, which is why the Boating Safety Act of 1972 was more encompassing (though even that has been amended since), but it did recognize an important reality: internal combustion engines can backfire. And so gasoline engines installed in any vessel after April 25, 1940, except outboard motors, must be equipped with an acceptable means of backfire flame control. The device must be suitably attached to the air intake with a flame-tight connection and is required to be Coast Guard approved or comply with SAE J-1928 or UL 1111 standards and to be marked accordingly. Never *ever* run a gas engine without its backfire flame arrestor (BFA)! And keep it clean to assure a good flow of air.

Visual Distress Signals (VDS)
These are used in a distress situation for one of two purposes (or in some cases, both): 1) to *alert*—that is, to let others know you're in distress; and 2) to *locate*—to help people find *you* among all other boats out there. Some devices are good only to alert, others only to locate. Some work only by day, others only at night. Some are good for "all of the above." We don't have space to discuss all the options (the International Rules of the Road recognize many different types of signals—Figure 25-2) but we can examine some of those most commonly used on small powerboats.

Please note that although federal regulations require carrying VDS on all boats over 16 feet while operating in "coastal waters," which means not only the obvious but also adjoining bays and inlets or river mouths 2 miles or more in width,

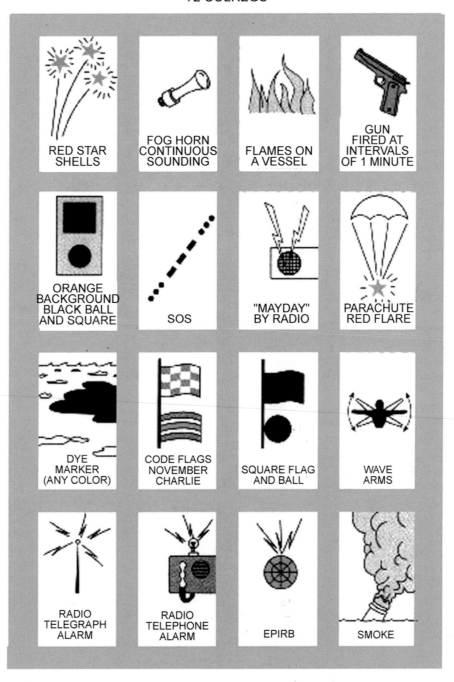

FIGURE 25-2. *International distress signals. (Courtesy U.S. Coast Guard)*

some states (New York, for one) require them on ALL waters. Note also that while three "day/night" devices are enough to make you legal, this will probably not be anywhere near enough should you ever really need them. The burn time for pyrotechnics is so short that it's wise to have plenty of backups. It's best to keep them handy in a red or orange watertight container, plainly marked "FLARES."

Remember also that pyrotechnics have a 42-month useful "life." That is, they expire 42 months after manufacture, and both dates are shown on each. They don't go bad immediately, however, so outdated flares may be kept aboard as extras. They'll probably still work for quite a while, though there's no guarantee, of course. Just remember to get new ones; out-of-date flares don't count toward your legal requirement.

Commonly Used Visual Distress Signals

- **Handheld red flares.** Good day and night. Excellent locator, OK as an alert device if other boats are within sight. Has only about a 2-minute burn time, and so should be used judiciously. NEVER USE railroad or highway flares; only the USCG-approved marine type will do. Three will satisfy your legal requirements, but you really should have more.

- **Orange smoke.** Works by day only but is quite effective as an alert device (what else produces *orange* smoke?) and can be an excellent locator, too. Just remember smoke soon dissipates. Can be handheld (like a flare) or dispatched from a toss-overboard floating canister.

- **Red meteor flares.** Excellent alert devices—if an observer happens to be looking in your direction. Best fired in pairs so that the second flare confirms sighting of the first. They have only a 6- to 10-second burn time, but are usually visible over 20 miles. Not terribly effective as a locator because of distances involved. Also, wind can carry them well away from where they're fired off.

- **Parachute flares.** Go higher and burn longer than meteors, and thus are even better as alert devices because more people can see them. They're also more affected by wind and so are less effective as locators. Some meteor and parachute flares require a "gun" for launching, others are self-contained. If a gun is required, you should use the same safety precautions you would with any firearm.

- **International distress flag.** Good by day only, useful only within range of sight. Can possibly alert (for passing ships or low-flying aircraft only) but is a very good locator, especially for search aircraft. It's inexpensive, has no expiration date, won't wear out quickly, and is easy to stow. It should be displayed as visibly as possible and is best if hung from a signal mast or pole; can possibly be flown from a kite. Davis Instruments also sells a distress flag that *is* a kite (Figure 25-3). It's not terribly expensive and will

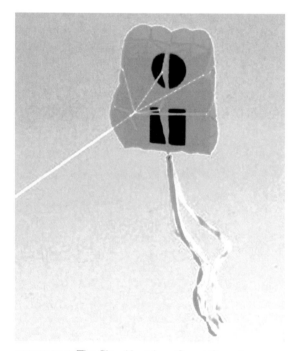

FIGURE 25-3. *The Sky-Alert is a Coast Guard–approved signal device that is self-contained and launches easily in breezes from 5 to 25 knots. (Courtesy Davis Instruments)*

be much more visible than any other form of signal flag.

- **Dye marker.** Good only by day. Excellent locator for search aircraft because its fluorescent sheen helps separate the distress boat—often a small white object—from the waves, which are also often small white objects (whitecaps). Only a so-so alert device; it only works if a plane or chopper happens to be in the vicinity.
- **Signal mirror.** Another relatively inexpensive day-only locator device that's easy to store and never expires, but it's effective only when potential rescuers are within sight.
- **SOS (Morse code).** Probably the best known of all "help" signals, it can work with lights, horn, foghorn—just about anything that can show the three dot—three dash—three dot pattern. There are signal lights on the market that are much brighter than a flashlight and capable of flashing SOS automatically. These are much better (and far less tiring) than manually "keying" a flashlight, but are good for night use only.
- **VHF radio (for Mayday signals).** Good day and night. Probably the VERY BEST ALERT signal of all. OK as a locator if those who hear it have a VHF radio direction finder (RDF) aboard, and the Coast Guard usually does. Doesn't count as a VDS, however. We'll discuss proper radio techniques shortly.
- **Emergency position-indicating radio beacon (EPIRB).** A must for offshore cruising; we'll cover these in greater detail in Chapter 34. Also does not count as a VDS.

There's another inexpensive Help signal you have with you at all times: Simply stand in the cockpit or on deck—anywhere you are plainly visible—and wave your arms up and down at your sides; sort of like doing jumping jacks without the jumping. This isn't strictly a distress signal, and it can be used when you need any sort of assistance. Of course, you have to pray other boaters who see you know this is a signal for help. And on that score, I should also add that fed-eral law requires you to help other boats in distress to the best of your ability as long as you don't endanger your own boat, or those aboard, in the process. There's a $1,000 fine for failure to render aid, and the "Good Samaritan" provision in the Boating Safety Act of 1972 protects you from being sued should your rescue efforts cause damage as long as you acted prudently.

Bells and Whistles

Sound-producing devices are required on all vessels. As we'll cover further in Chapter 26, there are situations in which sound signals are required, despite the reality that most vessels don't use them. As the table shows, for boats up to 12 meters (39.4 feet), the requirement is not too demanding, so complying with the law shouldn't be that difficult.

Safety Requirements Are Minimums!

For years, I've been critical of Coast Guard regulations for pleasure boats because I don't believe they're strict enough; you're better protected when you buy a $20 ticket for a ride on a sightseeing boat than when you pay so very much more for a boat of your own! I once said so rather plainly at a joint UL/USCG seminar that was held to introduce some new electrical and fuel system requirements back in the late 1970s. In response, the moderator asked me just how much regulation I wanted. "Ideally, none!" I answered. (I'm a free spirit at heart and really abhor regulation of any kind, though I accept it as often necessary.) "But if we must have regulations," I added, "I believe they should go far enough to really do the job. Inadequate standards create a false sense of security. People who don't know any better will figure if something meets federal requirements it must be OK. And well they should. But as many of the surveyors present today have already stated, the conditions allowed by these new regulations would not be acceptable in a thorough survey." I still feel the same way. And though some builders are willing to settle for meeting the minimums,

FEDERALLY MANDATED SAFETY REQUIREMENTS

Safety requirement	CLASS (BASED ON LOA)			
	A (less than 16 ft.)	I (16 to less than 26 ft.)	II (26 to less than 40 ft.)	III (40 to 65 ft.)
fire extinguishers	see table on page 159; all extinguishers must be Coast Guard approved.			
PFDs	One Type I, II, III, or V* for each person on board.			
		One Type IV throwable.		
visual distress signals	Three "night" signals if operating at night.	A minimum of three "day" and three "night" signals or three "day/night" signals (see text).		
bells and whistles	Vessels less than 12 meters (39.4 ft.) need a signaling device capable of producing a 4- to 6-second blast audible for ½ mile (as required per Inland Rules). A mouth whistle or horn is legal if loud enough.			Vessels over 12 meters must have a mechanical whistle or horn, and a bell.
backfire flame arrestor	Required on all gasoline engines installed after April 25, 1940, except outboard motors.			
ventilation	Required on all vessels with enclosed engines or fuel tanks (see text). Since 1980, powered ventilation is required for each compartment that has a permanently installed gasoline engine with a cranking motor for remote starting.			

*Type Vs, which are a hybrid—part permanent flotation, part inflatable—must be worn to count.

Note: For more details, please read the USCG booklet, "Federal Requirements and Safety Tips for Recreational Boats." Call 800-368-5647 for information, or read it online at www.uscgboating.org/safety/fedreqs/landing.htm.

I'm pleased to report the builders of better boats are not. They surpass them. That's why earlier in the book I suggested you look for ABYC or NMMA certification; a boat that merely "meets USCG standards in effect at time of manufacture" isn't necessarily good enough. But remember, the aforementioned certification only applies to construction and installed equipment. When it comes to added gear, it's up to you. So I suggest you also go beyond the minimum requirements in outfitting your boat.

Optional Safety Equipment and Knowledge You Should Have (or Know) Anyway

In Chapter 31, I'll discuss anchors and anchoring in terms of pure enjoyment—as in the pleasures of "hanging off the hook" in a peaceful cove. But an anchor is also a safety device; it's a boat's only "emergency brake." Be sure yours are adequate for your boat, and keep one rigged and ready to set at all times because it might be the only thing

that can keep you out of trouble—out of the shallows or off the rocks—in the event of mechanical breakdown.

Get a good compass (don't pinch pennies in this area, either) and use it. Follow compass courses even when steering by eye. Full coverage of the subject is beyond the scope of this book, but I'd suggest you learn the rudiments of navigation and practice the art routinely. It will add pleasure as well as safety to your boating experiences. We'll get you started on that track in Chapter 28, but please remember the navigation information presented in this book is just the very beginning—an overview, really—though I hope it encourages you to explore the subject further.

Get a good VHF marine radio. As I stated previously, it can be the best way to call for help in an emergency. Today's VHFs are pretuned and easily installed; it can even be a do-it-yourself project if you're at all handy. Time was when you'd then have to get an FCC license for your "Maritime Radio Station" and a "Marine Radiotelephone Operator" license for yourself. In those days the licenses were mandatory, but they were free. Now you have to pay a user fee for each, but unless you're operating your boat commercially or are traveling outside U.S. waters, having the radio aboard is voluntary. Currently you don't need any FCC license at all for "voluntarily equipped" vessels.

"Wait a minute," I can hear you say, "I have to carry visual distress signals, but I don't have to carry a radio?" to which I'd agree. So you might add, "Then why add the expense of a VHF if it isn't required when I have to have the other stuff anyway?" That's a good question. But I have a good answer: There are *distress* situations in which you can use the distress signals or call Mayday on the VHF, but there may be other times when a call for help could be a very good idea, and yet you might not actually be "in distress."

Aha! Now I have your attention, yes? Let me explain. *Distress* means life threatening—to anyone on board or to the boat itself. If no one is about to die and the boat isn't going to sink, it's *not* distress (even though it may be distressing for those involved). And so the visual distress signals should remain stowed, and any VHF call for help should not be started with "Mayday." Be advised that in addition to the "cry wolf" aspects (which could be bad enough, especially if the call took rescuers away from a real disaster), making a false distress call is a serious offense, punishable by some very stiff penalties.

These days the Coast Guard responds only to distress calls. For anything less—engine won't start; you're out of fuel, aground, or in some other less than life-threatening difficulty—there are private tow services that *will* respond and get you out of trouble. For a fee, of course. You can buy memberships in a number of organizations, which are akin to auto clubs, that allow you to pay annual dues and get the services for free—or at least at a substantial discount—when you need them. It's worth finding out what's available in your area.

"But I have a cell phone," you say. "I can use that to call for help." The only answer I can offer is "Maybe." Cellular coverage on the water can be spotty. Sometimes it's better than anywhere ashore because you have a clear, uninterrupted shot at a tower, yet in other places you can't get through at all because the cells were designed for coverage on land.

In many places you can use a cell phone and dial "*CG" to reach the Coast Guard (or use a similar shortcut to reach your state marine patrol), but there's a drawback here, too. Most CG communications centers have a standing order: radio calls have priority! If there's a call coming in via VHF and the phone rings at the same time, they'll answer the radio call before they pick up the phone. So even if your call goes through, it might not go all the way through immediately.

Now, cell phones have changed on-the-water communication in many ways, and mostly for the better, I'd say. If you look closely at the VHF channel allocations in Figure 25-4, you'll see several listed as being for "Public Correspondence," which means a marine operator, a connection to landlines via VHF. Marine operators have largely gone out of business because they were no longer being used enough to survive— cell phones have done them in. This is perhaps good, because talking to a landline phone via a marine operator was like being on a huge party line. Everything you said could be heard by anyone who happened to be tuned to the same channel—even people with scanners who were listening with criminal intent. This wasn't so good, especially if you were calling to discuss business matters. Cell phones are much more private (though not completely so, remember). But it's that "party line" aspect of VHF that makes it so great when you need help; everyone listening will hear your call. And if you make your call on Channel 16, the International Distress and Calling frequency, this includes almost everyone out there on the water as well as nearby marinas and yacht clubs.

VHF marine radio is intended for three types of transmissions: those involving **S**afety, **O**perations, and **B**usiness (SOB should be easy to remember, yes?). Of course, "business" can be *personal* business on recreational craft, but the VHF should not be used as CB radios so often were in their heyday. They're not intended to be for idle conversation or long-winded chats.

MARINE VHF RADIO CHANNELS

The chart below summarizes a portion of the FCC rules -- 47 CFR 80.371(c) and 80.373(f)

Type of Message	Appropriate channel(s)
DISTRESS SAFETY AND CALLING - Use this channel to get the attention of another station (calling) or in emergencies (distress and safety).	16
INTERSHIP SAFETY - Use this channel for ship-to-ship safety messages and for search and rescue messages and ships and aircraft of the Coast Guard.	6
COAST GUARD LIAISON - Use this channel to talk to the Coast Guard (but first make contact on Channel 16).	22
NONCOMMERCIAL - Working channels for voluntary boats. Messages must be about the needs of the ship. Typical uses include fishing reports, rendezvous,scheduling repairs and berthing information. Use Channels 67 and 72 only for ship-to-ship messages.	9(fn6), 68, 69, 71, 72, 78, 79(fn4), 80(fn4)
COMMERCIAL - Working channels for working ships only. Messages must be about business or the needs of the ship. Use channels 8, 67, 72 and 88 only for ship-to-ship messages.	1(fn5), 7, 8, 9, 10, 11, 18, 19, 63(fn5), 67, 72(fn7), 79, 80, 88(fn1)
PUBLIC CORRESPONDENCE (MARINE OPERATOR) - Use these channels to call the marine operator at a public coast station. By contacting a public coast station, you can make and receive calls from telephones on shore. Except for distress calls, public coast stations usually charge for this service.	24, 25, 26, 27, 28, 84, 85, 86, 87, 88(fn2)
PORT OPERATIONS - These channels are used in directing the movement of ships in or near ports, locks or waterways. Messages must be about the operational handling movement and safety of ships. In certain major ports, Channels 11,12 and are not available for general port operations messages. Use channel 20 only for ship-to-coast messages. Channel 77 is limited to intership communications to and from pilots	1(fn5), 5(fn3), 12, 14, 20, 63(fn5), 65, 66, 73, 74, 77
NAVIGATIONAL - (Also known as the bridge-to-bridge channel.) This channel is available to all ships. Messages must be about ship navigation, for example, passing or meeting other ships. You must keep your messages short. Your power output must not be more than one watt. This is also the main working channel at most locks and drawbridges.	13, 67
MARITIME CONTROL - This channel may be used to talk to ships and coast stations operated by state or local governments. Messages must pertain to regulation and control, booting activities, or assistance to ships.	17
DIGITAL SELECTIVE CALLING - Use this channel for distress and safety calling and for general purpose calling using only digital selective calling techniques.	70
WEATHER - On these channels you may receive weather broadcasts of the National Oceanic and Atmospheric Administration. These channels are only for receiving. You cannot transmit on them.	Wx-1 162.55 Wx-2 162.4 Wx-3 162.475

Footnotes to table
1. Not available in the Great Lakes, St. Lawrence Seaway, or the Puget Sound and the Strait of Juan de Fuca and its approaches.
2. Only for use In the Great Lakes, St Lawrence Seaway, and Puget Sound and the Strait of Juan de fuca and its approaches.
3. Available only In the Houston and New Orleans areas.
4. Available only in the Great Lakes.
5. Available only In the New Orleans area.
6. Available for Intership, ship, and coast general purpose calling by noncommercial ships.
7. Available only In the Puget Sound and the Strait of Juan de Fuca.

FIGURE 25-4. *Marine VHF radio channel allocations. (Courtesy FCC)*

VHF Radio Operation

The FCC has volumes of established rules for marine radiotelephones. Fortunately, the operating rules can be condensed into a few simple statements:

Maintain your watch. Whenever your boat is underway, the radio must be turned on and be tuned to Channel 16 except when being used for messages. Channel 09 has been designated as the new Alternative Calling Channel for pleasure boats (to free Channel 16 for better use as a Distress frequency). There are some problems in implementing use of Channel 09 for calling that will be with us until more radios have "dual watch" capability; it's currently quite difficult to monitor both 16 and 09 unless you have two radios. Most VHFs now do have a 16/9 button that will alternate between the channels, but they still only receive one at a time.

Power. Output is switchable between High and Low (1 watt). Try low power first if the station being called is within a few miles. If there's no answer, switch to higher power (25 watts on most installed units, less on handheld portables).

Calling coast stations (marinas and yacht clubs). You should try to call a coast station on its normal working channel. You may use Channel 16 when you don't know the working channel.

Calling other ships. Call other ships on Channel 16. You may call on ship-to-ship channels when you know that the ship is listening on both a ship-to-ship channel and Channel 16. For example, most commercial vessels also monitor Channel 13, the bridge-to-bridge frequency. To do this, the ship has to have two separate receivers.

Never carry on a conversation on Channel 16, and try to use Channel 09 to call other pleasure boats, though considering the realities, you might end up using 16 anyway. But try 09 first for pleasure boats, please; if it works, you'll be helping to keep 16 less busy.

Limits on calling. You must not call the same station for more than 30 seconds at a time. If you don't get a reply, wait at least 2 minutes before calling again. After three calling periods, wait at least 15 minutes before calling again.

Change channels. After contacting another station on Channel 16, change immediately to a channel that's available for the type of message you want to send. When you contact a marina or tow service on 16, they'll usually respond with "Acknowledge and switch to Channel whatever." This means they want you to repeat the channel number on 16 before you switch so they'll know you heard them and understand which channel you'll be using.

Station identification. Identify, in English, your station by your FCC call sign (which you'll have only if it's licensed), vessel name, and the state registration number or official number of your boat at the beginning and end of each message.

YOU **MUST NOT** TRANSMIT:

- False distress or emergency messages.
- Messages containing obscene, indecent, or profane words or meaning.
- General calls (these are messages not addressed to a particular station) on Channel 16, except in an emergency or if you're testing your radio. Avoid unnecessary radio checks. If you do make a radio check (and even that provokes a "why bother?" since if your radio worked last time you were aboard, why shouldn't you expect it to work this time?), it's better to use a "working" channel and call someone specific, such as the tow service you subscribe to.
- When your vessel is on land (for example, while it's on a trailer).

Remember, marine radio is a *simplex* operation—conversations flow only one way at a time. You have to press the microphone's push to talk (PTT) switch to transmit and then release it to listen. If it isn't clear by the words or your tone of voice, indicate it's the other person's turn to talk by saying "Over" before you release the microphone switch. You can also indicate you have nothing more to say by saying "Out" at the end of your final statement.

VHF Safety Calls

Distress and safety messages normally use only Channel 16—there's no need to switch channels.

But even within this category of call there are differing priorities:

- **Mayday** is reserved for distress only and should be the cue for everyone else to shut up (though unfortunately, it doesn't usually work this way).
- **Pan Pan** (pronounced "pahn pahn") is used for emergency calls when the danger is *not* life threatening. This, too, should prompt silence on the part of everyone else, though it rarely does.
- **Securité** (pronounced "say-cure-it-tay") is used to transmit information pertaining to navigation safety or weather advisories. Ships entering and leaving harbors will often precede their movement with a security call. The Coast Guard uses securité calls not only to inform mariners of potentially dangerous weather but also to advise us of other impending adverse conditions. Most of these calls will instruct you to listen to Channel 22 Alpha (22A), the Coast Guard's working channel, for details.

In each of these situations, the key word will be repeated three times, as in "Securité, securité, securité, this is the motor vessel Big Guy, motor vessel Big Guy, about to enter Tightsqueeze Canal, westbound. All concerned traffic should contact us on Channel 16 or 13. Big Guy out." Pleasure boats will rarely initiate securité calls, but you should always listen for them and react as appropriate. Listening for securité calls is just one more reason you should always monitor Channel 16.

Mayday Calls Making a Mayday call should never be taken lightly. Remember, this is reserved for life-threatening situations only. But should the occasion ever arise, it's best you know what to do. So I'll outline it here.

I can't overstress the importance of practicing simulated distress calls until the procedure is second nature. Knowing what to do (and knowing you know) can be a huge help in reducing stress in situations that are bound to be at least somewhat stressful at best. In fact, if you have everything already written on a "Mayday" script (ex-

cept your position, number of POB, and nature of distress, of course) the whole process will be easier in a real distress situation. You can use the same outline for Pan Pan calls.

First, it's important to know where you are. Before you make any emergency call (Mayday, Pan Pan, or even just a call to your tow service), take a moment to note your position either by Lat/Lon on a GPS (global positioning system) display or chart, or in general terms such as distance and direction from a prominent landmark.

Next, make sure the radio is turned on. Yes, this is obvious. But in a true emergency, you wouldn't be the first to start talking into a "dead" radio. Once you're sure the radio is on, select Channel 16 and make sure the power is on High. Then you can begin.

1. Key the microphone and speak slowly, clearly, and calmly.
2. Say "Mayday, Mayday, Mayday" (or "Pan Pan, Pan Pan, Pan Pan").
3. Give the name of your vessel: "This is (vessel name)."
4. Say "Mayday" and the name of your vessel again.
5. State where you are, your position (as discussed above).
6. State the nature of your distress.
7. Give the number of persons on board and the condition(s) of any injured.
8. Estimate the present seaworthiness of your vessel.
9. Briefly describe your boat, its length, type, hull color, trim, any canvas such as a bimini top, and any distinctive features that might help rescuers in recognizing your boat among all others.
10. Say, "I'll be listening on Channel 16."
11. End message with "This is (name of your boat), over."
12. Release the microphone PTT switch and listen. (Failure to release the microphone switch has caused more than one skipper to panic and believe no one heard him. Just remember, you can't hear an answer as long as you're holding that button down; you're still trans-

mitting until you release it, and you can't receive while transmitting!) Someone should answer. If not, repeat the process. If a second call on Channel 16 produces no answer, try other channels such as 68, 69, 10, 06, or 09. Despite the requirement to monitor Channel 16, boats are often monitoring other channels. But unless you're truly in "another world," someone *will* hear you and respond.

Digital Selective Calling (DSC)

Since June 17, 1999, marine radio manufacturers have had to include a digital selective calling (DSC) capability in their new radios in order to get FCC approval to sell them in the United States. No recreational boater is required to use DSC, but the radios you buy these days will have the capability nonetheless.

DSC radios are fundamentally different from the older marine radios in that 1) they respond to a unique maritime mobile service identity (MMSI) programmed into the radio to serve as a kind of "phone number"; 2) DSC automatically maintains a watch on marine VHF Channel 70, rather than your having to listen to Channel 16; 3) you can call other DSC radios or coast stations directly using their MMSI; and 4) you can communicate with commercial vessels (which have been required to carry DSC radios since February 1, 1999). DSC helps reduce the clutter on Channel 16, but for most pleasure boaters it's something that's not totally applicable to their use. By all means, if this service appeals to you, apply for and get your MMSI so you can take full advantage of your VHF radio's capabilities. (The dealer who sells, and probably installs, your VHF will be able to help you obtain your MMSI and make sure your radio is fully DSC capable.) Note also that many new radios also have automatic Mayday capabilities; you need only flip a switch, and the call goes out. If your VHF is interfaced with a GPS, it can even broadcast your position!

Learn First Aid and CPR

I suggest this not because of any greater danger aboard your boat but rather because outside help may be farther away than in a shoreside situation and thus will take longer to reach you should an emergency occur. If you know what to do and have an adequately stocked first-aid kit aboard, you can be the "first responder" who helps alleviate the situation until professional help can arrive, or until you can get the injured person to shore.

Practice Good Boatkeeping

It's no coincidence that *shipshape* is often a synonym for neatness. But really it means more. No matter how neatly it's piled, stuff left lying around can trip you up when lumpy seas make for unsure footing. Many things left out on deck, even if they're arranged with extreme neatness, can become unguided missiles if the going gets rough. Clear decks are safe decks. But there's more to it than just putting stuff out of the way. Properly stowed gear won't come flying out of a locker if the boat drops sharply off the face of a steep wave. Properly stowed gear won't interfere with other stowed gear. Properly stowed gear remains accessible. A secure place for everything and everything in its place should be your goal.

Finally, let me emphasize that the safety practices I've outlined are not meant to induce drudgery or take any fun out of powerboating. Quite the contrary. By making the effort to keep the sport safe, you practically guarantee that it will continue to be enjoyable, because it greatly reduces your chances of having an accident—an unwanted event that can quickly take the "pleasure" out of pleasure boating.

The only remaining elements of safety you need to consider involve the operating rules. We'll look at them next.

26

Rules of the Road

Before you head out on the water, you should be aware of the nautical "Rules of the Road," as the Navigation Rules are commonly known. These exist for one purpose: the prevention of collisions at sea. For this reason, the Rules are also known as the Collision Regulations, or COLREGs for short.

Prior to 1980, the United States had three sets of rules for inland waters alone (Inland Rules, Great Lakes Rules, and Western Rivers Rules), in addition to those that applied in offshore waters. Fortunately, things are much simpler and more uniform now. The International Rules apply to "ocean waters" (which begin at the mouth of each inlet in most areas), and the Inland Rules apply on federal waters everywhere else in the United States (for more on federal waters, see Chapter 27). The two sets of rules are identically formatted and very similar, differing only in a few particulars. Both sets are contained in the Coast Guard publication *Navigation Rules, International–Inland* (COMDTINST M16672.2D), which is generally available wherever navigation charts are sold (or go to www.navcen.uscg/mwv/navrules/navrules.htm). I suggest you get a copy and study it well. A thorough knowledge of the Rules of the Road is so important that the Coast Guard demands a minimum score of 90 percent on the rules section of its captain's license exams, while 70 percent suffices for passing other portions.

When you first skim through your copy of the Rules you'll be amazed at the extent and apparent complexity of its contents. But when you really dig in, you'll discover that although they are extensive, the COLREGs are not as complicated as they first appear. Indeed, when you consider only the basic *operating* rules (the "steering and sailing rules" as opposed to the rules regarding vessel lights and "shapes,") they're quite straightforward.

A friend once summed up the Rules in one simple statement: "Safety first, and keep to the right." Perhaps this is an oversimplification, but it's the essence of what they are about.

So, without intending to suggest that you shouldn't also study the Coast Guard publication, I'd like to expand a bit on my friend's statement and cover the practical application of the Rules in the hope that it will further your understanding of their intent.

Safety First

Though they make their points in formal terms (thus it takes four pages for Rule 1 to tell us the Rules apply to *everyone* on the water), in many ways the Rules merely ask for common sense. The requirement that "every vessel shall at all times maintain a proper lookout," for example (Rule 5), means simply that a skipper should always keep an eye on where the boat is going and what's happening around it. If other related activities (such as checking your position on a chart or looking through a guidebook for the location of a marina) cause you to take your eyes off the water for more than a few seconds, you should have another pair of eyes to watch the water for you until you can be your own "lookout" again. You should also engage the services of "extra eyes" whenever visibility worsens. Use of radar or an autopilot does not release you from the obligation of maintaining a visual lookout.

The Rules also require that you "at all times proceed at a safe speed" (Rule 6), and that in determining how fast is "safe" you take into consideration such important factors as visibility, sea and weather conditions, the handling characteristics of your boat, maneuvering room, potential hazards, and other vessel traffic.

Avoiding Collision

The Rules are quite specific as to the behavior of vessels when in sight of each other and describe the actions each should take to avoid collision. Fortunately, the nearly infinite variations that might occur in the real world can be grouped into just a few closely related "situations."

Meeting

In most *meeting* situations (you and another boat approaching each other head-on or nearly head-on), you should keep to the right. If the other vessel does the same, you'll go by port side to port side, just as we do on the highway. This precept holds particularly in narrow channels. If you're already so far to the left of the vessel you're meeting that "keeping to the right" would cause you to cross in front of it, stay to the left and meet starboard to starboard. *Most* of the time, however, you'll avoid trouble by holding to the right side of a channel or waterway. Note that in most such cases, neither vessel has a "right of way." There's one case where the Inland Rules go beyond the International Rules, however. The former hold that upstream of tidal waters, a vessel bound downstream has right of way over one heading upstream. This is because the down-bound vessel, which has the current behind it, will have more difficulty in maneuvering than the vessel with the current on its bow. As I stated, the Rules are quite logical. The International Rules, for obvious reasons, have no need to cover this situation.

In many cases, the question of who gives way can be puzzling to newcomers, yet the Rules are explicit. By establishing a definitive order of who yields when, we seek to prevent the "after you/no, after you" confusion we sometimes experience in doorways ashore. What is at worst an embarrassing inconvenience ashore could lead to collision on the water, and as Thucydides said, a collision at sea can ruin your entire day. If everyone in command of a boat knows and follows the Rules, there should be no confusion.

Crossing

Since you'll probably want a bit of experience under your belt before you begin operating after dark, a discussion of navigation lights might be premature at this point. The way lights are arranged, however, relates directly to who has the right of way, so it will help to consider the lights on your boat even if you don't plan to use them soon.

I should also point out that while we speak of "right of way" for convenience, the Rules never mention the term, nor do they grant anyone any "rights." In truth, only another skipper who knows and follows the Rules and thus gives way when the Rules require it can grant you the right of way when it's your due. Unfortunately, many pleasure-boat operators *do not know* the Rules, so one of the smartest moves on your part would be to always "drive" defensively, with a "Plan B" in mind that will keep you out of trouble if the other boat fails to do what it is supposed to, even if this means not following the Rules exactly.

The Rules actually anticipate this, by the way. Rule 2 has two parts: paragraph (a) states in essence that no one is exempt from the consequences of "neglect to comply with these rules"; and paragraph (b) cites the need for due regard for "special circumstances . . . which may make a departure from these Rules necessary to avoid immediate danger."

Lighting the Way Figure 26-1 shows the four basic "navigation" lights on a typical powerboat. The red sidelight is visible through an arc from dead ahead to 22.5 degrees abaft the port beam. The green sidelight covers a similar arc to starboard.

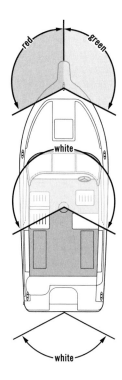

FIGURE 26-1. *Navigation lights.*

The white masthead light covers the arc of both sidelights (because it's displayed only by vessels under power, the masthead light is also sometimes called the steaming light), while the white sternlight fills in the gap—the portion of the circle not covered by the others.

The area from dead ahead to 22.5 degrees abaft your starboard beam is generally called the danger zone. It's no coincidence that this is the area covered by your green navigation light; skippers of boats within this arc are allowed to *stand on* [maintain course and speed] and can consider the green to mean "Go." Under the Rules, you must give way to nearly every vessel within this arc. In any *crossing* situation that could result in collision, these vessels would be showing you their red lights, which you can take to mean "Stop." Of course, you don't necessarily have to stop. You can also give way by slowing down or changing course (to starboard, please) or by taking any combination of these actions. You can even keep going straight ahead at the same speed if you're absolutely certain you'll pass well clear of the other vessel (as you would if it were going fast enough to pass ahead of you or you were going fast enough to pass ahead of it), but it isn't always wise to do so. Just remember, if you have a boat in your danger zone, it is incumbent upon *you* to avoid collision. The other boat is technically bound to stand on while you're charged with the obligation to give way. If you have a collision, "I thought I had room to clear" won't cut it.

Overtaking

You need only give way to those vessels that present a potential for collision; how to determine this is shown in Figure 26-2. There are other reasons for not giving way, such as those covered under Rule 9, which will be detailed later. In other situations the matter of who gives way, and when, doesn't seem quite as clear cut. But it is. For example, you must always give way to a vessel you are *overtaking*, whenever you approach within the arc described by the other vessel's sternlight. That doesn't mean you can't pass, it just means that until you are well ahead of the other boat, *you* are the one burdened with the responsibility of staying out of the way. (Though the current terms "stand-on" and "give-way" vessels are clearer in some ways, the formerly used expressions of "privileged" and "burdened" had some coherent meaning, too.)

We've now covered the three passing situations: meeting, crossing, and overtaking. "OK," you might ask, "but what about other circumstances? For instance, I've heard that sailboats always have the right of way. Is this true?" Good question. The answer is "Most of the time, but not *always*." For example, if a fast multihull under sail overtakes a slow displacement trawler under power, the overtaking vessel is still the give-way vessel, regardless of its means of propulsion. And then, too, as far as the Rules are concerned, an auxiliary sailboat is a powerboat if its engine is running, even if it also has sails up. And there are other instances in which sailboats must give way, as we shall now see.

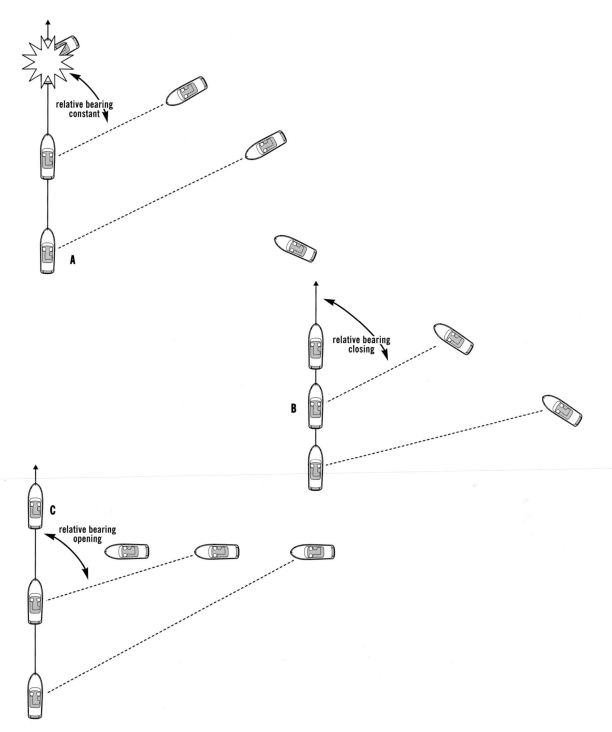

FIGURE 26-2. *Any vessel in your danger zone whose bearing doesn't change appreciably (**A**) represents a potential collision. If the bearing angle is closing on your heading (**B**), the vessel will cross ahead of you. If the angle is opening (**C**), the other vessel will cross behind.*

Pecking Order

As is often the case in life, there's a pecking order on the water. "New Reels Catch Fish, So Purchase Some" is a mnemonic to help remember it. From most privileged to least, the order is the following: **n**ot under command; **r**estricted in ability to maneuver; **c**onstrained by draft; **f**ishing boats; **s**ailboats; **p**owerboats; **s**eaplanes. Under Rule 18, each category must give way to *all* those above it.

"Not under command" doesn't mean no one is in charge. Rather, it refers to a vessel that has lost its steering or propulsion or both, and thus absolutely *cannot* maneuver—it's at everyone else's mercy.

You might think that the term "restricted in ability to maneuver" would mean the same thing. Under the Rules, however, this refers to a vessel that is able to maneuver but only with difficulty because of the work it is doing. The term covers dredges, buoy tenders, survey vessels, and such.

"Constrained by draft" refers to ships (or even large boats) that cannot leave the channel and go into shallower water and thus do not have the option of turning. Therefore, they have to give way only to vessels higher on the list, which have even fewer options.

"Fishing boats" means only the commercial variety, and only when they are dragging nets or trawls. Sportfishermen don't come under this banner, even when they're trolling (though it's thoughtful and considerate to avoid their lines), and neither do commercial fishing boats when they're not actually engaged in the act of fishing.

"Sailboats" is a clear-cut category, but as mentioned above, if they're under power they're powerboats under the rules.

The Law of Gross Tonnage

The common thread in all this is relative maneuverability. The intent of the Rules is for the more maneuverable vessel to stay out of the way of the less maneuverable. Simple as that. So, while bigger vessels aren't given special consideration in the Rules (other than in the constrained-by-draft category), practicality suggests that they should be given special consideration on the water. If you're zipping about in a 21-foot outboard-powered center console, you and that 110-foot steel sightseeing boat beside you are on equal grounds, legally speaking. But you have more maneuverability and carry less draft, so when push comes to shove (perhaps not the best phrase to use when talking about collision avoidance!), you would be well advised to stay out of the larger boat's way. This admonition takes on greater meaning when "the other guy" is even bigger, say a freighter or tanker. When you realize that a large ship underway at cruising speed needs a mile or more to stop or complete a turn, you can see why this is healthy advice. I hardly need point out who will come out second best if there is a collision.

The One on the Right Doesn't Always Have the Right

Rule 9 covers narrow channels and is another application of the Law of Gross Tonnage. Paragraph (a) reemphasizes the "keep to the right" aspects of the Rules. Paragraph (b) states: "A vessel of less than 20 meters in length or a sailing vessel shall not impede the passage of a vessel that can safely navigate only within a narrow channel or fairway." Paragraph (c) tells us "A vessel engaged in fishing shall not impede the passage of any other vessel navigating within a narrow channel or fairway." And paragraph (d) reminds us "A vessel shall not cross a narrow channel or fairway if such crossing impedes the passage of a vessel which can safely navigate only within that channel or fairway." This one is particularly important, because if you're in a small boat approaching a vessel in the channel from its starboard side, and you have any knowledge of the Rules, it's easy to think you have the right of way because "you're on the right." But you don't. Vessels that must operate within the channel have precedence over those that are more maneuverable and need less depth, even if those vessels are approaching from the traffic flow's starboard.

In keeping with this theory of relative maneuverability, though I've made the point that sailboats under power are powerboats under the Rules, keep in mind that your powerboat will still have greater maneuverability than most sailboats (particularly when the sailboat is larger). Remember that sailboats under power are most often underpowered, and act accordingly.

Sound Signals

This is probably one of the more confusing aspects of the Rules, for several reasons. To begin with, though the Rules require them, sound signals are rarely heard any more. This is why the table of required safety equipment shown in Chapter 24 lists what it does under Bells and Whistles. To be legal, your boat must have the equipment to produce the required sounds even if you rarely use it. Far too many pleasure-boat operators don't even know they exist, and most commercial operators "exchange signals" via VHF radio. But you're supposed to use them if you're going to follow the Rules to the letter. On the other hand, there's no point in creating more noise pollution, which is what sound signals become if the other skipper doesn't understand them, so I'm going to suggest a means of announcing your intentions without making a sound.

But before I do that, I feel obligated to at least acquaint you with the sound signals so you'll know what they mean when you hear them, even if you rarely initiate them yourself.

This is another of the areas where Inland and International Rules differ. Most inland sound signals are signals of intent (INland = INtent is a good mnemonic), while international signals indicate action. Inland signals are mostly exchanged. That is, one vessel signals its intent, and the other replies to either agree or object. While on the high seas, vessels only signal when they're changing course as the signal indicates, and unless the other vessel is also changing course, no reply is required.

Inland signals are required when vessels are in sight and within a half mile of each other (this is why whatever "signaling device" you have aboard must be audible for a half mile), while on the high seas they need only be within sight.

The signals are easy to remember if you relate them to the syllables in "port" (one) and "starboard" (two). In a head-to-head meeting situation, neither vessel has the right of way, so either may initiate the signals. One *whistle* [one short blast]

means "I'm going to show you my port side." Two whistles [two short blasts] means "I'm going to show you my starboard side." Thus, in a typical meeting situation, the vessels would exchange one whistle. And although what's called for here under the Rules would be a short blast on your horn or whistle, which is defined as "having a duration of about one second," most often the "exchange" of "whistles" will be done by commercial vessels via VHF on Channel 13: "One whistle, Cap?" "Yeah, one whistle is fine." Two whistles would be used only as described previously, in situations where the vessels are already set for a starboard-to-starboard meeting.

In a crossing or overtaking situation, the give-way vessel should initiate the exchange, thus indicating it does, indeed, intend to give way. Since it's most often best to give way to starboard when you have another vessel in your danger zone, one whistle works here, too. It only gets a bit confusing (and then only for a moment), when an overtaking vessel signals one whistle. But when you think about it, if the vessel coming by you intends to show you its port side, it will be coming by on your starboard. More often, especially if you're keeping to the right of the channel (your starboard) as you should, a vessel will overtake you on your port side, which means an exchange of *two* whistles because the overtaking vessel will be showing you its starboard side.

Again, an exchange of whistles means just that. One vessel signals its intentions, and the other says "OK" by giving the same signal right back. Never respond with a *cross* signal [answering one whistle with two or vice versa]. If, for any reason, you don't agree with the proposed action (say a vessel wants to overtake you on your port side, and you know you're about to turn to port), you should respond with the *danger* signal of five or more short blasts (effectively saying, "No, no, no, no, no!"). This signal should also be used in any situation that looks like it might become trouble, such as when a give-way vessel doesn't seem to be giving way.

There are a couple of other Inland Rules sound signals you should be aware of. Three short blasts means "I am operating propulsion astern." And a *prolonged* blast of 4 to 6 seconds indicates a vessel is leaving its berth at a pier or approaching a blind turn or junction in a waterway. These are the only Inland Rules sound signals that, like *all* those under the International Rules, are signals of action, rather than intent, and thus require no response or exchange.

You really don't have to concern yourself with International Rules sound signals because you should never be in a position to hear them. Whenever you see another vessel in waters governed by International Rules, simply give it a wide berth—in the ocean, there should be more than enough room to do this—and neither of you should need any signals.

Restricted Visibility

Whenever we operate in restricted visibility (which does not mean after dark, but rather fog, heavy rain, smoke, or other substance in the air that makes visibility difficult or impossible), we don't use the standard sound signals. Remember, they're called for when vessels are "within sight." Instead, we sound the *fog* signal of one prolonged blast every 2 minutes. It's also wise to listen, too. If you hear the fog signal of another vessel apparently forward of your beam, you must reduce speed to bare steerageway until you're sure there's no risk of collision. Of course, you should be going slowly to begin with, so as to be able to stop in half the distance of visibility, leaving the other half to the "other guy."

Actually, until you acquire more experience in navigating when you *can* see, I suggest you don't try navigating when you *can't*. At the first hint of encroaching restricted visibility, get out of the channel and anchor in a safe spot until visibility improves. Of course, this will call for another fog signal, the ringing of your bell for 5 seconds every minute (which is why the equipment requirements we discussed in Chapter 25 include a bell).

Timely Actions

I'd like to end this discussion of the Rules of the Road with a bit of advice that tempers the Rules'

stated operational requirements with some practical insight.

The Rules require that the give-way vessel give way in such a manner that the stand-on vessel can clearly see the first vessel's intentions. If you're the give-way vessel and are changing course, make one big, *obvious* change rather than a series of slight and perhaps imperceptible changes. Likewise, if you're slowing down or stopping, make the action clearly visible. In short, comply with the Rules' objective of removing ambiguity. Let the other skipper *know* you're giving way. And if you do this, quickly and clearly, the other vessel's skipper will see that you're giving way, which can be far more effective than any whistle signal—especially if he or she doesn't know them.

The Rules require that the stand-on vessel maintain course and speed to avoid confusion, but as I've suggested, there will be times when you should follow the more practical option of getting out of the way of a less-maneuverable vessel even if you are, technically, the stand-on vessel. In this case, too, be sure to make your intentions clear to the skipper of the larger vessel soon enough to avoid confusion and potential problems.

Incidentally, taking such action is not as much a departure from the Rules as you might think. Rule 17, the same one that tells us the stand-on vessel must maintain course and speed, also states that if it appears a give-way vessel isn't taking appropriate action, the stand-on vessel should do whatever is necessary to avoid collision. Since the Law of Gross Tonnage is involved only when common sense tells you it's necessary——that is, when the less-maneuverable vessel cannot take proper action as easily—your doing so actually follows the letter as well as the intent of the Rules. (And remember also, Rule 2, part (b) that tells us a "departure from the Rules" is OK if "special circumstances" demand it.)

There's more to the Rules of the Road than we can cover here, of course; that's why you should study the Coast Guard book itself. But if you understand what I've outlined above, you're nearly ready to go boating.

27

Boating and the Law

Powerboating is one of the few activities in life that still allows nearly unlimited personal freedom. You can pretty much get in your boat, head out on the water, and go . . . to wherever you wish, whenever you wish, as fast or slow as you wish, for as long as you wish. And all without asking anyone's permission.

That's not to say, however, there aren't any rules. Far from it. In the previous two chapters you got a taste of the regulations that dictate the safety equipment we must have on board and those that outline our responsibilities toward other boats. Now let's look at a few more rules—those that guide our behavior with respect to the interests of various government entities and our behavior in regard to our environment.

Fortunately, these regulations aren't that great in number. And most make sense (which can't always be said for all the rules that affect us ashore). Yet they're still far too numerous and varied for me to cover them all fully, though I'll do my best to explain their intent and scope as thoroughly as possible.

One of the prime reasons for the number and variety of regulations is that on any given stretch of water, we'll usually be under the authority of more than one set of laws. This is because of the way our governments work. In certain situations, we live by laws that apply universally, laws enacted by Congress in Washington, D.C. A good example would be the Inland Rules of the Road, which are valid on all "navigable waters of the United States" except those that lie outside the demarcation lines separating inland from coastal waters. The International Rules apply there, of course, as they do on the high seas—the ocean beyond our territorial limits.

The term "navigable waters of the United States" includes all waters navigable continuously from the high seas, including coastal waters and all connecting inland waters, even where access is by canals and locks; if you can get there from the ocean, they're federal waters. Also included are bodies of water that touch two or more states and thus—although not accessible from the ocean—are capable of interstate commerce. Federal waters are under the jurisdiction of the U.S. Coast Guard.

What tends to complicate things—though, as we'll see shortly, not unmanageably so—is a peculiar habit of Congress, which is to pass legislation that applies to the whole country but then leave the details of application to the individual states. This gives us not one law, but fifty, to cover each situation. This is not as bad as it may seem at first because you don't have to learn all fifty sets of laws. Just be sure you know the ones that apply where you go boating.

Layered Authority

State laws, those that are enacted by each state legislature and that apply on all waters within that state's boundaries, tend to complement (or, in some cases, supersede) federal laws. For example, some states' mandatory equipment requirements are more stringent than the Coast Guard's, and include additional items the federal regulations do not, such as a compass and anchor.

Though as we saw with regulations regarding children and PFDs, state laws often prevail even when they are less stringent; it's the nature of our republic.

State marine patrols are responsible for enforcing state laws and, where state waters are also navigable waters of the United States, federal laws as well. It used to be that coastal states would separate their saltwater and freshwater law enforcement activities and have one agency responsible for each. Since some state laws apply only to nonfederal waters, the plan made sense. But given that downsizing and budget consolidation seem to be as rampant in the world of civil service as they are in the private sector, this is changing. Currently, many coastal states have just one boating law enforcement agency to cover both saltwater and freshwater jurisdictions.

This drive toward a common approach actually started many years ago, when boating officials from the various states joined together to form the National Association of State Boating Law Administrators—or NASBLA, as it's generally known. One of their goals was to help create more uniformity in boating laws and law enforcement.

Though NASBLA has made great strides in helping develop regulations that are much more consistent from state to state, there's still a way to go on that score. So it's important to acquaint yourself with the specific laws of the state(s) in which you go boating; all are similar, but each state is different.

In many places you'll also encounter county and municipal marine patrols in addition to the federal and state authorities. Because people often think existing federal and state statutes aren't exacting enough for the needs of their communities, they pass local laws and ordinances that are more restrictive than their farther-reaching counterparts. So in addition to knowing the federal and appropriate state boating laws, you should also make yourself aware of local regulations wherever you go boating. When dealing with "The Law," "I didn't know that" is never a valid defense.

You can be thankful that learning local regulations usually isn't difficult. Most communities with enough maritime activity to prompt these added levels of lawmaking and law enforcement have enough related businesses to have engendered an association or two dedicated to promoting the local marine industry. One of the ways they do this is by publishing brochures and pamphlets that help explain the applicable laws and regulations. Just ask at a local marina, marine store, or bait and tackle shop, and most likely they'll give you some brochures, or at least tell you where to get them.

Regulations

You'll have your first encounter with federally mandated state law as soon as you take possession of your new (or new-to-you) powerboat. You must register it within 30 days of purchase. The Boating Safety Act of 1972 requires all undocumented motorboats to be numbered, but the numbering and registration process has been delegated to the states as long as they adopt a system equivalent to or more encompassing than the federal requirements (and all of them have, although Alaska didn't get with the program until 2001).

Just to complicate things a bit further, you're supposed to register the boat in its "state of principle *use*," which is not necessarily where you live (though your home state probably won't refuse the registration!). For example, if your home is in southwest Georgia, and you'll do most of your boating on the Gulf of Mexico from ports in the Florida Panhandle, your boat is supposed to be registered in Florida. That's the law. And it applies even if your boat spends much of the time sitting on a trailer beside your house in Georgia, and you sometimes use it on nearby inland lakes. Most of us don't have to worry about this aspect of federal regulations, but you should be aware of it nonetheless, especially if your favorite boating area isn't within your home state.

In many states, the Department of Motor Vehicles also is charged with handling boat registration, so where you register your car is a good place to start when you need to register your boat. At the time of registration you must show proof of ownership and pay applicable fees to the state or county tax collector. Registration fees vary from state to state. To cite a schedule I have handy, from my home state of Florida, as of 2004 the fees are:

- Class A-1—All vessels less than 12 feet in length, and motorized canoes, $7.25.
- Class A-2—12 feet or more and less than 16 feet, $14.25.
- Class 1—16 feet or more and less than 26 feet, $22.25.
- Class 2—26 feet or more and less than 40 feet, $54.25.
- Class 3—40 feet or more and less than 65 feet, $86.25.
- Class 4—65 feet or more and less than 110 feet, $102.25.
- Class 5—110 feet or more, $126.25.

Please understand such fees are by no means universal. For example, currently in California the fee to register and title a new vessel of any size is $9, while the fee to register a vessel that was previously registered in another state or country is $37. Obviously, registration fees are subject to change, and these examples shouldn't be construed as anything but an illustration of the wide variance you'll find from state to state.

Note that some states also issue titles as well as registrations, but as yet not all do. Most states also offer reciprocity, which allows you to use a properly registered boat in a different state for a designated period—usually between 60 and 120 days—before you have to register it there.

And remember, your certificate of number, which is another name for the registration, must be kept on board and available to boarding officers whenever the vessel is underway.

Registration Numbers

These are similar to an auto registration tag or license plate, but they're also quite different. For one thing, there's no plate! You have to purchase and apply the numbers individually. When you do this, remember to affix them to both sides of the forward half of the bow so that they read from left to right on each side. They must be bold block letters, not less than 3 inches high, of a contrasting color to the hull or background, and they must be placed as high above the waterline as practical. Letters must be separated from numbers by spaces or hyphens; CA 5678 ZZ or CA-5678-ZZ are OK, but CA5678ZZ is not. Also, no number other than that assigned by your registration can be displayed on the forward half of the vessel.

Many states issue validation decals, which offer visual proof that your registration is current. These decals usually must be displayed close to the boat's registration numbers, though exactly where and how close also varies from state to state.

Also varying are the term of registration and date for renewal. Some states require renewal on the anniversary of the initial registration, others on the owner's birthday, and still others on the same date every year for everyone—July 1, for example. In most states registrations are for a single year, though some offer longer terms, such as 2 or 3 years.

Hull Identification Number

All boats manufactured or imported on or after November 1, 1972, must have a hull identification number (HIN); it's another federal regulation. The HIN is a twelve-character number that uniquely identifies a particular boat by manufacturer, model year, model designation, and hull number (it's like the VIN for your car), and you'll need it to get a registration or title in most states. When you buy a boat, you should record the HIN and keep it in a safe place.

On the boat itself, the HIN has been located in two places since 1984. One HIN is permanently attached (or molded into) the transom on the starboard side, as high as possible above the waterline. The second is hidden inside the boat somewhere out of sight, usually beneath some piece of hardware. The location of the second HIN is generally known only to the manufacturer and is used to identify the boat if it's stolen and the thieves change the number on the transom. Some crooks have become so adept at doing this that the change is not easy to detect; having the second HIN helps foil them.

Federal Documentation

This is an option for recreational vessels of at least 5 net tons. Note that in this case a ton is a measurement of volume, not weight. Generally, 5 net tons means a cabin boat of about 30 feet. Net tons result when we subtract any space dedicated to essential mechanical equipment, such as the engine room, from the total interior space, which is the vessel's gross tonnage.

Documentation provides an exemption from the need to be numbered and is fairly easy to obtain, but there are some strings attached. First, the owner must be a U.S. citizen or a U.S. corporation. A certificate of documentation may be endorsed for fishery, coastwise, *registry* [foreign trade], or recreation. But there's a second "string." Although any documented vessel may be used for recreational purposes regardless of its endorsement, a vessel with only a recreational endorsement may NOT be used for any other purpose. This means a yacht that's documented solely for recreation must not be chartered. Chartering is a commercial venture, and if the yacht is so involved, it's not being used for recreation even if the people aboard are there to play.

One solution is to document your boat initially with endorsements for the activities you may someday decide to engage in, even if not until a later date. The downside of this is that it will cost more than documenting a recreational vessel; plus, many insurance companies issue policies based on severest possible use, so having "coastwise" on your document could make for more costly insurance than when you document the boat strictly for recreation. On the other hand, the ability to enter your yacht into charter service at any time without having to wait for a new endorsement could be worth it; processing paperwork can take a while these days. Then, too, many insurance companies will issue a policy based on current use, which should reduce the cost if your boat is used solely for recreation. Just be sure to update the policy before you engage in any commercial activity. If you don't, and should you later have reason to file a claim, you could discover you weren't really insured. Using a boat commercially usually voids a policy issued for recreational use only.

The Upside of Documentation There are quite a few advantages to documentation. Among them, no state numbers need to be displayed on the boat's exterior. There's an official number, however, which remains with the vessel for the duration of its life, regardless of changes in ownership, and which must be permanently affixed inside the boat in a place where it can easily be seen. In the days of mostly wooden vessels, the official number was required to be "carved into the main beam." Outlining the numbers with weld beads does the equivalent on metal hulls even today. But on fiberglass, the usual practice is to use an engraved plaque, which is attached with epoxy so it can't be removed without taking some substrate along with it. Times change, and techniques along with them. But the principle remains. The official number is intended to become a permanent part of the hull and now "must be affixed in a manner which would make alteration, removal, or replacement obvious."

Perhaps the biggest advantage of federal documentation is that it allows issuance of a *preferred ship's mortgage*, which is a maritime lien that has priority over all other liens should there be a default. As you'd expect, lenders are rather fond of the preferred ship's mortgage, and many require one as a condition of financing, which means that if your desired boat is 5 net tons or more, you'll have to document it to get a loan.

Documentation also provides a solid paper trail of ownership from the builder to the current owner and everyone in between. Every time a documented vessel changes hands, a Bill of Sale for Documented Vessels, which is a Coast Guard form (CG-1340), must be recorded with the U.S. Coast Guard. The vessel's file will always reflect all details of past and present ownership. This can be beneficial, and the lack of such a clear record of prior ownership can be an impediment to documenting an older vessel that was previously only numbered.

Documented yachts are officially "vessels of the United States," which can help cut some red tape when you're cruising out of the country; clearly establishing a vessel's nationality can be very important when "going foreign." In some countries, the lack of a national document precludes getting a cruising permit, and visitors with state-numbered boats must check in and clear customs in every port they enter, which soon gets expensive. (This advice may be premature for someone just getting started, but it's good to know. Besides, it pays to plan ahead.)

And the Downside Of course, documentation has some disadvantages, too. We've already discussed one (that legal use of the vessel is limited to the activities listed in the document's endorsements); another is higher costs. As of this writing, the initial documentation fee for a recreational vessel is $100. As we've seen, registration fees vary from state to state and often by size of boat, but on average they are much less than a "Benjamin." Also, while documentation exempts a boat from displaying state numbers, it still may have to be registered, which means twice the paperwork and having to pay both fees. The reason is that about half the states require that resident boats—those on the state's waters for six months or more—must be registered in the state even if they are federally documented. Though documented yachts that are also registered don't have to display numbers on the bow, they must show a current validation decal. And remember, documented vessels are not exempt from state or local taxes or other boating fees.

Documented yachts must display as their hailing port either the owner's city of residence or the boat's port of registry, which is probably different from the boat's actual home port. If the owner is a Delaware corporation (as many are—there are some tax advantages), it may be officially headquartered in Dover, Delaware, which is why you see that hailing port on so many large yachts. This regulation also explains the strange hailing ports you sometimes see, including some totally landlocked cities that could never be a real home to any boat too big to fit on a trailer, such as Denver, Colorado—or even Dover, Delaware, for that matter!

Another minor limitation is that you can't change the name of a documented vessel without involving the Coast Guard and some red tape that includes filing more forms and paying more fees. It's no big deal, but it does involve extra work, time, and expense.

Finally, documented vessels are also required to have the document on board at all times, not merely when underway, as with registrations.

You can get further information on documenting a U.S. vessel by logging onto the Coast Guard's National Vessel Documentation Center website at www.uscg.mil/hq/g-m/vdoc/faq.htm. Or you can contact the center the old-fashioned way at 792 T. J. Jackson Drive, Falling Waters, WV 25419 (800-799-8362).

There are also agencies you can hire to assist you with all the paperwork involved in documenting a vessel. You'll find them advertised in the classified sections of boating magazines.

Buying or Selling

Since registration and documentation involve government entities, there will be a certain amount of paperwork required whenever a boat changes hands. You'll normally need the following in order to satisfy the authorities that everything is legit:

- Proof of ownership, preferably a bill of sale.
- A title signed off by the current owner (if possible; remember, some states don't issue titles).
- The original registration, if it's a "numbered" boat from out of state.

A proper bill of sale will include the following:

- The buyer's name and address.
- The seller's name, address, and signature.
- The length of the craft.
- The year it was built.
- Its brand, or name of the manufacturer.
- The hull identification number (HIN).
- The previous registration number, if applicable.
- The date of purchase.
- The purchase price and, where applicable, proof that the sales tax has been paid (if it has).

Having the seller's signature notarized isn't a bad idea for every bill of sale, although not all states require it.

As noted above, the Coast Guard Bill of Sale form *must* be used in the sale of a documented vessel, or the new owner won't be able to get a new document. These forms must be notarized and submitted in duplicate. They also must be error free; the Coast Guard is notoriously finicky about perfection on the forms required for documentation. When I documented that 80-foot trawler I frequently mention, our application was initially rejected because one builder's form stated it was Hull Number 1, while another listed it as Hull #001. We couldn't get the document until all our papers agreed. Since a broker will usually handle the sale of most vessels large enough to be documented, the brokerage office will probably prepare all requisite paperwork so the buyer and seller don't have to give it a thought. But a little awareness never hurts.

Because You're There

Unlike ashore, where enforcement agents need probable cause to stop a vehicle on the highway, enforcement agents on the water can stop and board a vessel simply because it's there. The bad news: This means you can be stopped at any time. The good news: If you're stopped, it's not necessarily because you've done anything wrong, so you have no reason to panic when it happens to you. The better news: Boarding is usually routine, and if your paperwork is in order and you have all the mandated safety equipment aboard, you'll be left with a paper that states you passed muster (which you can show to future boarding officers to expedite the process next time), along with the boarding team's wishes for a continued good day on the water.

But be aware that boarding officers can terminate a voyage if they find an "especially hazardous condition." This term covers problems such as the following:

- An inadequate number of PFDs.
- An inadequate number of valid fire extinguishers.
- Overloading.
- A boat obviously unsafe for prevailing conditions or the proposed voyage (they may ask where you're headed).
- Failure to display navigation lights (at night).
- Fuel leakage.

- Fuel accumulation in the bilge.
- Excessive leakage or accumulation of water in the bilge.
- Failure to meet carburetor backfire flame arrestor requirements.
- Failure to meet ventilation requirements.

I once saw the Coast Guard terminate a voyage when the boarding team discovered an inoperative bilge blower, though the balance of the ventilation system was fine. Plus, the boat had been underway for a while before it was boarded, and no fuel vapors were detected at any time. Extreme? Perhaps. But it's within their authority to terminate a voyage for any patently unsafe and potentially life-threatening deficiency—an "especially hazardous condition."

Between "A-OK" and "termination of voyage" there are several possibilities. Minor deficiencies such as the lack of a required placard (which we'll cover shortly) will most likely earn you an oral warning or perhaps a written one, if the officer feels so inclined. Your attitude can be a big influence here, so always bend over backward to cooperate and be pleasant. More serious infractions, such as an expired registration, or none at all, will usually get you a citation, which can mean a court appearance and most probably a fine of $50 (or more). By the way, it's not wise to ignore a warning just because there's no hearing or fine involved. Written warnings are entered into a central computer, and should you get a second for the same offense (most likely from a different officer who would be unaware of the first), the computer will flag you as a scofflaw who ignored your first warning. There could be unfavorable consequences. But you can avoid this kind of problem by caring for your boat and its equipment and keeping everything in proper shape at all times.

Another thing you should avoid is negligent operation, which may be defined as "the failure to exercise the degree of care necessary to prevent the endangering of life, limb, or property of any person" (I love that phrase!). Another definition of negligence is the failure to do what a prudent person would do under the same circumstances.

Negligence can be the result of operator ignorance, inattention, indifference, or carelessness, or disregard for the Rules of the Road. Examples include the following:

- Excessive speed in a congested area.
- Excessive speed in fog or stormy conditions.
- Operating under the influence of drugs or alcohol.
- Operating in a swimming area with bathers present.
- Towing water-skiers where obstructions exist, or where a fall might cause them to be hit by other vessels.
- Cutting through a regatta or marine parade in progress.
- Operating in the vicinity of dams when such areas are known to be hazardous.

Not only does this behavior involve considerable risk of injury to others, but it can hurt *you*, the owner/operator, even if everyone else comes out unscathed. You see, negligence can carry some rather stiff penalties, which can apply even if no direct harm results. The objective, of course, is to make you think twice before ever being negligent again. So the enforcers can rap your knuckles quite severely.

Simple negligence can bring a civil penalty of $1,000. Gross negligence carries a civil penalty of up to $5,000 plus a year's imprisonment. But that could be just the half of it. The boat itself can also face matching penalties. Maritime law includes a concept called "in rem" by which the vessel itself can be, in essence, treated as a person and arrested (impounded), charged with violations, and required to pay penalties. Since the boat itself cannot pay anything, ultimate responsibility comes down to the vessel's owner; it's pay up or bye-bye boat. If you're also the operator, you could have to pay twice! Of course, you also face paying the boat's share of penalties, as its owner, when someone else is the operator at fault. So be careful about who you let take the helm.

A good example of in rem proceedings is the Coast Guard's zero-tolerance policy regarding drugs and controlled substances. Any amount found on board, no matter how insignificant, is cause for police action, which can include impounding the boat even if no one aboard is sufficiently connected to the substance to cause the arrest of any person. Think about it: If an illegal substance is found on board, the boat is considered "guilty" and penalized even when they can't tell which human aboard may be guilty also. And at least one person must be, of course; the boat cannot put something aboard itself! It's a tough policy, but that's the way it is.

Speed Limits

On most of our nation's vast waterways you can go as fast as you desire, or at least as fast as safety allows, because there are no speed limits. But in many places there are. Speed regulations are established for various reasons. In some cases speed limits are imposed to protect the shoreline; repeated *wakes* [the progressions of waves created by the motions of vessels—the tracks vessels leave behind] from speeding boats can do severe damage. In other places speed limits are put in place to protect us from each other because going slower allows us more time to react to other vessels where traffic is heavy.

You'll see a lot of speed-limit signs these days, but not all of them are posted legitimately. Those that are will conform to the uniform regulatory format (Figure 27-1). In some portions of some jurisdictions, the speed limits will be displayed as a number, such as 30 mph, but more often the limit will be stated in broader terms, especially for the slower limits.

Idle Speed—No Wake. This is the most restrictive limit. It's also the speed at which you should dock your vessel and the speed to use when you're inside a marina or going through a bridge. Idle speed is like putting a car with an automatic transmission in "Drive" but not stepping on either the gas or brake; the engine will idle, and the car will creep forward at a very low speed. On a boat, idle speed starts by engaging a clutch without advancing the throttle. The engine remains at dead idle, and the boat moves ahead slowly.

Just as that idling car might not roll up a slight incline until you step lightly on the accelerator, a boat operating at idle speed may at times require some throttle to overcome current. This is allowed because idle speed can also be defined as

FIGURE 27-1. *Official markers will have an orange border or, in the case of buoys, orange bands. The orange circle indicates some sort of traffic control such as this speed limit, while a diamond warns of a danger you should avoid. A cross inside the diamond means keep out. Buoys with a diamond and cross often mark the edge of restricted swimming areas along beaches, but they're also used to indicate other places boats must not enter.*

steerageway [the speed required to maintain control of the vessel]. But always start at dead idle first, to see if it's sufficient. If it isn't, throttle up until you just gain control. That way you'll know you're both morally and legally correct. If you should happen to be accused of excessive speed, using the above description of how you determined idle speed should clear you in court (though I can't guarantee it, of course). Just be sure that's what you really did by making it what you always do.

Slow Speed—Minimum Wake. Despite the "minimum wake," the primary purpose of this restriction is to regulate speed. It's often used in high-traffic zones to help reduce accidents. A major factor where I live in Florida is going slowly enough to be able to avoid manatees, lumbering, gentle (and currently endangered) sea

cows. But other jurisdictions have slow-speed zones also, and for a variety of reasons. To conform to this regulation you must have your boat completely off plane and fully settled in the water (not plowing); that is, it must be in the full displacement mode.

The law says both speed and wake should be reasonable under the prevailing conditions, but it fails to define "reasonable." The best solution is to make this another "when in Rome" situation. If you're being overtaken by everyone, you're probably being too cautious. If you're doing most of the overtaking, you may not be cautious enough.

Resume Normal Safe Operation. This is generally posted at the end of a regulated speed zone. In most cases it means you can go back to using the COLREGs definition of safe speed, which is the speed at which a vessel "can take proper and effective action to avoid collision." Please note, however, that sometimes the end of a speed zone will coincide with the approach to a bridge, and "normal safe operation" when going through a bridge is idle speed, right? So don't speed up until the bridge is behind you, and you're sure the way ahead is clear.

Speed limits will generally be well posted, often more universally than we may like. That said, I should also caution that there will be times you should slow down on your own without a posted limit. Going through bridges is one example; here are a few others:

- Around and within marinas.
- In or near fishing or swimming areas.
- Near vessels under tow or those servicing aids to navigation.
- Whenever you aren't sure of what's going on around you.
- When overtaking slower boats in congested waters.

That last example points up another important principle. Under the law, you are always responsible for your wake and any damage it may cause. The full significance of this may register if you recall that some years ago, a woman successfully sued McDonald's for merely *serving* the hot coffee she spilled, which then burned her. Imagine what could happen if someone were to successfully show it was your wake that caused the spill!

Port Security

Ever since September 11, 2001, security has become a major concern in all aspects of life. It's no different on the water. Cruising areas and activities that were once fairly common are now strictly off-limits. The waters in active seaports can be closed from time to time to assure the safety of vessels in port; and ships, especially military vessels, are no longer as approachable as they once were. Unauthorized vessels (that's us) now must stay 100 yards away from all ships in port and reduce speed to "slow" when within 500 yards of a military ship at sea.

Even bridges, which used to be great spots for fishing or for providing a degree of shelter for small open boats when a sudden shower came up, must now be considered in a whole new light. Since bridges are potential targets for terrorists, we are no longer allowed to dally around them for any reason. Now we must get through and get on our way.

Because port security regulations are in a constant state of flux and often change with varying threat levels, it's impossible to outline them all here. But most likely they'll be with us in one form or another for years. So let me offer this toll-free number—800-682-1796—which is a Coast Guard hotline that provides security information for ports and waterways all over the United States. The hotline is automated and menu driven, so you'll have to press a few numbers and probably wait a few moments before you get to the specific port you're looking for, but anytime you dial it, your patience will be rewarded with up-to-date information on the security regulations regarding port openings, closures, and restrictions. Incidentally, Puerto Rico has its own hotline (800-706-2415) with information on twenty-two ports. There's also information online for U.S. ports at www.uscg.mil/safeports.

And if you happen to see any suspicious activity on the water or around the shore, be sure to report it to your local authorities or call the terrorist hotline at 800-424-8802.

There's one final point I should add because it relates security to another issue I covered previously. It's the fact that I've been boarded more times since 9/11 (which as of this writing is a period of 3 years) than in all my previous 25 years of boating in Florida. How things are where you live, I can't say. But down here, enforcement activity has increased exponentially. Of course, Miami and Port Everglades are among the world's busiest ports, and we have a tremendous volume of cruise business, which adds a lot of people to the mix, so the authorities are ultracautious. The Coast Guard and other maritime law enforcement entities—including the Border Patrol and ICE (Immigration and Customs Enforcement)—each have their own boats, and are part of the Department of Homeland Security (which also has its own DHS boats!). These entities now have a much greater presence than ever before, and I must also add that boarding officers don't seem to be as friendly as they used to be, though they're still polite. But now they seem to approach each boarding with a degree of apprehension and increased wariness. And they're much more serious about "taking care of business" when they come aboard. It's hard to say how much this increased law-enforcement visibility actually helps, but it sure goes a long way toward making us feel more secure. We can see our ports are well patrolled.

Education and Licensing

This is another way in which boats are different from cars. Currently, you don't need a license to operate a boat strictly for pleasure in any state (though you do if you carry passengers for hire). In many states there isn't even an age limit! A child way too young to drive a car can freely command a powerboat without adult supervision in quite a few places. But this is changing, thank heaven. I doubt we'll see licenses as a requirement for noncommercial operators anytime soon, but more and more states are establishing mandatory education programs. As of 2004, thirty-seven states require boating education of some sort, and the number is growing. Exactly who is required to meet the mandatory education requirements varies by state, ranging from everybody operating a boat to only those born after a certain date. Each state also sets its own standards as to whether nonproctored classes will satisfy the requirement. Be sure to check the regulations where you live. Most states offer reciprocity on education; generally, evidence of completing a NASBLA-approved course in one state will satisfy the education requirement in all.

Mandatory education is good since formerly, people could go out in boats not only not knowing the Rules of the Road but also not even knowing the Rules existed! After passing a NASBLA-approved course, however, a boater should know the Rules, the equipment requirements, and other safety-based and operational essentials that are very important to the well-being of all of us out there. So all education requirements are a step forward.

What disappoints me personally is that NASBLA approval is, in many ways, the lowest common denominator. Getting all fifty state boating law administrators to agree on what constitutes "required knowledge" brought the minimum standards down too low, in my opinion. But I have to agree that *any* qualified education is better than none, so I can't complain too much.

I do suggest that you take one of the courses offered by the U.S. Coast Guard Auxiliary (www. cgaux.org) or the United States Power Squadrons (www.usps.org). These are also NASBLA-approved courses, but they go far beyond the minimums and are well worth the time and effort involved in taking them. The classes are usually free, though there's a small charge for the text and other course materials you'll need. You can learn more about classes in your area by calling 800-336-2628, the information number for BoatU.S. (the boatowners' advocacy group).

If you're pressed for time, you can also take approved courses online. These courses are not proctored and so do not qualify in all states. But if they work in yours, they're a good quick way to get some structured boating education—in a limited fashion, at least. BoatU.S. offers a course at www. boatus.org/onlinecourse. Others courses are available at www.boater101.net, www.boatingbasics online.com, and www.boat-ed.com. There are others also, but any of these is a good beginning.

Whichever course you choose, whether the more-intensive instruction of a CG Auxiliary or USPS course, or via a quicker Web-based program, I hope you'll decide to get some structured education even if it's not yet required in your state. Passing an approved course usually lowers your insurance premiums, but that's not the only reason I suggest it. In my opinion, there's a better one. I say this often, but only because it's true—one of the greatest joys I've found in boating is that you can never know it all; no matter how much knowledge you acquire, there's always so much more to learn. And the learning just adds to the pleasure. Because in powerboating, it seems the more you know, the more fun you can have.

Protecting the Environment

This should be a goal of all of us who venture forth on the water. After all, if we destroy our waterways with pollution, we'll have no place left to go boating. Nonetheless, our various governments have enacted laws to guide us toward a cleaner, "greener" environment. Many of them are federal regulations that apply everywhere within the United States, while some of them have been enacted in response to international treaties to ensure that U.S. laws are in agreement with the rest of the world. But let's face it—we have just one planet, and pollution doesn't recognize national boundaries, so international cooperation makes sense.

No Oily Waste One of the biggest concerns is the discharge of oil or oily waste, which is prohibited on navigable waters by the Federal Pollution Control Act if that discharge causes a film or discoloration on the surface, or a sludge or emulsion beneath the surface. Violators are subject to substantial civil and/or criminal sanctions including fines of up to $5,000 and imprisonment. Specifically, oil must not be dumped into the bilge or pumped overboard with bilge water.

Inboard engine installations must have a drip pan or other form of containment beneath the engine(s) to keep any leaked oil from spreading around the bilge or mixing with bilge water (which is normal, by the way; all inboards take in water, if only an occasional drop or two where the shaft penetrates the hull).

Skippers caught with oil in the bilge must be able to show how they intend to dispose of it properly. Specifically, you must demonstrate you are able to prevent it from being pumped overboard. Consider using oil-absorbent materials (which attract oil but reject water) or BioSok, an oil-absorbent "sock" that employs petroleum-eating microbes to get rid of the oil.

Vessels 26 feet or more in length must display an oil-discharge placard that measures at least 5 by 8 inches, is made of durable material, is fixed in a conspicuous place in the machinery spaces or at the bilge pump control station, and states the following:

Discharge of Oil Prohibited

The Federal Water Pollution Control Act prohibits the discharge of oil or oily waste upon or into any navigable waters of the U.S. The prohibition includes any discharge that causes a film or discoloration of the surface of the water or causes a sludge or emulsion beneath the surface of the water. Violators are subject to substantial civil and/or criminal sanctions including fines and imprisonment.

Note that these regulations apply not only to engine oil and fuel, but to hydraulic fluids as well, and also to cleaning products and other solvents that are not biodegradable—in other words, *anything* that might put a sheen on the water. You should report violations or spills by calling the Coast Guard's toll-free pollution-control number: 800-424-8802.

No Garbage Another worldwide problem is waterborne garbage, which can litter our beaches and make people sick. That's the reason for the International Convention for the Prevention of Pollution from Ships 1973. These regulations, which were modified by the Protocol of 1978 and are known as MARPOL 73/78, prohibit the discharge of specific types of garbage within certain distances from shore:

MARPOL GARBAGE PROHIBITIONS

GARBAGE TYPE	DISCHARGE PROHIBITED
plastics—including synthetic ropes, fishing nets, and plastic bags	in all areas
floating dunnage, lining and packing materials	less than 25 miles from nearest land
food waste, paper, rags, glass, metal, bottles, crockery, and similar refuse	less than 12 miles from nearest land
comminuted or ground food waste, paper, rags, glass, etc	on all navigable waters of the United States and within 3 miles of nearest land elsewhere

On boats with an LOA of 26 feet or more you must post (where they can be clearly seen by all persons aboard) one or more placards that clearly set forth these regulations. Often known as SOS (Save Our Seas) placards (Figure 27-2), they also state the serious penalties involved for failure to obey the regulations, which can include fines up to $500,000 (for organizations) and jail time up to 6 years.

Note the prohibition against dumping ground-up garbage, such as from a Disposall or In-Sink-Erator in a galley sink with direct overboard discharge, unless you are beyond the 3-mile limit. I'm not completely convinced this is necessary. After all, minuscule amounts of finely ground food particles should disperse and be eaten quickly by various sea creatures as long as there's at least some current in the area to keep it from just settling, as there would be most anywhere outside the confines of a cul-de-sac marina. Besides, the regulations were established primarily for ships, and there's a huge difference in the amount of food waste a small pleasure boat might discharge when compared to any ship, and especially when compared to a cruise ship. On the other hand, we have to consider the cumulative effects—I'm sure you recall the fable about the camel and the straws. And it *is* the law, so beware.

Note also that although some materials may be dumped legally if you're far enough offshore (though I don't recommend it), plastic is prohibited everywhere! Plastic refuse dumped in the water can kill fish and marine life and can foul

FIGURE 27-2. *Federal law requires that all vessels 26 feet and over display one or more MARPOL pollution placards in a prominent location so that they can be read by the crew and passengers. The placard must be at least 9 inches wide by 4 inches high; state that discharge of plastic or garbage mixed with plastic into any waters is prohibited; state that discharge of all garbage is prohibited in the navigable waters of the United States and, in all other waters, within 3 nautical miles of the nearest land. Note that stiff criminal penalties can be imposed for failure to obey these regulations. (Courtesy BoatU.S.)*

vessel propellers and cooling-water intakes. The best bet: DON'T DUMP ANY GARBAGE OR ANY KIND OF TRASH INTO THE WATER ANYWHERE. PERIOD!

In addition to the placard, the regulations also require a "written waste disposal plan" on ocean-going boats of 40 feet and up. This plan can be quite simple, such as: "First mate will collect all trash, stow it in plastic bags, and keep them secured until we return to the marina, where they will be taken ashore and put in the dumpster." But you must have a plan if your boat is 40 feet or longer.

You'll find the above-mentioned oil and trash placards in most marine stores, though to be honest, I really question their need. I like to think those of us who care about the environment won't pollute the water with anything and don't need placards to remind us. And let's face it, mere signs won't stop people who *don't* care, even if they contain the threat of a stiff fine and a jail term—we've seen that from numerous cruise-ship violations over the years. But the law requires placards, and the reminders can't hurt, so be sure you post them if your boat is 26 feet or longer.

No Raw Sewage Sewage is another concern. Any MSD (marine sanitation device; maybe it's this mouthful that prompts us to use the word "head" instead), installed on your boat must be certified by the U.S. Coast Guard and of a type authorized for the area where you will be boating. Local law takes precedence here, too, and not all types are acceptable everywhere. Be sure to check what's legal for you.

Remember, it's against the law to dump raw sewage overboard anywhere within U.S. territorial limits. You must contain sewage in a holding tank and have it removed at the pumpout station you'll find at most public marinas (Figure 27-3), or use an approved treatment device to treat the sewage prior to discharge. (These rules do not apply to portable toilets that can be taken ashore to be dumped.)

If you have a Type III MSD (which is a holding tank), you can opt to bypass it and discharge directly overboard when you're outside territorial limits. If you use a Y-valve to switch sewage flow from holding tank to overboard discharge, it must be set to "No Discharge" when you're inside territorial limits, and there must be some means of locking or securing the valve in this position. This is subject to inspection by boarding officers, by the way, and they *will* look.

FIGURE 27-3. *This sign on the end of the pier shows this marina has pumpout facilities. Look for one where you stop for fuel. You'll also find pumpout stations listed in most cruising guides.*

Remember too, some waters are NO DIS-CHARGE, period. You must not discharge sewage in these areas even if it has been treated. Again, the best bet is to check local regulations wherever you go.

And No Noise! Though it doesn't necessarily impact on our physical environment, noise pollution is also a growing concern because it adversely affects us, nonetheless. As a result, many states have enacted laws to control it on their waterways. In many ways, this is a manufacturing problem because the buyer has limited control over how loud a boat may be—it is what it is. And for that reason, many of the noise-prevention laws exempt boats built before a certain date, since newer models usually have been equipped with mufflers designed with current compliance in mind, while older ones do not comply. Maintaining a boat to continue to meet noise regulations is the owner's responsibility, however, so you should be aware of what's required on the waters you use.

Handle with Care There are also other local environmental concerns that may affect us when operating boats. For instance, here in my adopted home state of Florida, authorities are quite serious about protecting sea-grass beds because they are nurseries for so many forms of sea life. Heavy fines and reparation costs can be imposed on the owners of boats that go aground and damage sea grass, which only adds to the often-considerable cost of getting properly refloated, to say nothing about the cost of repairing any damage the grounding may have done to the boat. Talk about adding insult to injury!

Those of us who are active on the water here are routinely reminded of these fines and added costs, but groundings still occur. The fines just add more incentive for us to pay attention. Similar situations exist in other places, too, so always check the local environmental laws wherever you go, and always operate your boat with care. It could save you money. And your planet will thank you.

Accident Reporting
There's one more situation in which you may find yourself involved with the law. If you have an accident on the water, you must report the accident to your state boating law enforcement agency using an official accident report form whenever any of the following occur:
- A person dies within 24 hours.
- A person loses consciousness or requires medical attention beyond basic first aid.
- There's property damage in excess of $2,000. (It used to be only $500, but costs are rising!)
- A person disappears from the vessel under circumstances that indicate injury or death.
- There's a complete loss of a vessel.

Failure to report an accident carries some stiff penalties including a $10,000 fine and the possibility of 15 years in prison.

To end this chapter on a positive note, I should add that these accident-reporting requirements might very well be among those things you should know about but never really need. If you "drive" defensively, faithfully follow the Rules of the Road, and keep your boat in good repair, you should have a long and happy boating career that never involves a reportable accident.

28

Introduction to Navigation

Simply stated, navigation is the science—and art—of successfully guiding a vessel from one place to another. It can be as straightforward as steering toward a plainly visible object nearby or as complicated as steering toward an unmarked and unseen spot in the water (known as a *waypoint*) that could remain totally invisible even when we arrive there—though a good navigator will find it nonetheless.

Navigation can also entail steering toward something that's unseen because it lies beyond visible range, or even finding your way when seeing things has been taken out of the equation entirely by darkness, fog, or other elements of nature.

It should be obvious that you'll need to use some form of navigation if you're ever going to take your boat anywhere away from "home." Of course, you might scoot across the harbor and back by visual reference alone. But the offshore adventures I suggest in Chapter 34, or even shorter journeys closer to home, will require something more than this if you plan to go and return without getting lost—or stuck.

Admittedly, the subject of navigation deserves far more attention than I can possibly give in one brief chapter. Indeed, there are entire books, most of them much thicker than this one, devoted to nothing but navigation. Their sheer bulk, however, can often make them quite daunting. There's also another thorny aspect. Although all of the books are technically correct, many were written from the perspective of ship navigation, and reading them could lead you to believe the process is involved and difficult. But it really isn't, and because the realities of navigating a boat demand a different approach, I recommend you read—no, better make that study—one book: *Boat Navigation for the Rest of Us* by Captain Bill Brogdon, a retired U.S. Coast Guard officer with vast experience on ships *and* boats.

Bill's book is about the same size as this one, so it shouldn't be at all intimidating. And you'll find it informative as all get-out because the guy really knows his stuff; he's been on the water all his life. Yet it's also easy to read because not only does Bill know the subject thoroughly, but he also knows how to relate it so enjoyably that learning is practically painless. Most important, as the title suggests, the book is aimed directly at solving the problems we face in navigating *boats*.

I could stop there. After all, the purpose of this chapter is merely to acquaint you with navigation and the need to learn it, at least at a rudimentary level, if you plan to enjoy your boat to its fullest. Except I still sense a hint of reluctance on your part. "Listen," I can hear you say, "why do I need to know navigation? With the electronics available today, at least from what I've seen at boat shows or read about in magazines, all I have to do is buy the right equipment, and it will do all the navigating for me."

Well, you're partially correct. Today's navigational electronics are amazing in what they can do. Further, they're constantly improving to the point that some new systems now coming on the market were only science fiction not too long ago. And I'll be the first to admit that I find these tools invaluable. In fact, were I to begin an ocean passage tomorrow, I would pack a handheld GPS or two (and lots of spare batteries) as backup to the vessel's built-in system rather than bring a sextant, almanac, and sight-reduction tables. The reasons are accuracy and ease of use. GPS has celestial navigation beat by a mile. Literally. And on all counts. But, and this is *so* important, I can rely heavily on electronic devices because I also know how to navigate without them; I know what they're doing inside. I also know what they *can't* do, and therefore I don't ask them to do those things.

One thing you absolutely should never ask any piece of electronic gear to do is show you how to get somewhere. Oh, it will do it. And quickly, too; functional speed is one of the charms of electronic navigation. The problem is that when you ask how to get from where you are to where you want to go, electronics such as GPS or the older (but still in use) Loran-C will give you the shortest, most direct way to go from here to there. Always. And they will do this even if following that course would take you across a sandbar or rocks or even across land! Remember, even the most sophisticated electronic devices can't think; they merely calculate.

Of course, to give electronics their due, steering toward a visible object by eye alone could also take us across a sandbar or rocks in many places; usually the water isn't clear enough to see for more than several inches beneath the surface. So we often need to preview our course by first examining a chart to make sure the way we've chosen allows safe passage even when we're "eyeballing" (Figure 28-1). This is elementary. Learning how to read the essential information you'll find on a nautical chart should be the basis of your navigational knowledge if you never learn anything else. But learning to plot courses to steer should really be next, even if you don't do it on paper. And these days we so often don't. Electronic charts displayed on the colorful screens of GPS-linked computer-like (or PC-based) plotters are increasingly popular on even some very small boats. Much of the actual work of navigation can now be done for us. But even if you use electronics exclusively, it's wise to understand

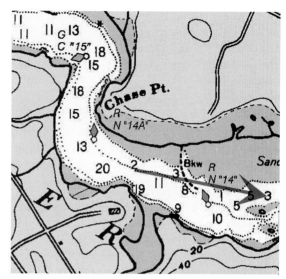

FIGURE 28-1. *This is a portion of the Saco River near where I grew up in Maine. Many an unknowing skipper has torn out the bottom of his boat by running onto that submerged breakwater (Bkw) curving out from the north bank. At many stages of the tide, the river appears to widen after you round Chase Point. And it does. Except most of that width is not navigable. Heading "straight down the middle," which would seem a good idea, takes you right across the breakwater (arrow). Using a chart, or even just paying attention to the channel markers, will guide you over toward the south bank where there's plenty of water. Eyeball alone is rarely enough. (Courtesy Maptech)*

what these devices are doing for you by learning how to do it yourself.

And of course, knowing how to navigate on your own will save you from being caught "up the well-known tributary without any visible means of propulsion" (as a friend used to put it) in the totally possible event your nifty electronic navigation devices don't have power, get dropped overboard, or otherwise leave you in the lurch by being unavailable or inoperative.

Besides, it's also possible to use good ol' paper charts and still rely on GPS for help. Not every boating budget is large enough to include electronic charting even if the boat itself is. So while I in no way intend to disparage the use of electronics, let me introduce you to some elements of the science of navigation. You should understand the principles thoroughly whether you use them with, or instead of, electronic systems. As for learning the *art* of navigation . . . well, as with any skill, you can only develop artistry over time through continued practice and a growing familiarity with the process. But this, too, can be part of the fun.

The Tools of the Navigator

Navigation requires little equipment, and learning to use it is as simple as learning to use a knife and fork. Of course, you can complicate things with some of the specialized gear you'll see in catalogs or marine stores. And if you really get into navigating, you just might want to. But the beautiful part is you don't have to. You can stick with the simple basics for as long as you go boating and never, ever need anything more. Among the essentials are the following:

Charts (see Figure 28-1). These are graphic representations of given chunks of water and their surrounds. Charts are to boating as road maps are to driving. But just as operating a boat is different from driving a car, so too are nautical charts very different from road maps. In many ways. There are no route numbers, but you'll see water depths, aids and hazards to navigation, prominent landmarks, directional references (to both true and magnetic north), shorelines, and more. While charts are printed in different scales (such as 1:40,000, where 1 inch on the chart represents 40,000 inches on our planet), nearly all charts show much more than you can see from the helm of a boat. Thus, you can plan ahead and have a preview of waters that lie beyond your visible range. Even if you forsake paper charts and go strictly electronic, you absolutely cannot navigate without a chart of some kind.

Note: In time, you'll be able to navigate familiar waters without consulting a chart, just as you drive familiar highways without looking at a map. This doesn't mean that a chart is no longer necessary, but rather that you have developed one in your mind and are constantly referencing it subconsciously. That's fine. But let me repeat, be-

cause it's so important, you absolutely cannot navigate safely without reference to a chart of some kind, even if it's only in your head.

Compass (Figure 28-2). This is your prime source of directional information aboard your boat. Its main feature is a circular compass card, which is marked around its circumference to divide all the directions that surround us into 360 degrees, measured clockwise from north. This makes east 090, south 180, and west 270.

Contrary to appearances, the card does not rotate as your boat changes course. Instead, because there are magnetic needles beneath it, the card constantly aligns itself with the earth's magnetic field to point toward magnetic north. Within the compass housing there's a reference mark, called the *lubber line*, which indicates your compass heading because it rotates around the card as the boat turns. The result is that you always know which way is north. But more important, thanks to the lubber line you can always know which way you're headed. And you should always pay attention to your compass heading even

FIGURE 28-2. *The compass is our primary directional reference on the water. Here the lubber line shows us here we're on a compass heading of 004 degrees. (Courtesy E.S. Ritchie & Sons)*

when you're steering by visual reference. Remember, the card is still, and the lubber line moves around it, so to change your heading, you must bring the lubber line to the number, not the number to the line.

Plotting tools (Figure 28-3). These are what we use to work with paper charts. Take the course to steer. It starts with drawing a line that runs from where you are to where you want to go. After checking to make sure the way is clear and that following it won't take you over a sandbar or rocks or into water too shallow for your draft, you then have to determine the line's direction so you can follow it by compass. *Parallel rules* allow you to transfer the line back to a *compass rose*, one of the representations of a compass card that, for convenience, are printed in several places on most charts.

The compass roses are actually a two-in-one deal. Within the outer rose, which shows directions in reference to true north, the same north as

the "pole" at the top end of the earth's axis of rotation, there's also an inner rose that accounts for variation, the element that results from the earth's magnetic field not aligning perfectly with its rotational axis, and thus places magnetic north to the left or right (west or east) of true. Using the inner rose to do all your plotting in terms of magnetic north is the easier way to go. If you plot as true, you have to allow for variation before you can steer by compass. This difference between true and magnetic north varies with your location on the globe—is that why it's called variation?—and also changes over time. Each compass rose will show the present variation in that area as well as the amount and direction of annual change.

A *course protractor* allows reference to a parallel of latitude or meridian of longitude. (These form the grid we superimpose on the globe and charts.) Since the parallels run east-west and the meridians north-south, they can serve as directional references, though you'll have to allow for

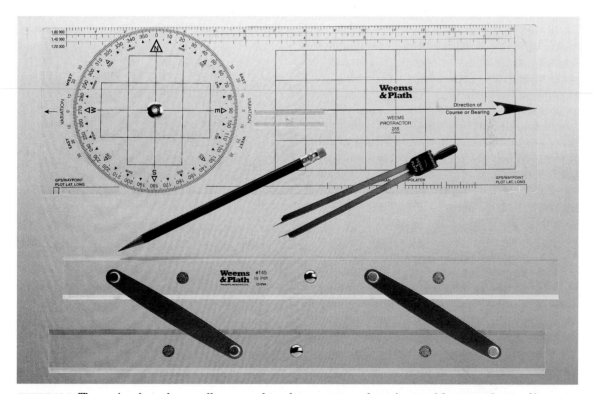

FIGURE 28-3. *These simple tools are all you need to plot courses and navigate with paper charts: (from top) course protractor, pencil, dividers, and parallel rules. (Courtesy Weems & Plath)*

variation before you can use the protractor directions effectively because the grid is aligned with true north. More important, the grid system allows each spot on earth to be identified by its intersection of parallel with meridian. Much as a city destination might be given as being "at the corner of 4th and Main," a spot on the water (or land) can be identified by its unique intersection of latitude and longitude. For example, the tidal reference station at the entrance to Miami Harbor can be pinpointed as being at 25° 45.9' N (latitude) 080° 08.1' W (longitude). A GPS numerical display will show you where you are in terms of latitude and longitude. Thus, with either the parallel rules or course protractor we have both a straightedge to aid in drawing the line and a means of determining the line's direction.

Incidentally, a similar approach will work when we draw a line that represents the bearing of a prominent landmark, the use of which can help us determine where we are. More on this later.

Needless to say, but I will anyway, plotting on paper also requires a sharp pencil and an eraser.

Of course, if you use an electronic plotter and charts, all the tools will be inside the equipment and activated by a mouse, trackball, touch pad, or other similar device that allows you to move and pin down a cursor.

Dividers. These allow you to measure the length of lines on the chart and relate them to the chart's distance scales so you don't have to stop and calculate as in, "Let's see. This line measures 6½ inches, which at 1:40,000 would be 260,000 inches on earth. If we divide that by the 72,864 inches in a nautical mile . . ." Well, you get the picture. Using the chart's scales is a much easier way to determine distance. Then again, if you're using an electronic plotter, the *range* [distance] and *bearing* [direction] of any waypoint, landmark, or object can be determined and displayed for you.

Watch or clock. Time is an essential element in navigation; the more accurate your timepiece, the more precise you can be all around. A stopwatch can be handy, too, for such things as determining the interval of the flashing lights on aids to navigation so you can tell them apart, or precisely timing the transit of a given leg of your route.

Depth sounder. Whether you use an old-fashioned *lead line* [a lead weight you drop to the bottom, which is suspended from a line that has markers along its length to indicate depths] or a modern device with a colorful graphic display that shows "pictures" of the bottom, or something in between, such as a basic rotary flasher or digital sounder that shows depth only as a number, you can usually benefit from knowing how much water lies beneath you. The bottom will often be the closest land, and knowing just how close it is can be extremely valuable.

As I wrote above, these are all the tools you'll ever really need, but here are a few more you might find helpful:

Nautical slide rule (Figure 28-4). This device allows quick calculation of the simple math involved in basic *piloting*, which is what we often call coastwise and inland navigation. The math is easy enough to do without the slide rule, but using one is so much easier and faster (as well as more accurate if your math skills are like mine!) that it's well worth having. You can also do the computation with a scientific calculator, though in many ways this is overkill because those things

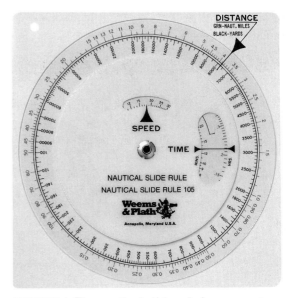

FIGURE 28-4. *The nautical slide rule is an easy-to-use device that helps us solve speed, time, and distance equations without actually having to do the math. (Courtesy Weems & Plath)*

are capable of so much more. But a "regular" calculator won't do. Since time is involved, and that requires counting in 60s rather than 10s and 100s, you need the scientific calculator so you can enter time as degrees, which are also based on multiples of 60. The nautical slide rule works just as well and costs a lot less. Plus, it doesn't need batteries, and you don't have to remember any formulas in order to use it.

Tide tables. I list these as an option, despite the importance of knowing the present tide stage if you boat in tidal waters, because this information is usually so readily available from many other, less formal sources. Cruising guides usually contain tide tables. In coastal communities, daily newspaper weather information usually contains some tidal data, at least the times of high and low tides, as do many weathercasts on local radio and TV. More complete information is usually available in regional boating newspapers. One of the nice aspects of these publications is that they often present tidal information in a graphic display that gives you a visual indication of the height of tide at any time.

You can also get tidal information online at several websites. My favorite (www.tides.com/tcpred.htm) is one posted by Nobeltec, a company that publishes some excellent navigational software. There you can find tide (and current) in-formation for the current day and the next day for any of the thousands of tidal stations and substations listed in the standard tide and current tables. The information is also presented in both graphic and tabular form (Figure 28-5). The only limitation of the site, in my opinion, is that you can't plan any further ahead than tomorrow. But hey, the information is free! And if you want to plan further ahead, Nobeltec has a tide and current program you can buy to have your very own reference source good for any time (www.nobeltec.com). You can also find tidal data, in tabular form only, if you go to the NOAA site at http://co-ops.nos.noaa.gov and click on "Predictions," or go to www.saltwatertides.com, a commercial site that also has complete information (though it's labeled as "not for navigation") for most U.S. tidal waters.

Just remember, basic tide tables are stated in standard time. During daylight saving time, you have to add an hour. But some of the above-mentioned sources show tides for the time basis currently in use, so no correction is necessary. But be aware that during daylight saving time, if you don't add an hour to standard time listings, your tide estimates will be an hour early. But if you add an hour to tables that have been corrected already, you'll be an hour late. So be sure you know the time basis of the tide tables you use.

FIGURE 28-5. *One sample (for New Harbor, Maine) of the tidal data available on line at www.tides.com/tcpred.htm. This website covers all the thousands of tidal stations listed in the government Tide Tables; information for the current day and the following day is free. (Courtesy Nautical Software Inc.)*

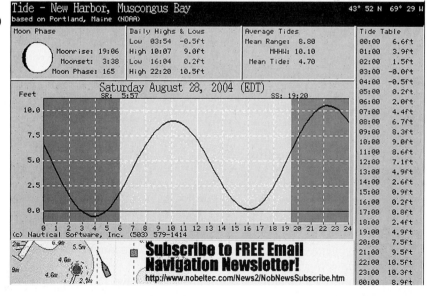

Actually, you could ignore tides completely and just use charted depths as your guide. But you'd be missing a lot. Charted depth is generally mean low or lower low water—the average, if you will, of *all* low tides. Thus, there most often is greater depth than that shown on the chart. The exception comes during the very low (and high) spring tides that occur during and after full and new moons. Then the tide is extremely low, often well below the mean, and thus there's less water than the chart shows—a *minus* tide, we call it. But most of the time there will be more. So you can generally look at charted depth as the least water available.

Since the increase in depth that results from a rising tide can often make available some of those waters the chart indicates are too shallow, being aware of the stage of tide can often open opportunities you'd otherwise miss. If you plan on entering these waters, it's a good idea to know how much more depth there should be at any given time. It can be well worth your while to gain an understanding of tidal action and acquire the complete information for your area—height as well as times—from some reliable source that gives you more than just the times of high and low tides.

Global positioning system (GPS). This satellite-based system is the most accurate navigation system yet devised—under optimum conditions it can place you within 12 yards of an exact spot. That's a mere 36 feet, barely a boat length for many people. Even in less than optimum conditions, a GPS brings you more than close enough for practical purposes. And much closer than you can determine by any other means.

I list a GPS as optional because you can navigate without it, though I honestly would prefer not to. And small handheld receivers can be inexpensive enough these days that you really don't have to go without it.

Not only can a GPS tell you where you are at all times, but most receivers have the ability to store waypoints in memory, both individually and grouped as routes. If you carefully check each route before you enter it, to make sure the path from waypoint to waypoint is safe and clear, the GPS memory can be a great help. Just remember

what I wrote above about these units lacking the ability to think.

Here's a perfect example. Say you have the entrance to your marina stored as a waypoint in your GPS. You go out with friends one fine afternoon and have so much fun you foolishly stop paying attention to where you are. After a while, you find yourselves out of sight of land. If you're not lost, you're at least considerably bewildered because, to tell the truth, you no longer have a clue as to where you are other than somewhere offshore.

"No problem!" you think, "I'll just select the waypoint at my marina entrance as a 'Go To' and the GPS will take us back." Please don't. Remember, the GPS will give you the most direct route, and that may not be such a good idea. Instead, use the GPS display of your current position to mark where you are on a chart and then see if the straight line back is wise. If so, fine. If not, you need to proceed differently and go around any obstacles. Often, this is as easy as deciding on a single waypoint to go to that will allow you to clear any obstructions, and then you can go straight to your ultimate destination. The chart will show what you need to do.

One of the most useful features of a GPS, as we'll see shortly, is that not only can it tell you where you are at any moment, but it can also calculate and display your actual speed and course over the ground as you go along. These data can be even more helpful than current position. In fact, it's the GPS displays of SOG (speed over ground) and COG (course over ground) that I use the most during routine navigation.

Autopilot. These devices can steer a straighter course than any human, which can be a huge advantage. It's unbelievably helpful when the course you actually follow is nearly as straight as the course line you drew on the chart!

Further, steering by autopilot can free your eyes from staring at a compass and free your hands from the wheel so they can do other necessary things, such as work with your navigational instruments or chart. But it should never free you from maintaining a lookout. That would be much too dangerous.

Another benefit of most modern autopilots is that they can be interfaced with a GPS to steer toward a waypoint or follow a route you've stored in its memory. Although this can be a huge plus, electronic interfacing isn't necessary to the mating of autopilot and GPS; you can also do it with a human interface. I'll explain how in just a bit.

Finally, most of today's autopilots use a flux-gate compass, which has a wire coil, rather than magnetic needles, to sense the earth's magnetic field. The unit's control panel will usually display your heading digitally. In addition to providing you with another source of heading information, that digital display can often be more reliable than your magnetic compass. First, being non-mechanical, it can respond much faster to the changing headings as you turn. More important, there's a sneaky devil called *deviation*, in which onboard iron or steel interferes with the ability of a magnetic compass to line up exactly with the earth's magnetic lines of force and thus prevents it from pointing straight to magnetic north all the time. Deviation can often be eliminated from an autopilot's functions by the magic of internal digital logic. (This correction usually isn't automatic until you program it, which is often as simple as pushing the correct buttons to let the system know your intentions and then swinging the boat through a few circles as the unit's internal computer calculates the differences between the magnetic headings it senses and the evenly spaced 360 degrees of change that should occur when the boat makes a circle. After a few such circles, the unit will apply the proper corrections to equate what it senses to an even 360 degrees and change its output and display to match, which effectively eliminates deviation.) Thus, the digital display on your autopilot can be a more accurate reflection of your heading than the one shown by your magnetic compass.

Binoculars. These "glasses" bring things closer—things such as aids to navigation or landmarks you can't quite identify with the naked eye. Though 7 x 50 is often considered the standard for marine use, that's just tradition. In practical terms, you should test many different models, in both brand and power, and buy the best binoculars you can afford that work comfortably and well for you. In the long run they'll be much better for your eyes—and your navigation.

A Closer Look

I must again remind you this chapter is not intended to teach you all you need to know about navigation, but rather to introduce you to some of the principles in order to 1) show you just how easy and logical the process is, and 2) perhaps whet your appetite to learn more. But I think it's still a good idea to examine some details.

Let's start again with charts. Because they're representations of relatively large areas of the earth printed on small pieces of paper, they use a shorthand of sorts to present the greatest amount of information with the least possibility for confusion and clutter. Once you learn the shorthand, you can tell a lot about an area with just a glance.

To begin with, there's a color code. Land areas are printed in beige, shallow water is blue, areas that become dry, or nearly so, at low tide but which are covered with water at higher tides are (a usually pale) green, and the deeper water is white. The depth at which the chart changes from blue to white depends on its scale, but with many charts, you'll be sure to stay afloat if you stay out of the blue, though this isn't always possible.

Of course, depth is also shown by numbers. But what units these numbers represent can vary. Traditionally on U.S. charts, *soundings* [depths] have been mostly in feet. But some charts still use the *fathom*, an ancient nautical measure that equals 6 feet. Newer editions of charts are going metric and show the depths in meters and *decimeters* [tenths of a meter]. Since there's a significant difference between a fathom, a meter, and a foot, it's important to know the units of measurement your chart uses for soundings. Fortunately, this will always be printed on the chart, usually quite boldly and in more than one place.

Another neat feature is that thin curved lines, called *depth contours*, will often connect areas of equal depth. In many cases, these depth contours can be a useful aid to either knowing where you are, or knowing which way to go. I'll explain this later.

There's much more to the system of symbols and other shorthand used on charts. For example, there are different ways of showing the shoreline, from semisubmerged marshes to beaches with breakers to steep, high and dry bluffs. Once you learn to recognize the symbols, you can get a detailed image of what you can expect to see when you get where you'll be going, even if you've never been there. If you plan to do much traveling, I suggest you obtain and study a copy of *Chart No. 1*, a book that explains *all* the symbols used on U.S. charts. But for now, I just hope you'll get the idea that a chart can be chock-full of wonderful, even if often rather cryptic, information.

Aids to navigation, the red and green channel markers you'll often see on the water, are shown on the charts also, allowing you to preview a route you may have to follow to stay in navigable water. Covering the entire subject of AtoN (as the Coast Guard often calls them) would take another chapter—or more! So let me just hit the highlights. Navaids can be identified by three elements:

- **Color.** As you proceed in from seaward or go up a river, red marks will be on your right, green on your left. The navigable channel runs between the red and green. A good way to remember this is with the alliterative mnemonic "Red right returning."
- **Shape.** Fixed red aids are triangular, while unlighted red buoys (called *nuns*) have a conical top. Fixed green aids are square, while unlighted green buoys (called *cans*) are cylindrical. The large lighted buoys marking deep-water ship channels won't

have a distinctive shape, though the smaller lighted aids, both fixed and floating, found on the Intracoastal Waterway and other protected waters will generally have the shape of their unlighted counterparts. The light on a lighted aid will usually match the mark's base color, though it may also be white.
- **Number.** Navaids in the lateral system (so called because the aids indicate which side to take them on) are numbered, which helps in correlating an aid you see on the water with the correct one on the chart; charts also show the colors and numbers of navaids. As a further help, red marks will always be even numbered, while green ones will be odd.

The numbers can also help you know which way is "returning" on the many waterways that are neither a channel in from the sea nor a trip upstream. Although I don't recommend navigating without reference to a chart, this method will do in a pinch. It works whenever you can see two or more aids. Just look ahead; if the next marker up has a higher number than the closer one, you're "returning" and want to keep the red ones to your right. If the next mark has a lower number than the close one, you are *not* "returning" and should keep the green ones on your right (Figure 28-6).

FIGURE 28-6. *You see some green markers ahead; which side should you take them on? In this case, because the numbers are increasing, you're "Returning," so you want to keep them on your port. (Remember "Red Right Returning.")*

The Process

In basic navigation, we're concerned with four elements: direction, time, speed, and distance; the latter three are inexorably interrelated. Their relationship is shown in our basic measure of speed, miles per hour, which is merely another way of stating that by definition, speed equals distance (miles) divided by (per) time (hour). Since these elements are so tightly linked, if we know any two of them, we can solve for the third. Of course, a nautical slide rule makes it easy; just line up any two known elements and the unknown becomes immediately apparent. But just so you can work without the slide rule, let's reexamine these elements and their relationships.

The mnemonic address "60 D St." is a good way to do this. It's a reminder of the formula 60 x D = ST, which tells us that 60 times D (distance), equals S (speed) times T (time). To get the distance traveled in any given time, we multiply that time by our speed. And since our time underway is most often measured in minutes, but our speed is measured in hours (mph), we divide that result by 60. (If it's been a while since you studied math, let me remind you that items above the dividing line on one side of an equal sign drop to below the line when they cross to the other side of the equation. Therefore, if 60 x D = ST, D = ST/60.)

By rearranging the formula to solve for the unknown, we can use math to do what the slide rule does for us—find the third element when we know any two. Thus to find speed, we use S = (60 x D)/T and to find time, T = (60 x D)/S. That 60 is in there, remember, because our measurement of speed is in miles per hour, while in more practical terms we'll be measuring time in minutes, which are $\frac{1}{60}$ of an hour. Incidentally, in saltwater areas we're more inclined to use nautical miles and knots than statute miles and mph. But it's essentially the same because a knot is 1 nautical mile per hour.

Let me interject something here briefly. It's not terribly important at this stage of your navigational knowledge (though I hope you find it helpful), but I offer it mainly because it's further proof of just how neat, orderly, and well structured the whole system is. While our U.S. charts are going metric in terms of depths, vertical clearances, and many other measurements (to keep up with the general metrification of the rest of the world), it's unlikely the nautical mile will ever give way to the kilometer. You see, a nautical mile is very, very close to being equal to 1 minute ($\frac{1}{60}$ of a degree) of latitude; close enough that for practical purposes we can consider them the same. This allows us to use the latitude scales at the sides of Mercator charts to also measure distance.

The process of converting the surface of our three-dimensional sphere of a planet to the flat two-dimensional surface of a chart is known as *projection*. There are several kinds, but on coastal charts the *Mercator projection* is most common. One of the features of the Mercator projection is that parallels and meridians are placed on the chart at right angles. This creates some distortions but allows the shapes of landmasses to be represented much as they actually look. One of the distortions is that meridians, which are actually converging as they approach the poles, become equidistant on the chart. This causes parallels, which are actually equidistant on earth, to be spaced farther and farther apart as they go north (or south) from the equator. While the difference in spacing is insignificant on charts of the scales commonly used for coastal navigation, you'll still achieve greater accuracy if you measure distance on the latitude scale immediately to the left or right of your position.

Yes, with the ease of working with the Mercator projection, the nautical mile is far too convenient, in both theory and practice, for us to ever abandon it for anything metric. This also explains why we use nautical miles rather than statute miles in marine navigation; nautical miles are more convenient. The difference? A nautical mile is 1.15 statute miles, so a knot is 1.15 mph. There. Now we can get on with things.

Position Finding

While the main objective of navigation is to enable us to get to where we want to go, in practice the process also involves determining our current position from time to time as we go along. After all, we need to know where we are in order to figure how to steer to where we want to be. Having more than one way to do this can be a huge help in not getting lost.

Ded reckoning (often written as "dead reckoning," though the *ded* is short for *deduced*) is a time-honored method of keeping track of where you are. It's simply a matter of applying elapsed time to determine the distance traveled as you proceed in a given direction at a known speed. For example, if you head east at 20 knots, after a half hour you should be 10 miles east of your starting point. The process is always that simple, though real-world speeds and times rarely allow you to figure the answer in your head so easily. Just remember to log or otherwise record your departure time, or you won't have any basis for measuring elapsed time. You should plot a DR position at regular intervals, say every half hour, to keep a running track of your progress.

The main problem with ded reckoning is that even if you know your boat's speed very well at different throttle settings (engine rpm), those are speeds through the water. But wind and current can make your actual speed over the ground either faster or slower, depending on their strength and direction(s) relative to your heading. Similarly, you can hold the lubber line on your intended course with as steady a hand as possible, or have an autopilot do it for you to hold even steadier, yet after a while, those same pesky natural elements can also push you toward one side or the other so you end up going slightly left or right of your intended track (remember leeway?). Thus, ded reckoning becomes less and less accurate with the passage of time. The farther you get from a known position, the less sure you can be of where you are.

This is where a GPS can come in. Let's look again at the above situation, heading east at 20 knots. If you steer to keep your GPS display reading of COG at 090 regardless of your compass heading, you'll know you're compensating for wind and current and following your intended course line. Similarly, you could either adjust your throttle(s) to get an exact 20-knot SOG or, if your boat operates best at the throttle setting that produces 20 knots through the water, leave the throttle(s) alone and use your actual SOG as

shown by your GPS in calculations of ETA (estimated time of arrival) and such. Either way, you'll be better off than you'd be without using the GPS. And, of course, you can cross-check the positions displayed by your GPS with the equivalent latitude/longitude on the chart to confirm you are where you should be.

If you don't have the accurate knowledge of course and speed that a GPS can provide, your DR positions will not be as precise. But even if your actual track wanders, and current distorts the accuracy of your estimate of speed by quite a bit, your DR positions will still be better than the "not a clue" you'd have without them. Besides, GPS technology is relatively new. Our forebearers were able to determine where they were without it, and we can, too. The answer lies in lines of position.

Line of Position (LOP)

An LOP is simply a line on which your position happens to fall. Because you can be anywhere along that line, a single LOP isn't much help, though it's still far better than knowing nothing! But with just one more LOP you have the basis of a *fix* [a very accurate position]. Add a third, and you're really pinning things down.

Here's how it works. Say you're headed north out of Port Everglades, Florida, on your way up to Palm Beach. Along the way you see the huge black-and-white steel skeleton tower of the lighthouse at Hillsborough Inlet. When the lighthouse is exactly west of you, you must be somewhere exactly east of it. So if you draw a line eastward (90 degrees) from the lighthouse on the chart, you have a line of position. Just label it with the time, and you're well on your way to determining your position at that time.

Now, that single LOP is only a start because you can be anywhere along it (though common sense will allow you to eliminate the extremes and narrow the possibilities to the section near your intended course line). Traditionally, another LOP from a visual bearing of a different landmark would be plotted to cross that first one. That works very well in a slow-moving sailboat, but in a fast powerboat, the time difference—and thus distance—between visual bearings can be enough to reduce the accuracy of your resulting position, though the method remains a viable solution. But what else can we do? Well, how about those depth contours? They can also be LOPs. And if you cross that visual bearing of the lighthouse with a spot that's equal to your observed depth at the same time, you'll have a pretty good fix. Of course, for utmost accuracy, you need to adjust the depth shown on the sounder to allow for stage of tide and the distance your sounder's transducer lies beneath the surface. But for practical purposes you can often use the displayed depth. It will put you somewhere close on the chart to where you actually are in the water, and again, much closer than you might be without it. It's important to note that the greater the range of the tide in that area, the more critical it is to compensate for it.

A visual bearing line that crosses your course line at or near a right angle (90 degrees) has another value, too; it's an excellent measure of your forward progress. So in the above example, if you were to measure the distance from your point of departure—the sea buoy off Port Everglades—to that LOP based on the lighthouse and apply the elapsed time between them, you'd have a very accurate assessment of your actual speed over the ground. You could use this speed to figure future DR positions that would be much more accurate than those based on your speed through the water. And they would hold quite true until you either changed your speed or heading, which would affect the actions of wind and current, or until you detected a drastic change in either wind speed or direction. In other words, that calculated SOG could be good for most of your trip to Palm Beach. Naturally, this process doesn't just work off the coast of South Florida; you can use it anywhere. You just need the tools and the knowledge of how to use them.

While we're on the subject of LOPs, let's again consider course lines and depth contours. Your course line is an LOP also, but a terribly unreliable one because, as noted above, the farther you get from a known point, the less sure you are that you're actually following the line you drew on the chart. But you can get some idea of how you're doing by comparing the charted depth at intervals along your course line with the depth shown by your sounder at the corresponding times.

And when your intended track takes you up a winding tributary where compass headings change too frequently to be of much real use, you can go safely, even in limited visibility, by following a depth contour, whether it's drawn on the chart or not. Just pick a depth—say 10 feet or so to allow a little "playing" room—and start following it. If your sounder starts showing less depth, apply left rudder; if it starts showing more, turn to starboard. This will take you up the right side of the waterway—believe me, even in a pea-soup fog. Just check the chart first to be sure there won't be any sudden surprises along the way, such as rocks or other outcroppings that might appear without the advance warning of a gradual change in depth.

Updates and Backups

When electronic charting first came out, we were cautioned to always carry paper charts as backups. In fact, the Coast Guard required it on commercial vessels. Now, commercial vessels are allowed to work solely with electronic charts as long as the ships meet two criteria: they must carry a backup plotter in case the main unit fails; and they must have a subscription to update their electronic charts frequently and routinely.

That paragraph contains two bits of wisdom we can apply to small pleasure boats. First, if you're going to use paper charts, either as your main plotting material or as backups, remember that all published matter becomes obsolete in time. You can get the information to correct and update your charts (and more!) from the Coast Guard's weekly "Local Notices to Mariners." These used to be printed and distributed through the mail, but now you can only get them online at www.navcen.uscg.gov/lnm.

Second, if you're relying on electronic charts, you need to keep them up to date also, and you need backup of some kind; electronics can fail from a variety of causes on even the most well-maintained vessels. Believe me, over the years I've been through electronic failure many times for many different reasons.

Your backup should be either in the form of corrected, up-to-date paper charts, or at least through having aboard a handheld GPS with reliable waypoints and routes in its memory. If that's your backup, remember never to ask your handheld to do anything you wouldn't ask of your main unit. I'll say it again for emphasis: they can't think!

This chapter is already longer than I intended, and I still haven't touched on everything. But I hope I've been able to give you at least a hint of how easy it is and also of the fun you can have in navigating, either by enjoying the process itself or in the ways it can expand your horizons. I must confess that, even after doing it for all these many, many years, I still get a huge charge out of being able to choose a destination on a piece of paper and then actually arrive there by boat. It's like magic! I'm not at all surprised that it works every time, but it remains an enormous thrill nonetheless.

The navigation processes I've touched on here, as well as the techniques and wrinkles I didn't get to, will help you enjoy boating more, so you should take the time to learn them. I assure you that what I haven't covered is no more complex than what I have. Remember, our nautical ancestors, the seafarers of old who initially developed our navigation system, were not educated people. They were smart enough, that's for sure. But they mostly lacked formal schooling. We benefit in that they developed a navigation system that did not require formal schooling or complicated math. They designed it to be so simple that uneducated people could use it and pass it on to others who were also uneducated. The system has evolved over time, and we now have many advantages our ancestors never even dreamed of, such as GPS, electronic depth sounders, more-accurate and easily updated charts, and even electronic chart plotters tied to our GPS. But the basic process remains as simple and straightforward as it ever was.

I'd like to wrap up this discussion of navigation with some advice you're unlikely to find anywhere else by passing along two observations that were given to me many, many years ago by a friend of my father's, a man who was instrumental in my early nautical education when I was just a youngster back in the late 1940s. His name was Seth Pinkham, and he sailed out of Cape Porpoise, Maine, from a cove where lobster-pot buoys were and are still scattered over the water as thick as dandelions on a lawn. It's truly an art director's vision of Down East. But it's also a real working port where "practical" is a most important concept.

Seth taught me many things. Among them were how to sail, how to navigate, and how to play cribbage. I think it's interesting that I still remember nearly everything he ever said about navigation, yet every time I play cribbage, I have to be taught it all over again. It could be that I've found navigation to be more fun, but it could also be that despite the nearly 60 years that have passed since Seth first presented me with these guidelines, I've found they remain very sound, and thus unforgettable, advice.

His first maxim was, "A good navigator always knows about where he is. But he also remembers that he only knows *about* where he is. You can really get in trouble if you overestimate your accuracy. Chances are you'll never be exactly where you think you are, so always retain at least a little bit of doubt."

His second piece of advice was related to the first: "We draw our lines on the chart with nice sharp pencils, and when we cross our course line with bearing lines we often get a neat, tight grouping. So it's awfully easy to think that's exactly where we are. Just remember, we use fine lines to have less to erase and to avoid obscuring important information printed on the chart. But you'll be far better off if you think of those lines as having been drawn with a dull carpenter's pencil—broadside! Because that's really our margin of error."

Applying Seth's advice to navigation today, I have to say that despite the extreme accuracy of GPS, we still never know *exactly* where we are. It's always a good idea to use as many means of determining your position as you possibly can, and even better to always keep a healthy degree of skepticism regarding the infallibility of navigational systems—and yourself.

29

Getting Underway

I think the time has come to get *underway* [a vessel is "underway" any time it's not anchored, aground, or otherwise made fast to shore, such as when tied to a pier]. Yes, you need to get aboard that new powerboat of yours and actually use it. In the next few pages I'm going to outline some procedures you should follow (at least in a general fashion) every time you take your pride and joy out of its slip. Developing a repetitive routine is one of the best ways to ensure you do things right every time. But even well-memorized and regularly repeated routines can go awry when an unexpected interruption derails our train of thought.

Aircraft pilots counter this by using checklists—always—in every size and sort of plane from Piper Cubs to 747s. And it's a practice we'd be wise to emulate on the water. Checklists help us in two ways: putting a task on the list reminds us it needs to be done, and checking it off saves us the needless worry of wondering if we've done it.

Listing the Lists

How many lists you have and exactly what each contains are entirely up to you. But as a rule, every detail you want to remember without fail every time you conduct some activity belongs on a dedicated checklist. Among my personal faves: a predeparture list for getting underway, an end-of-trip list for securing the boat on arrival, and routine maintenance lists—one each for daily, weekly, monthly, and seasonal chores.

The predeparture list is our main concern in this chapter. You want this list to contain everything you should do before leaving the pier, even those things you just know you could never forget. But before we get started, let's look at the others.

Your end-of-trip list should contain everything you have to do to be able to safely leave the boat unattended. This is important even if you're going ashore just long enough for a meal. But when you return home and leave the boat for several days . . . well, the peace of mind that results from really *knowing* you've done everything can be priceless.

When it comes to setting up daily, weekly, monthly, and seasonal maintenance lists, your owner's manuals are the best place to start—be sure to read them thoroughly. Putting the tasks on checklists merely saves you the trouble of either trying to remember what to do or having to look it up each time. It's a matter of convenience.

And speaking of convenience, I prefer to use a number of short lists. I find them easier to manage. For example, an engine inspection and an overall examination of your boat as a whole are both important aspects of a proper predeparture routine. But if you have all of the many requisite tasks on one large list, it could be too cumbersome for convenient use. By breaking it down, your master predeparture list can simply contain entries such as "Engine(s) OK?" and "Boat seaworthy for trip?" which can then be checked off the master list when the sublists are all properly checked off.

Doubling Up for Safety and Convenience

This duplication also helps two ways. Perhaps most important, it doubly assures that critical details will not be overlooked—ever! If your pre-departure list contains a reminder to check the engine compartment, and you use a separate list for all the details you must pay attention to there (Figure 29-1), the chances are pretty good you won't get underway with anything important left undone. But there's another benefit: having shorter lists also allows you to physically downsize them to more practical dimensions.

A big list almost demands that you carry a clipboard or notebook (even for a small boat), whereas short lists can often be printed on pocket-sized cards. When I'm doing chores I find it much easier to carry pocket cards than either a clipboard or notebook. And, of course, the easier it is to use your checklists, the more you'll be inclined to actually use them.

A suggestion: Have the cards laminated in clear plastic and do your check-offs with a grease pencil. To reuse a list, just wipe it clean, and it's ready to go.

The Float Plan

There's another list you should always use before you head out. Called a *float plan*, it's essentially a list of facts regarding your boat, the people and equipment aboard, and perhaps most important, where you're headed and when you'll be back (Figure 29-2). A float plan can be a great aid in locating you in an emergency. And it works whether that emergency concerns your boat or something ashore that suddenly needs your attention.

If you're just taking a day cruise, your float plan can be purely oral. Telling the dockmaster where you're going and when you'll be back should raise a question in his or her mind if you haven't returned by the marina's closing time. But if your trip will keep you away from "home" for overnight or longer, it's best to use a written float plan. Let's face it, it's way too easy for people to forget details when they're not in writing. Yet it could be disastrous if you were supposed to be gone for two days, and no one considered

you missing until you were gone for two weeks.

Be sure to leave the float plan with someone who will be responsible enough to report you overdue if you don't show up when it says you should. And remember your responsibility to notify that person of any change in plans. You don't want the Coast Guard out searching for you just because you were having so much fun you extended your cruise without telling anyone.

Getting People and Gear On Board—Safely

There's an old nautical saying: Always have one hand for the boat and one for yourself. What this means is you should always have one hand free for holding on and one to help you maintain balance. This is true at any time, but especially when you're climbing aboard. And with one hand for the boat and one for yourself . . . well, unless you're different from the rest of us, that leaves no hands for carrying things aboard. So don't! It's a bad idea at best. The ideal procedure is for one person on the pier to hand things to someone on the boat. If you're going solo, put the stuff down on the pier, climb aboard, and then reach back for your gear. This may seem awkward in description, but it's the safest way, believe me. Boats rarely sit still even when they're just lying there at the pier. They can bob and weave like a champion boxer. And that spot where you intended to plunk your foot as you step on board may no longer be just where it was when you first looked. So unless you're paying close attention, your foot can come down on empty space, in which case the nonslip soles on the boat shoes you should be wearing won't help you a bit. In addition to the possibility of spilling everything you were carrying, the tumble you take with that misstep can break things— and some of them may be body parts.

For similar reasons you should always help your guests board properly, guiding their steps and lending a steadying hand if needed. But we're not yet ready for guests. Just as new businesses usually have a "soft opening" days, even weeks, before the official "Grand Opening" to allow time to work out the kinks, you should do the same

Pre-Departure Checklist

___ Tank Levels -- Fuel P____S_____Day____ Water____Holding ____

___ Engine Room OK?

___ Boat Generally Seaworthy for trip planned?

___ Gear Properly Stowed and Secure?

___ Safety Equipment OK?

     ___ Fire Extinguishers sufficient & in compliance?

     ___ First Aid Kit on board and stocked?

     ___ Flares aboard and in compliance?

     ___ PFDs located, tried on and adjusted, and re-stowed for availability?

     ___ Throwable PFDs ready and quickly deployable?

___ Proper Charts Aboard?

___ Weather Conditions Favorable?

___ Tides & Currents Checked & Noted?

___ Nav Lights & Horn working?

___ Steering System OK?

___ Electronics On and Working?

     ___ VHF?

     ___ Depth Sounder ?

     ___ GPS ?

     ___ Autopilot on Standby?

___ Float Plan Filed?

___ Genset on Line?

___ Shore-Power Cable Secured and Stowed?

___ Shore-Water Hose Disconnected and Stowed?

___ Everyone Aboard?

___ All Lines Clear and Stowed?

___ Fenders In and Stowed?

___ **Is everyone aboard in a safe place for the prevailing conditions?**

FIGURE 29-1. *Checklists covering what you do before getting underway (above) and for routine daily maintenance chores (next page) can help prevent your forgetting important details. The lists here are just suggestions; your boat may require something different. But do use checklists of some sort; having them is great for peace of mind. They remind you of what needs to be done and allow you to keep track of what you've already done—you don't have to remember a thing.*

Pre-Cruise Engine Room Checklist (Daily Maintenance)

Date __11_ / _15_ / _04___   Time __0645_____

Engine Hours -- P _0936.9_ S _0939.0_ Gen _1200.0_

Lube Oil levels -- P _F-_ S _F-___ Gen __ADD___

Lube Oil Added -- P__0__ S __0__ Gen __1Q___

Coolant Levels -- P _OK_ S __OK__ Gen __OK__

Water Added -- P___0__ S__0___ Gen___0___

Anti-freeze Added -- P___0__ S__0__ Gen___0___

Gear Oil Levels -- P__OK_ S__OK___

Gear Oil Added -- P__0_ S__0___

Seacocks Open?

     P __X__OK _____Opened S __X_OK _____Opened

     G __X_OK _____Opened A/C_X_OK _____Opened

Sea Strainers OK?

     P _X__ OK ___Cleaned S_X____ OK ___Cleaned

     G_X__ OK ___Cleaned A/C_____OK _X_Cleaned

MSD Overboard Discharge Valve OK?

     _X_Closed & Locked ___Closed but Operable

Bilges Clean and Dry

     _X_OK ____Pumped

Drip Pans Clean & Dry

     P__X_OK____Cleaned S__X_OK ____Cleaned

Visual Inspection Only:

     _X_Hoses & Clamps_X_OK _____ Need Closer Inspection

     _X_Wiring & Terminals_X_OK _____ Need Closer Inspection

     _X_Belts & Drives_X_OK _____ Need Closer Inspection

     _X_Signs of Oil or Coolant Leaks _X_OK _____ Need Closer Inspection

Note: In addition to the tasks to do and check off, this checklist has spaces for recording pertinent information that can later be transferred to an Engine Room or Maintenance Log for a permanent record.

FIGURE 29-1. *Checklists (continued).*

Float Plan

Provided courtesy
the Oregon State
Marine Board

Leave this float plan with a friend or relative. If you make changes to it, let that person know before you go.

Name of boat operator:_____

Home phone number:_____ Business phone number:_____

Boat type_____ Color of hull_____

Color of trim_____ Registration number_____

Name_____ Make_____ Length_____ Other_____

Engine: Type_____ Horsepower_____ Fuel tank (gallons)_____

Number of persons aboard (including operator)_____

     Name   Age   Address/Phone Number

_____
_____
_____
_____

Survival Equipment:

   lifejackets (number)_____ flares_____ mirror_____

   flashlight_____ food_____ paddles_____

   water_____ cushions_____

VHF Radio - Frequencies_____Call Sign_____

Cell Phone # _____

Itinerary:

   Depart_____ from_____ on_____ (time, date)

   Going to_____ or_____

   Expect to return by_____ (time, date)

     and in no event later than_____

Other information_____

Auto license number_____ Trailer license number_____

If not returned by_____ call the Coast Guard or

   local authority at_____

• Upon your return, notify the person to whom the float plan was given.
• If you were reported to the Coast Guard as overdue, notify them of your arrival.

Oregon State Marine Board • PO Box 14145 • Salem, OR 97309 • (503) 378-8587
In case of emergency, notify local authorities.

FIGURE 29-2. *Using a float plan is an idea that's ridiculously simple—once you've thought of it. Oral float plans are OK when you're returning the same day. But for overnight or longer, always leave a written plan with someone you can trust. Many state marine patrols offer blank forms as a downloadable PDF file online; we thank Oregon for this one.*

with your boat. I know you're probably anxious to show off your new toy to all interested friends and relatives. But please resist the urge for at least a little while. Go out by yourself, or with the help of whoever will be your regular "crew," and spend some time developing your routines and skills before you invite any guests. There's nothing difficult about operating a powerboat, but when you've never done any of it before, you might be considerably less than totally confident. So you can do without the added pressure of an audience. Leave them ashore until you feel truly comfortable with your boat. Then you can invite guests. Lots of them.

And before you go, don't forget to apply sunscreen and bring plenty of drinking water. Even in northern climes, the combination of sun and its reflection off the water can take a toll on your body.

Keeping Shipshape

Before you even think of getting underway, be sure to stow all that gear you brought aboard. In the next chapter, I'm going to go into considerable detail on the hardware and techniques involved in achieving optimum trim. But let me say here that one of the important elements of trim faces you well before you get underway, and that's proper distribution of the added weight you just brought aboard. Yes, where you put people and gear can have a huge influence on your boat's behavior. What you should aim for is having the boat sit just as it did before the people and gear came aboard. A bit lower in the water perhaps, but not down by either bow or stern and not listing to either side. If this involves restowing gear or asking someone to move, so be it. But the closer a boat is to sitting "on its lines" at rest, the easier job you'll have in achieving optimum trim when you get underway.

And remember what I wrote in Chapter 25 about stowing things properly—it's not enough to merely put them away. Even when you plan to remain on well-protected, barely rippling waters, the going can get rough very quickly if a thoughtless idiot roars by too close to you, throwing a humongous wake. So always stow all your gear as

if you were headed for the North Sea—even for a short outing on Lake Calmandserene.

Also be aware that it's unwise for anyone to sit on the gunwales or up on seat backs, and in some states it's against the law—a ticketable offense! So always have folks properly seated before you cast off. (Line handlers excepted, of course.)

And remember your PFDs. Never stow other gear on or in front of them in such a way the flotation devices can't be easily accessed. Better yet, let me again suggest that before you get underway, you remove enough PFDs from their "in the slip" stowage locker for everyone aboard. Each person can then don one, adjust it for proper fit, and then, if anyone chooses not to wear it at all times, he or she can at least restow it within easy reach to grab quickly whenever necessary. This makes it a truly *personal* flotation device.

Starting Essentials

These probably should be on your predeparture checklist, but since I suggested that the lists we've shown are merely guidelines, I'm adding some detail here for emphasis. On commercial vessels, we're required to check our steering and signaling device (horn or whistle) before each departure. This isn't a bad idea for pleasure boats also; you wouldn't want to cast off only to discover you have no steering!

It's equally important to check for the flow of cooling water after you start each engine. It usually flows out the exhaust port. Since outboards exhaust through the propeller hubs, it's hard to see the flow, so outboards divert some of the water to squirt down from under the cowling. It may take a few seconds for the water flow to reach full volume; hence you may not see it immediately after startup. But if a flow doesn't begin soon, shut down the engines and find out why.

Power Patience

Be sure to allow your engines to warm up a little before you put them under load. It doesn't have to be for a long time. In fact, too long a warm-up wastes fuel, creates unnecessary pollution, and can cause excess carbon inside the engine. But you never want to make an engine "work" until it warms a bit, and the oil has had a chance to circulate fully and cover all surfaces. Similarly, it's always best to let an engine run at idle for a minute or two before you cut it off if it's been running at cruise or higher for a while. These days, the long idle-speed zones we often face on return to our marina may be enough of a cooldown. But it's still a good idea to let your power plants have at least a short no-load period before you *secure* them [shut them down] for the day. This also applies to your genset if you have one; let it run a bit before you put it online, and let it run with no load for a moment after you've switched back to shore power. These short waiting periods can add a lot to your engines' longevity.

Casting Off

The first time you depart from your slip, all those lines that have worked so well to keep the boat in place can be a bit intimidating. Where do you begin? Or does it matter where you begin? Maybe you can just cast 'em all free and take it from there. Well, which line you cast off when can be very important. And just as I suggested that you have a plan in mind before you try to dock a boat, you should also have one for getting underway. Observe Mother Nature: Which way is the wind blowing? How about current? Is it a factor? If so, which way is it flowing? The reasons for wanting to know these things before you cast off are the same as they are for all maneuvering—boathandling is easier when you don't try to fight Mother Nature.

Once you have an idea of what nature is doing, formulate your plan. Making your first moves into Ma Nature's predominant force will be easier all around. In Figure 29-3 we see a typical marina situation. You want to do what is shown in **A**: back out of your slip, turn toward the only exit, and get underway. But when you try to do that, the combination of wind blowing in and the low speed required when maneuvering inside a marina causes the result shown in **B**. Applied power pushes your stern to starboard—remember, stern swing is *always* the first result—while the wind pushes your bow. Ouch! Not what you want at all.

The easier solution is to take advantage of two peculiarities of powerboats: 1) they like to back into the wind, and 2) once you get them swinging around their pivot point, they continue to turn easily in the same direction. **C** shows what happens when you back out of your slip, continue backing around into the wind, and then spin the boat to head toward the exit. It may look like it could be complicated, but in practice, it's *far* easier than trying to fight Mother Nature.

Once you've formulated your departure plan, look at all your lines. The chances are that only one of them will be under any noticeable strain; all the rest will be hanging at least somewhat loosely. In essence, the line under strain is the only one holding you at the moment. The other lines are there to keep the boat in place when nature acts differently. But at the moment, those other lines are "on break" and not contributing to keeping the boat in place, so they can be cast off, and your boat will still stay put.

The only exception to leaving the line under strain until last can occur when you need a springline to get away from the pier. If the line currently under strain isn't going to be your spring, you'll have to leave the line that will serve as the springline for last and cast off the line currently under strain next to last, first transferring the tension to the spring line with appropriate power if necessary (which, of course, means that the spring becomes the line under strain, and the line you cast off next to last is the line that *was* under strain until you started to use the spring). If none of your normal docklines can serve as the spring you need, you'll have to rig one before you cast off the line formerly under strain. (Reread Chapter 22 if you need to refresh your memory on using springlines—but let me assure you, none of this is as complicated as it may first seem; it's all easier done than said.)

No Pushing, Please!

Please resist the urge to push your boat away from the pier. When the boat is small or you have plenty of help, this often seems the easiest maneuver. But here's why I say "Don't!" One day you'll either be operating a boat too large to push,

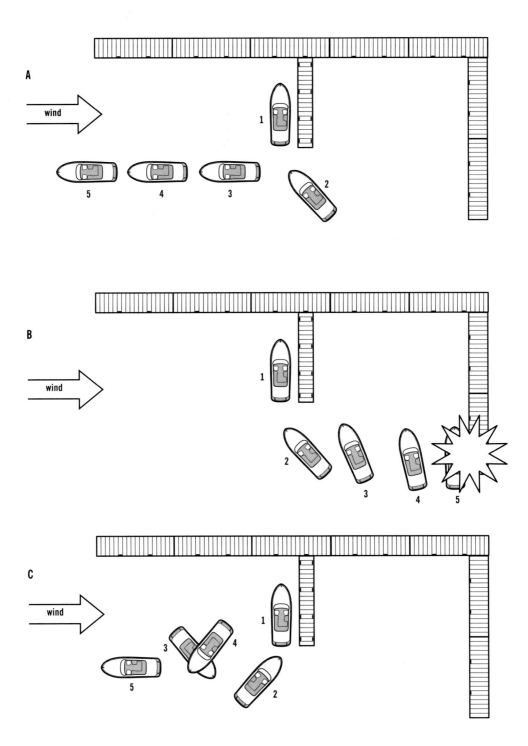

FIGURE 29-3. *Your boat will respond better if you work* with *nature's forces.* ***A*** *is what you want to do.* ***B*** *shows what will likely happen unless you do as shown in* ***C***.

or perhaps the wind will be pushing harder than you, or maybe you'll be alone with no one to push for you while you work the controls. Then what do you do? Use other techniques for the very first time? Believe me, every technique is easier when it's familiar. Use it all the time, and it's "yours" when you need it.

There's another good reason for not relying on a friendly, "helpful" push. You don't know how strong it will be, so it's another variable over which you have no control, a potential (unpleasant) surprise. And Ma Nature usually gives you enough "surprises" without you adding to them. When you use a springline (or rubrail to pier-surface friction, which often works just as well with small boats), you know how much power you're applying; you have control over when you'll change the thrust and release the line. In other words, using a springline removes some of the unknown. And that makes your work easier.

And Awaaay We Go!

When you first depart your slip, be sure to stow any lines you brought aboard, and then bring in and stow your fenders. Leaving the fenders hang-ing isn't anywhere near the crime of the century, but it's unsightly and indicates a skipper who doesn't really care for his or her boat. And it's not only sloppy, it's inefficient to boot. If you decide to stop at another pier during your trip, say, for lunch at a waterfront restaurant, you'll probably need to relocate the fenders anyway. And it's easier to get them out of stowage and hang them where needed than to have to untie them from where they are and retie them where they need to be.

Of course, since this is your very first trip, I suggest you explore the "get acquainted" procedures outlined in Chapter 16 before you do anything else. Just find a clear area and go at it. Then maybe you can practice a little docking and, well, just start the process of getting to know your boat. In the next few chapters, I'll suggest some other ways of doing this.

30

The Tools and Techniques of Trim

As I stated way back in Chapter 4, proper trim is essential to getting the maximum performance from a planing hull. Now, after many pages about many other things, I'm finally going to describe—in considerable detail—ways, means, and methods of achieving it.

The Objective

Our goal, in every case, is to move the boat ahead, on its lines (to achieve maximum lift, which is such an important element of planing hull performance), with the least possible thrust required to attain our desired speed. That's a simple definition of efficiency. And remember, this translates to using less fuel and usually to a better ride and better handling, too.

I must acknowledge that, taken to the extreme, powerboat performance is of greatest interest to those who value speed above nearly all else—either to win races or to be the first to arrive at prime fishing spots or simply for the satisfaction of achieving the ultimate, of knowing they've pushed a boat to its max. But in reality, everyone who operates a planing boat (and that's most of us these days) should be concerned with getting its best possible performance. Even when your objective isn't maximum speed, you'll enjoy your boat more (and probably get better fuel economy to boot) when your boat is operating at peak efficiency. And for a planing hull, this means running at the optimum trim for the speed you desire, whether that speed is WOT (wide-open throttle) or something comfortably slower. When a

boat is at optimum trim your engine(s) won't be working as hard (which tends to save fuel and increase longevity), and usually your boat will be the most cooperative in its response to handling, which is a decided boon to the operator (that's you).

The Tools of the Trade

In this section I'm going to delineate everything we may use to improve the trim of a planing hull, though not all methods are either applicable or desirable for every type and style of boat. Consequently, some gear won't be anything you might want aboard your particular pride and joy. But I've included the whole gamut so you can get an idea whether each item is something you merely need to be aware of, or something you absolutely *have to have*.

Drive Trim

Let's start with engine/drive trim. Obviously, if the boat of your dreams has conventional underwater running gear, this part won't apply. But please read it anyway, because every bit of this chapter relates to our goal: maximum enjoyment of your time on the water in a planing hull.

With outboards, sterndrives, and even most surface-piercing drives, you can adjust the propeller's angle of thrust, which in itself helps maximize engine efficiency.

This matter of most-effective propeller angle is one of the reasons that trimmable drives can be more efficient overall than conventional under-the-boat running gear—at least for planing hulls. When a prop's thrust is directed anywhere but straight back—that is, directly opposite, but parallel to, the boat's movement ahead—its power plant can't be operating at its best. This is why I tend to favor outboard power on boats up to about 35 feet LOA. With conventional underwater gear, the props are always aimed at least slightly down (though, as we'll soon see, this is not necessarily bad).

Optimum Trim

Ideally, the boat will run on its lines, and the prop will be perpendicular to forward motion; that is, the drive unit will be exactly vertical (Figure 30-1). If the balance of loads within the boat never changed, you might be able to set the drive unit angle once and forget it. But loads do change in the real world. Say your plump Uncle Paul insists on riding "up here in the front seat, where I can see everything." You'll need to adjust the trim angle to compensate. Usually you can compensate quite well.

One of the neat things about drive trim is the balance of forces working in a propeller's thrust is such that the prop will try to run at its optimum angle (perpendicular) no matter what, and since the drive unit forms an effective lever between the prop and transom mount, it can exert a pretty strong force on the boat as a whole, changing the boat's trim angle extensively. (Note: Figures 30-2 and 30-3 are exaggerated slightly for emphasis.) While some boats will not react quite so much to a change of drive trim, remember that the load on your engine(s) will be least when trim is correct, regardless of what happens to the trim of the boat as a whole.

When you trim the drive(s) *in* (Figure 30-2), the resulting forces tend to lift the stern and push the bow down. Since this is far from the best running angle, you might wonder why on earth we'd want to trim a boat this way. Well, there are several reasons. Say, for example, you have a bait well full of water and bait, a fish box full of fresh catch and ice, and a few fishing buddies in the cockpit along with a huge cooler full of cold

drinks. You'll need more stern lift just to stay on plane. Even with a normal load, most planing hulls can use a little help getting up on plane when you start out. Remember, in climbing out of displacement mode, the natural tendency is for the stern to settle—and many actually "squat." Forcing the bow down by trimming the drive(s) in to lift the stern helps the boat plane sooner. Indeed, some stern-heavy boats would never plane if you couldn't trim the bow down when you first hit the throttle.

Trimming the drive(s) *out* (Figure 30-3) tends

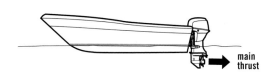

FIGURE 30-1. *With proper trim the main thrust is parallel to the surface; the boat runs on its lines.*

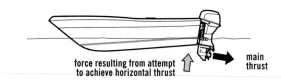

FIGURE 30-2. *Trimming the drive unit(s) in (negative trim) adds stern lift. This can lead to bow-down "plowing" if continued at cruise speeds, but it can be extremely helpful in getting a boat on plane more quickly.*

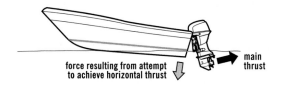

FIGURE 30-3. *Trimming the drive unit(s) out (positive trim) adds bow lift. A slight degree of positive trim is usually necessary for proper planing, but too much can cause porpoising. Positive trim is great for counteracting the effect of too much weight in the bow.*

to lift the bow, which is just what you have to do when you have big old Uncle Paul up there in the bow seat. Of course, it's possible to trim out too far. When you do, many planing hulls will begin to porpoise, romping across the water rather than gliding across it smoothly. Again, it's a balance of forces. Drive trim causes the prop thrust to lift the bow only to have gravity bring it back down, and the action keeps repeating itself over and over until you retrim the drive to lower the bow to a running angle the entire hull can support. So when your boat begins to porpoise, trim in slightly to bring the bow down a bit, and the boat should run at its best.

The Trim Drill Here's the basic procedure for achieving optimum trim underway. (The process of controlling trim underway is easy because most outboards and sterndrives have the trim switch in the single-lever control, right where your thumb can flip it to adjust trim in or out as the rest of your hand grabs the handle to advance or retard the throttle.) Trim the drive(s) all the way in before you start. Hit the throttle(s), and advance steadily and smoothly to wide open. When you get on plane, trim out until you reach maximum speed (or until the boat begins to porpoise, at which point you should trim in slightly). Once you have the boat running at its best, throttle back to your intended cruising speed and fine-tune the trim to that speed. Strangely enough, it usually takes less time to make these moves than it does to describe them.

If you make a tight turn or slow down for any reason, you'll usually have to readjust the trim by tucking the drives slightly in to compensate for the drop in speed and the changing attitude of the boat, and then trim out again when you regain your original speed. (Because planing hulls tend to bank in turns, the outboard engine's prop may get too close to the surface and ventilate excessively unless it's trimmed in during the turn.) That's the advantage of power trim—you can fine-tune trim as you need to with just a flick of your thumb. Note that with some hull forms it's neither necessary nor desirable to retrim in turns. You'll have to judge what works best for your boat by trying turns both with and without trim adjustment.

In my observation, a 35-foot hull is about as much as can be trimmed effectively by changing the drive trim, which is one of the reasons I set this length as a cutoff for outboard propulsion, though I daresay any hull that can be pushed at reasonable speeds by outboard power is a viable candidate for having it—and that applies to displacement hulls also.

Trim Tabs

Back in Chapter 13 I noted that boats with transom power "rarely need the added lift of tabs to get on plane." Now it's time to expand on that thought.

Because fuel, engines, batteries, and other loads are often all located quite well aft, some sterndrive boats have so much weight just forward of the transom that drive trim alone can't produce the lift it takes to get them on plane easily—the stern just squats. In these cases, trim tabs help, though the tabs usually must be retracted once the boat does get on plane.

Of course, with conventional under-the-boat running gear, trim tabs are the only way to get this added lift, especially on boats with V-drives, whose engines also sit well aft. Now, some designers will claim their hulls don't need tabs. And they may be right much of the time. Their design's hull shape and the slight lift that results from the down-angled props trying to make themselves perpendicular to the boat's forward motion work together to get the hull to lift up onto plane with little difficulty. (This lifting force, which we saw so clearly with trimmable drives, also exists with conventional drives, though usually to a far lesser degree since they lack the leverage inherent in an outboard or sterndrive and because they are under the boat, rather than attached to the transom, and their thrust goes mainly against the "thrust bearing" that is in the transmission, closer to the boat's center of balance. Unfortunately, with many hull designs this lift is negated by other factors, so you won't see it on every boat.) The problem is this lack of need for tabs disappears when the boat owner or guests start placing additional weight aft, thus upsetting the designer's intended balance. Boats in use are *almost* living things that constantly change; we have to be able to adapt with them.

So know that trim tabs can be helpful at times on any planing hull even if they're not always necessary. Remember also that trim tabs don't have to be used solely for fore-and-aft trim. Adjusted independently, trim tabs can also correct lateral trim. And because one of the sometimes-frustrating traits of deep-V hulls is the tendency to lean into the wind, it's nice to be able to counter this with a slight tweaking of the tabs.

One thing you have to be very careful to avoid is using too much tab once you get the boat up on plane. This will give a slight bow-down attitude that may not be noticeable from the helm. Quite honestly, your visibility forward will probably be better than it is when the boat is running at a more efficient angle, so you might like it. But most planing hulls are designed to plane with at least a slight bow-up attitude, so if you use too much tab, you aren't letting the boat run on its lines, which is our goal. If you have a way of measuring your speed accurately, such as with a GPS, you can see the effects of trim, both positive and negative, by observing your speed over the ground while adjusting trim without changing the throttles. When you have the maximum speed at any given throttle setting, your trim is perfect.

If you're wondering about the drag created by sticking things down from the bottom of the boat, even if ever so slightly, I must confess it does exist; trim tabs do create some drag. But unless they are down too far, and thus are upsetting ideal trim in other ways also (by creating too much stern lift and pushing the bow too far down), the resistance to forward motion will always be much less than what would result from "dragging" the whole stern. The stern lift that properly adjusted tabs create should more than offset their minimal drag.

But sometimes you don't want the action that tabs produce. Whenever you're in a situation in which the seas tend to wallop your stern excessively, such as when running an inlet or in heavy following seas, your best bet is to retract the trim tabs as far as they'll go. When you're getting kicked in the butt, you want to make the "butt" as small a target as possible by keeping it low. Having fully retracted tabs will do this by keeping your stern down and your bow as high as possible (Figure 30-4).

Note also that most trim tab controls, whether they're rocker switches, a joystick, or toggles, are usually labeled "Bow Up" and "Bow Down." Just remember the bow action is a direct result of stern lift occurring on the opposite side. That is,

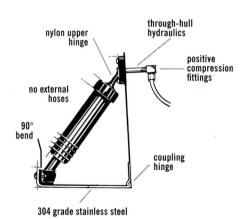

FIGURE 30-4. *Adjustable trim tabs are an excellent means of adding stern lift and lateral trim to planing hulls. Just be sure to have them all the way up when running inlets or in following seas—two of the few times you absolutely don't want added stern lift. (Courtesy Bennett Marine)*

to get the port bow to go down, you have to lower the starboard tab to bring that side of the stern up. And as for bow up, once a tab is full retracted, its opposite bow won't go any higher—at least not through the action of trim tabs.

Performance boats often have indicators (usually tied to the tabs through a direct mechanical linkage) to show the present tab positions. These indicators are nice but not absolutely necessary. Most of the time, pleasure-boat skippers should be more interested in the boat's resulting attitude and performance than the tab settings that cause it. One highly desirable option is the one that automatically retracts the tabs whenever you turn off the ignition. This way you *know* you're always starting with fully retracted tabs. In other words, you're always starting from square one. The result is you should never have any more *tab action* [stern lift] than you need at that particular time because you have to reset the tabs to suit prevailing conditions and get the best running angle every time you start out. Yes, this means a bit more work, but it saves you from having the wrong running attitude by forgetting to reset the tabs.

A final thought on trim tabs. In some ways, the behavior of planing hulls resembles that of airplanes in flight. When using trim tabs independently to correct lateral trim, it's possible to create a tendency to turn from the resulting "bank," just as ailerons help guide a turning airplane. If you feel your boat start to turn when you're adjusting the tabs individually, you've gone too far. Trim back the other way until the boat regains a straight track. At this point, whether you've completely corrected lateral trim is moot; any further trim tab adjustment will be too much for your directional stability. And though it's possible to level out a boat and correct for the resulting turning force with some answering rudder, the added drag from the more-extended tab and the off-center rudder can overcome the gains acquired from getting the boat on its lines. So the total result is less than optimum efficiency. It's better to let the boat heel a little (sailors don't seem to mind a little heel—in fact, they often carry it to extremes) but have minimal tab and rudder drag.

Jack Plates

As Albert Hickman discovered with his early sea sleds, and as modern surface drives such as Arnesons have proven since, it can be a huge advantage to have your prop(s) close to the surface. In fact, the ideal profile for prop thrust is often just behind the transom, just below the waterline, and pushing straight ahead, with as little drive unit as possible in the water to reduce the drag the appendage creates. Trimming out a drive sort of accomplishes this, though not without some negative side effects. When the prop is tilted up this way, it tends to produce too much bow lift, which not only may lead to porpoising but also reduces engine efficiency. You want your thrust pushing the boat straight ahead, not upward.

Then, too, thrust from near-surface propellers, while absolutely beautiful for driving a boat that's already on plane, isn't so good for helping a boat *get up* on plane unless you can angle the props downward, as you can with most surface-piercing drives, or move the props way behind the boat. (Brackets can help with this, though not all that much). But what about outboards or sterndrives? If the motors were mounted this high on the transom (or were built with such short lower units), they'd probably only work well once you somehow got the boat to plane by other means. As we've seen, you most often need the props down and in to get boats out of the displacement mode.

The answer lies not in telescoping lower units (which is an intriguing idea, though they'd be an engineering nightmare), but rather in adjustable mounts that raise or lower the whole outboard called *jack plates* (Figure 30-5). The best ones are electro-hydraulically operated and allow you to have the motors way down and trimmed way in when you hit the throttles, and then once you're on plane and have trimmed the motors out to the optimum, you can raise the plates until the props are up where they often work best, just below the surface. As with other trim systems, you'll know when everything is set just right because you'll see the maximum speed at that throttle setting. Note that it's quite possible to lift the motors too high and get the ventilation you don't want. But if the installation is carefully planned, the upper limit of jack plate travel will be such that the

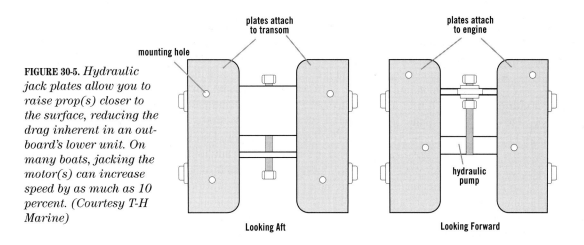

FIGURE 30-5. *Hydraulic jack plates allow you to raise prop(s) closer to the surface, reducing the drag inherent in an outboard's lower unit. On many boats, jacking the motor(s) can increase speed by as much as 10 percent. (Courtesy T-H Marine)*

props are just high enough and no higher, thus taking some guesswork out of their operation.

Granted, not everyone is interested in the extra speed you can gain by raising the props this way, but if you are, and if you have outboard power, jack plates are a great way to wring out every last bit of performance your rig may have in it. Another advantage of raising the motors to bring the props nearer the surface is less draft. This means you can run in thinner water with no danger of hitting bottom. You still have to be aware of depth and draft, however; this "magic" only goes so far.

Jack plates are also a good way to help keep all of your power plants out of the water when the boat is just "sitting." Sometimes the extreme tilt position still leaves part of the skeg and lower gearcase submerged where it will collect growth whenever the boat isn't underway. This growth, though it covers a small area, will have a negative effect on your motors' performance until you clean it off—it causes unnecessary drag. Lifting the motor with the jack plate, while also using full tilt, keeps the whole drive system high and dry—and clean.

Ballast Tanks

So far, everything we've discussed does its work at the stern. This shouldn't be too much of a surprise; most every move we can make with a boat starts with something happening at the stern. So we shouldn't expect that trim would be any different from steering in this respect. But there is one exception. Weight up forward could be a good antidote to weight in the stern except that it's counterproductive in the long run; we want to keep the total weight of planing hulls as low as we can. But what if we had a *variable* weight up there? Weight we could add or remove as we desire. That might be a solution, yes? And it is. A ballast tank in the bow allows us to have weight forward when we need it—fresh water weighs nearly 8.4 pounds per gallon, and salt water even more—and release it when the weight would be a detriment. The mechanism is simple: a well-vented tank, which allows water to flow in and out with ease, a remote-controlled valve we can open or close from the helm, and an intake/discharge opening that's underwater in the displacement mode but up in the air when the boat is on plane.

In use, the system is simplicity itself. While sitting in the displacement mode you open the valve. Because the tank is placed below the static waterline, water flows in until the tank is full, and then you close the valve. The added weight forward helps you get on plane, but once up there you lighten the boat by opening the valve to let the water flow out (Figure 30-6). It couldn't be easier.

This isn't a new idea, by the way; racing boats have used ballast tanks for years. It isn't even brand-new in pleasure boats, though I never ran into one on a "beginner" boat until the late 1990s.

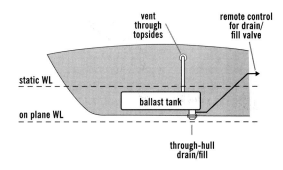

FIGURE 30-6. *A ballast tank adds an adjustable weight to the bow. Because the fill/drain through-hull and the tank itself are below the static waterline when the boat's at rest, opening the valve fills the tank. Opening the valve when the boat's on plane empties it.*

Then, I had the opportunity to test a 28-footer, a boat that was billed as an entry-level go-fast. One of its features was a ballast tank, included as standard equipment. And it helped. The boat could reach only 85 mph, which is slow for a die-hard go-fast skipper, but it's probably fast enough when you're just getting started in the sport.

Out of curiosity, and to add "meat" to the article I was writing at the time, I used a stopwatch to check the boat's time-to-plane both with and without the aid of the ballast tank. It was long enough ago that I no longer recall the exact numbers, but I still remember that using the tank really helped shorten the time. By a lot! And so I now also believe that if you're looking for the absolute ultimate in performance, you have to consider a ballast tank along with the other, more conventional aids to better trim.

Trim—with All the Trimmings

Earlier in this chapter, I outlined a drill for getting a transom-powered boat on optimum plane using drive trim alone. Now, for sake of illustration, I'm going to go through the drill on a boat that has trim tabs, outboards on jack plates, and a ballast tank. And just to make it interesting, let's say we've somehow loaded the cockpit with so much "stuff" we need every bit of the help these devices have to offer, or it would take forever to get on plane.

Here's the drill. While sitting in the displacement mode, fill the ballast tank, drop the jack plates to their lowest, extend the tabs, and trim the drives all the way in.

When you're ready to go, hit the throttles and advance them steadily as the boat gains speed. When you reach WOT, open the ballast tank valve and trim the drives out. Raise the tabs, perhaps all the way (you may no longer need them) and adjust drive trim to compensate for the changes resulting from the dropped ballast and lack of tab-induced stern lift. And then, when you seem to have maximum speed, raise the jack plates to lift the props closer to the surface. You'll be amazed at what happens.

At this point you might want to back off to a cruise speed less than WOT. If so, you'll probably also have to readjust drive trim ever so slightly to make up for the lesser thrust. You can generally leave the jack plates up until you again need to start from point zero, at which time you'll have to lower them all the way, trim the drives in, fill the ballast tank, and extend the tabs.

The drill I just described may look like a lot of work with a number of "When do I do what?" decisions. Actually, it's one of those routines, like the basic drive-trim drill itself, that take longer to explain than do. And as to when you make each move and in what order, what I wrote isn't chiseled in stone, and the clues to boat behavior are so obvious after you've done it a couple of times that you won't have the slightest doubt as to what to do when. You'll feel it, believe me. And as with other such procedures, the more you do it, the more sensitive you'll become to the proper order and timing of each step for *your* boat under the conditions of the moment, which is what ultimately counts most.

One of the common traits of almost all planing hulls is that they'll remain on plane at a lower throttle setting than the setting that enables them to get on plane. That is, a boat requires less power to stay on plane than to get there. Many boats remain quite level while coming down off plane, while a huge majority have to go though a *plow-*

ing stage on the way up. (Plowing occurs when a planing hull is still in the displacement mode, but more power is being applied than the displacement mode requires. Bow-up plowing can be corrected by the application of sufficient power to get the boat to "climb out of the hole" and get on plane, with the aid of drive and tab trim adjustment, if necessary. Bow-down plowing is most often a result of improper drive trim or excessive use of trim tabs, either of which can create too much stern lift. The correction, of course, is to readjust trim until the boat runs level or slightly bow-up.) A boat that's plowing has its stern way down, its bow way up, and it's throwing a huge wake. It's probably the least-efficient attitude a boat can be in and gives the operator the poorest forward visibility. Always make this stage as brief as possible by either throttling up to stop plowing and get the boat on plane or by backing off on the throttle to reenter the pure displacement mode.

If you're trying to stay on plane at the lowest possible speed, experiment with trim. Sometimes it helps to have the drives a bit out and then counter the bow lift with a bit of tab. This can work similarly to the flaps airplane pilots use when landing. It will probably require a bit more throttle than that speed may normally call for, but many times it will keep you planing, rather than plowing, at the lower speed. It's worth a try to see if it works for you.

It's also a good idea to let other folks aboard know whenever you're about to change a boat's speed, especially if you have a boat with quick acceleration. A Coast Guard *coxswain* [pronounced "COX·un"; the term for the operator and person in charge of a small boat such as a 41-footer] will often yell out "Going up!" to warn the crew before he or she hits the throttles, and "Coming down!" when about to ease off. Emulating this procedure on pleasure boats can prevent a lot of unnecessary falls and bumps, though a slow steady hand on the throttle can often accomplish the same goal.

To recap, let me say once again that trim tabs are nearly a must on any planing hull. If you have trimmable drives (and in the United States, more boats are powered by outboards than any other drive system), tabs may not always be necessary, but you'll often appreciate having them nonetheless. Jack plates only work for outboards, of course, and they're only for those who want the very most from their rigs. Ballast tanks are probably only a plus for boats that otherwise don't have much weight forward, as is the case with so many performance boats that have a minimally furnished "cabin," especially way forward. Whether you need, or even want, any of these extra aids to better trim on your boat is entirely up to you. But at least now you know about them and can make an informed decision.

31

Anchors and Anchoring Techniques

In much of this book I've written as if your destination will always include a place to tie up. You can go boating that way, of course, but if you limit your trips to cruising from one marina to another you'll miss a lot of fun, because one of the great pleasures our sport offers is the ability to get away from it all. Though we were all born too late to venture boldly where no one has ever gone before (at least on this planet), we still have the opportunity to visit where others seldom go. And that calls for "hanging off the hook."

Choosing an Anchor

Anchors so typify boating that we use them as symbols of our sport—putting them on hats and blazers to announce to the world that we're involved with the sea. Anchors have been a part of boating since nearly the beginning, and for centuries they changed very little. In fact, boats changed more than anchors did. Through all that time, weight was the prime consideration. The heavier, the better.

But with the development of the modern anchor, most notably the Danforth lightweight type (circa World War II), things changed dramatically. The shape of the modern anchor enables it to penetrate the bottom and hold by strength rather than weight. So now, when choosing an anchor, we have to consider "which type?" in addition to "how big?"

Anchor Type

The best place to start the anchor-selection process is at ground level. Rocks, sand, clay, mud, coral, kelp, and other substances, along with various admixtures, form the bottoms of our anchorage areas. No two are identical, and no one anchor works best in all bottoms. (If you do your boating in areas where coral abounds, try to avoid anchoring directly on the coral itself. Anchors can damage and sometimes kill coral, so always set your anchor in nearby sand, even when you're there to enjoy the beauty of the reef.) So the type of anchor you'll use requires that you first consult a chart to determine what type of bottom you'll be anchoring in. Usually one type predominates in a particular area. Base your selection of a primary anchor on your home ground, with a nod to what you'll encounter when you go cruising. The anchors used by the majority of boaters in your area were most likely chosen because they work. If you buy your boat from a knowledgeable local dealer, you can usually trust his or her advice in this matter, too. Your dealer should know what other customers are using and why.

But as in other purchasing situations, the more you know, the better able you are to make an intelligent decision. So let's examine a few of the currently available anchor types to see how they fit in the real world.

Yachtsman Anchor These are the old-fashioned anchors commonly used as symbols (Figure 31-1). They hold in rocks, where penetration (the claim to fame of newer varieties) is impossible, and they may gain a purchase in grassy bottoms,

FIGURE 31-1. *The yachtsman anchor is good for anchoring in rocks, but not the best choice for all-around use. The one shown here is small and light; you'd be more apt to see a 50-pounder on a boat over 31 feet long.*

FIGURE 31-2. *Though stockless or "Navy" anchors come in small-boat sizes, they're best suited to large yachts where they can be hauled up into a hawsepipe with a mechanical windlass. They have to be heavy to work well.*

which, again, Danforths and plows may fail to penetrate. But they're awkward to handle, and since they must be comparatively large to have sufficient weight for holding power, they aren't easy to stow. Unless you spend a lot of time in rocky areas and have a salty-looking old-fashioned yacht you don't want to "spoil" with a modern contrivance, best let them be decorative.

Navy-Type Anchor These anchors don't belong on small boats. Sure, they come in small-boat sizes and look shippy (Figure 31-2), but unless they're very large, stockless anchors aren't much good. Their main virtue is that, being stockless, the shank can be drawn up into a hawsepipe, which is fine for ships and large yachts. Pound for pound (or fluke size for fluke size—a better correlation), they don't hold as well as the yachtsman.

Danforth Anchor These granddaddies of all modern anchors (Figure 31-3) still have a lot going for them. Their holding power (in the right bottom) goes *far* beyond mere weight, particularly in the Hi-Tensile series. They can lie flat in deck chocks or lockers, so stowage and handling are relatively easy. They work best in solid mud, clay, or hard-packed sand, where they can burrow unbeliev-

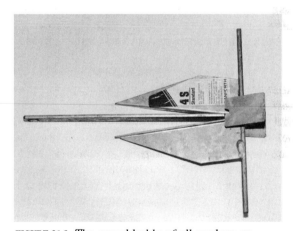

FIGURE 31-3. *The granddaddy of all modern anchors, the Danforth anchor holds well in most bottoms. Beware of imitations; if you want a Danforth, be sure it says Danforth.*

ably deep in very short order if set with sufficient scope.

They become less efficient as bottom density lessens, and they don't work as well in soft sand or near-liquid mud. Because they depend on penetration (a result of fluke angle), kelp, grass, or other weeds can prevent them from taking hold even if the bottom beneath the weeds is ideal. They are nearly useless in rocks, but if they do grab a crevice, they can then be difficult to retrieve.

A Danforth depends so much on the angle of pull against its flukes that when this angle changes, the anchor can come out of the bottom. Thus, Danforths are prone to losing their grip when your boat swings on a change of wind or tide. When the anchor is easy to set initially—no kelp or other impediment—it will usually reset itself with no problem. If there is *any* hindrance to easy reentry, however, it will most likely start to drag. But the Danforth is still a prime choice for general use.

Danforth Followers The success of the Danforth anchor both in use and in the marketplace has prompted a number of clones and derivatives. Some of the clones look so much like Danforths you have to check the shank to be sure. If it looks like a Danforth but doesn't say so, beware! Imitators usually use a different fluke angle to avoid patent infringement and may not achieve proper penetration.

Derivatives are another story. Danforths, as good as they are, suffer the fate of many pioneers. The trail they blazed has been followed by others who had no intention of imitating (a form of flattery closely resembling rip-off) but rather chose to improve upon progressive thinking.

Fortress anchors (Figure 31-4) are one example. Fabricated of a hardened, marine-grade aluminum-magnesium-silicon alloy, they take the strength-with-lightness concept to the nth degree. My experience with them has been limited, but reports (including one released by the U.S. Navy) and their use by many well-known megayachts (including transatlantic speed-record-setter *Gentry Eagle*) suggest they're well worth considering.

Plow or CQR There are several varieties, all having a single fluke. This practically eliminates dislodging when the boat swings, since a single fluke will better follow the rode—a tendency encouraged by one of several design variations depending on the brand you choose.

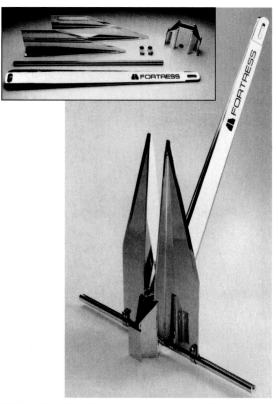

FIGURE 31-4. *The Fortress anchor is the lightweight principle carried to the nth degree. These aluminum alloy anchors hold exceptionally well by design rather than weight. (Courtesy Fortress)*

The original CQR plow (Figure 31-5) uses a hinge to pivot the shank. The Bruce anchor (Figure 31-6), which its manufacturers don't call a plow because the single fluke is less plow-shaped than that of the CQR, relies on shape alone—the side humps work to reposition it after a swing.

A relatively new entry from the manufacturers of the CQR is the Delta (Figure 31-7). It incorporates aspects of each of the other plows and boasts two special abilities: 1) it's designed to free-fall unattended, which makes it especially good for pulpit/automatic-windlass applications; and 2) no matter how it lands, it will always flip over to the proper attitude for best penetration. I've found it works very well in sand and mud, even where there's a lot of grass or other weed.

In my experience, any single-fluke anchor

FIGURE 31-5. *The CQR plow is particularly good for anchoring where weed or grass hinder bottom penetration. (Courtesy Jay Stuart Haft)*

holds better in sand than a double-fluke anchor, and although no anchor is *great* in grass or weed, the single-fluke type usually gets through and holds better. The main drawback to single-fluke anchors is that they don't stow as easily, but

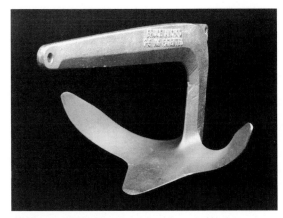

FIGURE 31-6. *The Bruce anchor is a variation on the plow theme, but with no moving parts. Good for most bottoms and well suited to hanging from pulpits. (Courtesy Imtra Corp.)*

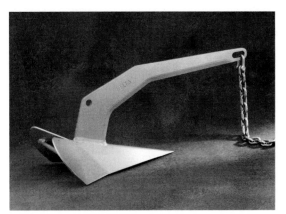

FIGURE 31-7. *The Delta anchor is more "plow-like" than the Bruce anchor, but still with no moving parts. A relative newcomer from the manufacturer of the CQR, the Delta is intended for lighter duty than the plow. (Courtesy Jay Stuart Haft)*

they're perfect to hang from a pulpit, even one just large enough to handle the anchor.

Anchor Size

Total load, not merely the overall length of the boat, is the critical factor for determining anchor size. A high-sided family cruiser with a lot of gear aboard will need more holding power than a low-profile, center-console fisherman or sport boat of equal length. Keep this in mind when you look at manufacturers' guidelines.

Keep in mind, too, that although anchor weight is no longer the sole factor in holding power, it still matters. That is, within a given brand and style of anchor, the larger (heavier) it is, the better it holds, and the better it's able to penetrate the bottom under adverse conditions. (With the Fortress anchor, which is so very, very light, a larger, and thus heavier, model is better able to reach the bottom in a strong current, which can tend to make a light anchor "kite" in the current before it settles down to penetrate the bottom.) So when you consult the manufacturers' tables for recommended sizes, if you must err, do so on the large side. Then, too, consider that we should be talking in the plural. One anchor isn't enough. There are times when you'll need two just to keep in proper position (we'll see how in just a bit), and because anchors are part of your safety gear, a backup is good insurance.

The old admonition to carry a lunch hook, a working anchor, and a storm anchor is still valid. The theory is that your lunch hook can be light, small, and easy to handle because you'll use it only when the weather is good and you're anchoring for a short time. Chances are someone will be aboard to keep an eye on things, so you don't need the full security of a heftier anchor.

Using one that's easy to set and weigh makes anchoring more pleasurable, and some anchors especially designed for lunch-hook use have quick-release mechanisms for even easier removal from the bottom. This is nice, but it's possible to rig your own quick-release on any anchor (see below).

A working anchor should be large enough to hold under average-to-good conditions—such as anchoring overnight in mildly disagreeable weather. As its name implies, your storm anchor should be the big gun for really nasty conditions.

After suggesting that the old rule of thumb has

merit, I'll acknowledge that carrying, stowing, and using three anchors can be physically impractical on many of today's powerboats. So, as we get on with other aspects of your anchoring system, I'll show you how to make two do the work of three. But first, let's look at the rest of the system, because anchors don't work by themselves.

Ground Tackle

Tackle (traditionally pronounced "TAKE·ul") refers to *all* gear associated with anchoring, or holding a boat to the ground beneath it. The anchor line, or *rode*, does more than connect the anchor to the boat. Properly employed, it also helps the anchor hold—particularly anchors that depend on fluke angle for penetration. Generally speaking, anchors need the pull against them to be as close to horizontal as possible. Obviously, unless you're anchoring a submarine, a truly horizontal pull is out of the question. However, we can approach it through catenary action and *scope* [the ratio of rode length to water depth]— (Figure 31-8).

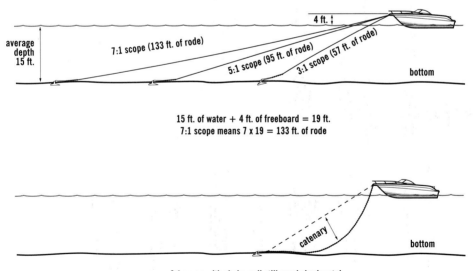

15 ft. of water + 4 ft. of freeboard = 19 ft.
7:1 scope means 7 x 19 = 133 ft. of rode

3:1 scope with chain: pull still nearly horizontal

FIGURE 31-8. *With a combination chain-and-fiber rode, a scope of 7:1 or better produces the near-horizontal pull required by anchors, especially if wind and wave action put a lot of strain on the line. An all-chain rode, being heavier, produces a sag, or* catenary, *between boat and anchor. This acts as a shock absorber whenever wind and wave cause the boat to tug against the rode, and the pull on the anchor remains more nearly horizontal even with shorter scope.*

An all-chain anchor rode is the most secure option. The added weight (as compared with a similar length of line), greater breaking strength, resistance to abrasion, and natural catenary action make it superior on all counts. But a chain rode is not always practical. Many small pleasure boats can't carry that much extra weight up forward. Even if yours can, hauling chain back aboard is a royal pain unless you have a windlass. The standard compromise is a short length of chain (anywhere from 6 to 40 feet) between the anchor and a fiber (usually nylon) rode. This provides chafe protection for the part of the rode that can be expected to come in contact with the bottom and adds weight to the end of the line to help keep the pull on the anchor more nearly horizontal.

Because chain can rust—which not only is unsightly but also causes stains—and can scratch shiny gelcoat, many boaters opt for vinyl-covered chain. The covering protects the chain from rusting (for a while, at least) and protects the boat from being scratched by the metal. In my opinion, however, the commercially available vinyl-covered chains are too short (often about 3 feet). I suggest you buy at least 6 feet of proper-sized chain (the more the better) and then coat it yourself if you wish. The vinyl coating is available in liquid form at most marine stores and isn't difficult to apply.

Since part of the chain's purpose is to add weight to the end of the rode, you should err on the large side here also. If you have a small boat, strong enough may not be heavy enough.

TYPICAL GROUND TACKLE HORIZONTAL LOADS

WIND SPEED (KTS.)	BOAT LENGTH (FT.)												
	10	15	20	25	30	35	40	50	60	70	80	90	100
15	40	60	90	125	175	225	300	400	500	675	900	1,200	1,600
30	160	250	360	490	700	900	1,200	1,600	2,000	2,700	3,600	4,800	6,400
42	320	500	720	980	1,400	1,800	2,400	3,200	4,000	5,400	7,200	9,600	12,800
60	640	1,000	1,440	1,960	2,800	3,600	4,800	6,400	8,000	10,800	14,400	19,200	25,600

FIGURE 31-9A. *Working loads (in pounds) placed on anchors and ground tackle as a function of boat size and wind speed. (Courtesy American Boat and Yacht Council)*

RECOMMENDED ANCHOR WEIGHTS, RODE SIZES, AND CHAIN SIZES FOR YACHTS BETWEEN 21 AND 50 FEET LONG

LENGTH (FT.)	ANCHOR WEIGHT (LBS.; BASED ON PLOW OR CQR)	CHAIN DIAMETER (IN.)	RODE DIAMETER (FOR THREE-STRAND NYLON; IN.)
up to 21	18	$\frac{1}{4}$	$\frac{7}{16}$
22–25	22	$\frac{5}{16}$	$\frac{9}{16}$
26–30	27	$\frac{5}{16}$	$\frac{9}{16}$
31–34	31	$\frac{5}{16}$	$\frac{9}{16}$
35–41	35	$\frac{3}{8}$	$\frac{3}{4}$
42–50	44	$\frac{3}{8}$	$\frac{3}{4}$

FIGURE 31-9B. *Using Figures 31-9A and 24-3, you would conclude that a 50-foot boat in a 42-knot blow needs a rode of 1- to 1⅛-inch diameter, not ¾-inch as this table indicates. But keep in mind that the breaking strength (as opposed to the recommended normal working load) of ¾-inch nylon rode is 14,200 pounds, and in a 42-knot blow you would want to share the load between two anchors. (From* Anchoring, *by Brian Fagan. International Marine, 1986)*

Don't shortchange yourself on the rest of the rode either. It should be long enough to provide optimum scope for your intended anchorages, and large enough in diameter to be easy on the hands and resistant to chafing. This often means a bigger line than working-load tables alone would suggest. How long should it be? I've already alluded to the importance of scope, and we'll cover it more thoroughly when we get to anchoring techniques. An average scope of 7:1 is a good place to start. This means that to anchor in 10 feet of water, you'll need a minimum of 70 feet of rode. My recommendation for coastal cruisers is 300 feet, which is enough for most situations. Obviously, if your boat's rope locker can't carry that much, you have to pare it down. But anchor rode, like money, falls in the "never-too-much" category (Figures 31-9A and 31-9B). Carry as much as you have room for; eventually you'll be glad you did.

Deck Gear

These days, many small boats (even some in the 20-foot range) sport the bow pulpit, electric windlass, and permanently mounted anchor once as-

sociated exclusively with large yachts. Believe me, such a system makes the task of anchoring much easier, often allowing you to set and weigh your anchor with almost no physical effort. There are other pluses, too. The windlass and pulpit allow you to use an all-chain rode, if your boat can carry the load, and eliminate the need for a lunch hook, since handling your main anchor is so easy. In fact, with the help of a windlass and pulpit, your heaviest anchor can be your normal working anchor. Your spare can then be lighter and thus easier to handle on those occasions when two anchors are needed (Figure 31-10).

Modern windlasses easily handle both chain and line on one drum that has indentations into which the links of a chain fit perfectly (the sizes must match for the device to work properly). The raised surfaces—the parts that go around the links of the chain—also grab the line and create pull for fiber rode as well. These new windlasses are much easier to use than the old style, which required manual shifting of the rode from a notched drum for chain to a smooth one for fiber (which also required several turns of rode and some added tension in order to provide the necessary friction to haul the rode). With a remote

FIGURE 31-10. *Pulpit and windlass setups like those at right and opposite (top) have been common for years, but now we're beginning to see the idea in smaller boats. Though it hasn't yet been rigged, the Donzi, a 23-foot center-console fisherman (opposite, bottom), sports a built-in pulpit.*

switch at the helm, these new windlasses can often be employed without anyone on the foredeck, though this isn't always possible for one reason or another. For example, sometimes their grip on fiber isn't good enough, and you still need to provide some tension on the line coming out of the windlass and into the rope locker so the drum won't just slip.

FIGURE 31-10. *Pulpit and windlass setups (continued).*

Setting the Anchor

We'll start with a single anchor, since that will do for most situations. Before you set the anchor, seek out a good spot, meanwhile evaluating conditions of wind, water, bottom, and traffic in the anchorage. Among the questions you should answer before anchoring are:

- How deep is the water?
- Will the water get deeper or shallower while you ride to anchor?
- Which way is the wind blowing, and is current a factor?
- How much swinging room do you have and will your swing change when the tide changes?
- Are there rocks or other shallow hazards you might swing over?
- Are there other anchored boats to consider?
- And finally, in view of your answers to the other questions, where do you want the anchor to be? (Remember, this is *not* where your boat will end up; you have to allow for scope and lower your anchor far enough ahead of where you want to sit so that when you fall back on the rode, you'll be in the right place.)

This is all less complicated than it sounds now, and with very little practice you'll know exactly where to drop the hook for any given amount of scope.

In Figure 31-11, we see the drill. You should move slowly up to the drop point (usually heading into the wind) so that you can stop easily when you get there. When you're ready to set the anchor, lower it (there's no need to throw it) until it touches bottom. Next, pay out the rode as you slowly back away, continuing until you have paid out the length you need, and then belay the rode on deck. If you can measure the necessary length of rode and belay it before you start to anchor, you'll be ahead of the game. When the anchor sets, you'll stop backing even with an engine astern at idle speed. If the rode gets taut, you'll know the anchor is set. If it vibrates (a result of the anchor bouncing along the bottom) and does not quickly become taut, haul in the anchor, go back to your drop point, and try again.

Incidentally, while 7:1 is a generally accepted scope, you'll set the anchor better and faster if you use more rode initially. Remember, the more nearly horizontal the pull, the better the penetration. You can shorten up to your desired swing-

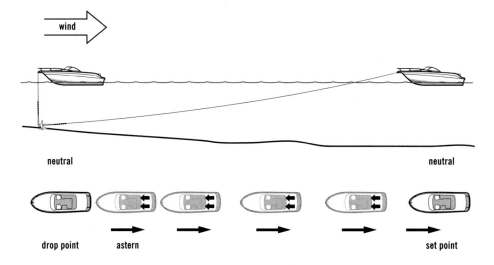

FIGURE 31-11. *The anchoring drill. Premeasure your desired scope and secure the rode to the cleat or post at that point. Loosely coil the rode you're going to pay out, taking care to arrange it so it won't snag or tangle. Then, after lowering the anchor at the desired drop point, simply back slowly until the rode becomes taut. If the rode remains slack when you've paid it all out, the anchor isn't set. Haul it in and start over!*

ing scope after the anchor is set. And if you're in a lunch-hook situation, you can (and often will need to) swing on shorter scope than 7:1. If the anchor is well set, the shorter scope shouldn't matter as long as you keep an eye out for possible dragging. Take bearings on objects ashore using a hand-bearing compass or the ship's compass. As long as they stay the same, you're in the same place, but if the bearings change appreciably, you've dragged your anchor and should let out more rode to increase your scope or move and re-set the anchor.

How do you know how much rode you have out? You can guess, of course, but if you mark the rode every 5 or 10 feet (or in 6-foot intervals to indicate each fathom), you won't have to. Chain links and braided nylon can be painted, and you can get numbered vinyl tabs to insert into twisted nylon. Marking the rode is well worth the time and effort.

One more note on scope. Though I've suggested that 70 feet of rode in 10 feet of water gives you a 7:1 scope, that's not quite true. It would be if you belayed the rode at the waterline, but since it will be belayed a few feet higher, the above-waterline distance should be considered also. If your foredeck cleat is 2 feet above the waterline and the water is 10 feet deep, you'll need to put out 84 feet of rode (7 x 12) to ensure a 7:1 scope.

Weighing Anchor

When it comes time to get the anchor out of the bottom and back aboard, you can usually use the same principle that helped you set it—only in reverse. If near horizontal pull makes the anchor penetrate and hold, vertical pull will break it free. Go ahead slowly, taking in slack, until the rode is vertical (Figure 31-12). Secure the rode at that point, power ahead a moment, and the anchor

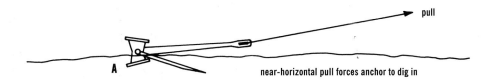

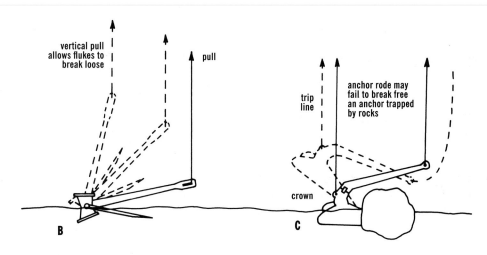

FIGURE 31-12. *Near-horizontal pull makes an anchor hold (A); vertical pull will break it loose from mud, clay, or sand (B). Shorten scope until the rode is straight up and down, secure it, and apply a little power—it should break free easily. When anchoring among rocks, you might wish to attach a trip line and float to the crown (C). Then, if the flukes become wedged under a rock, and you can't free the anchor with the rode, you just haul in the trip line, and the anchor should come with it.*

should break loose. If it doesn't, try pivoting around that point. Often pressure from a different direction will break the anchor free. Then all you have to do is haul it back aboard.

This technique will work in mud, clay, or sand. If rocks are involved, you'll more likely want to pull the anchor out just the opposite of the way it went in. One way to do this is to attach a trip line to the crown. To pull the anchor up, leave slack in the rode and haul in on the trip line.

It's also possible to use the rode to pull an anchor out backward. As I mentioned, some lunch hooks are rigged to do this automatically. The shank is slotted (Figure 31-13) so that as long as the pull is basically horizontal, the rode stays at the end of the shank, but when the pull approaches vertical, the rode slides down toward the crown to pull the other way. Voilà! The anchor comes loose. Figure 31-14 shows a way to rig any anchor to achieve the same effect. Attach the rode to the crown, and then bring it up alongside the shank. Wrap a few turns of moderately heavy

FIGURE 31-14. *Secure the rode to the crown with a shackle and add a secondary connection to the shank with twine. A vertical pull will break the twine and move the application of force to the crown for easy extraction.*

twine around the rode and shank, and the anchor will set and hold as long as the pull is basically horizontal. Shorten scope so the pull approaches vertical, and the twine will break, allowing the anchor to be pulled free easily. You may have to experiment with the size and amount of twine it takes to work with your particular boat and anchor, but with the right combination, it *will* work.

Comfort in Pairs

Though a single anchor will work nicely in the majority of anchoring situations, at times you need to set two. Say, for example, you're anchored in a narrow spot where there isn't enough room to swing on a change of tide (Figure 31-15).

The simplest solution is to set an anchor astern in addition to the one off the bow. The technique is easy. Set the bow anchor in normal fashion, and then pay out about twice as much rode as you'll finally use. Drop back on the extra rode as far as you can, then lower your spare anchor over the stern. Go ahead again and pay out the stern rode, taking in the bow rode until you're about in place (Figure 31-16). Make the stern rode fast to a stern cleat, leave the boat in gear for a moment to set the stern anchor, and there you are.

With this arrangement, you absolutely will not swing. This can be a plus, but it can also be a minus. If other boats in the anchorage are able to

FIGURE 31-13. *Even in soft bottoms, pulling the anchor out by the crown is often the easiest way to recover it. Slotted-shank anchors aren't meant for unattended use but work nicely as lunch hooks. As long as the pull is horizontal, the anchor holds. Bring the pull to vertical, however, and the rode slides toward the crown for easy retrieval.*

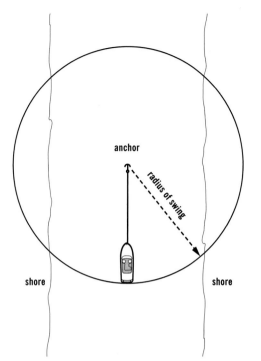

FIGURE 31-15. *Whether the restriction is a nearby shoreline or other moored boats, you'll encounter occasions when the scope you need for proper holding creates a bigger swinging circle than you can realistically use.*

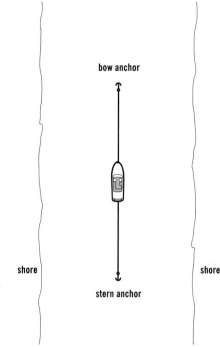

FIGURE 31-16. *Setting anchors ahead and astern can keep you securely anchored with enough scope and no swing. Beware of other boats that can swing!*

swing, you'll discover that not all things that go bump in the night are imaginary! You may also find that should the wind kick up astern, you'll take boarding seas at the point of lowest freeboard.

It's far better to be able to swing with the wind and tide but on a limited basis. The solution is the so-called Bahamian moor (Figure 31-17). The procedure is similar to that for setting bow and stern anchors, but after the second anchor is set astern, its rode is led forward to belay. Your swing is limited, you have a secure anchor for each side of your swing (often better than relying on a single anchor to reset itself), but your bow will always point into prevailing weather.

Sometimes you need two anchors just for holding power. Say, for instance, you need to ride out a storm. Sheltering behind protective land is a possible solution to handling rough weather (Chapter 33), but although you *could* do this without anchoring, you'd have to resort to constant

maneuvering to stay in place. You could lie to one anchor, but if the blow were strong enough, you might drag. After all, anchor selection is based on normal conditions. If you use two anchors, however, you can be reasonably sure of holding.

Figure 31-18 gives us the picture. If you set an anchor somewhere between 30 and 45 degrees to either side of the line of approach of the strongest winds and seas, you'll get maximum benefit from both anchors. Be sure to set each anchor securely with a direct pull and then use maximum scope.

While it's possible for one person to handle both the boat and the anchor, realistically anchoring is a two-person job. If you have the benefit of pulpit and windlass, anyone can handle the anchor end. If more physical strength is involved, many boating couples find that it's easier for the man to handle the anchor and rode while the woman handles the throttle(s) and clutch(es). However you do it, you'll find the drill goes more smoothly if you develop teamwork. A set of hand

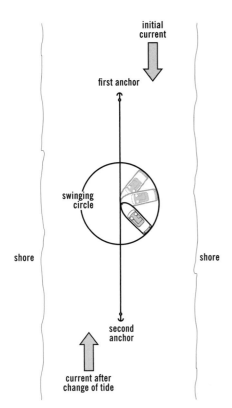

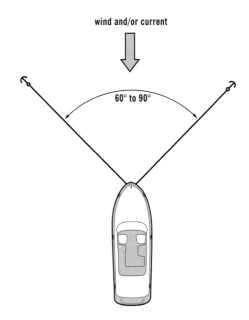

FIGURE 31-18. *Two anchors are better than one when extra holding is needed. Set them 60 to 90 degrees apart.*

FIGURE 31-17. *Setting two anchors 180 degrees apart but with both rodes brought to the bow— a Bahamian moor—lets you swing in a very restricted circle.*

signals for come ahead, go back, stop, haul, lower, secure, etc., makes the process easier and eliminates a lot of shouting. It doesn't matter what the signals are as long as both teammates understand them. Make up your own. That can also be a part of the fun.

One final comment: If you're anchoring overnight, and unless you're in a "Special Anchorage Area," which will be so indicated on the chart, be sure to display an anchor light, an all-around white light placed high on the boat, so that other boaters will know you're there. The Rules of the Road require it, but so does common sense. The bump in the night that results when two boats swing differently at anchor will be mild compared to the bump that results from a boat running into you under power because no one could see you! The anchor light is a must.

32

Inlet Running

Inlet running, like most boathandling skills, is best learned by experience built up gradually over time—a luxury seldom granted those of us who don't encounter barred inlets in our boating backyards. All is not lost, however, and there's a quick way to gain gradual experience in running inlets at any stage of your boating career. First, let's examine the difficulties. As with other skills, running inlets begins with an understanding of what we have to overcome and why.

The Problems

The difficulties encountered at the mouth of a river or creek (or sometimes at a break between barrier islands), actually begin far at sea in wind-generated waves. The stronger the wind, the bigger the waves. If the wind blows from the same direction for an extended period of time or has the opportunity to blow unimpeded over a great distance, or *fetch*, the waves get even bigger.

Ocean waves generally resemble sine waves (Figure 32-1, A and B), though in real life they're more confused because several individual waves will traverse a given spot at the same time. The result is a complex wave, similar to a complex sound wave, in which individual waveforms combine to reinforce or cancel each other (C). This pattern of reinforcement leads to the observation that "every fifth (or third or seventh) wave is bigger." As long as the water depth exceeds one-half the wavelength, the seas maintain a smooth form and are, except in severe storm conditions, no real threat.

The problem develops when ocean waves

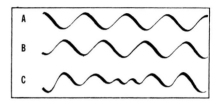

FIGURE 32-1. *Individual ocean waves are essentially simple sine waves. However, the seas we encounter in boating are complex waves that result from the interaction of two or more simple wave systems of differing wavelength. The combination produces irregular, but often predictable, patterns of smaller and larger seas.*

move into shallower water (Figure 32-2). When a wave begins to "feel" the seabed, its sinusoidal movement is restricted, and the wave slows, permitting the next wave behind it to catch up. The top portion of the wave is less affected and thus tends to overrun the bottom portion, and the result is steeper, sharper, more closely spaced peaks, and eventually, as the seabed continues to shoal, the familiar curl of a wave approaching the beach. Forward motion and gravity combine to bring the curl downward, forming a breaker. A series of breakers is called *surf*.

The second element of the problem starts with the sand and silt brought downstream by outflowing current (Figure 32-3). The amount of suspended solids a given current can carry is directly related to its velocity. When an outflowing stream encounters the incoming surf, it slows and deposits some of the silt across the mouth of the inlet to form a sandbar. When the bar develops

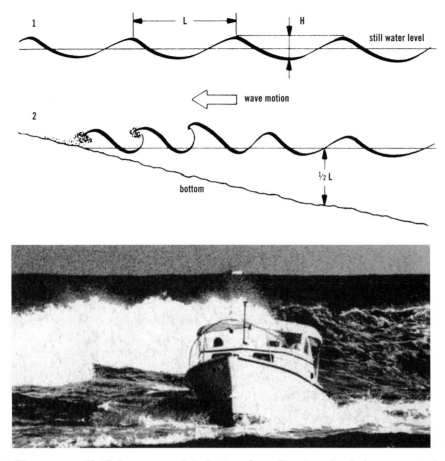

FIGURE 32-2. *When waves "feel" the ocean or lake bottom (usually when depth decreases to about one-half the wave length), the result is steeper, sharper seas and eventually cresting breakers, or surf.*

sufficiently, it changes the course of the stream, which in turn changes the development of the bar. Thus, inlets are in a constant state of change. A major ocean storm or runoff after a heavy inland rain can produce a big change in a hurry. Even in calm weather, change is constant and inevitable.

This presents several problems for boaters. For instance, the meandering course of the outflow can eventually produce a channel that runs parallel to the breakers in the incoming surf. Fortunately, these stretches are often short, but even a few minutes of beam seas in heavy weather can be both uncomfortable and dangerous. Another problem is that buoys must be constantly moved to mark the best water. Thus, it's impossible to chart their location, and a cruising boater has no

way to preview the course through an inlet by studying the chart.

Human Improvements?

Though constant change is the nature of the beast where inlets are concerned, we humans often can't resist trying to stop it. As a result, we have "improved" many inlets by adding breakwaters or jetties and by dredging and redredging the channel to make it go where we want it to. The truth is that while these man-made changes can slow down nature's changes, they can't eliminate them. Even improved inlets change, though the change is often slowed enough to render them more predictable and easier to run.

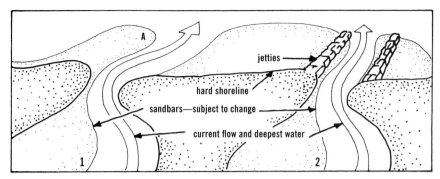

FIGURE 32-3. *A typical natural inlet is shown in (1). Eventually silt will deposit to the right of point A, and the current will either continue farther down the beach or perhaps break through the bar to the left of A. The same inlet "improved" (2). The jetties will help stabilize the inlet, but frequent dredging will be required to maintain the channel depth and remove the bars that will tend to form along the jetties.*

Strategy and Tactics

The most practical way to learn inlet running is to go ahead and do it. But begin gently. For your first attempt, pick a time when you have an offshore wind and slack water, or the early stages of a rising tide. Starting with an improved inlet helps. If you can't get ideal conditions, two out of three aren't bad, but be sure to avoid onshore winds in your initial attempts. Even under the best conditions a problem inlet should have enough surge to give you a good indication of what you must work with (and against) and of what to expect under worse conditions.

If you're starting on an unimproved or natural inlet, be sure to go out through it before trying to come in. This will give you a better picture of the sandbar and surf patterns. In fact, this brings up one of the biggest dangers in inlet running. From the outside it's very hard to determine the state of the seas, since the backs of waves all look very much alike; the clues to roughness are mostly on the inside. With practice, you'll note subtle indicators visible from the outside, but this degree of observational skill takes time to develop.

Beginning with the easy surge of ideal conditions, practice the proper techniques until they feel natural. If the surge is very gentle, technique won't really matter, but take advantage of the opportunity to get used to feeling the rhythm of the sea. Next, try the inlet on an outgoing tide with all other conditions ideal. You'll notice a difference. When you've mastered that, move on to gentle on-

shore winds. Ultimately, you'll be ready to face the worst conditions—an outgoing tide against a strong onshore wind.

Throughout your practice sessions, your objective is to maintain control. Just how you do that depends greatly on your boat and how it handles. If you have twin screws and a lot of power, often you can just pour on the "coal" and outrun, or at least ride *with*, the seas. If you try to use speed alone, be sure you can go fast enough to skip across the crests or stay with one. Remember, shallowness is one of the problems presented by inlets. This is accentuated in the troughs. More than one speedster has torn off underwater running gear and holed a boat by coming off the crest of a wave and down into so little water that the boat momentarily grounded—hard! So if you opt for the fast lane, do so with care.

A more cautious approach is to enter the inlet on the back of a wave, neither too close to the curl nor too close to the wave behind (Figure 32-4). This is easier said than done, but you can learn with practice; developing the proper pacing is one of the reasons for practicing under gradually worsening conditions. Entering on the back of a wave is step one; adjusting your speed to stay there is step two (and in my opinion, a wiser choice than barreling onward, even if you have the power). If you don't have the power to keep up with the wave system, you'll have to learn to use the power you do have with finesse and let the waves outrun you without upsetting you.

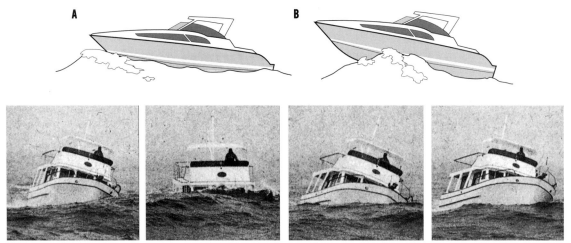

A   B

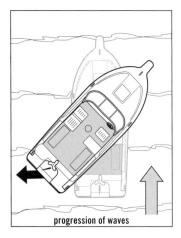

FIGURE 32-4. *The second secret of inlet running is to try to stay on the back of a wave near the crest (**A**). Getting ahead of the crest (**B**) can lead to either dropping into the shallows or surfing out of control. Dropping too far behind the crest may leave you in dangerously shallow water and invite the wave behind to come crashing down into your cockpit. A boat that lacks the power to either outrun or even keep up with the waves must let them pass. The toughest moments come when the crest of the overtaking wave passes beneath you.*

If the seas are overtaking you, try to keep your stern square to the waves so that there will be less tendency for the boat to swing sideways—a move known as *broaching* (Figure 32-5). You should avoid this because heavy beam seas can lead to capsizing if their frequency should happen to coincide with the rolling moment of your boat. Repeated beam seas, like the repeated gentle pushes of a child on a swing, can accomplish more in total effect than a large, strong single wave. Staying squared away has to be a prime objective.

Square It Up

At times the sea will win out and swing you around. When it does, take corrective action immediately. Back off on the throttle(s), and turn the steering wheel to swing the bow in the direction you want to go. Then give a burst of power ahead. The purpose of this operation is to swing the boat back stern to the seas, so you'll have to ease off on the throttle(s) and straighten out the rudders as soon as you near the desired heading, or you'll overcompensate and swing the other way. You have to act fast, because you want to be squared away before the next wave can catch you abeam. This sort of throttle and steering-wheel game can go on repeatedly until you reach calmer water. It's work, but it will get you through some really rough inlets unscathed.

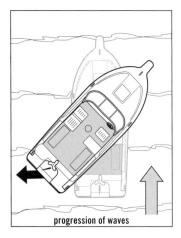

progression of waves

FIGURE 32-5. *The first secret to safe inlet running is to stay square to the seas. While staying square is often impossible, the trick is to get squared away again quickly before the next wave can kick you.*

Pitchpoling [turning end over end] is another possibility one faces when running a treacherous inlet. Pitchpoling occurs when the bow buries itself in the wave ahead while the wave behind lifts the aft section up and over. It *can* happen, though the shape, relative lightness, and shallow draft of most powerboats make it more of a theoretical problem than a practical one. It would be most apt to happen after a wild, out-of-control ride on the curl of a wave followed by a slide down the steep front face (surfing, if you will). Although pitchpoling is less likely than broaching, its mere possibility is another good reason for trying to stay on the back of a wave. Here's another. Remember, you only have control when your prop(s) and rudder(s) are in the water. Get too far up onto the top of a wave, and it will lift your after section out of the water. And that can lead to trouble. On the other hand, staying too far back leaves you open to being *pooped*—a calamity in which the wave behind breaks and comes crashing down on you. This presents two not-so-pleasant possibilities. Having a wave's worth of water coming down on you can do considerable damage in its own right, and worse, since the trough is the thinnest water you'll encounter, being pooped can cause the same kind of grounding damage to a slow boat that flying off a crest can do to a fast one.

As I said, keeping a boat constantly squared to the seas and on the back of a wave (if possible) requires nearly constant work with the throttle(s) and steering wheel. And *work* is the operative word. In fact, a trip through a rough inlet can be downright exhausting. But the results are worth it.

Final Caveats

No matter how adept you become at running inlets, never lose your respect for the power of the sea. A treacherous inlet can be difficult (and sometimes dangerous) even for the experienced. Size up every situation before entering to make sure that both you and your boat are up to it. When in doubt, stay out.

33

How to Handle Heavy Weather

The best way to handle heavy weather is to avoid it—as much as you possibly can! And I don't mean that facetiously. Too many people find themselves in uncomfortable seas simply because they fail to pay attention to the weather. With NOAA radio stations now broadcasting in nearly every boating region and with inexpensive weather receivers available everywhere in so many different types and models, there's no excuse for the skipper of even the smallest boat not knowing what major weather activity is forecast. NOAA Weather Radio is directly available to approximately 70 to 80 percent of the U.S. population. The National Weather Service is currently engaged in a program to increase coverage to 95 percent. Weather receivers are suitable for use at home or on board, if you don't have a VHF marine radio. But if you have a VHF, reception of the weather channels is built in, available any time at the push of a button—another reason to have a VHF aboard. Beyond that, you should work on developing a good weather eye (along with all your other seaman's tricks). The indicators are many and too varied by regional and seasonal influences to go into here, but the old-timers in your area will undoubtedly know them well. Cultivate friendships among other boaters (which should be easy, because boaters are usually the friendly sort) and pick their brains. Soon you'll be recognizing the signs yourself. Typically, particular changes in wind direction, certain cloud formations, and specific combinations of wind direction and cloud type will be the forerunners of bad weather. Nature can be very predictable—at least in the short term.

Weather Signs

I remember from my early childhood that I knew it was about to rain whenever I could hear carousel music at our home. The amusement park at the beach was over a mile away, and we hardly ever heard a sound from it. But when that music came wafting in, the rain soon followed. I thought it was magic! When I got older, my father explained the reason: Whenever our summer wind backed around from its usual southwesterly flow to come out of the east, it was a sign of impending bad weather—an approaching low-pressure system. Since we lived west of the amusement park, we could hear the merry-go-round at our house only when there was wind out of the east. It wasn't magic, but it was a reliable omen. Various sights, sounds, and smells can all work the same way to tip you off to changes that portend trouble. All you have to do is learn what they are for your boating area and keep that weather eye peeled. It doesn't do much good to know the signs if you're too "busy" to look for them.

When the Going Gets Rough

One of the corollaries to Murphy's famous law ("Anything that can go wrong will go wrong") is that despite your best efforts to avoid it, bad weather will sneak up on you sometime during your boating career, and usually when you least expect it. Since it's this sneaky kind of heavy weather that we most often encounter in small pleasure boats, we'll forgo discussion of mid-ocean gales, tropical storms, and other such extreme conditions and concentrate rather on what to do when sudden storms surprise us in inland and coastal boating areas.

Some of the nastiest chop I've ever encountered was on so-called protected waters. Just as the seas can be challenging in inlets, small, shallow bodies of water can get nasty *because* they're shallow. When a strong wind kicks up, the water doesn't have the depth to accommodate the long, gentle swells encountered offshore. Instead, we get short, steep, and often very confused seas.

Chapter 1 suggested that a fair-weather boat on inland waters need not be as seaworthy as a craft intended for serious ocean-tournament fishing. I'll stand by that advice. In this context it means that you'll probably have a more lightly built boat for sheltered waters than if you had planned to go offshore, and that means comparable seas are going to toss you around more than they would a heavier craft.

Yet, since boats as a whole can usually take much more punishment than their occupants, this is often more a matter of comfort than safety. Properly handled, that small, light boat you never expected to have out in the bad stuff will keep you safe indeed. The key, of course, lies in the phrase "properly handled."

Examine Your Options

Your exact approach to heavy-weather boat-handling depends a lot on your boat, of course. It also depends on where you are, where the bad weather is when you first realize it's coming your way, how bad it's going to be when it gets to you, and how fast it's coming. There's no simple panacea that will work every time. Let's examine a few strategies.

Run Away

Even if you can't avoid bad weather entirely, you may be able to escape the worst of it by outrunning the storm. If you have a fast boat, there's a distinct possibility that you can move *much* faster than the weather. Using your potential speed to get away from heavy seas is often your wisest choice (Figure 33-1).

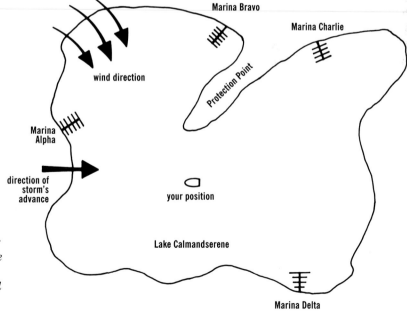

FIGURE 33-1. *If "home" is Marina Alpha, Charlie, or Delta, you might be able to get there before the storm. Head for Alpha only if you're quite sure you have enough time. If home is Marina Bravo, consider other options—it's not as close as Alpha or Delta, doesn't offer the potential protection of Charlie, and will expose you to a lee shore that could be dangerous if the storm arrives before you make it home. Delta is closer than Charlie but will probably be rougher when the storm hits. Charlie will probably be calmer, but will take longer to reach and will put you farther from home.*

Marina Bravo

Marina Charlie

wind direction

Protection Point

Marina Alpha

direction of storm's advance

your position

Lake Calmandserene

Marina Delta

Where do you go? Home is the best bet if you can get there safely. Even if heading home will take you toward the storm, it can still be a good idea *if* you have the speed to get there and get your boat secured *before* the storm hits. On the other hand, you absolutely *do not* want to be caught by high winds and choppy seas just as you're coming in. Adding storm conditions to the other elements of close-quarters maneuvering is begging disaster. Never run toward a storm unless you're absolutely certain you can beat it to your destination.

Find a Harbor of Refuge

If getting home safely is questionable, perhaps there's a closer port, or one that lies in a direction away from the storm. It should offer the opportunity either to escape the bad weather entirely (not always a sure thing under any circumstances) or to properly secure the boat before the bad weather hits. You'll need a marina with available slip space or an anchorage area with good holding ground, and some kind of shelter ashore would certainly be desirable. (After all, why not try to get *completely* away from the weather by going ashore for a while?) The most important attribute of your harbor of refuge, however, is that you should be able to get there in time to beat the weather.

Hide

Even if you can't make port in time to avoid the storm, you might be able to escape the brunt of it by sheltering behind an island or some other protective piece of land (Figure 33-2). Generally speaking, the seas in the lee of a point or island will be considerably calmer than those receiving the full force of the wind. Check your charts. If limited protection is available and you can reach it quickly, it can often be safer and more comfortable than "better" shelter you can't reach before the storm does. Be sure the waters are *bold*, with adequate depth right up under the land and few if any ledges lurking.

Dodge the Storm

Lacking radar, weather instruments, and other gear that operators of large craft may have to help define a storm's boundaries, small-boat skippers have a poorer chance of taking this action effectively. Yet the old eyeball can help here, too, at least to a degree. The center of a storm is usually darker and denser, while the edges fade to a whiter shade of pale. Using such hints as a guide, you can often work your way to the edges of a storm and eventually completely away from it. This tactic carries no guarantee, but if begun soon enough, it can work. It's often worth the try.

FIGURE 33-2. *If you can't make it to a marina, find some protective land to hide behind. You can anchor or just sit and wait, depending on how long you expect the bad weather to last.*

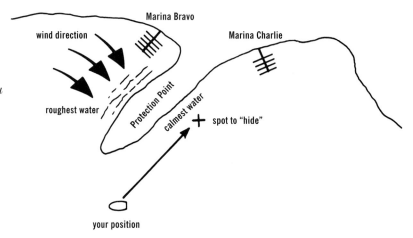

Riding It Out

If you can't avoid a storm and are forced to ride it out, you can take a number of actions to make a bad situation better. Probably the first is to find deeper water. Though you may think staying close to land is your best bet, this simply isn't true. Deeper water will usually be calmer because the waves have room to develop a smoother, gentler form. Heading away from shore is, many times, the path to a more comfortable ride.

You particularly want to avoid a *lee shore* (Figure 33-3). When you get too close to the shore the wind is blowing onto, not only do you risk the danger of being driven ashore should you lose propulsion, but you also face the worst waters in the storm sector.

Here's the problem. As the storm seas approach shore, they encounter shallower and shallower water, which creates a steeper and steeper chop. Then, as the waves crash against the shore and rebound, they generate conflicting seas from the opposite direction. Add the fact that the shore is rarely a straight line so that rebounding seas can come back from several directions, and you have confusion of the first order. Stay well away from any shore that doesn't offer protection.

In summary, if the shoreline is between you and the direction from which the wind is blowing, that's good. You have at the very least a degree of shelter. If you're between the wind and the shore, that's bad. You're in the worst possible position, so get out of there fast, or as quickly as conditions allow. Which brings us to the next point . . .

Adjust Your Speed to the Seas

Running away at full throttle is a practical option only before the bad weather hits. Once it's upon you, you must adopt a different strategy, and that inevitably calls for slowing down. Inexperienced skippers often make the mistake of slowing to a dead crawl. Sometimes this is your only choice, but more often you'll find that the most comfortable speed, while certainly slower than full throttle (or even normal cruise), is faster than flat idle. Look for a balance between the pounding you get from going too fast and the bobbing-cork, limited-control feeling you get from going too slow. Remember, rudder action is largely dependent on a good flow of discharge screw current across it. If you slow down too much, steering suffers. On the other hand, going too fast can be not only uncomfortable but also counterproductive—you also lose control if your props come out of the water! Experiment a bit, and you should be able to find the optimum speed for the conditions you're facing.

Please note, however, that in many seas there

FIGURE 33-3. *Don't put yourself between the weather and a lee shore. The water will be rougher there, and engine failure could put you on the beach. In this instance, running for Marina Bravo would be a bad idea.*

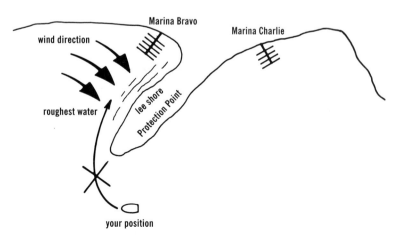

won't *be* one comfortable speed. To maintain both control and comfort, you'll have to adjust the throttle constantly, much as you would in running an inlet.

Take the Seas at the Proper Angle

Most of the time, this means slightly off the bow, although sometimes it can be comfortable to take the seas *on the quarter* [on the corner of the transom]. As much as possible, avoid taking seas either directly on the bow or against the transom. Avoid beam seas no matter what.

Since taking the seas at an angle more or less dictates the direction in which you must proceed, you'll often have to zigzag toward a destination, particularly if that destination lies in the direction from which the storm is blowing (Figure 33-4). The easiest method is to take a given number of waves on one side—say on the port bow— and then to swing and take the same number on the starboard bow. This will allow you to make good a course over the ground (straight into the storm) that would be uncomfortable or even unsafe if pursued directly into the teeth of the wind and seas.

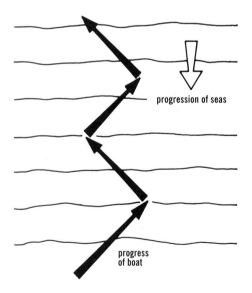

FIGURE 33-4. *In steep seas, a straight line is the roughest distance between two points. Taking the seas on alternate sides of the bow may make the trip take longer, but the ride will be smoother.*

Many of the principles of inlet running apply here. You don't want to broach, you need to maintain control, you don't want to surf or be pooped, and you want to keep props and rudders in the water and working. In short, you're probably going to have to do some work with both steering and throttle(s) to maintain the boat's most comfortable attitude, which is, as in inlet running, close to but slightly behind the crest of any wave you're riding.

Another way of putting it: *Try to stay on the "high ground."* Just as you might smooth out a ride down a rough dirt road by steering around potholes, you can often smooth out rough seas by following a wave train from crest to crest. Though each is to some degree an individual entity, waves tend to run in groups. You can't see it when you're in a trough, but when you're high on the back of a wave you can often discern a bridging pattern between adjacent crests of even the most confused seas. If you try to follow that pattern (and *try* is the best you can do, since the "high ground" at sea doesn't hold still as it does ashore), you'll usually have a smoother ride than if you ignore the pattern and slide repeatedly back down into a trough. Staying up offers another advantage: You can see better, which is a practical and psychological plus. In both respects, it beats looking at the walls of water that are all you can see when you're in a trough.

Heave-To

Sometimes, making headway, even with the slightest progress, is just too much for comfort. In that case you should try to sit still until the storm blows over. You still may need to work with the steering wheel and throttle(s), but your objective now is merely to help the boat hold its most comfortable attitude to the seas. This can call for an occasional burst of power to nudge the boat around, but before you get carried away, see how it rides when you take a hands-off approach. You could discover that the boat and nature work well together; the boat may lie stern to the seas, which is fine as long as the waves are not short and steep enough to break over the transom. Just be ready to take corrective action if the boat wants to lie with the seas abeam. Chances are it won't, and you'll find that the boat drifts with the weather more comfortably than when you try to fight it. Of course, you have to keep an eye out to make sure you don't drift into danger, and you must be ready to apply power at any time if corrective action is called for.

If you have to heave-to, it usually won't be for long—maybe just through the very worst of the storm. In fact, the upside of all this (yes, even bad weather has an upside) is that the kind of storm that develops so quickly that it sneaks up on you most often blows over just as quickly; long-lasting bad weather usually provides better advance warning. No matter how rough the water gets, you can take heart in the thought that it should soon calm down.

General Precautions

Whatever actions you take to minimize the effects of nature's nastiness, there are other actions that should accompany them. I've saved them for last because they're probably the *most important* elements of heavy-weather boathandling and apply universally.

Act Quickly

As I've already said, avoiding bad weather is still the best thing you can do, and that entails reacting quickly to the warning signs. Even when it's too late to avoid bad weather completely, however, you shouldn't delay making your move to run, hide, or find the best of the worst. This advice applies particularly to the next two items.

Secure Anything Loose

If your boat is going to start bouncing around, you don't want things within it bouncing, too. Naturally, it's easier to secure loose gear while you still have a relatively stable platform—hence the advice to act quickly. Anything you can't get lashed or stowed before it gets rough may have to remain on the loose until the weather calms down again. Depending on what they are and where they are, such objects can range from mere mess makers to potentially destructive missiles.

Wear PFDs

This is an unpleasant prospect for some people, who equate the wearing of PFDs with impending disaster. Actually, to wear a flotation device is only to recognize the simple fact that if you're aboard a small, bouncing boat, you have at least a possibility of making a misstep that could put you overboard. The odds are great that it won't happen, but it can. Be prepared for the possibility no matter how remote it may seem.

One of the easiest ways to get others to wear their PFDs (without resorting to issuing an order) is for the skipper to don his or hers first. Leading by example is often best. As the captain, you're responsible for everyone aboard. If all else fails, insist! Make sure there are no exceptions.

Stay Put

One way people aboard can increase their odds against falling overboard is to find a seat and stay in it. If you aren't moving about, you can't make a misstep. It's that simple. This, too, may call for an order, although it's usually easier to get people to sit than to wear a PFD.

That's really all there is to it. The worst part is that the first couple of times you get caught in heavy weather, you'll be doing things from scratch. Advice and suggestions are fine, but you can't beat having been there. You can, however, get your basic skills well under control. If you do that, the rough stuff will be much easier to handle.

34

Offshore Boating

I thought of calling this chapter "Beyond the Blue Horizon." OK, that's the title of an old (old!) song. But it also suggests a wonderful, magical, mystical realm that eventually beckons to all of us who venture out onto ocean or large-lake waters.

We start out in powerboating by puttering around near home. And it's fun, no doubt about it. Big fun! But after you become totally familiar with your local coastline and nearby ports of call, you'll find the horizon, which initially may set a limit to your personal cruising grounds, will cease to be a formidable boundary. Instead, it will seem more like a threshold to new adventure, and an urge to cross it will inevitably grow within you. The urge may arise from a desire to catch bigger and better fish or perhaps to visit the heretofore "unknown." But whatever the root cause, the desire to explore new territory will ultimately become an itch you'll want—or maybe even need—to scratch. Rest assured, if the craving hasn't hit you yet, sooner or later it will. And when it does, my advice is "Go for it!"

But first, and this is extremely important, make sure that you and your boat are ready for the trip.

The good news is that going offshore for either fishing or cruising isn't really any more difficult than staying close to home; it just requires a level of preparation you don't need for shorter, close-to-shore voyages. Even better, you don't necessarily need a bigger boat. In fact, to build upon what I wrote back in Chapter 1, how your boat is designed, built, rigged, and operated can be far more important than its length, though, for many reasons, I would set the lower limit at roughly 18 feet LOA.

Indeed, operation is such a key part of the equation I'm going to discuss it first. Then we'll get to some specifics about your boat.

Like the Boy Scouts

The Scout motto, "Be Prepared," really means leaving nothing to chance. In our case it means having everything ready before you cast off. Getting *yourself* ready to cruise is most important and begins with becoming comfortable with your boat—in every respect.

Before you venture far from safe haven, not only should you become intimately familiar with your boat's handling characteristics under a wide variety of conditions—including rough water—but you should also gain some experience in basic *piloting* [coastwise navigation]. This experience should be sufficient that you can plot courses on a chart and follow them accurately without undue strain or tension, whether you do it on paper charts or on the screen of an electronic chart plotter. Navigation doesn't quite have to be "second nature," but you should be thoroughly comfortable with the procedures and reasonably confident of your abilities (for more, refer back to Chapter 28). Your first offshore trip isn't the time to wonder, "Am I doing this right?"

If you plan to get into cruising in a big way, you may want to expand your navigating system to include a handheld radio direction finder (RDF), a hand-bearing compass, and a handheld GPS if you aren't already using one. These devices aren't absolutely necessary, but they're useful tools that can make offshore navigation much easier. Likewise, while none of them is difficult to use, you should at least become familiar with the operation of any tool before you take it offshore—though cruising is a grand way to improve *all* your navigational skills.

It's also wise to have some after-dark navigating experience before you go offshore, even if plans for your blue-water trip are for daylight hours only.

There are several reasons for developing considerable personal experience before heading offshore. One is that whenever you try something new and even mildly adventurous (such as heading into new and unknown waters), there's bound to be some apprehension. The more secure you are with the basics, the less that apprehension.

A bigger reason is that Murphy's Law will often intervene and force you to formulate new plans underway. The more varied your previous experience, the better you'll be able to adapt to changing circumstances.

Some examples? Say Ma Nature didn't listen to the morning's optimistic forecast, and the afternoon weather turns rotten. Running offshore often means that your distance from safe haven can, in itself, rule out several of the rough-water options I outlined in Chapter 33. If you're past the point of no return (that is, beyond the halfway point), and there are no intermediate ports of refuge, scooting home or seeking alternative shelter will be out of the question. Need I explain the many reasons your first offshore trip should not be the first time you experiment with some of the other ways of handling rough water?

Similarly, nasty weather, or perhaps mechanical problems or other unforeseen circumstances, may force you to run slower than planned. This could change your ETA to after dark even if your original plans called for reaching your destination long before sundown. I think it's easy to see why the last legs of your first offshore run shouldn't also be the first time you turn on the running lights.

All this is to point out that the biggest difference between cruising around your home harbor and actually taking a *voyage* is often the shorter list of viable options you have offshore. Many times it will be a list of one: *keep going*, as prudently and safely as possible. And that's the biggest reason for building a fairly broad base of experience before you head offshore.

But the best news is that this experience doesn't take years—or even months—to develop. Of course, in powerboating, as with many disciplines, the more you practice, the better you should be able to handle things when Mr. Murphy has his way. But the real key is *variety* of experience, not length. And you can get a wide variety in a short time simply by doing a lot of boating and expanding your skills as your confidence grows. Just keep trying new things. On the other hand, if you spend 10 years going out only on the nicest days, scooting home at the slightest hint of nasty weather, and never (never!) being caught out after sundown, you still won't be truly prepared to go offshore. So get yourself ready first.

Ready the Boat

The ideal boat for offshore use would be a ruggedly built craft of any size that's been designed for serious fishing. Die-hard anglers tend to pay less heed to disagreeable weather, and boats built with them in mind usually are more capable of withstanding long exposure to the rough stuff. But nearly any boat—even a lightly built lake boat—will do if you plan and prepare properly.

Having said that, let me add a few qualifying statements. First, when going offshore, it's best to have a boat with a foredeck—no bowriders, please. The reason should be obvious. If the weather acts up, you may occasionally take some seas over the bow despite your best efforts to avoid it. When that happens, you want the water to flow back overboard, not into the boat. One exception I'd make to my "enclosed bow" rule would be a Boston Whaler. Being unsinkable (they'll float when fully flooded) and possessing the ability to drain *very* quickly, the totally open Boston Whaler models are capable of taking seas over their bows with only minor consequences. I'll admit this can be wet and uncomfortable, but not life threatening as it would be with many open-bowed boats.

The ability to deflect water back into the sea is also important at the stern. As I wrote in Chapter 33, sometimes it's best to go *with* the heavy weather. But even when you're running ahead of (or with) the rough stuff, you can still take an occasional wave against the stern. Obviously, a full transom is your best protection. But that doesn't rule out using outboard power. Just be sure there's something between the motor(s) and the rest of the boat to divert water back into the sea.

The ideal would be a full transom with bracket-mounted motor(s). Next best is a molded-in splash well with good drainage. Third best is a flip-up splashboard that can be secured forward of the transom cut-down. Good drainage is important here, too. In fact, a self-draining cockpit is critical when going offshore because even with a fully enclosed foredeck and a full transom, some water will find its way aboard. Your objective is to get it back overboard as quickly as possible.

Another important consideration is hull form. Racers often turn to deep-Vs on rough days because they've proven themselves in heavy seas. Translating this to offshore cruising doesn't mean you should go only if you have a deep-V. Rather, it means that the greater your hull's deadrise (the sharper the V), the better it will cut through big seas without your having to back off on the throttle too much. (Though for comfort's sake—as well as safety—you'll want to slow down at least a bit in any boat.) The only hulls I'd personally rule out completely would be those with flat, or near-flat, bottoms. Yet, as I'll explain in a moment, even this rule can be broken if you're careful.

Freeboard is also important; boats with gunwales very close to the water are best run in sheltered areas only. Of course, even a boat with ample built-in freeboard will be unsuitable if it's overloaded, which not only reduces freeboard to unsafe levels but also makes the boat sluggish and slow to respond to changes of throttle or rudder. Since running offshore in foul weather can be a test of your seamanship at best, there's no sense hampering yourself with a boat that's not on its best behavior.

Regardless of what you have for a boat, you're probably going to have to make at least a few special preparations before you head offshore.

One way of preparing is to consider typical daily weather patterns, the resulting sea conditions, and their relationship to your boat's operational characteristics. Here's an example. A friend of mine years ago cruised Down East extensively in a high-sided, flat-bottomed, shallow-draft houseboat. As you might guess, this floating home was never meant to go offshore. Not by a long shot. It was definitely a "lakes, bays, and rivers" boat. But my friend often went on *long* cruises to remote islands. Yet he never compromised safety or abandoned the principles of prudent seamanship. His secret? He used his boat's substantial calm-water speed to good advantage. Knowing that the early morning hours in summertime New England usually bring near-calm winds and flat seas, he'd head out *very* early (often before first light) on fair days only. He planned his route to arrive at his destination by midmorning, well before the normal daily breezes could develop and start kicking up the seas. As a result, he mostly cruised in near-flat-calm conditions.

As I said, this was not a reckless approach. He was an excellent navigator, plus he had radar aboard and used it, so the early morning haze (or fog!) was never a hindrance. Most important, he fully understood his boat's limitations and planned his trips with all of them in mind. He would always revise his schedule when the next day's forecast was nasty, or even just questionable. But since his boat had all the comforts (and nearly the space) of home, bad weather rarely made much of an impact on his overall cruising enjoyment. And though I personally preferred my flying bridge cruiser's ability to keep going, comfortably and safely, after the seas built up, I had to admit that for him (and the way he used it) the houseboat was ideal.

I recall this only to reinforce the position that *you* are the most important element in the offshore cruising equation. But how you prepare your boat is nearly as crucial, so let's discuss it.

Take safety, for example. Since the availability of potential aid is generally related to your proximity to land (and especially harbors), the farther you venture, the more self-contained your boat must be. You'll want a number of things aboard that you didn't need for those shorter trips close to shore and home.

To the basic safety items listed in Chapter 25 I'd add meteor flares (and a gun for shooting them off, if necessary) when your legally mandated signaling kit doesn't already include them. And be sure to have at least a few suitable parachute flares as well. Also, if you decided to pass on having a VHF radio for everyday operation, I'd definitely get one installed before heading offshore.

If you're going *way* offshore—beyond VHF range, which is about 20 miles—an EPIRB (emergency position-indicating radio beacon) would be wise also. EPIRBs are designed to save your life if you get into trouble by alerting rescue authorities and indicating your location without the need for *visual* signal devices. Since an EPIRB can be expensive and may not be something you need every day, the BoatU.S. Foundation has a rental program for the occasional cruiser. For information, go to www.boatus.com/foundation/epirb. Among EPIRB types are:

Class A (121.5/243 MHz). These are designed to free-float and activate automatically. They're detectable by aircraft and satellite. Coverage is limited.

Class B (121.5/243 MHz). These are manually activated versions of Class A. On November 3, 2000, NOAA announced that the satellites processing 121.5/243 MHz emergency beacons would be terminated on February 1, 2009. Class A and Class B EPIRBs must be phased out by that date. The U.S. Coast Guard no longer recommends these types of EPIRBs, though you still may find them for sale.

Class C (VHF Channels 15/16). These are manually activated, operate on maritime channels only, and are not detectable by satellites. These devices are also being phased out by the FCC and are no longer recommended by the Coast Guard.

Category I (406/121.5 MHz). These free-float, activate automatically, and are detectable by satellites anywhere in the world. The prime signal frequency (406 MHz) has been designated internationally for distress use only. Other communications and interference are not allowed on this frequency. Its signal allows the Coast Guard to accurately locate the EPIRB and identify the vessel (the signal is encoded with the vessel's identity) anywhere in the world. These EPIRBs also include a 121.5 MHz homing signal, allowing aircraft and rescue craft to quickly find the vessel in distress. These are the only type of EPIRB that must be certified by Coast Guard–approved independent laboratories before they can be sold in the United States.

A new type of 406 MHz EPIRB with an integral GPS navigation receiver became available in 1998. These EPIRBs will send an accurate location as well as identification information to rescue authorities immediately upon activation. This type of EPIRB is the best you can buy, and the Coast Guard recommends it for offshore cruising. Needless to say, it's also the most expensive.

Category II (406/121.5 MHz). These are similar to Category I, except they are manually activated. Some models are also water activated.

I'll admit that's a lot of info on just one type of safety device, but I've included it because I firmly believe anyone going *way* offshore should have a 406 MHz EPIRB. If you ever need to holler "Mayday!" an EPIRB will work better than anything else when you get out to where visual distress signals are less likely to be seen and VHF can't be heard unless there's another vessel nearby, which is depending too much on good luck to suit my tastes. Note also a 406 EPIRB must be registered in the name of the vessel and owner (that's how they identify the vessel), and batteries must be kept up to date. Full instructions come with each unit.

I'd also like to amend what I said earlier about not wearing a PFD at all times. When heading offshore in a small open boat, I usually modify that position in recognition of the reality that the chances of meeting a suddenly bigger wave—with its potential for giving you an unexpected nudge overboard—are much greater in open water. Wearing your PFD all the time is simply prudent insurance.

You should also realize that a person overboard could be harder to spot in offshore swells than in the flatter seas of a protected bay or harbor. A PFD is much more visible than a person, plus it will generally keep you higher above the surface than you can hold yourself by swimming or treading water. Both factors make for easier spotting. Of course, a PFD will keep you on the surface with no tiring effort on your part until those still aboard can get back to you and pick you up. This is important, because conditions can make that interval considerably longer in open waters than it would be in calmer seas. So, when heading offshore, don't stow it, *wear* it!

An expanded first-aid kit and the knowledge of how to use everything in it are also welcome offshore companions. It's not that being in open water makes you more accident prone, but rather that if you should need it, outside help is even farther away than when you cruise close to home. Take a Red Cross course if you haven't recently had one. And knowing CPR also takes on even greater importance when you head offshore.

Think about "first aid" for your boat as well. You don't have to become a fully qualified mechanic, but you should at least learn about the parts that are prone to break down underway (pump impellers, alternator, and water-pump belts to name a few) and have spares aboard as well as the tools and knowledge to make the repairs.

Then there's the matter of your extended comfort. This covers many aspects from food and drink to clothing. Any offshore cruise requires more in the way of "creature comforts" than a simple afternoon outing close to home. Extended time on the water can expose you to more varied temperatures. Foul-weather gear will be most welcome when heading home is not among your options for getting out of the rain.

Now, once you really get into cruising, you'll want a boat with permanent shelter from the weather, berths for resting (even if you don't sleep aboard), a real galley so you can actually prepare *meals*, plus a head with a built-in shower. But you can easily start cruising in a totally open boat such as a center-console fisherman or runabout. Just be sure you carry more food, clothing, and drinking water than you think you'll need for your intended cruise. This way, if Murphy interferes, you won't run out before you reach your destination. Water is especially important. Carry enough so that even if you have a total breakdown and wind up drifting for a while (a worst-case scenario, I'll admit), you'll still have water to drink.

Portable coolers (such as those made by Igloo or Coleman) are excellent additions to an open boat. Besides being good for food and drink, a cooler without ice and water makes a good, reasonably weather-tight stowage box for extra clothing and such. Plus, coolers can provide some extra seating—another comfort often lacking in small boats.

You don't want to overburden your boat, but in the area of provisions and clothing, as well as in spare parts and safety gear, it's best to follow the advice of a French adventurer I once met. He and his colleagues were running the Mississippi River from headwaters to mouth in outboard-powered inflatables. Their goal was to retrace the trail of the French explorers who first traveled the route back in the 1600s. These adventurers were very well prepared, and like their earlier countrymen, they were also well sponsored; the boats and motors they were using had been provided gratis for the exposure and credit they'd receive in the TV documentaries and magazine articles the adventurers had contracted for before starting their trip. They were very smart men who planned their expedition exceptionally well. They had enough spare parts to nearly rebuild all the motors and a new fleet of boats. I asked why they carried so much, especially considering the extensive portaging they had faced at the beginning of the trip when food and other stores were also at their heaviest. He replied, "To have it and not need it is merely an inconvenience. To need it and not have it could mean disaster." So follow their lead and plan accordingly.

Once you start cruising, you'll discover that the horizon is not only physically impossible to reach, but psychologically impossible as well. Because just as varied initial experiences may lead to that first offshore cruise, your varied cruising experience may only whet your appetite for more and longer trips. Fortunately, the cruising "bug" is unlike many insatiable desires that can never be quenched. Rather, each trip, regardless of its length and destination, will undoubtedly bring you many pleasures—pleasures that will surely be quite satisfying in themselves even if they do leave you wanting more. And, in my eyes, that's a hard-to-match situation.

35

Practice Makes Perfect

Although I've tried to make the learning process easier by providing basic knowledge to build on, you can only complete your education by getting out there and putting it into practice. And "practice" is the operative word—learning through repetition. If you think I'm suggesting that you buy a boat to have a good time and then turn it into nothing but work, think again. Boats are meant to be fun, and this part should be no exception. If you handle it right, the learning can be fully as enjoyable as any other boating activity. The bonus is that by quickly (relatively speaking) getting to know your boat better, and becoming a better boathandler, you make the other activities more fun than they ever could be otherwise.

Take docking for instance (see Chapters 18, 20, and 21). It can be traumatic. Crowded marina, minimal maneuvering room, tight berth, people watching, inexperienced skipper and crew—these are definitely the elements for embarrassment (if not calamity) and pain. But if you add the knowledge gained through experience, you can perform magic, transforming this horror show to a veritable symphony of deft maneuvers. If the only docking practice you get is that which you can't avoid in the course of your other boating activities, you'll remain inexperienced for a long, long time.

The solution is to make practice fun in itself by setting up practice days as special boating events. Want to become more proficient at docking? Then create a practice pier. Buy a piece of Styrofoam to use as a float, a couple of small anchors to hold it in place ("fisherman's mush-rooms," those 10-pound mushroom anchors, will do), and enough line to secure the float to the anchors. Take your practice float to a quiet area where you won't be disturbed by other boats, nosy spectators, or other distractions, and set it in place. Then start practicing. Come in for landing after landing after landing, and critique yourself each time. The Styrofoam won't damage your topsides if you come in too hard, and being out there away from everyone else should prevent your mistakes from damaging your pride.

When you get to be pretty good at handling the conditions at the chosen location, find a different spot that will offer greater or different challenges. Or, lacking another location, at least raise one anchor and swing the float so it presents a different face to the prevailing conditions. Then try again. And again. And again.

Don't Forget Your Crew

You should make an effort to remember (because it can be so easy to overlook) that the learning experience should extend to everyone who will normally be boating with you. Amateur captains often envy us professionals because we have an equally professional crew to help us. Well, we often do. However, *more* often we have only slightly experienced beginning professionals. After we spend a lot of time and effort training them, they move on to a better job (such as a novice captain), and we start training again. As a pleasure-boat skipper, you can have the advantage of a reasonably permanent crew—your family—if you play your cards right. The essentials are getting them involved, keeping them involved, and treating them with respect and kindness through it all. Always remember that they're beginners, too. That's why it's important to have them practice with you. Whatever the maneuver, assign everyone a job, explain what you want done, and then let them learn to do it with you.

I had to learn this lesson the hard way, from a boating companion many years ago. She was a very attractive and bright young lady who enjoyed boating as much as I did and was a delight to have aboard. But she had not been involved with boats as long as I had, and we had just begun cruising together. Consequently, she didn't always do what I thought was right, and I let her know it in no uncertain terms. One evening as we watched a large British motor yacht being put through a rather tricky maneuver with near effortless precision, I couldn't resist commenting.

"Did you notice how efficiently each crewmember performed?" I asked, with an expression that made it obvious I expected the same efficiency aboard my boat.

"Yes, I did," she replied with a bigger smile than I thought appropriate. "And did *you* notice," she continued as her smile grew even broader, "that the captain never yelled at them once?"

Ouch! She was right. You shouldn't yell at your crew unless they are in immediate danger, and you want them to move quickly out of harm's way. In any other situation, you'll get better cooperation by staying calm. A yelling skipper is an insecure skipper who does *not* have the sort of control of the situation we all think a person in command should have. No matter how much experience you have, there will be times when you'll feel out of control. "The secret of professionalism," a very talented Down Easter I worked with once told me, "is knowing how to correct the situation when things go wrong. Anyone can learn to do the job when there isn't a problem, but a professional will make it come out right even when there is." He was right. And the better you feel about the situation, the more competently you'll think and act. Practice helps here, too.

Here's another way to avoid the need for yelling: Make sure all your crewmembers know what you expect them to do *before* you need to have it done. Then all it takes is a nod or a hand signal meaning "now," and they'll know it's time to do it. When you're prepared and they're prepared (as you will be if you practice together), you and your family can look just as sharp as any white-uniformed professional crew.

Take It Slow and Easy

Training experts tell us that learning takes place on a curve. Whether we're trying to shape up our bodies or our minds, the first few repetitions don't do much. Then we begin to see some gain. But if we work at it too long, the gain diminishes in proportion to the effort put forth. So don't overwork any single exercise. After you've practiced docking for a while, either quit and go play or try something else. Don't push to the point of boredom or diminishing returns. It's supposed to be fun, and it will be, as long as you keep a healthy attitude.

Practice well enough, and you'll be able to handle a boat like an old-time harbormaster I once knew in Maine. The man could make a boat do nearly anything; any watercraft he operated was like a marionette in the hands of a master puppeteer. One day I watched him back a single-screw lobster boat into a tight slip as easily as most landlubbers could put a Volkswagen Beetle into a Cadillac's parking space. Someone else on the pier saw him, too, and commented, "Wow, you parked that boat just like a car!" The old-timer drew himself up proudly, looked his observer squarely in the eye, and announced, "I did not! I handled her like a boat."

Appendix

A Gallery of Powerboats

A great variety of powerboats ply North American waters. The photographs that follow barely scratch the surface and are intended mainly to illustrate some of the most common styles. Designations such as "express cruiser," "center console," and "convertible" are convenient, though each of these embraces a substantial variety of sizes and configurations. Every boat pictured here is a good one, but I must remind you the inclusion of any boat in this gallery should not be construed as a recommendation or endorsement by either the author or publisher. Unfortunately, not all the good boats are pictured. Far from it. Space limitations and the availability of good photographs were the primary considerations.

Runabouts

Runabouts are the essence of speedboating; they exist solely for the purpose of having a good time on the water. You can't really fish from them, and though some have a small enclosed area forward, most runabouts offer little in the way of shelter or other amenities, so they aren't well suited to cruising, either. But they are fun!

You can ski behind most of them, but serious skiers usually demand the kind of dedicated performance—flat wake, towing pylon, etc.—offered by boats such as the MasterCraft Prostar 190. The downside to a pure ski boat is that its hull shape doesn't always take well to rough water, so they're usually best kept just for skiing.

As I mentioned back in Chapter 1, good ski boats also produce too flat a wake for really good wakeboarding, which is why I'm including a second MasterCraft in this series; the X-Star is the company's top-of-the-line wakeboarder. As you can see, the two boats are quite different, even above the waterline.

Runabouts have been popular since the earliest days of powerboating. The Chris-Craft, despite being totally modern in systems and construction, reflects some of the style and flair of that era (though the company disparages the term *retro*). This is only fitting, since Chris-Craft is one name that has been around since those early days. The Packard, on the other hand, unmistakably replicates the appearance of those marvelous varnished-mahogany speedboats of old, but in easier-to-maintain fiberglass. The other builders seem to prefer a totally modern look, which leads me to add that although the appearance of runabouts may have changed over the years, the fun sure hasn't. Runabouts remain among the best possible choices for your first boat.

The Cobalt 200, Four Winns 180 and Sea Ray 240 Sundeck typify the *bowrider* [open at the bow] form, a design that came on the scene in the mid-1960s and is well liked because it creates more usable space, which can be especially important when the boat is small to begin with.

I'm not that fond of bowriders (though I must confess to being very much in the minority; bowriders are perhaps the most popular of all boats in terms of sheer numbers out there on the water). I guess my main concern is that the bow seats are so attractive that everyone wants to sit there. At displacement speeds, this can make bowriders quite hard to handle since a boat trimmed bow-down doesn't respond well to changes in rudder. Though you can often overcome this at planing speeds by trimming the motor(s) out and thus the bow up, the seats may then be quite uncomfortable at best—and actually unsafe at worst—because the bow is the bounciest part of a boat. The only solution is to ask folks to move back where their weight would be more desirable. This inevitably hurts some feelings, but it's often the safer thing to do. In my opinion, a bowrider's bow seats should really only be used when the boat is *not* underway.

The lack of a covered foredeck also makes bowriders more susceptible to taking on water when seas kick up. Though runabouts are meant mostly for fair weather, even a sizable wake can be a problem for the unprotected bow of a bowrider. Here's a tip for bowrider skippers. When a huge and possibly breaking wave approaches, instinct tells you to slow down. Don't. If you give a brief but strong burst of power ahead (and I emphasize both *brief* and *strong*), the sudden acceleration will cause the stern to drop and the bow to lift. So instead of taking water in across the open bow, you'll ride over the wave and stay relatively dry. The move is definitely counterintuitive, but it works, believe me.

Runabouts are often offered in packages that include boat, motor, trailer, and all necessary accessories. Volume buying on the part of the manufacturers allows you to get "the package" for less than you'd probably pay if you gathered the individual components yourself.

PRINCECRAFT

CHRIS-CRAFT CORSAIR 25

COBALT 200

MASTERCRAFT X-STAR WAKEBOARDER

PACKARD 2600

FOUR WINNS 180 FREEDOM

SEA RAY 240 SUNDECK

MASTERCRAFT PROSTAR 190 SKI BOAT

Performance Boats

Performance boats might be considered run-abouts on steroids. Boasting hulls that are often derived directly from past or current winners on the racing circuit (such as the Cigarette, a name that has become so recognizable many people call *all* go-fasts "cigarette boats"), they carry a lot of horsepower and may get you where you want to go faster than your car! They are indeed very macho (as more than a couple of the model names would suggest) and are often called muscleboats.

Performance boats are part of the boating scene and can be a lot of fun, but I believe the skill required to handle them properly and safely takes them out of the "getting started" category, though they sure are something to aspire to if raw power excites you.

Incidentally, while muscleboats are largely an American phenomenon, we in the United States are not alone in either enjoying or producing them; the Hydrolift is built in Norway.

CIGARETTE 1

FORMULA 382 FASTECH

BAJA 245

HYDROLIFT S-24

FOUNTAIN 35

Center Consoles

Center consoles are pure fishing machines. No cabin to clutter the deck, no frills to get in the way. Nothing but hull, power plant(s), a place to hang the controls, electronics, and your fishing gear. They are the very essence of efficiency.

Center consoles were once mostly less than 25 feet, but that's no longer true. With larger boats has come the option of a fair-sized tower for even greater fishing efficiency, as well as room for more anglers and gear.

The center console's simplicity permits little shelter and risks the loss of full support from non-fishing family members, most of whom want some sort of cabin. However, shelter need not be totally lost. Some of the boats sport T-tops (in either aluminum/canvas or fiberglass), which offer protection from the sun and could be rigged with removable side curtains if you so desire. Some consoles are also large enough to contain a head, which provides both the facilities themselves and also some privacy when using them, albeit often in a somewhat "space-challenged" form.

WELLCRAFT 32

MAKO 31

OCEAN MASTER 31

AQUASPORT 201 OSPREY

COBIA 314

SEA FOX 210

DONZI 23

Cuddy Cabins

Their interior accommodations range from a vestigial berth space for catnaps to a "house" with a semblance of a galley and dining area, but the small cabins we call cuddies all have two things in common: they provide shelter—a place to get away from full exposure to weather; and they offer privacy—a place where a person can change into or out of a bathing suit, go to the head, or escape the crowd. Because these amenities so enhance the enjoyment of a boat, cuddies in all their forms are very popular.

Many of the models are designated "walk-around," and even some that aren't so named have the feature. The concept, which first saw the light of day in the late 1970s, makes possible a fishing boat that has most of the advantages of a center console plus shelter as well. Side decks around the cabin permit an angler to work a catch no matter what. With the "conventional" cuddy, this isn't so.

Cabin space varies with the size and style of the boat. If you want to be able to walk around the cabin, you have to accept that it won't be as roomy as one that extends from gunwale to gunwale. As is the case with all such designations, the point at which a "cuddy" becomes a small but full-blown "cabin" is usually a bit blurred. Thus the Cruisers 280 CXi might just as easily have been placed in the next section, Express Cruisers.

WELLCRAFT V21

FOUR WINNS 205 SUNDOWNER

HYDRA-SPORTS 230 WALKAROUND

CRUISERS YACHTS 280 CXI

COBIA 210

RINKER 282

WHITTLEY CRUISER 550

Express Cruisers

The often-used model designations give you an inkling of what this style of boat is all about— Sunbridge, Mid-Cabin, Sundancer. The idea is to have an open cockpit, with the bridge or console area raised somewhat, which permits extending the cuddy in several directions. Raising the cockpit, or at least the forward end of it, enables the foredeck to be raised also, and this makes possible a stand-up cabin with a galley and an enclosed head. The space beneath the bridge becomes what is generally known as a midcabin. How much of a benefit this is depends greatly on the size of the boat and the cleverness of the designers, but at the very least it offers another berth (even if you have to crawl in and out of it), and in many models—generally from 30 feet up—it really enlarges the saloon both in usable square footage and in effective use, adding more seating and perhaps a cocktail or game table. Raising the bridge has a third benefit—better visibility from the helm.

Given that the area beneath the forward portion of the cockpit is occupied by the midcabin, the engine(s) must go farther aft. This means that most raised-bridge, midcabin cruisers have either sterndrives or V-drives. Some models manage enough room for both the midcabin and an engine compartment far enough forward to use conventional underwater running gear, but this is rare in boats less than 36 feet long.

Other features common to the genre include ample benches and seats for lounging and transom doors for better access to the transom platform.

There are two boats in this series that almost don't belong: the Ocean 40 and the Rampage 38. They're here because, if you were to remove the towers and outriggers, they would look quite similar to the other raised-bridge models. As the towers suggest, these are die-hard fishing machines. Indeed, we used some of the cockpit features of the Rampage to illustrate what's desirable in a fishing boat back in Chapter 1. The raised bridge does, however, offer better visibility than a center console as well as the room to expand the forward area from a mere cuddy into a full-blown cabin with a lot more in the way of creature comforts and amenities than you could possibly find in a walkaround.

FOUR WINNS 248

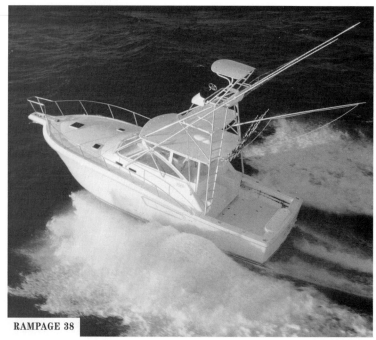

RAMPAGE 38

RINKER FIESTA VEE 312

FORMULA 48

SEA RAY 460 SUNDANCER

WELLCRAFT 330 COASTAL

OCEAN 40 SPORTFISH

Convertibles

These are boats with real cabins: fully equipped galleys with stoves and "like-home" refrigerator/freezer space, enclosed heads with showers, and full-size hanging lockers that are often as big as shoreside closets. In other words, these are boats you can comfortably spend some time aboard. Because they are convertibles, they have fishing cockpits, too; *real* fishing cockpits, not merely the convenient "back porch" often tagged onto motor yachts.

If any boat comes close to being all things to all people, it's the convertible. There's enough room inside and out for just about any aspect of boating you'd want to consider. The drawback is the size it takes to gain such versatility. Though there are convertibles on the market in the 28-foot range, other styles are often more practical in smaller sizes. Thus, the smallest boat I show here is a 38-footer. Likewise, the Hatteras 90 demonstrates what's generally the upper limit for the type. Though I don't believe this represents an entirely practical application of the style, the Hatteras is not the only convertible of its size in the marketplace.

RAMPAGE 45

LUHRS 38

CAVILEER 48

BERTRAM 390

HATTERAS 90

VIKING 56

Flying Bridge (Sedan) Cruisers

Keep the cabin and flying bridge of the convertible and (usually) reduce the cockpit to less than tournament-fishing dimensions, and you have the flying bridge cruiser, sometimes called a sedan. It, too, can represent the best of both worlds in that all but the most serious tournament anglers will probably find the cockpit adequate.

Sedans used to be very popular, and most builders offered several models and sizes. But in recent years, the convertible seems to have become the first choice for those who want a flying bridge, while the express cruiser has gained in popularity among folks who aren't so interested in fishing (and even with some who are!). Similarly, in the same boats that might previously have qualified as sedans, the "house" has been enlarged, and the cockpit deemphasized, enabling the builder to call the boat a "cockpit motor yacht." As I said at the beginning, sometimes the builder's model designation is less important than how you see (and believe you can use) the boat. A perfect example of this is seen in the Cruisers 455. There's no inside helm as there would most often be in a true sedan, and the cockpit layout is typically express. Yet I've included it among the sedans because it is an aft-cabin cruiser with full accommodations belowdeck and a much greater elevation to the bridge than you'll find on most express models. (Similarly, I could just as easily have included this model in the next section with other motor yachts.) The company's director of marketing notes, "With only one step separating the helm and cockpit seating area, the 455 Express Motoryacht has the same feel and functionality of an express cruiser without compromising the spacious interior that boaters expect in an aft cabin [cruiser]." In the final analysis, you make the call!

SABRELINE 36

CRUISERS YACHTS 455 EXPRESS

SEA RAY 560

OCEAN 57 ODYSSEY

Motor Yachts

The line between "cabin cruiser" and "motor yacht" is probably arbitrary, but 40 feet used to seem a reasonable length at which to draw it. But that may no longer be the case. I'd say size is now less important than the real key, which is comfort. And that's something you'll find aplenty in each of these boats.

There are motor yachts so big that it takes more crew to run them than there are berths on any of the boats shown here. Megayachts (generally defined as those over 90 feet long) are virtually small ships. Such vessels are not the concern of this book (we have generally figured our up-

per size limit to be about 70 feet, though we have included one just slightly larger).

A motor yacht might not seem the ideal candidate for a first boat, yet many newcomers to the sport have begun with boats of this size simply because they offer accommodations and cruising ranges smaller boats can't match. It's easier to start smaller and work your way up as your experience grows, but this isn't the only way. I've known a number of people who started with big boats and overcame their lack of experience by hiring a professional captain on a part-time basis to give them hands-on training. It works.

LAZZARA 76

CARVER 420 MOTORYACHT

HATTERAS 64 MOTORYACHT

Trawler Yachts

To the purist, only a working, payload-carrying fish gatherer deserves to be called a trawler. But the term *trawler yacht* persists. It began in 1962 with a boat dubbed the Grand Banks 36. Partly because of the deep-sea fishing image conjured up by the name, and partly due to the various traditional workboat lines that were amalgamated into the Grand Banks design, the boating public came to call the boat a "trawler," and the appellation stuck. You can see a Grand Banks 46 in Figure 3-1.

Trawlers are excellent for extended cruising and offer a lot of living space in a generally seaworthy hull. Because early models were either full displacement or barely into the semidisplacement mode and were built mostly in Asia, trawler yachts have sometimes been disparaged as "slow boats from China." These days, however, it's not unusual to see them move considerably faster. The Maine-built Sabreline, for example, has a sprightly semidisplacement hull capable of speeds into the 20s.

SABRELINE 47

KROGEN 48 NORTH SEA

MAINSHIP 34

PRESIDENT 47

Houseboats

Houseboats were once more house than boat and meant for use on only the most protected waters. They still offer much more in the way of interior accommodations foot for foot of overall length than any other type of boat. But although they're still not meant for real offshore cruising, you'll note from the bows of these boats that they're no longer necessarily flat-bottomed "river" boats. Today's houseboats often reflect the marriage of houseboat superstructure and cruiser-like hull. See also Figure 1-3.

HOLIDAY MANSION COASTAL CRUISER

BLUEWATER

Catamarans

The advantages of twin hulls are many, and as folks in the United States are slowly discovering, cats can make great cruising boats.

I mention this because "down under" in New Zealand (a nation well known for its seafaring tradition), twin-hulled cabin cruisers and motor yachts are very common and have been for many years. I learned this firsthand a few years ago when I visited Auckland on a magazine assignment to see the Mares 46 prototype under construction. In the process, designer Scott Robson also showed me some of his earlier efforts, and during some at-sea demonstrations I learned another important fact. While narrow-beamed cats often defer to deep-Vs when the going gets rough on the race circuit, the wider cruising cats remain very stable and comfortable at cruising speeds. In fact, I witnessed some incredibly smooth going in the neighborhood of 40 mph aboard a couple of different cats off Auckland in seas that would have loosened my fillings had I been aboard most monohulls I've ridden.

Cats also ride and handle well in offshore swells. I learned this firsthand not long ago when I delivered a 63-footer from Fort Lauderdale to Port Lucaya, Bahamas, for an "offshore" sale. On the trip across, the Gulf Stream was on its best behavior, and we made a comfortable 26 knots with ease. I was originally supposed to fly back after turning the boat over to its new owner, but he hired me to make the return trip also. This time, the seas were running a good 6 feet most of the way. And we still made a smooth and comfortable 26 knots. Most impressive was the fact that from the bridge helm, it didn't seem like we were in 6-footers. Only by going down to main-deck level and looking out (and occasionally up) was it possible to detect the true height of the seas.

Catamarans also offer the cruising yachtsman a wider range of destinations because they carry a shallower draft than comparable monohulls. This means you can go places, in spacious comfort, that would otherwise be appropriate only for much smaller boats.

The overall size of some new cats might put them outside the range of "getting started." However, another advantage of having two rather widely spaced hulls is that the distance between the props allows for some truly inspirational (yet easy to manage) "twin screw" maneuvering. From a practical standpoint, even the largest cats may not necessarily be beyond the reach of a neophyte.

GLACIER BAY 3400

TED HOOD 52

MARES 38 PERFORMANCE CAT

Index

Numbers in **bold** refer to pages with illustrations